Social Exchange Theory:
its structure and influence
in social psychology

European Monographs in Social Psychology

Series Editor HENRI TAJFEL

EUROPEAN MONOGRAPHS IN SOCIAL PSYCHOLOGY 8
Series Editor HENRI TAJFEL

Social Exchange Theory:
its structure and influence
in social psychology

J. K. CHADWICK-JONES

*Saint Mary's University,
Halifax, Canada*

1976

Published in cooperation with
EUROPEAN ASSOCIATION OF EXPERIMENTAL
SOCIAL PSYCHOLOGY
by
ACADEMIC PRESS *London, New York and San Francisco*

ACADEMIC PRESS INC. (LONDON) LTD.
24/28 Oval Road
London NW1

United States Edition published by
ACADEMIC PRESS INC.
111 Fifth Avenue
New York, New York 10003

Library of Congress Catalog Card Number: 75 19623

ISBN 0 12 166350 7

PRINTED AND BOUND IN ENGLAND BY
HAZELL WATSON AND VINEY LTD
AYLESBURY, BUCKS

Preface

I have brought together, for discussion, the major explanations of social behaviour as exchange—the works of John Thibaut and Harold Kelley, George Homans, Peter Blau. I say "brought together" because usually psychologists refer to Thibaut, Kelley and Homans as the exchange theorists, sociologists to Homans and Blau.

I examine these theoretical contributions, their content, the questions they raise and their influence since their publication more than a decade ago. In what directions, using which methods, has "exchange theory" developed?

As we shall see, exchange notions influence many research designs, across laboratory experiments and field observations. They have a vitality suggesting a theory with autonomy, both in concepts and hypotheses about empirical social situations, and they take us far beyond their behaviourist origins in reinforcement postulates. The theory deals with social process not merely as a matter of rewards and costs but as a matter of reciprocal behaviour, of different degrees of reciprocity, unequal power, and the social conditions for interpersonal behaviour—as complementary in some situations, competitive in others and, in yet others, altruistic. Ideas of social justice dominate in many of the recent studies.

There are numerous difficulties in building a theory of social exchange: for instance, the problems of finding rational criteria for behaviour, of assuming rational actors, of finding basic "premises", of reduction to "fundamental laws" of psychology and there are questions of tautology. These are problems which are important to any theory in social psychology. We can observe how exchange theorists try to circumvent them and the divergencies in the ways they do so.

The book shows that exchange theory has developed in certain directions and, more than this, that it is a changing entity in the mid-flow of discussion between its exponents and critics. Viewing the whole range of empirical and theoretical work in the chapters to follow, the book aims to present a thorough appraisal of exchange theory and of some of the current misconceptions about it.

I set out to demonstrate the emergence of exchange notions in empirical research over the last ten to fifteen years. What are the hypotheses or sectors of exchange theory which appear most frequently in this large amount of research? The ideas of Thibaut and Kelley emerge in many studies of the process of negotiation, of contractual norms and bargaining. From Homans' work, hypotheses about equity and distributive justice often attract researchers. Blau's interest in actual social situations has subsequently led to research in bureaucracies and in the family. His emphasis on the asymmetry of social relations raises problematical issues, yet to be fully taken up by social psychologists.

Beginning mainly as an American product, exchange theory now has its European contributors. It has become the object of a critique maintained over the years and more recently represented by French authors. Above all, we must recognize that social exchange ideas flourish as a theoretical, critical, empirical enterprise with variations of approach and method.

This book is intended for those who wish to discover the nature of exchange theory, to explore the controversial questions and most recent developments. I hope that it will encourage some to pursue their own research and that it will give them a better understanding of the theoretical context in social psychology.

September 1975   J. K. Chadwick-Jones

Acknowledgments

I would like to thank authors and publishers for permission to reproduce or adapt figures and tables from the following sources:

John Thibaut and Harold Kelley (1959). *The Social Psychology of Groups*. John Wiley and Sons, Inc., New York.

John and Jeanne Gullahorn (1963). A computer model of elementary behavior. *In* Edward Feigenbaum and Julian Feldman (eds), *Computers and Thought*. McGraw-Hill, Inc., New York.

Peter Blau (1964). *Exchange and Power in Social Life*. John Wiley and Sons, Inc., New York.

Otomar J. Bartos (1967). *Simple Models of Group Behaviour*. Columbia University Press, New York.

George Homans (1974). *Social Behaviour: Its Elementary Forms* (revised edition). Harcourt, Brace, Jovanovich, Inc., New York.

Guy Swanson (1965). On explanations of social interaction, *Sociometry*, **18**, 101–123.

Harold Kelley (1966). A classroom study of the dilemmas in interpersonal negotiations. *In* Kathleen Archibald (ed), *Strategic Interaction and Conflict*. University of California, Institute of International Studies, Berkeley.

Erika Apfelbaum (1967). Représentations du partenaire et interactions à propos d'un dilemme du prisonnier, *Psychologie Française*, **12**, 287–295.

Claud Faucheux and Serge Moscovici (1968). Self-esteem and exploitative behaviour in a game against chance and nature. *Journal of Personality and Social Psychology*, **8**, 83–88.

Gerald Marwell, Kathryn Ratcliff, David Schmitt (1969). Minimizing differences in a maximizing differences game. *Journal of Personality and Social Psychology*, **12**, 158–163.

Harold Kelley and Anthony Stahelski (1970). Social interaction basis of cooperators' and competitors' beliefs about others. *Journal of Personality and Social Psychology*, **16**, 66–91.

Acknowledgment is made for permission to reproduce passages from:

Robert Luce and Howard Raiffa (1957). *Games and Decisions*. John Wiley and Sons, Inc., New York, p. 95.

Serge Moscovici (1972). Society and theory in social psychology. *In* Joachim Israel and Henri Tajfel, (eds), *The Context of Social Psychology: A Critical Assessment*. Academic Press, Inc. (London) Ltd., London and New York, p. 26.

Contents

S.E.T.—I*

Araceli

Contents

1

Introduction

Social exchange: a unitary body of theory?

It has been my aim to describe the nature and content of what is frequently termed "social exchange theory"—in reality a collection of explanations, propositions and hypotheses, embodying certain general assumptions about social behaviour. At the same time, I have aimed to present a report on the progress of recent empirical work and to describe some of the most representative studies claiming to test social exchange explanations or at least to offer plausible support for them. I had hoped to show which aspects of exchange theory had the greatest influence, even which of the exchange theorists had had most influence. I did not expect to find a formal theory in the sense of a logical structure of general premises and hypotheses deducted from them. Obviously anyone who looks for such a formal structure will not find one in psychology and the social sciences. Yet, I found that exchange explanations, although they are not without their inconsistencies, comprise a source of very marked influence on recent research.

There are many references to "exchange theory" in empirical studies and theoretical essays of the last decade. At the beginning of this book I shall continue with the quotation marks, using them occasionally as a reminder that we do not wish to reify, but later on when I discuss Homans' contribution I shall drop the commas as his is an outright attempt to sketch a theory of social exchange. There is another reason. Thibaut and Kelley are *de facto* exchange theorists, part through the influence on them of Homans' earlier work. They have no intention to construct a theory. However, their work occurs as a reference jointly with that of Homans and Blau, over and over again.

Psychologists bracket them with Homans; sociologists cite them with Blau. Here, in this book I intend to study the social exchange position in the round—including all major contributions.* What is it about social exchange theory that interests researchers and is of use to them? How have they added to the original theoretical statements of social exchange as found in Thibaut and Kelley, Homans and Blau? To answer these questions I have tried to make a comprehensive and currently accurate report on progress and to present a more adequate appraisal than exists in the very few short summaries that are available.

Homans has come nearest to a formal theory and has attempted the most ambitious statement, at least in outline, of such a theory. He has sketched the outline of a theory of social exchange. Thibaut and Kelley concentrate on an empirical, experimental paradigm which they use to test exchange notions. Blau, following on from these two major contributions, has drawn attention to elements of social context which should be included into the exchange hypotheses. Social exchange propositions are always contingent on evidence, but the exchange theorists have different views on the research methods which should be used: Homans is eclectic in this, indicating that careful observation is essential but not preferring one research design more than others. Blau follows Homans, but Thibaut and Kelley are in favour of, and have themselves actively implemented, one particular design, the payoff matrix, although both they and their followers accept and occasionally utilize other experimental designs (see Chapters 4 and 6).

What is the common characteristic of these contributions to social exchange theory? They all declare a central interest in the interdependence of relationships between persons and in the actual process of social behaviour. The theory is truly social psychological since the interdependency of persons is at once the problem area for research and the unit of study. The set of problems, the problematic, concerns the

* The major contributions to a theory of social exchange are as follows: John Thibaut and Harold Kelley, *The Social Psychology of Groups*, 1959; George C. Homans, *Social Behaviour: Its Elementary Forms*, 1961; Peter Blau, *Exchange and Power in Social Life*, 1964. In his revised edition (1974) of *Social Behaviour: Its Elementary Forms*, Homans has introduced a discussion of aspects of the Thibaut and Kelley payoff matrices which concern the exercise of interpersonal power and he has elaborated on his own theoretical propositions. Homans discussed the same points in two other recent publications (1967a, 1970). These developments will be described in Chapter 9 below.

interdependence of motives, perception, behaviour and empirical work
has also to comprehend such many-sided relationships.

As will be discussed in Chapters 3, 8 and 12, the exchange theorists
find their starting premises by taking analogies from reinforcement and
learning theory or from statements about supply and demand in classical
economics. We shall see that they differ in degree of explicitness about
these sources and that Homans has formulated them the most clearly.
We discuss these sources at length but, in the remaining chapters
attention is focused on how this theoretical effort, centring on basic
notions of exchange, has developed subsequently and we shall find out
where exchange theory stands currently.

Later on, we will conclude that one advantage of exchange ideas is
that they encourage a diversity of research. This is a very important
feature, that explanation may be developed by many different kinds
of research method and should be a means to great flexibility in theory
construction. Social exchange theory offers an advantage in encouraging
a diversity of methods and evidence of different kinds such as the sociometric analysis of interpersonal choice, attitude scales, performance in
laboratory tasks and in experimental games, and observation and recording of communication in actual situations of occupational behaviour,
friendship, family relations. The nature of the measurement assumption behind this diversity of method is agreed by Homans and Blau as
no more than the assumption of ordinal scaling because the most a
researcher can hope to show is that more or less of one variable is
associated with ordered amounts of another. Thibaut and Kelley go
further to the point of assuming cardinal scales for their payoff outcomes. I argue in Chapter 3 that Thibaut and Kelley have overstated
the case for the payoff matrix to the extent of limiting the field of
evidence which might be used to support their hypotheses; they have
attached too much importance to one kind of experimental paradigm.
Plon (1972) makes a similar criticism; it is one which can only be refuted
by results yielded by this paradigm and the issue is currently in doubt
pending further empirical work.

Let us now open the discussion to a broader question which especially
belongs to theoretical development in social psychology. As a body of
statements about social process and interdependence, exchange propositions illustrate the difficulties which are raised by theoretical statements in the so-called interstitial discipline of social psychology.
Primarily this is a question of the relationships of social psychology to

psychology, and to sociology, and requires us to express a view about the degree of autonomy that such statements can have. The question of "reductionism" is discussed in Chapter 14 as a general problem for social psychology which, to some extent, social exchange explanations exemplify because they draw on both psychological and sociological variables. This problem is not met in quite such an acute form in theories of social perception and personality, for example, where the explanation is more closely attached to individual psychology.

Usually, when reductionist arguments are presented or attacked, the general debate occurs between psychology and sociology. Autonomy for social psychology, either in theory or research, is an issue which has, comparatively, been neglected. By their very nature, from a sociological point of view, theories in social psychology are reductionist. Yet neither the concepts involved for explaining individual behaviour nor those used to explain the organization of social structures, or collectives, can be suitable for explanation which is contingent on research in primary groups. Social exchange theory, in taking the interdependency between persons as the unit of study, is truly a social psychological theory; at the same time its explanations are explicitly related to the psychological premises of reinforcement and cognitive theories, as will be discussed later.

Lastly there are two yet wider issues which social exchange theory shares with the general enterprise of theory-building. The first of these is the question whether its basic premises are tautological and the second involves what Homans (1972) terms the "vexed question of rationality" in the study of human behaviour. I shall refer to the former question later in Chapters 2, 9 and 13; exchange theorists argue that their propositions are contingent on evidence and therefore cannot be tautological. On the second question the views of rational behaviour which are encountered in exchange theory, are discussed mainly in Chapter 7 but receive attention also in Chapters 3, 8 and 12.

Exchange theory is sometimes criticized as suggesting acceptance of the existing allocation and distribution of rewards. This is not a topic which I intend to discuss very fully here but there are a number of current publications, some of them very extensive, which take as their central topic the ideological position of social psychology as a whole. For instance, Plon and Preteceille (1972), Bruno *et al.* (1973) and Pecheux (1970) consider that much of social psychological research is vitiated because it reveals an ideological position which can be stated rather broadly as one which allows that only certain forms of conflict are allowable within the structure of the *status quo*. Plon (1967, 1972, 1974) states this position most clearly. He argues that, at its most basic, exchange theory involves a utilitarian view of man as *homo economicus* or as a risk-taking rational individual *homo aleator* and that both views as models of individual behaviour ignore the political-social issues between classes, the economic distribution of power in society and so on. Plon, Bruno *et al.* and Pecheux take issue with the model of Thibaut and Kelley as the most behaviouristic explanatory scheme yet attempted in social psychology. They do not discuss exchange theory as such, but there are a number of innuendos and passing references which perhaps could be best summarized as leading to the conclusion that exchange ideas consist of a kind of theory of the market-place, both a diminution and diversion of empirical study to narrow issues of bargaining. This criticism is by no means confined to ideological arguments because it can be found in earlier attacks in the academic journals from the mid-sixties but it rarely goes beyond a relatively brief statement ignoring the breadth of substantive content and the further development of social exchange theory in recent years. I shall describe its vigorous influences on a body of research and the ways in which this research raises many questions. If the starting premises are behaviouristic, then research has subsequently forced attention to non-behaviouristic issues. Exchange explanations by no means constitute a formal theory, nevertheless they do have the greatest advantage which it is possible to derive from any theoretical enterprise—they offer an orderly framework for the counter enterprise of criticism, refutation and critical modification.

In Chapters 3, 8 and 12 I discuss in detail the content and problematical issues in exchange explanations, in order to follow up their expression in research studies subsequently and in current theoretical discussion. In Chapter 2 there is an outline of reinforcement theories from which "exchange theorists" have borrowed propositions, by analogy. We shall see that reinforcement theories are vulnerable to criticisms of tautology or circularity and these criticisms, originally directed against reinforcement notions, have been passed on to exchange explanations. The criticism of tautology may be discounted in the case of exchange hypotheses which are contingent on evidence. Even if some of the general or basic propositions are tautological as "logical truths", the explanatory statements at the level of working hypotheses are open to verification. A more difficult criticism to counter is that exchange research and explanations are trivial. This is a criticism which might easily be made against some studies, in a technical sense, that the experimental manipulations are so strong that they can produce only one kind of result. In this sense, research is trivial if it tells us no more than we know in advance of the investigation or experiment. In another sense, the topic for study may itself be considered trivial* but this could only be a matter of opinion. There are no doubt instances of exchange hypotheses which are trivial in one sense or another but it is unlikely that the criticism will be sustained against the large body of exchange research across many different situations and methodologies. Even in experiments where the variables are highly controlled and abstract, the experimenter may claim that the results have a bearing on actual social problems. For instance, Harold Kelley takes an extremely pragmatic approach towards simulating and isolating variables thought to pertain in the wider society, although their bearing on actual social problems may be quite difficult, or impossible to establish (see my discussion of Kelley and Grzelak, 1972, in Chapter 7).

The Prisoner's Dilemma revalued

In Chapter 4 I describe the use of the Prisoner's Dilemma design by Thibaut, Kelley and others; the research which they have carried out places them with the foremost protagonists of this design. They are protagonists with an awareness of the criticisms which can be made against it and they offer their counter-arguments in its favour. In Chapter 4, some criticisms of the Prisoner's Dilemma are described which emphasize its over-abstract nature: any "social" relationship that might form is extremely attenuated. These criticisms are well summarized by Nemeth (1970, 1972), for instance. Other criticisms have been made against the barriers to communication in the P.D. design, often no conversation is allowed and no communication over and above the actual choice of alternative options—this is why Homans rejects the P.D. design. Plon (1974) adds another emphasis, that the Prisoner's Dilemma is ahistorical and ignores any sort of contextual or cultural influence.

---

* Murstein (1973) suggests that "the amount of research devoted to a topic in human behaviour is inversely proportional to its importance and interest". He states this "law" in order to underline the neglect of his own area of research—the choice of a marital partner.

Kelley, particularly, has made some interesting developments in the design from its original and arid classic form, by introducing communication of various kinds and by using pre- and post-experimental questionnaires. He has begun an exploration of cultural influences, in company with several other researchers in the transnational project (1970, described in Chapter 6).

One way of regarding the P.D. design would be to see its value as a way of examining the conditions producing antagonistic exchange. There is still a good deal to be clarified about the meaning of "competitive" choices, whether they are refusals to reciprocate, retaliation or attempts to exploit. The design has been surprisingly resilient in the face of criticisms and it is possible that there will be further useful work. However, it could also be that the P.D. design is a lure, a trap, in which the efforts of researchers are frittered away in endless, trivial modifications. Plon's (1974) critique rests largely on his view that in this design, as in others in social psychology, the experimenter is making his own projection of conflict and negotiation and ignoring the realities of conflict such as exist in actual situations within a given social structure.

In the original anecdote of the Prisoner's Dilemma, the two men arrested on suspicion, have a choice: either to confess or not to confess. If they both confess they receive a moderate sentence; if they both do not confess they get off with an extremely light one; but, if one does not confess and the other does, the former receives a heavy sentence and the latter gets off scot free.

Plon reminds us that in the original anecdote concerning the dilemma between two prisoners there was also a third person, the judge, who places before them the alternatives—"Confess and take a relatively light sentence. Otherwise, if you do not confess and the other man confesses, I will throw the book at you" (see Luce and Raiffa, 1957, p. 95; Ost, Allison, Vance and Restle, 1969). From this viewpoint the situation of the two prisoners results from a stratagem invented by the judge, representing the established order, in order to settle the conflict between the latter and the two prisoners. Plon argues that the judge has invented a conflict between the two prisoners and has substituted it for the true conflict which is actually between him and the prisoners. The Prisoner's Dilemma, created by the judge, now makes it difficult for them to remain allied against him. Looking at the P.D. design in this way, the end result is not an expression of mutual confidence between the two players in making *their* co-operative (not confess) choice, considered by some to be the rational choice. On the contrary, the result is to divide the two players, to prevent them remaining allied against the experimenter who is now in the judge's place. Plon also sees in the anecdote of the two prisoners that the dilemma created for them could be a means to social control by which they are persuaded to follow their "individual rationality" at the expense of maximizing their joint payoff.

So often in the literature social exchange theory is thought to assume, as if it were its sole assumption, that a person will maximize his own profit.* This is incorrect for several reasons. For instance, it presumes that exchange theory concentrates empirical attention on individual behaviour and the individual's calculation of rewards and costs. This is not so, because a basic assumption of exchange is the reciprocal relationship. Blau, for example, provides a notable definition of exchange in which he distinguishes between the psychological process of reinforcement, relevant for each individual taken separately, but not sufficient to explain the exchange relation between them. The relation is a joint product of their interdependent actions. It follows from this assumption that an individual's action must be studied simultaneously with the actions of others. It is a basic research tenet which follows from the social exchange propositions we shall discuss. And more than this, the reciprocal relationship is itself a problematical issue because the degree of reciprocity will vary depending on the characteristics of the persons involved and, in particular, their role and status in a given social context. Conditions must be studied in which reciprocity may be equal and where it may be unequal; or where it may be equal but negative in the case of individuals in antagonistic exchange. Empirical studies that are influenced by exchange theory must focus on these conditions for greater or less reciprocity or on the attainment of equity. The latter is a topic which, as we shall see in Chapter 11 has attracted much empirical attention. So now we see that it is not a matter of maximizing or optimizing individual gains but of understanding the meaning of such "gains" relative to the relationship with other people, or the realization

---

* See Chapter 7 below for a discussion of maximizing, optimizing and satisficing. It would be erroneous to make too much of maximizing, or satisficing, postulates even though they provide adequate hypotheses in some situations. This still would not mean that they are postulates suitable for explaining social behaviour in general.

of joint gains or gains at the expense of others; it may be a question of altruism or social responsibility. When we consider the recent empirical developments in social exchange explanations, we must recognize the breadth in substantive content of this body of theoretical statements.

of joint gains or gains at the expense of others. It may thus justify of
behaviour, social relationships. Which we can interpret, recent empirical
developments in social exchange explanations, we must recognize the
in mind in subsequent discussion of this body of theoretical material.

2

Reinforcement Theories and Exchange

Introduction: reinforcement propositions in social psychology

It is my intention now to illustrate how social exchange theory is based
on the explanations in psychology which attempt to link behaviour to
rewards or punishments (more technically, to positive or negative
reinforcers). Because of the very frequent use of reward propositions in
the theoretical discussion and in the empirical studies of social exchange
theory, we would be justified in adopting the term "reinforcement-
exchange theory" as Shaw and Costanzo (1970) have done and in
rejecting Nord's (1969) term "economic exchange theory" which is
misleading in its over-emphasis of similarities or analogies with economic exchange. The latter term ignores that social exchange theory
aims to explain what is not economic in social behaviour. Homans
(1961) and Blau (1964) refer to their basic propositions as psychological
and indeed they are, as we shall see. Thibaut and Kelley (1959) give
little explicit attention to this matter but reinforcement concepts are
predominant in their hypotheses and postulates.

This would not be the place to treat the meaning of the term *reinforcement* as it has been used in individual psychology so much as to examine
it for its meaning in social psychology. In laboratory studies of individual behaviour, animal or human, reinforcement is usually defined in
the form of quantitative measures—the frequencies of a particular
behaviour which are consequent on certain specified conditions.
Frequency as used by Hull is a measure of drive energy; as used by
Skinner it is a measure which indicates degree of reinforcement, i.e. the

frequency of a designated behaviour is a function of the reinforcement which is consequent on that behaviour. Skinner is concerned with the fact of reinforcement, as observed in a purely empirical set of operations, and not with the hypothetical mechanisms which produce the effect. Gregory A. Kimble (1967) who is one of very few text-book authors to take the Skinnerian view, sees it as an unfortunate accident that the term reinforcement may seem to imply acceptance of some version of drive-reduction theory, pointing out that there has been "a further unfortunate tendency for 'reinforcement theory' to be equated with all of the other aspects of the most important theory of this type (Hull, 1943). Thus, the term *reinforcement theory* has become surrounded by . . . illogical connotations" (p. 86). Much of the discussion in the earlier reinforcement literature centres on the controversy over making inferences about drive-states in the actor. Nevertheless, reinforcement theories concur in the Thorndikean tradition that the consequences of behaviour have an effect on that behaviour itself. Thus, reinforcement is a matter of the repetition of behaviour and the choice of that behaviour in preference to alternatives. Since the basic explanations of social exchange theories involve statements about the effect of reinforcement or reward on behaviour we should be clear at the start about their wider theoretical background. In so far as theories of reinforcement derive from Thorndike's work on the law of effect—the importance of positive actions or rewards on subsequent behaviour—these theories are psychological, to that extent. It is interesting that McDavid and Harari (1974) refer to "behaviouristic reinforcement theories", suggesting that they are useful to explore social motivation (gregariousness, affiliation, power) and aspects of social reinforcement—for example, approval, acceptance by others, and social controls over behaviour.

There are several problems to be considered in the use of reinforcement propositions in social psychology. In the first place there are the difficulties which arise in attempting extrapolation from laboratory experiments on infra-human species to human behaviour. Secondly, these are compounded in extrapolating from experimental results on individuals to complex human social situations. For example, the Hullian interpretations of drive-reduction can be tested against induced hunger- or thirst-states in animals, but how is this procedure to be adapted to situations where motives cannot be measured in this way. Furthermore, in order to "translate" the law of effect from the animal laboratory to human situations, it is necessary to qualify and reformulate the concept. Some of the difficulties are soon apparent if we consider transferring notions such as the "strengthening" of the behaviour which follows reinforcement, where this is so precisely defined by Skinner as the rate of response during extinction, i.e. after the last reinforcement. The chief danger in transferring the terms applied to the laboratory behaviour of animals to human social situations is that the same terms when they are used to cover events both in the laboratory and in complex social behaviour may become merely homonyms (see Chomsky, 1959). Chomsky sees a problem in the limited degree of generalization which may be justified from the results of carefully controlled experiments, and the psychologist may choose between alternative approaches to this problem: he may decide to restrict his attention to a highly limited area in the hope that behaviour can be demonstrated to show regularities, giving support for "laws" which are also confined to highly specific segments of behaviour. Or he may choose to study more complex behaviour but he now finds that his descriptive accounts of uncontrolled situations cannot establish lawfulness. Chomsky attacks Skinner for not taking either course consistently because, having carried out studies of limited content, he extrapolates from this to a much wider and more complex area by means of "analogic guesses" (p. 30). There is a further danger, mentioned by Chomsky, in the possibility that all one is doing is taking a term defined with the precision available to laboratory control and using this term to interpret complex uncontrolled behaviour; this does not make for any more progress than applying the ordinary vocabulary but it gives a spurious impression of precision: this is "mere terminological revision, in which a term borrowed from the laboratory is used with the full valence of the ordinary vocabulary . . ." (p. 38). Certainly, Homans' use of the term *emit* in his *Social Behaviour* (1961) seems to invite this criticism as is argued in Chapter 8 (p. 158) below.

Chomsky accepts that reinforcement is significant, among a variety of motivational factors, but he draws attention to the disadvantages of this form of explanation because it involves extrapolation of terms and propositions validated in the controlled, simplified animal laboratory to situations where similar control and measurement cannot be used to isolate and define reinforcements. For example, it would be difficult to deal with schedules of reinforcement in very rich social environments and the notion of covert reinforcement in humans raises even more difficulties. Chomsky does not confine his criticism to the extrapolation of Skinnerian reinforcement hypotheses; "drive reduction" is similarly criticized as a cover term which is used to explain every occurrence of learning: whatever the activity, some "drive" must have been reduced. Chomsky's arguments in favour of substitutes for reinforcement are backed by experimental work on brain stimulation, observations of imprinting in animals and imitation in children, but the value of his criticism lies in drawing attention to the importance of taking reinforcement seriously "as something identifiable independently of resulting change in behaviour" (p. 42) and to the exaggeration of claiming that reinforcement is necessary for all learning or behaviour maintenance. Thus, Chomsky points to the tendency to use reinforcement as a cover term for explaining any or all conditions where behaviour is acquired or strengthened. This suggests an obvious direction for research in order to sharpen the reinforcement notion, if only by listing the exceptions to its operation. For instance, Logan and Wagner (1965, p. 11) described maze-learning in rats without reward, concluding that learning occurs but that it is less effective than learning with reward and we shall see that attempts to explain social behaviour by reinforcement concepts do include specific statements on the limits as well as the generality of reinforcement.

Another related criticism, frequently encountered in the literature is that the reinforcement principle is a tautology; and social exchange theory, because it is based on it, incurs the same criticism.

Reinforcement explanations as tautologies

The basic hypothesis of reinforcement, in its simplest form, consists of an if-then statement: that, if the occurrence of a given behaviour is followed by reinforcement then its strength is increased. This statement has many qualifications and elaborations which will be dealt with presently, but for the moment it is important to recognize that this is a testable hypothesis under research conditions where increases in strength can be defined and measured and the reinforcing conditions identified. Annett (1969) mentions that the use of reinforcement as a descriptive term means that "anything which leads to the selective repetition of previous behaviour or increases the probability of a given response to a given stimulus situation is . . . a reinforcer . . . Reinforcement in this sense has no explanatory value" (p. 122). On the other hand, reinforcement studies, if they are descriptive of the amount and frequency of behaviour which can be connected with measurable stimuli or conditions do provide a means of explanation, or at least a step towards it. It is only when the "explanation" takes the form that the strengthening of behaviour is *said* to be the result of reinforcement, *irrespective* of whether the latter can be identified or isolated, that it becomes a procedure without value. The explanation in this case is circular: behaviour is strengthened by the operation of reinforcement and a reinforcer is what strengthens behaviour. Basically this is no more than a statement that a reinforcer is what reinforces and the question of why reinforcement takes place is not answered.

While the reinforcement proposition is circular if it is put in the form that a given event strengthens behaviour because it is reinforcing, the protagonists of reinforcement theories do not of course say this—rather, what they have to say becomes a matter of empirical and objective measures. By this emphasis, the argument that reinforcement propositions are circular receives a direct refutation in the form of the counter-argument that "there is nothing circular about classifying events in terms of their effects" (Skinner, 1953, p. 73). The problem of why reinforcement should occur is also considered and dealt with by Skinner. He has acknowledged that it is not possible to be anything more than conjectural. Many reinforcers may have biological advantages which have obscure origins and "A biological explanation of reinforcing power is perhaps as far as we can go in saying why an event is reinforcing" (Skinner, 1953, p. 84). Even if it is claimed, in the Hullian manner, that reinforcement implies reduction of drive, the explanation need not necessarily be followed through; as Miller and Dollard (1961) point out, "it is not necessary to be able to identify the drive which is reduced and the manner in which it is reduced in order to be able to determine empirically that certain events are rewards under certain circumstances and to make practical use of this information" (p. 34). The case in favour of reinforcement theories concepts seems to rest on the possibility of measuring the reinforcers. According to this view there is no circularity where prediction is possible from the basis of information concerning certain reinforcers and the behaviour effects which follow them.

Burgess and Akers (1966) in their article "Are Operant Principles Tautological?" cite one of Skinner's propositions in order to illustrate its tautological nature. The proposition they take states that "If the occurrence of an operant is followed by the presentation of a reinforcing stimulus, the strength is increased" (*The Behavior of Organisms*, 1938, p. 21). Since strength of behaviour is defined as its frequency of occurrence, the proposition can be re-stated as no more than the following: if behaviour is followed by a stimulus that will increase its frequency of occurrence, then its frequency of occurrence will increase. Burgess and Akers contend that this effect is obtained because definitions are confused with propositions and that definitions are stated as if they were propositions. Once the distinction is made clear between a definition and a proposition, then the tautology disappears. Definitions are of necessity tautological, anything "true by definition" is tautological and if propositions merely restate the definitions they will have the same quality. In fact, Homans (1961) makes this point when he comments that "all definitions are tautologies" (p. 41). Distinguishing between the value of an activity to a person and the amount of that activity which that person actually undertakes, Homans states the proposition: the more valuable a reward (x) the more activity (y) a man exerts to attain that reward. He argues that if the only measure of value is the quantity of activity then the proposition turns into a tautology because (x) and (y) have the same measure and are the same variable. This proposition becomes "a real proposition and not a tautology" when x and y are independently measured.

One of the characteristics of reinforcement principles if they are to be considered as tautologies, should be that they explain everything—for instance, one would have the somewhat crudely expressed statement that behaviour which is learned or maintained at strength is reinforced behaviour and that therefore the reinforcement explanation is appropriate to all contingencies. It is the characteristic emphasized by Annett in the illustration given above. This cannot be so, argue Burgess and Akers, because reinforcement propositions are empirically discriminating both of different conditions and degrees of reinforcement and of exceptions which are made empirically explicit by identifying such exceptions or classes of exceptions.*

Burgess and Akers touch on two characteristics of tautologies which the reinforcement principle might be thought to possess: firstly, the

---

* The pursuit of exceptions is well developed in social exchange theory. For example, Homans discusses exceptions to the hypothesis that interaction leads to liking (see below, Chapter 11, p. 268). Blau specifies conditions of power and conflict where no social exchange occurs (Chapter 12, p. 293).

definitional characteristic where a statement merely expresses the equivalence of two concepts and secondly, the logical circularity where subject and predicate are more or less the same. The first of these Burgess and Akers defeat by arguing that propositions should be clearly separated from definitions; secondly, they counter the accusation of circularity by showing that reinforcement principles can be tested, confirmed or disconfirmed. They assemble 67 explicit statements, starting with definitions and listing a number of general "laws" which they extrapolate from the empirical and experimental context of Skinner's research. They allow for "empirically established exceptions" (p. 308), for example respondent behaviour mediated by the autonomic nervous system where "all events produced by it are irrelevant to its future occurrence". They argue that an extensive effort at stating general and derived propositions, such as they attempt, may clear the ground for the application of such propositions to "more and more complex social situations" (p. 309). Their efforts at compiling such a list, with qualifications and possible exceptions are intended to emphasize the point that reinforcement propositions are testable. This is the counter-argument to the view that there is nothing more in reinforcement principles than the tautologous statement that reinforcement takes place whenever behaviour is followed by a reinforcer. Burgess and Akers seem to identify reinforcers in empirical terms. However, the important disadvantage still remains that we are left with no general "law" about what constitutes a reinforcer although we may have a large number of empirical statements about what stimuli or conditions reinforce in specific instances.

A final argument in favour of the non-tautological nature of the reinforcement explanation can be added from the recent empirical work on computer simulation of some reinforcement propositions by Gullahorn and Gullahorn (1963, 1965a, 1969). If the reinforcement principle is a circular explanation then this would preclude simulation, as indeed it has done in the case of the Levi-Strauss functionalist explanation cited by Gullahorn (1969, p. 5) as a proposition concerning social organization which cannot be translated into a computer model—because its vagueness does not allow for measurable results. In detail, the Levi-Strauss explanation is as follows: preference for marriages with maternal branches within a family occurs more frequently than does the alternative choice of marriage with paternal branches because this rule has greater functional value for social organization. It is not, however, possible to express functional value in measurable units.* The Gulla-horns go on to suggest formulations of social exchange between two persons in their computer program. If social relations are successfully simulated in this model and exchange hypotheses tested, this will be a further exemplification that exchange (and reward) propositions are not tautological. The program itself and its current stage of validation, are discussed later in Chapter 10.

It should by now be clear that social exchange theory by its depend-ence on reinforcement concepts draws the criticisms which are usually made against these concepts and especially that they involve a tautology. In Chapter 9 I shall show that Homans and others are by no means deterred by this particular criticism and they insist that the cry "tau-tology!" is a "positivist" error which ignores the fact that in the social sciences theories can only be sketched in outline and cannot avoid hav-ing tautologies at their definitional centre. Blau's position is discussed in Chapter 12. He expresses a practical awareness of tautological implica-tions which occur if the reward notions inherent in a social exchange theory are indiscriminately made to apply to all social interactions, "even conduct toward others that . . . is not at all oriented in terms of expected returns from them" (p. 6). Blau points out that it is important to confine the use of the concept of exchange, so that tautologies are avoided. For this reason, he pushes strongly towards a discussion of those issues which show the limits and the exceptions to social exchange explanations. The fundamental test of the reinforcement notions that have been incorporated into the starting definitions of social exchange theory is therefore to be attained by means of deriving hypotheses to be confirmed or disconfirmed by the evidence. This seems to be a funda-mental shared position of social exchange theories which has led to the considerable subsequent influence on research of all three major sources which I shall discuss in Chapters 3, 9 and 12. However, this does not take social exchange theory out of the wood. For instance, Asch (1959) uses some effective arguments, taking issue with the assumptions behind reinforcement explanations in social psychology. First, he draws attention to Allport's (1924) view that social behaviour is based on similar biological needs as nonsocial ones and that the satisfaction of these needs constitutes the guiding principle of social interaction. Asch argues that this view by-passes the problem of group behaviour by

* I have no intention of going further into functionalist arguments. Functionalist propositions are often criticized because they are not amenable to testing.

denying the reality of groups on "elementaristic" grounds (a term similar to "reductionist"). Furthermore, Asch continues, by defining an all-inclusive basis for motivation, it leads to the conclusion that all group behaviour can be interpreted in terms of self-centred motives. Referring to early postulations of "group mind", Asch points out that the group mind theorists were seeking to express "what they sensed to be an essential feature of social life—the capacity of individuals under some circumstances to transcend their own particular interests and to act in the interest of their group" (p. 370). Asch sees these contrasting viewpoints as attempts to reconcile an apparent antimony between the requirements of social behaviour and the individual's "private existence" (p. 370). Both views, according to Asch, miss out the process that does overcome this paradox—the representation by an individual to himself of the situation that includes himself and others. Thus, in a group there are similar and mutually relevant representations in individuals. Nor is the mutual reference of participants in a social situation consistent either with a purely egocentric account of cognitive or motivational events. Asch discusses the egocentric view as an error of some magnitude: "To it we should trace the accounts of group belonging as a kind of business transaction having the motivational principles of a watered-down Hobbes" (p. 372) and he goes on to conclude that if social psychology is to make progress account must be taken of "the vectors that make it possible for persons to think and care and work for others". Mutually held representations which group members share concerning the aim of their group involve more than the intellectual assessment of a given situation, they involve consensus on needs: "the needs or goals of one person can, given certain conditions, arouse forces in another person toward fulfilling them, without exclusive reference to the latter's 'own' needs. This relation to another, when it is mutual and known to be such, seems to me to be an indispensable condition of mutual trust and of group coherence" (p. 373).

　　Thus, Asch points to the major shortcoming of reinforcement theory —the egocentric conception of motives which provides an explanation for all contingencies. The question must be answered of whether social exchange theory, by incorporating propositions from reinforcement theory, has also acquired this major failing?

　　Buckley (1967) discusses this kind of consideration drawing together the views of Blau with those of Coleman (1963), Parsons (1963) and G. H. Mead (1934) as these all underscore the importance of self-identification with others. Buckley indicates the importance for these writers of the "explicit notions of investment of *self* in others" (p. 112) and he argues that to interpret behaviour as profit-seeking is to engage in tautology and is one reason why the viewpoint of egoist hedonism and its derivates do not survive rigorous analysis: "to appeal only to the Hobbesian or classical economic sense of 'self interest' is to miss G. H. Mead's interpretation of this concept, and thus to ignore the all-important distinction between an exchange in which 'the self' is not directly involved and that in which it is" (p. 140).

Rewards and reinforcement

Although "reinforcement" and "reward" are often treated as equivalent terms, reinforcement is, strictly speaking, used in laboratory studies without the meaning of "reward" in its usual sense. In general, reinforcement is the term currently used among experimental psychologists because reinforcement need not involve reward. It might involve escape from electric shock (negative reinforcement) or behaviour may be strengthened by brain stimulation—and such conditions as these do not fit the concept of reward. Woodworth and Sheehan (1964) draw attention to the difference between "reinforcement" and "reward", noting that reinforcement was the term used in Pavlov's conditioning experiments while Thorndike, in explaining the law of effect, preferred reward. Reward seems a more appropriate term in experiments on human behaviour although it is interesting that the kinds of rewards used, from Thorndike onwards, are of a quite restricted range. Thorndike, for example, used the spoken words "right", "wrong" or small sums of money to demonstrate the law of effect in verbal learning and this is illustrative of the simple, even trivial, class of reward to which it is feasible to apply laboratory measures.

Experimental psychologists whose work on reinforcement, incentive and drive has been carried to a high degree of certainty in research designs for laboratory studies on animals, do have a tendency to apply interpretations of what their results may mean, to human social behaviour. Plausible though the application always is, it is anecdotal. The extrapolation is usually done in order to use an additional confirmatory source for the explanations which are presented of the laboratory findings. If the explanation accords plausibly with a familiar human illustration then this seems to assist the experimental case.

It seems that it might be a useful enterprise to attempt to classify situations and events that are, or are not, rewarding. Followers of both Hull and Skinner would agree that it is possible to catalogue rewards. If a reward strengthens behaviour in frequency or intensity, then the next step is the attempt to measure the nature of reward as an independent variable. It should be possible to proceed by observing, describing and classifying, experimentally or *ex post facto*, the evidence of reinforcers in operation. Still there are a number of difficulties. Money, attention, approval, affection or liking are all generalized reinforcers which represent or facilitate the attainment of a number of other associated rewards. But it may be argued that these are entities not easy to isolate, as Skinner writes "they are not things but aspects of the behaviour of others" (Skinner, 1953, p. 79). Blau has discussed this difficulty at length in this treatment of "intrinsic rewards" which are personal, adhering to particular individuals or to a fairly unique relationship between persons who cannot easily find equivalent rewards with others (see Chapter 12, pp. 286, 295). Social exchange theorists emphasize approval or liking (Homans) and status, esteem or compliance with others (Blau) as generalized reinforcers equivalent to money in economic exchange. So it is a matter of direct importance for social psychology to determine how far these authors and those influenced by them, have succeeded in the task of measurement. If an assessment can be made, and it is my intention in this book to work towards one, then we may also discover some indication of the direction in which future efforts may press forward in the next five or ten years.

Social exchange and learning theory

Much recent work on social reinforcement concerns problems which are of interest to the exchange theorists. One example is the influence of a person's past history on the effectiveness of a particular reinforcer in influencing his behaviour. The importance of past reinforcement history; of awareness that rewards are contingent on particular behaviour; and the principle of stimulus generalization are very often mentioned in the reinforcement literature. For example, Baron (1966, p. 528) states the assumption "that an individual's past history of social reinforcement defines for him the baseline against which the adequacy or appropriateness of present social reinforcer inputs is judged". Luetgert (1967) mentions that "the total reinforcement value of a given social reinforcer (or class of social reinforcers) would consist partly of its general objective value in relation to the situation in which it occurs and partly of a subjective value which would vary across individuals as a function of previous experience with those reinforcers". Furthermore the statement by Rotter (1966) on social learning that a reinforcer to be effective has to be contingent on a particular behaviour is reminiscent of the contingency effect which has been observed in experimental games (see Chapter 4 below). Thus Luetgert comments that "social learning theory predicts that expectancy level will change in the direction of reinforcement received, but only provided that the subject perceives the reinforcement as contingent upon his own behaviour" (p. 6).

As we shall see (in Chapter 8) Homans' Proposition 1 is clearly a general learning principle, stating stimulus generalization and is sufficiently well-established to apply to behaviour in many contexts. The fact that it is a basic precept of learning theory and that it is also a basic proposition in social exchange theory seems to be worthy of more attention than it has, in fact, received. In particular, it should exemplify the psychological nature of social exchange theory, which has sometimes been obscured by the consideration of economic parallels which the theory invites. The emphasis on immediate past history which is also characteristic of learning theory and the experimental work on social reinforcement also suggests a close similarity with the discussion of comparison levels by Thibaut and Kelley. Again, Luetgert comments that "the greater the number of cues present in a given situation which have previously been associated with positive reinforcement, the greater the expectancy of positive reinforcement and the higher the level of performance" (p. 8). This statement is virtually duplicated by Thibaut and Kelley in the comparison level definitions (Chapters 3 and 5).

I have tried to illustrate the major problems which are encountered if we wish to explain behaviour as a function of rewards and punishments. The problems are twofold. First, there is the question of tautologous propositions which many writers assume to be inherent in this kind of explanation. Secondly, any form of reinforcement theory can be criticized as involving a self-centred concept of the individual. In discussing these problems, aside from the question of whether they are soluble— and at the present state of theoretical discussion this is only a matter of opinion—I hope that it has now become obvious that any theory in social psychology which adopts a reinforcement model of man or includes reinforcement concepts into its propositions will encounter these two problems and draw a similar attack on account of them. Asch's criticisms which I have included at length were directed broadly at self-interest concepts within social psychology, so that this is a problem which is not merely of concern to social exchange theory but affects other research and theoretical approaches. Thus, in borrowing from reinforcement theory, exchange theorists have adopted an explanatory framework with these particular problems but they are by no means specific to this orientation.

In recent researches influenced by exchange ideas there are a number of attempts to encompass "intangible" as well as tangible rewards within their scope. Notably, Foa (1971) has suggested a classification of resources in social exchange as love, status, services, information, goods, money. He presented those who assisted in his study with six hypothetical situations in which they had given a certain resource to a friend and were then asked to indicate what they would prefer to receive in return. He notes that for each resource given there was one resource which was most frequently chosen in exchange; this enabled him to construct an order for the six classes showing relative proximity of any two resources. Thus, love is near to services and status and most distant from money. Differences were analysed on several dimensions including the delay of a reward: love is a relatively long-term resource with delayed returns. In contrast, an exchange of money with another resource is completed immediately. Later on, in Chapter 13 we will examine further empirical studies which focus on the question of delay and the development of trust in the long term. In an earlier study of intangible rewards Marsh and Stafford (1967) undertook a comparison of attitudes of academics with those of non-academic professions, presenting the hypothesis that academics seek non-financial "income", in compensation for their strictly monetary "losses". They argue that non-monetary values are an alternative currency. This study is also of interest mainly because it concentrates on non-material rewards.*

Rogers, Heffernan and Warner (1972) provide us with an interesting discussion of exchanges between individuals and the voluntary organizations to which they belong. Although their study uses a "one-shot" questionnaire and therefore presents only a static, surface analysis it raises some worthwhile points. These authors try to explore the relationship between the benefits, noneconomic as well as economic,

* In Chapter 13 below, the exchange of intangibles in family relationships is discussed.

received by members and the amount of their contributions to that organization. They mention that the

> application of the exchange model to most voluntary associations is seriously complicated by difficulties in calculating costs, benefits, and alternatives for organisations dealing with nonmaterial and relatively intangible inputs and outputs. The extent that such calculations are made by either the organisational leaders or members, the manner in which they are made, the frequency, and other aspects are simply not well understood or documented (p. 185).

They define noneconomic benefits as fellowship, education, information, identification, personal influence. They also asked their respondents for assessments of their economic benefits, present and anticipated, from these organizations. Having defined the reward variables, they take, as a second variable, the members' performance defined as attendance at meetings, recruitment of new members, and support of organizational policies. The analysis of questionnaire replies is less clear because the benefits mentioned above show varying degrees of association across the performance or contribution measures. All the same, noneconomic benefits rather than economic ones seem to have larger effects. For example, both identification and personal influence seem to have stronger associations with performance than anticipated income benefits. But noneconomic and economic effects were interrelated and the investigators can do no more to answer questions concerning *how* they interrelate, than to suggest closer study. These researches in actual situations, influenced by social exchange theory, are doubtless an effective expression of the set of problems which a theory deriving from reinforcement notions must try to resolve.

3

A Model of Social Interaction: the payoff matrix

Introduction

Thibaut and Kelley (1959) in their *Social Psychology of Groups* have a modest aim: to present a framework for explanation rather than a structure of deductive statements, but they claim to make "a rather new approach" and they do attempt to apply the same explanatory propositions to a variety of research findings.* Moreover they attach importance to defining the concepts which are in their propositions, so that some conditions belonging to formal theoretical systems are fulfilled: basic assumptions, defined concepts, and propositions—even though no attempt is made to derive them in a systematic structure of deduction from basic or general statements to more specific hypotheses. Their approach is to begin with a few relatively simple statements to which they will add only as it becomes necessary against the facts. Although they renounce any attempt at a formal deductive theory, this approach seems similar to that of proceeding from general propositions and then on to low-order statements to include special conditions. Some of the propositions will be listed later in the Chapter. It could be justifiably argued that it would be premature to attempt to order them formally. Even so, at least we shall see how near the model comes to a formal structure and how it resembles other social exchange theories. We are

* We will use the present tense in this discussion although some parts of the theory may have been modified since it was first presented in 1959.

going to examine the substantive content of the model and what Thibaut and Kelley have achieved. I have set out to capture the style of their theoretical effort and to explore the extent of its debt to game theory, economics and psychology.

It will be useful to recognize the general frame of reference assumed by Thibaut and Kelley as the empirical and propositional basis for the explanations they offer. In most of the nine chapters comprising the first two-thirds of the book, Thibaut and Kelley define their concepts, with illustrations from relationships in dyads. They concentrate on the relationship between two persons, taking the view that achieving a clear understanding of the influences at work in the dyad will lead to greater understanding of problems in larger social entities. In the last third of the book they show how the same concepts have a more general application to larger groups. Secondly it is important to emphasize what they see as the central problem for the study of social behaviour—the mutual *interdependency* of persons. Thibaut and Kelley focus on the aspects of relationships which they term the pattern of interdependency —a pattern which expresses the possibilities of reciprocal control. Each person may have ways of influencing the outcomes, and eventually these may form a discernible pattern, allocating rewards or costs to each. The interdependency can be seen as an objective and a subjective pattern. They point out that there is an objective interdependency of which a person may have knowledge,* there is also the likelihood that his perception and understanding of the interdependency depart from its objective values. Thibaut and Kelley examine the factors influencing this likely difference. They emphasize that it must first be possible to describe the objective interdependency, then one can compare actual social processes with the outcomes, as objectively stated, and explore the influences producing the difference or the correspondence between the objective or optimal, and the actual social outcomes.

The outcomes are to be evaluated against two criteria: what follows for the viability of a group or social relationship and, more basically, for the individual's own interest. This notion of viability is defined when they point out that "for a dyadic relationship to be viable it must provide rewards and/or economies in costs which compare favourably with those in other competing relationships or activities available to individuals" (p. 49). They argue that the behaviour of individuals,

---

* This is similar to the ideal condition of perfect information in game theory.

their enacted roles, can be evaluated against what is required functionally for group achievement, assuming that this can be measured: "one might wish to consider . . . the prescribed or enacted roles, on the one hand, and the functionally requisite roles on the other, relating this discrepancy to group achievement" (p. 145). We will return to this comparison issue again because it forms a main theme of the approach argued by Thibaut and Kelley.

Before discussing the substantive content of their model, its background and derivation should be examined rather more closely than has been the case in other summaries. I propose to discuss: (a) its similarities to game theory; (b) the limitations on using game theory; (c) the assumption of calculative decisions in social behaviour; (d) the extent of its derivation from experimental psychology; (e) the concepts borrowed from economic theory. In the course of this chapter it will emerge that some major problems are associated with the model—such as its relationship to S.-R. models, its development beyond them and the questions which arise about its possible uses and applications.

Similarities to game theory

A good deal of the discussion in social exchange theory, whether conducted by Blau, Homans or Thibaut and Kelley, is an attempt to define outcomes—that is, the payoffs to participants in interaction. To some extent each of these writers attempts to specify the choices, preferences and consequences, so that the affinity to game theory must be a very large one. Game theory, especially in economics, is intended to solve the problem of choice between alternative strategies, in favour of the optimal decisions in a two-person bargaining situation. It is also a branch of mathematics dealing with the formal statement of rational decisions—formal in the sense that the outcomes are abstracted and presented as a logical numerical statement of alternatives. The broad similarity to game theory is obvious, since Thibaut and Kelley take as their starting assumption only that two or more persons should act in order to optimize those gains and losses which are related to the behaviour of the other. This can take the form of collusive, equally advantageous behaviour from each, a "trading" agreement, or of dominance by one or more persons. The model allows for egotistic competition and it also allows for co-operative behaviour, similar to the mixed-motive or non-zero solutions of game theory.* Furthermore, Thibaut and Kelley present matrices which hold the values of outcomes from reciprocal behaviour; and from these values, just as in game theory, can be inferred the possible actions which a person may take to improve his outcomes. If we compare the matrix used by Thibaut and Kelley in its most general form, as shown in Fig. 1a with the general paradigm depicting the strategic structure of a game as

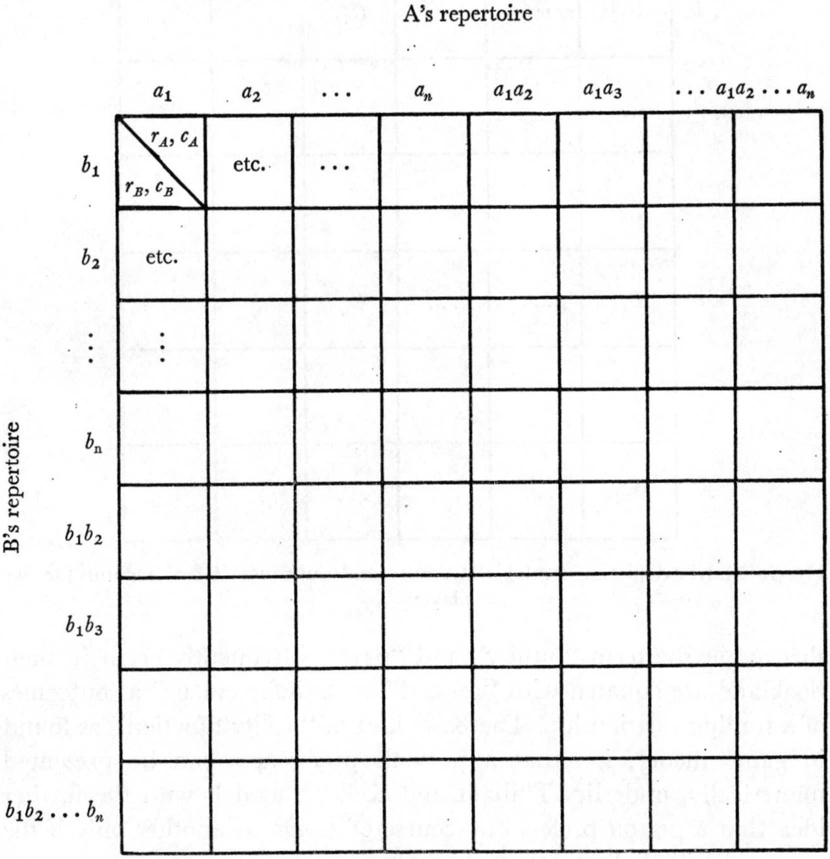

A's repertoire

	a_1	a_2	$\cdots$	a_n	a_1a_2	a_1a_3	$\cdots$ $a_1a_2\cdots a_n$	
b_1	r_A, c_A / r_B, c_B	etc.	$\cdots$					
b_2	etc.							
$\vdots$	$\vdots$							
b_n								
b_1b_2								
b_1b_3								
$b_1b_2\cdots b_n$								

B's repertoire

Fig. 1a Matrix of possible interactions and outcomes

r = rewards

c = costs

* A prototype of the mixed-motive game is the Prisoner's Dilemma, offering a conflicting choice between co-operation with mutual advantage and competition with divergent advantage. Some versions of this have been used to test social exchange theory and will be discussed in later chapters.

shown in Fig. 1b we see that the appearance of similarity is very great indeed.

Besides a brief reference to the influence of Luce and Raiffa's (1957) book *Games and Decisions* Thibaut and Kelley do not discuss game

	1	2	.....	j	.....	M
1	O_{11}	O_{12}	...	O_{1j}	...	O_{1M}
2	O_{21}					
⋮						
i	O_{i1}	...	...	O_{ij}		
⋮						
N	O_{N1}	...	...	...	...	O_{NM}

Fig. 1b Matrix depicting strategic structure and outcomes (O) of a game for two players (i, j)

theory but the terms "utility" and "payoff" frequently occur in their book and are equated with "reward" or "reinforcement" as outcomes of a trading relationship. The basic idea of "utility function" as found in game theory, i.e. that a person's preferences can be presented numerically, underlies Thibaut and Kelley's model, with the further idea that a person prefers one course of action to another only if the expected utility is larger than alternatives.

Utility, in game theory, represents the evaluation of an outcome, which a person makes by whatever criteria he considers important.* Some limitations on the adaptations from game theory begin to appear

* Subjective utility, as dealt with in the theory of games, and particularly as it refers to apparent objective values (for example, money rewards) is discussed in Chapter 7.

when we see that Thibaut and Kelley do not assume that outcome values are fixed over time, as in game theory. They point out that satiation and fatigue reduce the rewards and increase costs and optimal strategies will therefore tend to fluctuate.

Thibaut and Kelley adopt the term *set* which seems to be equivalent to the game theorist's *strategy* where a constant intention or orientation is assumed throughout a period of interaction. They assume that when a behaviour sequence is observed "we may say that the individual has assumed a certain set" (p. 11). A set or strategy can be identified through *repeated observations*: "if enough observations were at hand, the elements of a given sequence could be identified on the basis of certain statistical regularities: the elements would be found to occur together repeatedly and to be performed in certain sequential arrangements" (p. 11). Thibaut and Kelley take, as their unit for analysis, the behaviour sequence directed towards a goal. Thus, change from one set to another can be identified by observing that serial dependency becomes low, where actions of one sequence allow little evidence for continuity with what follows or for predicting from the actions of one sequence to the next. We can infer that the person's orientation or set is not so precise a concept as a strategy in the game-playing sense of providing for every possible choice on the part of another person, but at least it has the quality of overall consistency of aim.

Limitations of game theory for social psychology

It should be understood that the game theory matrix provides only an approach to the possible and optimal, against which Thibaut and Kelley intend to match the actual.* *Explanation* of the differences between observed social process and what might be optimal patterns is the point of departure for Thibaut and Kelley from the game theory model. Nevertheless, much of their explanatory framework is derived from game theory conventions and before their ideas are further examined, a little more should be said about these conventions and how they have adapted them.

* Note, though, that Deutsch and Krauss (1965) make the criticism that the matrix outcomes are not measured independently of the behaviour they are to predict. This point will be taken up again in Chapter 5 when I shall argue that Deutsch and Krauss expected too much of the model. Thibaut and Kelley take a very cautious view about prediction—see below, p. 44.

In classic game theory there are strict constraints on the representational model which is proposed of a two-party transaction. Each participant makes his move without knowledge of the intended move of the other and what communication takes place is confined to the solutions chosen by the actors, which may be the one-off action of the zero-sum game—winner takes all. In general Thibaut and Kelley follow the continuous model where each party makes a series of decisions and modifying decisions which depend upon the choices made by the other. In this version of game theory reference is often made of the analogy to economics, each party making decisions which depend upon the choices made by other members of the economy. In both zero-sum and non-zero-sum versions of game theory the variables which influence the outcomes for each participant are assumed to be well specified and the outcome values too can be precisely stated. Perhaps the most formidable question is whether research findings on social behaviour are expressed in sufficiently precise forms for a model using numerical values. In other words, is the descriptive material, at least as it is currently available, suitable for this model, and is the model appropriate for the available data? Much of the Thibaut and Kelley discussion concerns this question and in the section on *Numerical Values* we shall see how far they have gone towards resolving it.

The use of the game theory model in the explanation of social exchange raises some interesting questions and problems.* For example, there is the extremely important convention where there are successive moves (choices) of a termination rule to make precise the end of one move and the beginning of another. In chess for example, a move which produces checkmate ends the game. Do we apply this kind of rule in social psychology, and if so, how? Despite what Thibaut and Kelley have said about observing one sequence or set changing into another, the difficulty remains in analysing social process, of specifying the equivalent of choice points.

In view of the limitations on applying game theory, especially the difficulties introduced by the requirements for numerical precision, termination rules, choice points and the restrictive conventions we have mentioned, it is unlikely that the use of the matrix representation

---

* For some discussion of game theory applications in the social sciences, see Rapoport (1966), Bartos (1967), Archibald (1966) and Schelling (1963). Ost, Allison, Vance and Restle (1969) offer some interesting practical exercises in two-person games.

would be successful in social psychology if the aim were only to indicate outcomes. Thibaut and Kelley make clear that their aim is to present a framework for explanation in order to work towards the eventual development of theory, and this implies that the use of the game theory matrix might lead to greater insights and understanding of the subtleties in social relations. It could lead to a more systematic treatment of a large number of empirical findings and research results. We are getting near to answering the question: Why use the game theory structure? Does it generate hypotheses which are more advantageous for theory-building in social psychology than other approaches? One criterion to which I attach some weight is the influence that Thibaut and Kelley's theoretical effort has had on subsequent researches, since its publication in 1959. Much could be inferred from this, and the whole of Chapter 4 will be devoted to examining the extent of the influence that their model has had since then, with particular emphasis on the last five years.

It is perfectly clear that Thibaut and Kelley intend to represent in the matrix borrowed from game theory the mutual effects of the actions of one person on another and the effects also of switching courses of action. It is inevitable that there is an over-simplification in a matrix which delimits most conveniently the outcomes of dyads and does not easily treat the multiple relationships of groups of larger size. It is useful to note, at this point, that they mostly use a 2×2 matrix, each cell containing a numerical value to express the rewards or costs to each person from association or communication with another. Although their first matrix is not introduced until almost half way through their book, the total number of matrices (46) demonstrates the numerous possibilities of interaction, where the interdependent outcomes vary with the environment, and with the skills and influences of the parties. Much of their book is a discussion of rewards in the matrix form of a 2×2 table where each of two partners has his choice between two alternatives, each of his alternative choices carrying consequences for the other. From this simple matrix further elaboration is possible into 2×3 or 3×3 tables; obviously, to represent more choices may be impracticable, even where such multiple choices can be analysed by computer. One is reminded of the problems encountered in programming computers to play chess: just the first four moves can occur in 197,299 ways.

It is immediately apparent that there will be tremendous problems in representing and including an array of alternatives such as may be present in a complex situation, and there are perhaps insurmountable difficulties in translating what is significant in a social relationship into the matrix cells. The fact is that no-one has yet shown a satisfactory way of assigning numerical values to the cells, if the matrix is to represent social behaviour, whether this occurs in actual situations or in laboratory simulation. This kind of problem is inherent in the game theory matrix and it is not at all singular to the Thibaut and Kelley adaptation of it. Rapoport (1966) argues that very often in real-life situations it will not be possible to assign value magnitude to payoffs or to state the possibilities, other than arbitrarily or in such a way that the game theorist fills in the cells untuitively.

However, if we leave aside this problem for a moment and consider what the game theorist achieves and what the psychologist may achieve, we see that the former aims at stating a rank order of preferences and probabilities: the game demands definition of payoff magnitudes. For the game theorist these magnitudes are the "givens", the goals to be reached by alternative strategies, and he is not concerned with how such magnitudes are assigned by the players to the outcomes. Why these goals are sought and why one is preferred more than another seem to be questions for psychology rather than for game theory. Rapoport (1970) has termed game theory as "depsychologized" decision theory—and it could be that the psychologist's contribution will be to point out what it is that prevents a purely logical solution. However, the payoffs in the game theory matrix reflect the psychological worth of the outcomes and this, at least in principle, can be ascertained by the psychologist. So it seems that an approach to social behaviour within the matrix convention of game theory, as pursued by Thibaut and Kelley may have the very positive result of identifying the psychological process underlying the trading and mixed-motive relationships.

Thibaut and Kelley take the course of assigning plausible outcomes to the matrix cells and working back from these to a number of illustrative and supportive cases in social psychological research. In adopting the game theory convention, even to the limited extent that they have done, Thibaut and Kelley encounter difficulties, and I do not think they have underestimated these, which are shared by any attempt to represent social outcomes in the cells of a matrix.* How to assess the

---

* Some of the difficulties in applying game theory to the social sciences have been discussed in Archibald (1966) and Schelling (1963).

probability of outcomes as perceived by a person, involves a very large number of unresolved questions. To have some empirical justification for assessing probability there should be observation of recurring identical situations, but many social events are non-repeatable and therefore probability as an objective attribute evaporates, together with the notion of expected average payoffs. Similarly, Louch (1966) makes a relevant comment when he notes that economic game theory cannot be extended to aspects of behaviour which lack the assumptions of rationality and perfect information. There are several outstanding problems creating obstacles for any application of a game theory matrix to social behaviour where one has to admit of irrationality, uncertainty and subjective satisfactions. Thibaut and Kelley can make only very tentative statements of what the larger numbers in the cells may mean for higher probabilities (and vice versa) or when they discuss extending the matrix to a person's estimates of conditional probability. A sensitive question is raised when they refer to the number entries in the cells as representing the motivation of a person, that is the motivation of one person to change his behaviour to suit the behaviour of the other. Again, as far as scaling the values of outcomes is concerned, and we shall discuss this in a moment under *Numerical Values*, Thibaut and Kelley recognize a number of technical difficulties and take care to emphasize that their aim is explanatory and that their "present interest is in theoretical consequences of such an operation (real or imaginary) rather than its technical properties or even its feasibility" (p. 13).

The matrices

Thibaut and Kelley accept, and argue for, the general explanation that social relationships are influenced by the ratio of rewards and costs for each participant, a ratio which is represented in the payoff matrix. Basically, they seek support from reinforcement explanations in experimental psychology (animal and human) but, as we shall discover, their approach to social behaviour has an especial richness because of the number of conventional psychological concepts which they show to be consistent with their explanatory scheme. This foundation they combine with the game theory format and promise to afford a systematic consideration, through the matrices, of the possibilities of mutual accommodation: for example, simultaneous sharing of rewards or alternating rewards and costs, by agreement of the participants. More than this, the matrices can allow for unequal advantage by representing coercion of one participant by another. In this sense then, Thibaut and Kelley go further than an analysis of reciprocal behaviour which depends on the notion of equity. They are able to add degrees and conditions of inequity and to represent in the matrices, the actions of persons in opposition to each other.

The two-person relationship provides the prototype for the matrix and the illustrations for triads and larger groups follow the structure of a dyad: for example, in triads, the main illustrations used by Thibaut and Kelley involve coalitions of two persons interacting with one other person and in larger groups a consensus of the majority is shown to interact with the individuals or minorities: so that in each instance there are still two parties only in the exchange. The matrix itself represents a one-step strategy but in principle this can be extended to cover a sequence of interaction. The model is similar to those devised for continuous exchanges in game theory where there are series of matrix outcomes, each one developing from the last. I have already referred to the difficulties which would be encountered in trying to apply termination rules, fitting the steps to the empirical data and trying to find discernible starting points and ends for each matrix in a series which must represent sequences of social interaction. For a sequence of some duration one sure way of doing this would be to fix arbitrary closures between one matrix and another, of the sort feasible in the laboratory. This would place a heavy limitation on the model by confining the methods used to test it to the laboratory. This is an important point to which we will return later in the chapter. Thibaut and Kelley get round the problem to some extent by stating, as has already been mentioned, that in actual situations it should be possible to observe where the serial dependence of the actions in one behaviour sequence ends and another begins.

Thibaut and Kelley make a thorough analysis of the possibilities available in alternative courses of action. From the point of view of the individual, they ask, what will be his action in relationships with others? And they illustrate the kinds of action he may choose, as far as this action affects the results for him. However, the essence of their approach is to consider joint outcomes, the mutual dependence of rewards and the range of combinations which could result. The notion of exchange involves reciprocal services, return of favours, exchange o one kind of advantage for another, or of threats, coercion—or even of the trivia of casual sociability. Although they discuss the nature of particular rewards of costs when they come to examine existing research evidence in support of their explanations, they do not do so at first, being more concerned with the general outcomes of the exchange, expressed as high or lower numerical values. They consider that social exchange is a matter of the relative advantage or disadvantage of the persons involved and they argue that there are three broad types of exchange relationships: (i) a trading relationship, (ii) a relationship of dominance of one person by another (fate control); (iii) a relationship of compliance, persuasion or influence over the other person (behaviour control).

The easiest way to understand what this explanatoiy scheme has to offer will be through an outline of the major mutual strategies as Thibaut and Kelley present them in matrix form. Later, we will examine the explanations which they introduce for the process underlying the strategies and the supporting research evidence which they attempt to match to the different matrices.

THE TRADING AGREEMENT

First, outcomes may be optimized by the reciprocal *agreement* of the two persons who are in contact. The actions of each can be equally rewarding or there may be agreement, implicit or otherwise, to share rewards and to share costs, perhaps on an alternating pattern. For example, a given communication may involve one of the two persons in more costs than the other; on subsequent occasions this reward/cost ratio may be reversed, by agreement between the two. Thibaut and Kelley discuss examples of this alternation, including the experiment by Mintz (1951) where subjects pulling cones from a large bottle found that if they tried to do this simultaneously the cones jammed. However, with the condition that prior discussion was allowed, those participating were able to co-ordinate their activities *conjunctively* by alternately waiting and extracting cones.

POWER AND CONTROL

Secondly, and with more emphasis, Thibaut and Kelley are interested in situations where one person has power over another, and is in a position to allocate rewards to himself, irrespective of the choice of action by the other. This is called *fate control*. Fate control is illustrated in the payoff matrix shown in Fig. 2. By changing his behaviour from a_1 to a_2,

A can increase B's outcomes from 1 to 4. Conversely, he can reduce them and B has no possibility of counteracting. The person with fate control can direct to himself a greater share of rewards; he can decide whether to withhold rewards or make them available to the other. However, a limit is set to this kind of control by the weaker person's degree of dependence on the dyad—if his costs increase to a point where alternative relationships are more attractive and, if escape is possible, he may leave the relationship altogether.

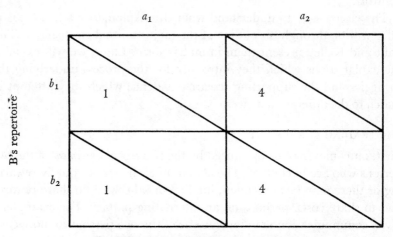

A's repertoire

Fig. 2 Illustration of A's fate control over B

It is consistent with their definition of power that there is this limiting case, and therefore B is gaining some rewards from the relationship when he submits to the wishes of A, unless there are also conditions of extreme coercion where escape itself is accompanied by stronger sanctions. Fate control may be implemented either through formal authority in an organization or through coercion in interpersonal behaviour. It is the inclusion by Thibaut and Kelley of the condition "irrespective of the actions of the other" which is interesting, as contrasted with the situations of social exchange considered by Homans and Blau (see Chapters 8 and 12). The latter see social exchange as largely a matter of interpersonal actions in *voluntary relationships*, whereas Thibaut and Kelley give explicit attention to coercive power such as may be found in prisons, the armed forces, or even in industrial organizations. But always there is some possibility of options for counteraction. One could think of the relationship between employer and employee as an instance where the matrix could represent conflict, with management decisions and withdrawal of labour as coercion and counter-coercion. Thibaut and Kelley seem to recognize this when they consider that fate control may give way to behaviour control, where the person with greater influence does take into account the actions or payoffs of the other, and arranges that these are improved providing they correspond with his own preferred outcomes. This introduces the mutual interaction effect which is implied in the interdependency, the double contingency in social relationships (see p. 55 below).

Thus a different kind of power, *behaviour control*, is achieved by a member of a dyad who varies his behaviour in such a way as to influence the other member to vary his. In Fig. 3, A has behaviour control over B by changing his behaviour from a_1 to a_2. B is induced to follow this move by changing from b_2 to b_1, because in doing so his rewards from

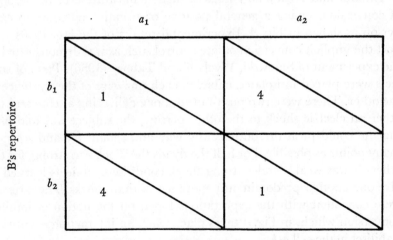

Fig. 3 Illustration of A's behaviour control over B

interaction with A are increased, his costs decreased. The amount of A's influence over B's depends on the values to B of the different outcomes—the more B stands to gain, the greater is the degree of A's control.

The a_2b_1 cells show an interaction effect, in the statistical sense, of joint behaviour of A and B. "That is to say, B's outcomes vary not as a function either of A's behavioural choices (fate control) or of his own, but as a function of the interaction between them" (p. 104). Thibaut and Kelley suggest the possibility of using a measure of statistical interaction by analysis of variance which would provide an index of behaviour control, although they do not take this any further than the statement of its possibility.

When a person with *fate control* acts to reward a particular course of action on the part of the other, this becomes *converted fate control*—converted, that is, to behaviour control. In this case, the more powerful person declares or follows his intentions of rewarding the weaker person providing he takes a particular course of action. Because rewards are given and costs reduced only (but consistently) for certain actions, control is achieved. This is illustrated in Fig. 2 where "Person A can make it desirable for B to perform set b_1 rather than b_2 by always performing a_2 when B does b_1 and a_1 when B does b_2," (p. 104). Person A must apply "matching rules" so that only two of the four combinations occur: a_2b_1 and a_1b_2.

Thibaut and Kelley now make a further illustration of this process of conversion, giving a general positive or negative outcome to each person as shown in Fig. 4. Experimental results of the late 1950s support the implicit conversion of fate control such as was demonstrated in the experiment of Sidowski, Wyckoff and Tabory (1956). Pairs of subjects were placed in isolated cubicles, each unaware of the existence of the other. There were two push-buttons, one delivering a score and the other an electric shock to the other person; the subject was told only that he could push the buttons any way and should try and score as many points as possible. For half the dyads the shock was strong, for the others it was weak. Under strong shock conditions, subjects learned to give one another predominantly more scores than shocks. These results were consistent with the expectations based on the notion of implicit conversion which, in Fig. 4 takes place when an interaction eventually stabilises in the cell a_1b_1.

Thus, the matrix is used to represent the joint outcomes of different behaviour and of different ways of controlling rewards and costs in the dyad. In listing three main types of strategy (trading agreement, fate control, behaviour control) only the broadest outline has been made of the alternatives, but this can be countered to some extent if we consider the matrix outcomes from the point of view of analysis of variance.

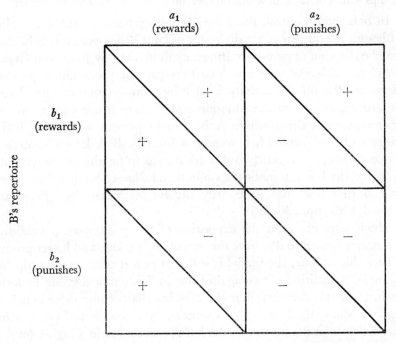

Fig. 4 An illustration of mutual fate control, which gives rise to implicit conversion

There would be three components underlying the outcomes for a particular individual:

(1) A main effect for outcomes produced for oneself (self- or reflexive-control).

(2) A main effect for outcomes produced for the other (fate control).

(3) An interaction term for outcomes conditional on joint behaviour (behaviour control).

No relationship would result if only reflexive-control were present and, as Thibaut and Kelley have since written (personal communication, 1972):

... reflexive-control combines in various ways with the other two components to affect the correspondence of outcomes in the relationship and hence the relative ease with which favourable joint outcomes can be attained. The trading relationship entails mutual fate control combined with "bilateral reflexive control" so that outcomes are highly correspondent, each person producing at low cost to himself (or even with

enjoyment) something of high value to the other. "Dominance" relationships would be those in which one person's fate control is overwhelming.

In behaviour control, there may be no exchange, strictly speaking.
Although the outcomes are the result of joint behaviour, this behaviour
may be the kind of pseudo-contingency illustrated by Jones and Gerard
(1967, pp. 506–508) where each party pursues his predominant personal
aims and the other's activity is of minor importance to him. Later,
Gerard elaborates on the situation where there is cue control by one
person over another—where A is able to present a stimulus which
triggers off well-established responses from B. If A knows enough of
B's past history of rewards and punishments to be able to present cues
to B's habitual or automatic responses then he has cue control and power
over B that does not necessarily involve exchange (see Jones and
Gerard, 1967, pp. 530–535).

Much later on, after the exposition of many different possibilities,
the matrix is used to illustrate the outcomes in triads and larger groups.
Where this is done, the model is still that of a dyadic relationship (for
example, a coalition of two against one individual or a group majority
against a single member) but the matrix cells become more complex.
Figure 5 shows the fate control exercised by a coalition of two persons
over a third. In the matrix on the left A can maintain a higher level of
outcome by taking account of the behaviour of either B or C, than by
disregarding both. But he can make a maximal adjustment only by
taking into account the behaviour of both. In the second matrix A
makes no average gain by watching either B or C; both must be
monitored.

In their forty-second matrix, an illustration is given of the collective
action of a group as one party to the dyad and the behaviour of an
individual member as the other. Here, in a trade union, the local
branch exercises influence on a member to act as secretary for its
meetings. In this illustration one of the members has to perform a
special service by preparing the minutes of their regular meetings.
Recording and transcribing the minutes may not in itself be an attractive job and so the other members have to persuade one individual to
undertake this task by means of other rewards which can be made
available. This is an interesting example of *converted fate control*, now
illustrated by Thibaut and Kelley for group behaviour outside the
laboratory. The members act together to convert fate control either by
rejecting the individual, if he fails to prepare the minutes, or by other

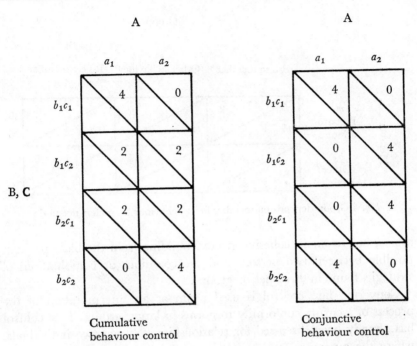

Fig. 5 Examples of types of behaviour control that the joint action of two persons can exercise over a third

behaviour sanctioning him, or praising him if he prepares them. The matching rule that g_3 (reject member) will be matched with m_2 (member's other behaviour) and g_1 (praise member) will only be matched with m_1 (prepare minutes) and this can be conveyed verbally or by enactment; the group must monitor the individual's activities and then act to produce the connection between behaviour and outcomes.

Although the illustration is taken from a very plausible situation involving the transactions of a group and its members, it is fair to remind ourselves that its application is still only illustrative and the numbers in the cells are arbitrary. They are there to indicate what may be the attractions of different choices of behaviour, expressed as the value of the rewards which accompany them. As in all the other instances of the matrices, there is no attempt to make the values convey anything more precise than this, or in any way to link empirically the values of the behaviour described.

Thibaut and Kelley give a number of illustrations of how these explanations apply to group behaviour, conformity, association with

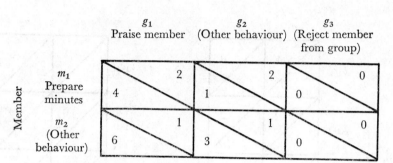

Fig. 6 Group depends on member for a behaviour he prefers not to do

others, behaviour in cohesive groups, building from the basic patterns possible between two persons and the coalitions or combinations of strategies found in three-person groups.

Converted fate control is used again as an interpretation of the process of securing conformity to norms in larger groups. Fate control has already been discussed for relationships between two individuals, where the outcomes to the more powerful person A (possessing fate control) cannot be affected by the actions of another person B. A can convert his fate control to behaviour control by matching his allocation of rewards to B's actions in such a consistent fashion that B's actions follow the matching rule. Now, at the group level, in order to achieve appropriate matching of the behaviour of individuals to group norms, individual actions must be monitored by other members and collective sanctions applied to the individual in such a way that preferred behaviour is attained. Thus the mechanisms of converted fate control, applied initially to dyads are used to explain conformity to norms and the use of collective sanctions and "highly cohesive groups have a relatively great amount of fate control to convert for the purpose of gaining compliance from deviate members" (p. 259). In low cohesive or unattractive groups where there is no widespread sharing of values, matching rules cannot be applied and members have to be coerced. The examples cited to support this explanation cover a variety of approaches from experiments to field studies.

We have now been shown how the model can be explicitly directed to larger groups and the collective action that takes place in them. But it is not really surprising that subsequent research has not produced applications of the matrices except in laboratory studies of dyads. The two-person laboratory design is so much more suitable for formal testing. In principle, it should be possible to apply the model to a variety of bargaining situations, for example, as has been suggested above, between an individual and his employer. In fact, this sort of application has not been made. Part of the difficulty derives from the complexity that will arise in action and counteraction once the matrix is extended beyond the laboratory situation. And there is still the problem of filling in the numerical values in the cells. This seems to be an intractable difficulty outside the laboratory, yet if research is to be confined to the laboratory this will narrow down the usefulness of a theory which is quite eclectic in its sources.

We have seen that in some matrices plus and negative signs are used to express the direction of values, of rewards and costs, while numbers are used to show the degrees of advantage of behaviour in different cells. I think there are two questions to be answered: how much importance do Thibaut and Kelley attach to these numbers? And how far has it been possible to make them represent empirical data?

A good deal of their discussion concerns the likelihood of different strategies and of moves from one matrix cell to another. In principle, it does seem that the cells can be filled by means of measures which they refer to as *comparison levels*. Since they have expressed the outcomes in numbers they must expect that transformation measures can be made of the social behaviour observed.

NUMERICAL VALUES

Thibaut and Kelley state a number of cautions on the use of the matrices, they intend them to be illustrative and to suggest conjectural outcomes from the interaction of two persons. As we have noted, the numbers in the cells cannot be fixed as they are in game theory; outcomes may fluctuate during interaction if only by the operation of fatigue and satiation effects. (When they point out that repetition is an important cost factor, they also accept that such sequential effects cannot be included into the reward-cost matrix.) While the matrix represents alternatives, the choice of one line of action or even a move from one line of action to another, it cannot represent the actual sequence of interaction and therefore unavoidably gives a partial representation, showing maximum rewards and minimum costs which "set the limits within which the actual interactions must occur" (p. 19). But the course of interaction itself is missed out and there are limitations to prediction because the matrix "is only a description of the *consequences* of behaviours themselves. Only under certain conditions does it seem possible to predict behaviour from such a matrix" (p. 16). This may not mean very much since explanation is nearly always predictive in purpose but it does tell us something about the cautious viewpoint taken by Thibaut and Kelley concerning what the model is intended to achieve.

Still, Thibaut and Kelley do assume that there is a strong correspondence between behaviour in the dyad and the numbers in the cells and that they can be used to represent the probability of the behaviour occurring. Their views on the imperfections of the matrix approach are stated as follows:

> We have chosen to use a very simple behaviour theory which we believe to be largely compatible with more sophisticated models and precise enough for present purposes. We assume that the probability of any one of A's behaviours being elicited is a function of two factors: (1) the strength of instigation to it (either from external or internal stimuli) and (2) previously experienced reinforcement resulting from it. The probability of occurrence reflects both of these factors whereas the objective reward-cost matrix reflects only the reinforcement consequent on the act (p. 26).

Clearly, the notion of probability here is very different to that found in game theory where it is a matter of averaging, and probability is important as a multiplier where utility magnitude is multiplied by the probability of its occurrence. For Thibaut and Kelley, the probability of an outcome lies in individual and situational factors and also in the amount of previous reinforcement which influences the incentive value of a particular kind of behaviour. They say later that it would be a reasonable extension of the model in some situations to treat the numbers as showing conditional probabilities. As we have mentioned, difficulties arise in game theory where assessment of probability values requires repetition of the matrix many times in order to arrive at average values; and we could expect even greater obstacles in social situations. (see p. 29 above).

Granted all the cautions, by introducing numbers into the cells, Thibaut and Kelley have implicitly assumed that the values of different behaviour can be assessed and they do make an attempt to show how, in principle, they can be measured. We can now briefly summarize this attempt, as follows. The assignment of values to the different outcomes is made against two criteria. The first of these is called the *comparison* *level* (CL). The second is called the *comparison level for alternatives* ($CL_{alt.}$). CL gives an assessment of the relationship itself, how far it is satisfying to the individual. $CL_{alt.}$ involves the lowest level of outcomes acceptable in the face of available alternatives. There is a close relationship between CL and $CL_{alt.}$, and the two will tend to be positively correlated. The magnitude of rewards which are sought after will depend upon individual needs and a person evaluates his outcomes by making the comparison with what he feels he deserves.* CL is influenced by his present situation, his skills, and the available opportunities. But his frame of references in assessing his outcomes is especially related to his past experience and Helson's (1948) adaptation level theory is brought in to show how past experiences will be important. To state the matter plainly, if one has received much, one continues to expect it. The degrees of *more* or *less* are perceived largely by comparisons with past experience. Outcomes above the CL will be relatively satisfying, those below it unsatisfying and unattractive. Outcomes of which he has experience, direct or symbolic, will influence the position of the person's CL which "may be taken to be some modal or average value of all known outcomes" (p. 21). The $CL_{alt.}$ will be related to what a person knows of other available relationships and it follows that as soon as outcomes in a given relationship drop below $CL_{alt.}$ the person will, if possible, leave that relationship. The position of the $CL_{alt.}$ will depend on the "reward-cost positions experienced or believed to exist in the most satisfactory of the other available relationships" (p. 22).

Thibaut and Kelley now make the nearest to a direct statement of how the numerical values are to be ascertained. The numbers in the cells will be scaled from the zero point belonging to the comparison level for alternatives—the least a person will settle for in his current relationships. In the simplified matrix this scale, from zero point of the $CL_{alt.}$, represents the individual's degree of dependence on the relationship relative to alternative relationships: the lower is the value of the $CL_{alt.}$ the greater will be his dependence. For instance, an index of A's fate control in Fig. 2 would be the average in reward-cost units that B achieves, above his $CL_{alt.}$.† As his outcomes in a relationship rise, B's

---

* The reader will notice here a similarity with Homans' notion of distributive justice (see Chapter 8)—that a person expects his rewards or outcomes to be proportional to his investment or efforts.

† Averaging of values means repetition of a situation. While it is easy to agree that this is the kind of mechanism which occurs in natural situations the question of how to apply averages as an objective measure has not been resolved.

dependence on that relationship will also rise. But it is possible that while outcomes are above the CL_{alt} they may fall below a person's CL, which also "constitutes a kind of zero or neutral point on the outcome scale" (p. 97), and in this case the relationship may not offer much attraction although the person will be coerced into it for lack of available alternatives. Stated in these terms a cohesive dyad is one where the members achieve for each other a relatively high number of reward-cost units above $CL_{alt.}$: thus, each one has high power over the other. Note that Thibaut and Kelley extend their definition of power by stating it as the capacity to reward others and therefore to produce return obligations, due from them.

The complexity of the assessment will be increased because the CL value depends on what outcomes a person has experienced in the past *and* which of these are actively stimulating. This latter weight will reflect how much the outcome is *instigated* for the person in the situation or by his own awareness, his self-reminders of what he might expect. At another point they conclude that "The CL thus begins to approximate the modal value of the range of outcomes over which the person believes his control prevails" (p. 86). This is largely what the individual feels he deserves and relates to a lesser extent to all the outcomes he has experienced. The reason for this, according to Thibaut and Kelley, is that outcomes are instigated according to how the person perceives he has responsibility for them, how far they are under his control.

A single scale is proposed (again, in principle) for the outcome values although the question of how reward-cost units are to be translated into standard units is left open.* This proposal does not avoid the obvious difficulties which would be involved in any attempt to transfer the alternative choices on to a unidimensional scale. Not only do short term goals have to be evaluated against long term ones, but material versus non-material, and internal goals (individual needs) against external or group goals. It is not shown how these are to be represented on one numerical scale. This is a major weakness in the model—it is not established how the perceived value of social activities and relationships, on the part of an individual, is to be expressed as a numerical outcome. Argyle (1969) notes that it is not shown how the subjective payoff matrix can be discovered. Argyle also mentions that in experiments the payoff is simply provided by the experimenter, but Thibaut and Kelley (1959, p. 25) do make the point that their matrix outcomes are not the

* An introduction to the difficulties of a single scale is given by Tversky, 1972.

same as values determined by an experimenter since the outcomes represent *all* subjective sources of value.

In summary, although Thibaut and Kelley give attention to the measurement possibilities, both for the CL and the $CL_{alt.}$ the statements made are brief and scattered through the book. Nevertheless, some guide-lines are offered which are consistent with the general explanatory statements. They suggest that reward values are reducible to a single psychological scale, even though they are not concerned with its technical properties or even its feasibility at this stage. This is a problem which is really left unresolved. It is the very important problem of expressing the rewards and costs in a measured form, and of measuring them in equivalent units. Presumably this could be done by ranking preferences. Thibaut and Kelley seem to incline to the view that they should not attempt any specification of a valuation formula, clearly this would have too many difficulties. They imply that their explanation should proceed without one, because the insights that may be obtained are a sufficient, if transient, objective.

Notions of a comparison level are applied to some very plausible cases. For example, the behaviour of a low-status person is explained adequately as follows: by avoiding occasions for contact with higher status persons he is able to screen the instigations or stimuli and to avoid comparing himself with them. By this stratagem "he does not ordinarily compare himself with that other person, hence the superiority of the other's outcomes does not afford grounds for dissatisfaction with his own fate" (p. 227). The question obstinately recurs of how the transformation might be made from the satisfactions and dissatisfactions of these plausible hypotheses, to the numbers in the cells?

A discussion of the conditions for survival of a group is brought down to the analysis of individual outcomes, where "the ultimate requirement is that it must hold its members, that is, keep each one consistently above his current $CL_{alt.}$. This means that for each member adequate rewards must be provided and costs of participation in the group must be kept down to reasonable levels" (p. 274). A number of propositions referring to behaviour which advances task performance and maintains the satisfactions of individual members, are now put forward. There is a discussion of behaviour sequence which serves both the purposes of a group and realizes individual expectations, as expressed by the notions of the CL and $CL_{alt.}$. By considering the influence of rewards and costs on the individual member's comparison of himself with other group members (CL) and of his comparison of his own group with the possibilities offered by other groups (CL_{alt}), we are brought back to the combination of a cognitive model with the game theory treatment of strategies: and especially to the possibilities for moves which this treatment makes explicit, from one strategy to another in order to maximize gains.

CONCEPTS

Some of the issues involved in adapting the game theory matrix to social behaviour have been discussed, and it will now be appropriate to consider Thibaut and Kelley's main body of explanation which deals with the process leading up to game theory outcomes. First to be considered will be their general theoretical frame of reference. Afterwards we will examine the extent to which the social process is explained by their use of psychological concepts.

Theoretical sources: reward propositions

First, let us consider the theoretical sources of this model, at their most general. Thibaut and Kelley are explicit about the influences and antecedents of which they are indebted. They consider past attempts at theory building: William McDougall's (1908) attempt to classify "social motives"; the sociologist Edward A. Ross's (1908) contrasting emphasis on "social interaction", Dashiell's (1935) comments on reciprocal relations, each person being "stimulable and reactive" and so on, down to Sears' (1951) definition of the two-sided social relationship as a "double contingency". Beyond this, as they elaborate the theme, the debt to economics resides in not much more than the general postulate of a trading or bargaining relationship between persons, with the principal aim of reducing costs. Thus, social norms may be interpreted as trading rules or agreements to reduce cost and maximize outcomes. This diffused influence of economics is seen again in the concept of advantages accruing to an individual's "psychic economy" (p. 119); in the activities of some group members who assess the reward/cost position of others, allocate their rewards, and sychronize this allocation with "cost peaks" (p. 276).

In Thibaut and Kelley's explanation of actions which result in particular outcomes in the matrix, the concept of reinforcement is central: outcomes are referred to as the "rewards, payoffs, reinforcement and utilities" (p. 4).* They make the point that interaction is a highly selective matter: some relationships are more satisfactory than others and selectivity in interaction results in a tendency for satisfactory interactions to recur. In a discussion which is occasionally tautologous,† they conclude that satisfactory interactions are those followed by rewards, which are defined as "the pleasures, satisfactions . . ." (p. 12) of the person. What constitutes a reward is the means by which drive is reduced or a need fulfilled. Thus, without specific mention of the notion of reinforcement in general psychology, a Hullian position is followed. In this way Thibaut and Kelley differ from Homans in the learning theory basis for the propositions, using the strong and not the weak version of reinforcement theory and incorporating, albeit with few explicit or developed references to them, the assumptions of Thorndike and Hull about the internal mechanisms of drive reduction. There is quite a large amount of discussion around the processes underlying behaviour, following the Hullian emphasis on the internal mechanisms of drive and reinforcement learning. Mixed with this are a number of statements of self-evident, common-experience observations concerning, for instance, the consequences of the use and over-use of power in two-person relationships.

Although some general terminology is borrowed from economics, the basic explanations are psychological. Thibaut and Kelley subscribe fully to reinforcement theory as a general orientation. The magnitude of rewards to be gained will depend on the individual's aims but in a "true trading relationship" (p. 15) all of each person's rewards are derived from the other's efforts. They do not argue for the primacy of any one kind of reward providing it is recognized that the rewards develop out of social relationships. What could be taken as their major premise is that "the most socially significant behaviour will not be repeated unless it is reinforced, rewarded in some way" (p. 12); what constitutes a reward is left as a matter for empirical research but Thibaut and Kelley avoid seeking explanations in individual motives—they consider it would be too unparsimonious and there would be too

---

* There is good precedent for this. Neal E. Miller in Stevens (1951) holds that "reward and reinforcement are roughly equivalent" (p. 435). But see also Woodworth and Sheehan (1964, p. 87) for a discussion of differences between the terms.

† In Chapter 2 there is a full discussion of the criticism that reinforcement theories are tautologous, and of the view that tautologies serve a constructive purpose in social psychology. This is discussed again in Chapter 9 when the arguments of Liska (1969) and Maris (1970) are summarized.

many propositions. Successful interaction between persons has to be functional for the group or social relationship, the end-purpose is group viability. However, they immediately link this notion of group viability to the satisfactions of the individual comprising it—what is functional for the group has also to be functional for its constituent members and thus "the group functionalism becomes an individual functionalism" (p. 5). Kelvin (1970) has pointed out "it seems possible that a quasi-economic model such as that of Thibaut and Kelley is itself a product of a particular social environment in the United States" (p. 175). This is not a very significant criticism because the model does not emphasize either monetary or economic gains or the exploitation* of one person by another. The economic aspects of trading are not assumed by Thibaut and Kelley, for example, in the relationships of the family, marriage, or friendship. The related issue of whether rewards are pursued only as an egocentric strategy has been discussed by Asch (1959), as a broad problem for social psychological theory. In fact, Thibaut and Kelley take quite a tentative position on this because, as they state, the positive outcomes of interaction and what forms these may take are discovered by research; they emphasize both individual needs and group viability as contributing to these outcomes, thereby avoiding the assumption of self-centred action. The question of ego-centric assumptions in exchange theory is one which is to be discussed again in Chapter 7. We shall discover that altruism is by no means excluded and that, as Sawyer (1966) argues, the rewards of two indi-viduals may not be clearly separable because the welfare of one person provides a reward to the other: altruism is not necessarily opposed to egotism, one can be equally concerned with one's own and another's welfare. Asch has probably made the most memorable statement about the wider issues of whether individual needs are fulfilled by rewards accruing to the self or to others:

> an error in thinking and in psychological analysis made it appear that there is no alternative to an egocentric formulation. To be sure, mothers have been known to starve in order to feed their children, and persons have endangered their lives for others. There are, then, actions which at least appear to be quite the opposite of self-centred. [But] contrary data are weak reeds against winds of doctrine. The ready answer stood at hand that the need to help others is egocentric because one enjoys it; it is

* For an instance of an exploitation approach run wild, and with clinical interpre-tations added, see Berne *Games People Play* (1964).

egotistic to enjoy one's unegotistic action ... The issue is, of course, a factual one; conceivably the most seemingly disinterested action may be work of calculation and self-interest. Admittedly a decision about this question is difficult, perhaps mainly because much of human behaviour is a function of both kinds of vectors. But science does not justify dogmatism when a problem is beset with difficulties.

A re-examination of a range of problems in the light of this issue could provide a challenging task. One may safely say that if social psychology is to make progress, it must take into account the vectors that make it possible for persons to think and care and work for others. It will need to find a place for the capacity of persons to relate to the needs of a situation so that they become the needs of the person; it will have to acknowledge that the desire to play one's part meaningfully may at times be strong, and that it may even make sense to speak of an individual's desire for the realization of a better society (Asch, 1959, pp. 371–373).

Touching on the question of egocentric behaviour is the related question of whether an individual's decisions are calculated, deliberate or rational in the economic sense of maximizing personal gains. How much deliberate calculation is assumed by Thibaut and Kelley? They point out that "adaptive performance need not be construed as evidence of continuing, deliberate purposive hedonism" (p. 29). Usually, solutions are not worked out in this way but are provided by routines, that is by the rules that other persons have found useful and which are expressed in role-prescriptions. There is an assumption of awareness where the individual surveys his situation and forms "an adequate conception of the interdependency pattern" (p. 29), although as already pointed out his information may be incomplete. They emphasize that if the individual has "ability, the means of acquiring information and of rehearsing his response alternatives, he does make the decision with awareness" (p. 29). Rational evaluation of an egocentric type seems to be assumed at some stages of the discussion of comparison levels. We are given a number of instances where the choice is calculative, but with an assurance that this would not necessarily be so. For example, although there is evaluation of likely outcomes by participants both at the start and during social interaction, the amount of deliberative planning may be slight. Presumably some decision-making will take place in the initial phases but here they point out that the initial test of outcomes, where the sampling of another behaviour takes place, is implicit and not rationally planned. They describe the sort of cues which may be important in the perceptual process at this initial state (p. 62). Appraisal of initial contacts "is not a rationally planned thing, it is more an implicit test" (p. 65) and changing from one course of action to another may follow a day-to-day coping with immediate situations, or vicarious learning from others, rather than a deliberative forecasting of trends. If they are unwilling to assume a hedonistic calculation or a deliberate optimizing of rewards, neither do they accept a random trial and error sequence of behaviour. Instead there is "a kind of natural selection of appropriate sets" (p. 62).

Despite this, Thibaut and Kelley do not succeed in completely throwing off the calculative bias of the model in so far as it shows whenever they discuss the objective possibilities of the reward-cost matrix. When they start to discuss a person's use of power to change outcomes, to change another person's behaviour or attitudes, they refer to what he perceives and believes to be the facts of the interdependency and, in some cases, he is assumed to have accurate understanding of the facts presented in the matrix. Again, when they discuss coalitions between two or more persons who act jointly to affect the outcomes of others, they make the point that the actions of a coalition will usually be done with awareness, "although we do not care to insist that they must be so" (p. 205). Recently Kelley and Thibaut (1969) have been concerned with the individual process of information-seeking and with information distribution in groups and they explore thoroughly the perceptual and cognitive skills involved. One of their central topics for discussion is the individual's acquisition of information about the payoff contingencies (see Chapter 6).

Whatever the influences on decisions, the subjective choice of appropriate action may be quite different to an objective estimate of the values which *optimally* should be sought. The possibility of discrepancy is at the centre of the explanatory attempt by Thibaut and Kelley. It would be wrong, clearly, to think that their approach allows only for the calculation of material payoffs. The notion of exchange nowhere implies this and to that extent Kelvin (1970) and Mann (1969) take an inadequate view in asserting that exchange theory presents only a materialistic model. Mann gives much emphasis to terms such as reward, cost, investment and profit, which occur in exchange theory and arrives at the merely superficial conclusion that the theory treats with "the more calculated and mercenary aspects of interpersonal attraction" (Mann, 1969, p. 42) and we have already seen that the issue should not be foreclosed in this way. It is true that when exchange propositions are tested in laboratory games, the gains and losses are easily quantified in points or money but there are recent instances where the measurement of payoffs is extended to trust and liking (Worthy, Gary and Kahn, 1969). In other developments of exchange theory by Homans and Blau, justice is a value exchanged (see Chapters 8 and 12).

Psychological concepts: S–R terminology

The influences on individual decisions and the social process which culminates in a given outcome form the major part of the explanations offered by Thibaut and Kelley. As we have described above, the reward-cost matrix may be considered to represent objectively available outcomes but it could be made to represent subjective anticipations, which may not be the same thing. In an attempt to clarify the question of discrepancy between objective estimates of best possible outcomes and the subjective view of the actors, a stimulus-response (S–R) framework is adopted. The objective possibilities, *assuming that means exist for describing them* provide the stimulus, and subjective perceptions are the response. Thus a form of analysis is suggested following the S–R conventions of measurement pertaining to laboratory experiments. Thibaut and Kelley point out that the aim of experiments on perception in classical S–R psychology is to examine discrepancies between objective phenomenon and the subjective response. Similarly, they argue that by comparing actual social behaviour with the outcomes predicted by objective criteria, a contribution may be made to our understanding. For instance there may be influences inducing a person to act, such as coercion by others or his own emotional states, or else the information he has available upon eventual consequences may be only partial. Such influences they term the *instigations* to behaviour: external or internal stimuli producing a response which may well be different to what is required for an optimal outcome, by the objective criteria. Or there may be situations where response interference occurs, when, say, powerful instigations from the behaviour of other persons are incompatible with internal needs or drives, and there may be competing demands from alternative social activities.

Discussion of these mainly experimental findings emphasizes the mechanisms of "sets, or response sequences", that lie behind behaviour and the potential outcomes. Using this frame of reference for social behaviour suggests that "interpersonal interference" will raise costs (p. 52) and that this kind of cost may be reduced by the joint activity

of two or more participants. Social interaction, with favourable outcomes, is a matter of combining and synchronizing compatible responses; and social roles frequently embody such synchronization.
Rights, privileges, precedence, seniority, can be seen in this light and so
can the "high serial dependence of items of behaviour specified by
roles" (p. 61). Social roles are interpreted as routines providing the
high degree of over-learning that in experimental studies has been
shown to make it easier for individuals to resist the effects of anxiety, or
of interference from others in performing tasks. They point to natural
situations where the intensive practice and drill of police, firemen and
the armed services can be explained in this way.

Thus, Thibaut and Kelley make considerable use of S–R terminology,
explaining social behaviour in terms of competing responses and
response strengths, high anxiety levels or high drive towards competing goals. The problems which derive from competing responses in a
relationship are discussed. Conflict may be minimized by "giving close
attention to relevant stimuli and selectively excluding the irrelevant.
The cues which tend to keep one in a single set may be multiplied and
other cues avoided . . ." (p. 55). This analysis in terms of cost avoidance
is similar to the S–R theoretical analyses of conflict-avoidance drives.
Further S–R instances of the effects of anxiety levels on learning
and task performance are quoted as giving hypotheses for behaviour in
dyads. Experimental citations of Berlyne (1957) and other researchers
are combined for the purpose of these explanations with plausible
examples from common-knowledge situations. The conclusion is reached
that individuals tend to select perceptual cues and to economize in the
attention given to incoming information. An instance of such economiz-
ing is the primacy effect which occurs in the initial contacts between
two persons, importance being given to early information at the beginning of a relationship. Following Attneave's (1964) development of
information theory leads to "the general principle that perceptual processes operate to minimise the cost of information intake" (p. 73).
Here again is a hypothesis taken from another branch of psychology
and applied to social behaviour. But note that this is done in order to
explain the perception and learning of social responses by individuals
and it is not a hypothesis applied to the social pattern itself, nor to the
double contingency.

This is especially the weakness of the S–R conventions—which are
not well suited to reciprocal social sequences. Thibaut and Kelley do

emphasize this when they say that separating out the stimulus side from the response side "does violence to the two-way flow of interaction" although they add that "it seems justifiable for the purpose of analysis and organization of topics" (p. 68). The S–R framework seems to run counter to their principal aim of examining social interaction in its own right, it presupposes that stimulus and response can be isolated and measured whereas in the mutual feedback of interaction sequences clearly this cannot be done. The matrix approach allows for social situations with no apparent separation between independent and dependent variables and Thibaut and Kelley have stated at the beginning of their book: "Each subject's behaviour is at the same time a response to past behaviour of the other and a stimulus to future behaviour of the other; in no clear sense is it properly either of them" (p. 2). While they conceptualize the independent variables as the mutually related strategies, and dependent variables as the characteristics of the interaction process, Thibaut and Kelley argue that in reality the independent and dependent variables blend. They have therefore made an explicit attempt to treat the interdependence of social relationships, which, as they point out, much of experimental social psychology tends to by-pass.

Although Thibaut and Kelley have shown that S–R concepts can be used to explain some social phenomena, they conclude, without further discussion, that the S–R conventions are not suitable for the double contingency in social interaction. We can infer that this is largely a matter of method. S–R analysis cannot be applied to the reciprocal pattern because, although the S–R theorist might say that the stimuli and responses are there and it is only a question of defining them, the problem is *how* to measure them in the interaction sequence. But there is probably more to it than this; the S–R paradigm also implies that the subject is passive, responding to the experimental stimuli, whereas in social relationships we need a frame of reference that incorporates the individual's active intervention in continuous interaction with others. The laboratory presentation of measured stimuli is not the way to explore the individual's tactics in presenting himself advantageously, his management of the impression he makes on others, or his strategy in deliberately setting out to enhance another's self esteem. In brief, the S–R convention fails to allow for the interdependency and it fails as an approach to the individual's active intervention in social sequence. While S–R conventions abound in their source material, Thibaut and

Kelley have dropped this approach in order to take account of the double contingency and they replace an S–R paradigm by their own experimental model.

As has been illustrated, in order to test their model we need a particular form of experiment where we can conveniently observe behaviour in units suitable for translation to the matrix values. Can we now extrapolate beyond the model to natural situations? If we were to decide to pursue research along the lines of this model, describing or predicting matrix outcomes, would we be restricted to these explicit events or could we extrapolate beyond them? Tajfel's (1972) discussion of game theory models of social conflict is relevant here. He has drawn attention to a situation where the hypotheses "are experimentally tested in contexts which are selected on the basis of the properties of the model rather than of those of the modelled phenomena" and "no extrapolation from the *findings* can be made to social conflict . . ." (Tajfel, 1972, p. 14). Thibaut and Kelley have shown they are eclectic in the cause of arguing for the plausibility of their model, by their willingness to use evidence from very different kinds of research, in support of their propositions. But it remains to be seen, and this will be a main point for discussion in the next chapter, whether the model which they offer has generality.

Thus, the S–R approach of individual psychology is rejected and a model for reciprocal strategies is substituted, although this model is demonstrated as providing explanations which are consistent with the findings and concepts of experimental individual psychology. Anticipating the reduction issue of Chapter 14, we may now ask: to what degree is the model independent of individual psychology? All it means is that a certain paradigm for research has been put forward as more appropriate for testing hypotheses about social interaction. This does not alter the fact that the premises of the model, tentative though they may be, are to be found in general and individual psychology. It seems fair that the explanatory connection with general psychology should not compel the use of a method of analysis where behaviour has to be isolated into stimulus and response units. And while this is so, the model still rests on general propositions derived from individual experimental psychology. That these take a somewhat unrefined form does not alter the main conclusion that the possibility of a logical reduction remains. It cannot be formally spelled out, and in fact need not be at the current stage of theory building, but it is very clearly implied by Thibaut and

Kelley in their major explanatory propositions, derived as we have seen from reinforcement theory, and in others which we will discuss in a moment.

Learning theory

Let us now examine how "elementary considerations of learning" (p. 110), associative or motivational, are cited to explain some of the behaviour of participants in social relationships. Thibaut and Kelley use Hullian terminology in interpreting the resolution of conflict between two courses of action—greater vigour of drive developing for the chosen alternative. Association learning is mentioned where "A will reward B in order to get B to produce behaviour that he, A, finds rewarding. By doing so, A creates conditions under which, through association in learning, B is likely to learn to like this behaviour himself. The greater A's ability to reward B, the more this learning will occur" (p. 115). The further distinction is made between cognitive and reinforcement learning in order to explain the development of interpersonal norms. The differences between these two kinds of learning are given in the following illustrations. Cognitive learning is suggested for new situations which are seen to be similar to previous ones "the behaviour rules applicable to the old are generalized to the new". Other norms may develop by a process of trial and error, a given rule comes to be adhered to because following it makes the situation more predictable and comfortable for participants; reinforcement learning has taken place.

It is interesting to notice the number of heterogeneous illustrations supplied by Thibaut and Kelley supporting alternative possibilities for two-person exchange: some are analogies taken from experiments on animal behaviour and others are taken from everyday familiar experience. While there is heterogeneity of illustrations, the nature of the explanation offered is itself well specified, developing on to individual courses of action and it is therefore reductionist in the tentative logical sense that I have used for this term. However, if the explanation derives from the premises of individual psychology, how do we adduce them to the double contingency? Thibaut and Kelley do not really pursue this line of development.

It would therefore seem that the prolonged consideration and conjecture about individual drives, learning and courses of action are only indirectly supportive to the matrix of outcomes. However, the efforts made by Thibaut and Kelley to bring psychological process into the framework of social exchange has been worthwhile. They have presented a model of choice and alternative strategies but they examine the strategies as representing underlying process. At the same time, there is no doubt that the section of the argument which deals with hypotheses concerning individual process is the weakest, far weaker than the later discussion of group events. This weakness lies in the separation between individual process, as explicated in the laboratory, or recognized from common experience, and the interdependency of social phenomena.

Supporting evidence

Thibaut and Kelley draw on a variety of research studies to provide supporting evidence for their model. We can now consider some instances of how they do this. They review a number of general propositions or suggestions each one backed up with illustrations either from field or experimental studies. After an initial statement of the conditions under which two persons can achieve their best reward-cost positions, the first illustration is well within the tradition of S–R research— a study of "co-operation in rats" (Daniel, 1942) which is now translated into reward-cost terms. Next, they move on to non-experimental evidence from Moreno (1934) and Jennings (1950) who used sociometric questionnaires to measure friendship choices of some 400 adolescent girls. One conclusion of the many verbatim illustrations from these studies is that however subtle the motives satisfied in a dyad may be, "the relationship may be viewed as a trading or bargaining one" (p. 37).

Some discussion takes place about what makes a good partner in a dyad, the evidence showing that intelligence may have some general value, as do such qualities as ability to empathize. Relationships also depend very much on situational or ecological factors; although the effects of proximity are sometimes inseparable from those of similarity between persons. Similarity, it is suggested, has "learned reinforcement value" (p. 43)—persons similar to each other tend to express agreement and thus provide rewards for each other. Further instances are cited of how perception that one is liked or accepted by others leads to reciprocated positive choice. Status is another factor which influences sociometric choice, and association with people of higher status yields rewards. Thibaut and Kelley point to several topics for future research including (1) perceptions of being liked or disliked and how these come about. Their examination of the early stages and formation of relationships is notable for a sociological citation: that of Merton's (1940) description of the bureaucrat's trained incapacity—the incapacity to differentiate among individual cases. Other topics they suggest for study are (2) rewards from high status persons and the nature of these rewards; (3) the contribution of similarity as against complementarity in relationships between persons. The discussion of complementarity relies on research results of the period up to the later 1950s which Thibaut and Kelley regard as giving an inconsistent picture, possibly because of inadequate methodology and "failure to measure needs and abilities at the appropriate level" (p. 47). More recent research into this topic will be dealt with in the next chapter.

The wide sweep of evidence on which Thibaut and Kelley draw in order to suggest or support the hypotheses accounting for the reward/cost matrix outcomes, lends conviction to their model as do their arguments demonstrating that existing psychological theories fit with the matrix solution. Their explanatory attempt gains general plausibility, but thereafter relationships still require to be stated more precisely. It should be remembered that the illustrative material which is used as support for descriptive hypotheses—for example, that X reciprocal behaviour will vary under Y conditions and that there may be N alternative hypotheses—does not connect up directly to the numerical values of the matrix. Neither is it established that Thibaut and Kelley's matrix approach is itself any more fruitful than some other conceptual presentation. Furthermore, it is clear that the representation of behaviour by numerical values, the connection of actions to numbers in the cells, can best be done under controlled conditions, where weights are allocated to the outcomes in simplified (perhaps monetary) forms. It seems inconsistent, that further construction of the theory may have to depend on the use of laboratory designs with their inevitable artifacts, even though there is no such restriction on the body of research which is used to launch it.

Larger groups

The last third of Thibaut and Kelley's book (pages 191–291) deals with the relationships in groups larger than the dyad. It is not really surprising that when group process, as distinct from individual strategies, is discussed, the arguments and illustrations are brought much closer to the matrix outcomes and the reciprocal solutions, than has been possible for the S–R and individual learning examples. We shall now consider some of the major points which arise.

They make clear that they intend to derive explanation of behaviour in larger groups from the concepts and "the theory developed to this point for the dyad" (p. 191). The differing conditions of larger groups are pointed out, for instance where the mutual choices of dyads are shown as not necessarily compatible with the general functioning of the larger group of which they form part—they may divide it up. There follows a discussion of a number of ways of raising a member's rewards that are not possible in a dyad, but are possible in larger groups. For example there may be "joint cost cutting" (p. 196) where the costs are distributed over a larger number, although Thibaut and Kelley illustrate this only from groups of three (triads). It is shown how there can be trading agreements for three people or more which could not be worked out by a pair. A further pattern unknown in the dyad exists where A is dependent upon C but can offer C nothing directly in return; a third person acts as an intermediary by being able to transform A's product into something of value to C.

Despite these conditions which pertain to large groups and are not found in dyads, Thibaut and Kelley consider situations where several persons combine to take action as two partners or coalitions. Thus, cohesiveness and power in groups, as investigated by Festinger, Schachter and Back (1950), is translated into a dyadic framework. The dyad is a relationship between an individual (as Actor A) and the concerted actions of the other group members (as Actor B)—a reasonable translation where members of a group strive to make a particular individual conform to their norm. They act as a coalition to reduce deviant behaviour, since on this particular issue their interests are in agreement. At the same time it is acknowledged that under other conditions "the assumption is seriously in error" (p. 208)—for example, if the degree of consensus among members is low.

Next, Thibaut and Kelley introduce triadic relationships to illustrate something of the alternative combinations of changes of values in the cells and hence the probability of control, when outcomes correspond or conflict or where synchronization becomes necessary as we saw in Fig. 5, above. The matrices are now extended to the eight cells needed to represent the triad.

The discussion returns to game theory considerations when coalitions are considered between two or more people who act jointly. Thibaut and Kelley discuss various ways in which two persons can mobilize themselves to influence the outcomes of a third. There are some quite interesting examples given of this kind of alliance, which they term *conjunctive fate control* by two persons who can act separately either to lower or increase the outcomes of a third. Co-ordination of outcomes may become relatively more difficult as the number of persons increases and in these situations group norms may specify the appropriate behaviour: "because of the proliferating problems of co-ordination with increase in size, group norms that specify the behaviours necessary for co-ordination gain in urgency as groups become larger" (p. 201). In other instances the co-ordination problem may be avoided where the group formation consists of "many overlapping dyadic relationships, all of which have one member in common. . . . Examples are the cheer leader and the coxswain" (p. 201). Much of the discussion of what may happen in the dyads and triads making up a larger group, is based on appeals to what is plausible in common experience.

The example of triads is extended to situations where there is imperfect correspondence between the outcomes of members. Where there is some conflict of interest a person with less power will be unlikely to influence the coalition towards his own preferred aims. He would therefore be likely to seek a coalition in which he is more powerful. On the other hand, he would also be expected to seek a coalition with the highest overall effectiveness in the social or physical environment. In the end he may have to compromise and enter a coalition in which he is relatively weak for the sake of its overall effectiveness in gaining rewards, of which he will have a share. Thibaut and Kelley describe experimental evidence where tasks are arranged so that individuals have a number of possibilities of combining to improve their joint outcomes, and they speculate on these, connecting once again the reward/cost matrix to a game theory approach—for example, a person may maximize his outcomes by certain strategies and some attention is given to the case where a person's expected outcomes are equivalent to the product of the probability of completing a task effectively and the outcome value.

Translation of Homans' Theory

The relationship between liking and rates of interaction as postulated by Homans (see Chapter 8), and by Newcomb (1953) is introduced in order to interpret the experimental finding that triads tend to develop into a mutually supportive pair and an isolate. Data from an experiment by Mills (1953) involving the observation of 48 triads demonstrated both that interactions which yielded mutual support right from the start tended to persist, and that relationships of conflict tended to be unstable, converting to mutual support. Thibaut and Kelley argue, in effect, that the interaction-liking hypothesis is explained at a more basic level of underlying process as an expression of *converted fate control*. However, it appears that this is itself explained by the tendency "to repeat acts that are rewarding and discontinue acts that are punished" (p. 212)—the reinforcement premise which we referred to earlier in this chapter (see p. 49 above). At this point the explanation of Thibaut and Kelley and of Homans truly seem to merge.

A number of statements are congruent with Homans' Proposition 1 (the more similar is a situation to one in the past where a man's activity has been rewarded, the more likely he is to repeat that activity) and Proposition 2 (the more often a man's activity is rewarded by another, the more often he will repeat it); they are specifications of conditions for the process of social learning. Although, unlike Homans and Blau, Thibaut and Kelley do not give special attention to altruistic rewards, they do have in common the considerable importance which they give to past experience. Much of their discussion is an examination of how past experience influences present action and they draw on Helson's (1948) experiments to emphasize this. Note too their discussion of association learning; the effects of liking on perception; the importance of initial impressions on subsequent relationships; the effects of strangeness on perception; how past experience leads to mutual accommodation and to converted fate control.

Their treatment of the influences of status on behaviour is very similar to that of Homans and can be summarized as follows. Higher status persons have more power to give rewards. Therefore the more rewards an individual wishes to attain, the more he will associate with high status persons. However, as he does this his profit per unit activity will tend to decrease because he will incur obligations to the higher status person. Each additional unit of reward will show a diminishing margin of utility and the more his reward, the more his obligations. It is possible to extract further propositions from Thibaut and Kelley's discussion, although they themselves do not state them explicitly as propositions. For example, they argue and provide supporting evidence for the propositions that: the less power an individual has to compel another's actions, the more he will be likely to accommodate that person; the more influence a person has the less likely he is to consider the outcomes of the other—followed by the limiting proposition—the more a person uses power to coerce another, the more is the other likely to use counter-power. In their model the individual is assumed to optimize his outcomes, material or non-material, and he may do this by mutual accommodation with another in a trading relationship or by fate control, converted fate control or behaviour control. Here again, further propositions can be stated such as: the more information the individual has, the more his decision will approach the objective interdependency, and: the fewer the situational and emotional instigations, the more likely is his decision to approximate the objective interdependency. There are many more propositions presented by Thibaut and Kelley in the course of their explanations of the different conditions for individual strategies and social outcomes, but they do not attempt to systematize them to the extent that Homans has done.

Among a large number of propositions derived from self-evident assumptions, from learning theory, from anecdotal references and from a variety of social research findings there are also two propositions familiar in the context of economic exchange: one refers to the diminishing returns of repeated rewards and the other deals with the choices offered by alternative relationships. These, however, are really psychological propositions referring to economic behaviour, and as I have emphasized in this chapter, the influence of economic theory goes no further than the use of a few concepts, and in this respect the explanatory framework is very similar to that of Homans.

Conclusions

Propositions concerning problem-solving, the matching and judging of the likely outcomes of interaction with others, take up a good deal of the discussion. As far as the influence of cognitive aspects of perceiving and judging social relationships are concerned, although this takes up a large part of their argument, Thibaut and Kelley do not entirely resolve the question of whether the explanations are to assume a calculative, deliberative choice of actions or merely action which follows the direction of previous reinforcements, without cognitive awareness or planning. Where Hullian theory is called on, it applies only to the latter kind of action and learning, and even then the Hullian hypotheses can refer to social situations only by analogy from rein-forcement conditions tested in the animal laboratory. In any case, Hull's concepts seem to be included rather as token references reflecting ultimate loyalties, but they have no direct bearing on the substantive content of the model or of the research findings presented in support of it.

For these reasons, Thibaut and Kelley have not brought us nearer the possibility of making a formal attempt at reducing explanations of social interaction to more basic assumptions in psychology. But there are a number of positive effects of their model for theory-building. Psy-chological explanations form the starting point and a major feature of their theoretical approach to social behaviour. Their approach does fit with the assumptions and research findings of individual psychology, although they do not attempt a systematic derivation. Moreover, they defend the study of interpersonal behaviour against a reduction to collective or structural concepts. In this respect they mention that "At this point in the development of social theory it seems unwise to rely too heavily on social stratification as a model for small group status systems or to test hypotheses about these systems by reference to evi-dence from larger aggregates" (p. 223).

In short, the propositions which are found in Thibaut and Kelley's work are for the most part derived from psychology, although their sources are empirical studies rather than theoretical statements. The brevity of their references to Hullian terminology reveals the slight extent to which they draw on basic theory and they do not refer their model formally to psychological propositions. From this they go on to define a variety of conditions of rewards and costs in social interaction and to discuss the possibility of measuring "the criterion of reward value" (p. 57). However, having provided a sophisticated analysis of social behaviour, they fail to carry this through. The relationship of social exchange theory to general psychology is one which, in the future, will be developed, inevitably, in the process of testing concepts and hypotheses—and other exchange theories will contribute. Furthermore, the game theory matrix as used by Thibaut and Kelley is an approach which has brought further insights into the process of accommodation and conflict. In game theory itself it is the outcome values which are important, while the social psychological process is taken as given. Game theorists, however, tend to pin their hope on future advances by social psychologists (Rapoport, 1966). Thibaut and Kelley have given this hope some encouragement. There are several questions outstanding such as the problems of defining the beginning and end of sequences, of transforming social actions into matrix values, of experimental definitions and social applications, of generating hypotheses and the methods of subsequently testing them. Thibaut and Kelley present a variety of evidence which, as they have shown, fits their speculative reward/cost matrices. The end result is a model by which it is proposed to test the many propositions they have included, particularly in the experimental laboratory, where values can be conveniently measured in reward or cost quantities (see Gergen, 1969).* The question now remains of how productive the approach has been for research and this will be the topic of the chapter to follow. The further question remains of the general validity of the model outside the laboratory. Will it become unproductive in the long term, if it cannot be used for actual conditions of social behaviour? I have suggested the possibility, at the risk of being repetitive, several times in this chapter (pp. 33, 43, and 56) that Thibaut and Kelley may, by presenting the paradigm, have put too severe a restriction on the methods that can be used to test their model. Homans places no restriction on the methods that can be used to test his theory. On the other hand, some investigators have considered it a disadvantage of Homans' propositions that they do not offer a research paradigm (see Komorita, Sheposh and Braver, 1968).

* Note the difficulties in practical situations to which Collins and Raven, 1969 (p. 120) draw attention.

4

The Development of the Model

Introduction

Thibaut and Kelley have made it clear that their aim is to present a tentative but systematic approach to a theory. They claim only to begin with a few relatively simple statements to which they will add as more evidence accumulates and they disclaim any attempt at a formal deductive theory. They make no assumptions, similar to those of the natural sciences, about what a theory should be nor that there should be a structure of general propositions and hypotheses to be tested empirically. They do not attempt anything so ambitious, nor do they accept such a theory as an appropriate immediate aim in social psychology. Instead, they suggest that their use of the game theory matrix should at least lead to greater understanding of the subtleties in social relations. What has been the contribution of the recent research influenced by their model? We can now hope to answer a question raised in the previous chapter: is their model more advantageous for explaining social behaviour than other approaches?

Since the publication of *The Social Psychology of Groups* (1959) the model of Thibaut and Kelley has had wide influence; something of this is indicated by the many psychological and sociological journals in which citations are currently to be found. Thibaut and Kelley themselves have continued with research and have personally encouraged or supervised a number of research workers. Most of this research is within the general area of experimental games, defined by Apfelbaum (1966) as any simulation of conflict where there is interdependence of the participants and they have both common and divergent interests. Since the largest body of work in experimental games uses the Prisoner's

Dilemma matrix it is not surprising to find that Thibaut and Kelley also have used it and are, in fact, among its strongest protagonists in social psychology. But we must make a distinction between the objectives which the Prisoner's Dilemma was originally intended to achieve in game theory and those of its current psychological adaptations.

In the previous chapter I argued that the game theorist is concerned with the goals to be reached by a variety of strategies and is not concerned with *how* magnitudes are assigned to the outcomes by the players. Why one goal is preferred to another is a question for social psychology, and the stated purpose of Thibaut and Kelley (1959, p. 4) is to discover what it is that prevents purely logical solutions. We will see later that there are a number of criticisms that can be made against this approach. In this sense, Thibaut and Kelley take over the payoff matrix as their main experimental design, at the point where game theory leaves off. This is Rapoport's (1970) view of what the psychologist's contribution might be. But what is the actual achievement of Thibaut and Kelley and the many scholars influenced by them? Most important of all, have they added significantly to our knowledge of the social relationship? They have set out to examine the interdependency. Do they and their followers in fact cast light on the social conditions facilitating competition, co-operation or exploitation? We shall seek an empirical answer to this question. We could, it is true, argue right at the outset that the payoff matrix is not likely to be useful as a design for investigating social problems. Later on we will refer to this kind of criticism, but in the meantime we should not forget that we are interested in an empirical assessment. Moreover, the work of Thibaut and Kelley and their "school" is not entirely confined to the payoff design; they use other forms of experiment and their work has influenced the general theoretical discussion of exchange propositions.

Generalizing from the experimental game

The work carried out by Thibaut and Kelley themselves, or supervised by them, or in some way influenced by their model, has focused mainly on exploring the social process of exchange in two-person relationships in the course of laboratory games, tasks, bargaining or negotiating. By adopting the paradigm, have they chosen the most effective model or one which is merely restrictive? How far can we proceed by clarifying why one alternative is preferred to another in a simplified laboratory game? The answer is largely a matter of whether observations made in the context can be generalized to social situations where individuals are members of groups with continuity and a deeper identification than the brief laboratory session. A full statement of these questions is made by Plon (1967, 1972) who seeks to emphasize the superficial nature of experimental games as a bar to further generalization. Thibaut and Kelley are entirely opposed to this viewpoint. Generalizing is a preoccupation of theirs which expresses itself on many occasions when they argue from their results in support of a generalization to actual situations or give this as their aim. (Thibaut and Kelley are completely consistent in their pragmatic approach; above all they are exponents of one kind of experimental paradigm.) Nor are they at all convinced by criticisms that such generalizing cannot be justified and they present several strong counter-arguments. One characteristic of their approach, strengthening their counter-arguments, is their capacity to assimilate criticisms by taking them into account in subsequent designs. For example, they have removed some of the restrictions in the Prisoner's Dilemma game, by allowing face-to-face interaction, a degree of communication of intent, and they have attempted comparisons for cultural effects. All these modifications are found in the large scale study by Kelley, Shure, Deutsch, Faucheux, Lanzetta, Moscovici, Nuttin, Rabbie and Thibaut (1970) which will be discussed later in this chapter (pp. 70, 84).

The advantages of the model are stated by Kelley (1963) when he contrasts Irving Goffman's undocumented analysis of social situations in *Encounters* with his own preferred approach by "clear and hopefully systematic analysis of limited problems" (p. 51). To some extent, Thibaut and Kelley have tried a variety of designs, for example, Kelley and Grzelak (1972) and Kelley (1966) attempt to simulate bargaining and choices between alternatives which go well beyond the simplified structure of the 2 × 2 matrix. Thibaut and Ross (1969) also use different designs in their study of judgements of social stimuli; Thibaut and Faucheux (1965) do likewise in their experiments on contractual agreements. But their most recent influence has on the whole continued to be expressed in the payoff matrix; and their model tends to derive most support from it. Needless to say, field studies enter into the theoretical enterprise extremely rarely although several investigators including Yuchtman (1972) and Murstein (1971) have attempted to broaden the empirical basis of the model.

The problem of generalizing is one which workers in the field of experimental games have been much concerned with in the past. For instance, Fouraker and Siegel (1963) refer to the gap between this restricted experimental context and the "fullblown richness of empirical conflict situations" (p. 206). Their own observations of students take place in a radically simplified situation, as compared to actual conditions of economic conflict. This obvious gap they see as deriving "more from the shortcomings of the theory than it does from innate deficiencies of the experimental method" (p. 206) since most economic theory assumes simple objectives. However, they argue in favour of their experimental method from the fact that results show consistent trends across a large number of experiments and they see an answer to their doubts in the further accumulation of experimental results. The external validity of their results has been a continual concern of Kelley, expressed several times in his recent work (see pp. 72, 80, 84, 113, below). When Kelley (1964), in his review of Fouraker and Siegel, refers to evidence that a pair of completely self-interested negotiators may reach solutions maximizing their joint interests, a phenomenon he calls *implicit* co-operation, he asks whether these are unique conditions in experiments that do not prevail in ordinary group situations. Or did the results reflect a general process "common to a wide range of interpersonal negotiations" (p. 241). Kelley and his colleagues frequently confirm that generalizing beyond the laboratory is the underlying aim of their experimental investigations. Benton, Gelber, Kelley and Liebling (1969) again raise the question of whether some of their results might be a function of particular conditions, or can they be generalized to other situations? We shall see that Kelley takes an optimistic view.

Kelley, for example, uses the Prisoner's Dilemma game as a means of sampling interpersonal behaviour assumed to be consistent across a variety of social contexts. His view of the degree of possible generalization is stated explicitly in Kelley and Stahelski (1970). Here he suggests that there is ample evidence for "the generality of the phenomena found in the laboratory gaming research" (p. 69) and he regards the Prisoner's Dilemma as a means to improving our understanding of social perceptions in many environments.

Laws of general validity

Kelley *et al.* (1970) make an outright statement of methodological belief when they say that the goal of their research is the formulation of laws of general validity in social psychology. They show their concern about criticisms of artifacts in the laboratory and about the uncontrolled effects of the attitudes of experimental volunteers. They are well aware that the game paradigm, restricted as it is, still leaves much that is uncontrolled. While they recognize that there is no evidence to show that laboratory artifacts and subjects' attitudes are *not* important variables, they advocate that bargaining experiments should use "complex miniature social situations which subjects are likely to associate with their everyday social systems" (p. 413). The miniature situation, they think, is likely to reflect the influence of norms from the wider society rather than a motivational response simply generated by the experiment. They have therefore sought to conduct the same experiment in laboratories in different countries in order to discover such situational influences. This seems to contradict the view expressed by Kelley and Stahelski (1970a) that austerity of design is an effective means to discovering a person's consistent orientation and not the demands of a particular situation (see p. 81 below).

Kelley *et al.* (1970) focus on negotiating between two persons, with long-term incentives for joint agreement (after a sequence of agreements the values obtained were to be increased), conflicting with short-term incentives. The latter were provided by high values in immediate individual gains, rejecting agreement with the other. Complete face-to-face communication was allowed: the experimenters were concerned particularly with the distributive aspects of the negotiating process, that is, with the division of rewards between the two persons. The task also allowed for the integrative aim of increasing the total rewards of both by means of co-operation. We shall return to this experiment later, but it is worth noting here some of the cross-cultural effects on the enterprise of generalizing from the results to other contexts.

The study consisted of eight international experiments; differences in the results suggest that the distinction between co-operative and competitive choices does not have a constant meaning between cultures, nor even between locations.* On the contrary, they suggest varying

* See the full discussion of this below p. 84.

definitions which can be given to the same objective bargaining situation. In this case, differences were reported between experimental locations in the definitions which volunteers gave to "co-operative". For some it implied a moral position—this tendency was evident in the Paris, Leuven and Dartmouth data. In the experiments at Columbia and North Carolina, volunteers seemed to see their situation more in task or achievement terms, defining "co-operative" as a weak or passive orientation. Nevertheless, these eight applications suggest the same functional relationship between pairs of variables, such as the relationship between higher (monetary) incentives and increased agreement between players. Kelley *et al.* emphasize the caution that the underlying reasons for this relationship may be different between locations and add that this possibility is especially likely to be a focus for further research in negotiation studies where attention is focused on *process* rather than on summarized results. In this series of experiments, orientations and tactics within a negotiation are the focus of study although, as the authors say, there is still the possibility that their interpretations of the process are vulnerable to ambiguities. They conclude that exactness of replication will be extremely difficult to attain, but they see an advantage, at the least, in exploring the problems of replication and in knowing what are the limits of comparability, since, as they comment, "undetected incomparability is a danger because it promotes erroneous generalisation" (p. 437). They consider it eventually necessary to assess and interpret for greater degrees of incomparability than those found in laboratory replications. In other words, it would be necessary to cope with the differences between laboratory and natural situations. For the moment, their aim is to deal with the immediate problems of laboratory replications as a way towards making the more ambitious generalizations which are their ultimate goal. The discussion at the end of this research report sets out the philosophy which is apparent in several of Kelley's recent articles: it is their aim to "generalize from the laboratory to the natural world, and from one real situation to another . . ." (p. 437). We can now appreciate the pragmatic bias of the payoff matrix. In the following sections I will describe the subsequent work by Thibaut and Kelley on the Prisoner's Dilemma design, on the comparison level concept (Chapter 5), on negotiation and bargaining (Chapter 6) and on the formation of norms (Chapter 6).

External validity

Thibaut and Kelley are very much concerned with the problem of extrapolating from their experiments to actual situations. For them generalizing from an experiment to other situations where similar conditions or processes may be found, could also be considered as strictly a methodological question. In this same frame of reference it is true that there exist criteria for the generality, usually termed the external validity, of a given experimental design. The degree to which external validity is obtained depends on such factors as the representativeness of a sample and experimental arrangements which may involve specificity of the results to a limited set of conditions. It is clear that the external validity of a research investigation can be improved by attention to such factors. Campbell and Stanley (1963) provide a discussion of designs to be preferred on the grounds of increased external validity. But they also warn that the degree of generalization that may be made from a particular design, cannot be established in a neat, conclusive way. It becomes a matter of suggesting a plausible match for the conditions and effects observed with a particular research design and those observed in other designs or in everyday life; it may be possible to show such a match between one set of effects and similar ones observed under different conditions. One comment by Campbell and Stanley concerns this attempt to match: "The sources of external invalidity are thus guesses as to general laws in the science of a science: guesses as to what factors lawfully interact with our treatment variables, and, by implication, guesses as to what can be disregarded . . ." (p. 17). This leads to the conclusion that while the complexity of relationships may confuse attempts to generalize, such confusion is "more to be expected the more the experimental situation differs from the setting to which one wants to generalize" (p. 18). Campbell and Stanley call for a greater similarity of experiments to the conditions where the results are eventually to be "applied", granted that the degree of similarity to be attempted must be tempered with concern for technical controls necessary in the internal design of the experiment itself. These points touch on some of those already raised by Kelley and others in discussing their experimental results and on the viewpoint which they share with Wilson and Bixenstine (1962) who stress that isolation of variables by the experimental design will lead to successful generalization, providing the variables abstracted are significant ones.

We have noted the continual preoccupation of Kelley and others with generalizations to actual situations of social behaviour. At the moment, we have no way of assuring ourselves of the success of their research unless it is that of the accumulation of results which all corroborate particular hypotheses. But there is another sense, other than this strictly methodological or technical one, in which the validity of the whole enterprise of the payoff matrix may be brought into question. The representation of competition and reciprocity within this experimental paradigm, the enterprise which centres on the two person game, is justified usually by the rather loose analogy between, on the one hand, situations of competition created in experiments and, on the other, actual social situations which the former is intended to simulate. We have no way of knowing, other than by analogy, if the simulation is effective and often our inferences about the experimental results have to be quite tentative. Plon (1972) argues that the analogy by-passes the work of explanation, substituting a pseudo-reality by means of some facets of resemblance which the experimental game is thought to have with interpersonal relations. By definition, Plon emphasizes, a model based on analogy does not represent anything; it can only illustrate relationships for which the valid task of explanation must be carried out within a systematic theory. In reply to this, it must be recognized that the accumulation of evidence which is discussed below, particularly on negotiation and bargaining now seems well on the way to a more general theoretical view of bargaining across a variety of situations (see Chapters 6 and 13).

The Prisoner's Dilemma

Seventy-eight forms of two-person games are identified by Rapoport and Guyer (1966), of which the "mixed-motive" Prisoner's Dilemma game is among the most frequently encountered. In this game the participant is presented with a choice between only two alternatives: he can decide to share the outcomes equally with the other person or he can try to maximize his own gains at the expense of the other.

The Prisoner's Dilemma Design is derived from the anecdote about the two persons arrested on suspicion of committing a crime. Luce and Raiffa (1957) describe the situation as follows:

> Two suspects are taken into custody and separated. The district attorney is certain that they are guilty of a specific crime, but he does not have

adequate evidence to convict them at a trial. He points out to each prisoner that each has two alternatives: to confess to the crime the police are sure they have done, or not to confess. If they both do not confess, then the district attorney states he will book them on some very minor trumped-up charge such as petty larceny and illegal possession of a weapon, and they will both receive minor punishment; if they both confess they will be prosecuted, but he will recommend less than the most severe sentence; but if one confesses and the other does not, then the confessor will receive lenient treatment for turning state's evidence whereas the latter will get "the book" slapped at him.*

In the typical matrix representing the dilemma, the first entry in each cell represents the choice (and payoff) for Prisoner A; the second entry represents the outcome for Prisoner B. Thus, in the co-operation cell both only receive one year; in the joint defection option both receive several years. In the "temptation" cell, Prisoner A gets off with only two months; the other prisoner, refusing to confess, receives (the "sucker" option) the heaviest sentence. Many variations of the payoff matrix, with different ratios of outcomes, have since been developed.

The Prisoner's Dilemma

Prisoner B

	Not Confess	Confess
Not Confess **Prisoner A**	C, C 1 year, 1 year (Cooperate, Cooperate)	C, D 9 years, 2 months (Sucker, Temptation)
Confess	D, C 2 months, 9 years (Temptation, Sucker)	D, D 6 years, 6 years (Defect, Defect)

First entry = Prisoner A
Second entry = Prisoner B

In summary, letters in the cells represent the choices and consequences for each person. The analogy is made to the dilemma of two prisoners simultaneously arrested on suspicion of having committed a crime. The prosecution offers each prisoner, separately, a choice of confessing or not confessing. If he confesses, and the other does not confess,

* Reproduced with permission of R. D. Luce and H. Raiffa, *Games and Decisions*, John Wiley and Sons, New York, 1957, p. 95.

he receives an extremely light, nominal sentence (the D, C or "temptation" cell). If the prisoner chooses not to confess and this is also the decision of the other, they can both be convicted only on a minor charge—this is the co-operation cell (C, C). However, should they both confess, as represented by the defection (D, D) or "punishment" cell, then they both receive a moderately heavy sentence. The prosecution warns the prisoner that if he does *not* confess and the other *does*, then he will receive a very severe sentence indeed (C, D, the "sucker" option).

In the game situation the player may choose the co-operative option (A1 B1 in the Figure below) or he may go for the "temptation cell" in order to gain more for himself, "defecting" from the co-operative option to a competitive one. This brings the danger, in the next game, that the other person will also become competitive or defensive and so in the long term they may both lose points. The participants are guided in their choices between the alternatives by the joint outcomes they observe and anticipate. A matrix similar to the one shown in the Figure below, with numbers representing points or money, is shown to each person at the start. Usually he is seated in a cubicle where he can indicate his choice of cell and is presented with the choice of the other more or less simultaneously. He is told that neither "partner" sees the other's choice before he sees his own and generally there is no other person, the latter's moves are simulated by the experimenter according to a pre-arranged schedule. Note that the structure of payoffs in this version of the Prisoner's Dilemma has a rather different bias from that of the original anecdote discussed in Chapter 1.

A Prisoner's Dilemma Matrix

	B1	B2
A1	+1, +1 (C, C)	−2, +2 (C, D)
A2	+2, −2 (D, C)	−1, −1 (D, D)

D, C > C, C > D, D > C, D

As we saw, A1 B1 is the joint co-operative cell. Mutual defection or competition yields a comparatively poor joint outcome but one which is preferable to being the victim of the other person's exploitation in a

Cooperate-Defect cell. (B's position in cell A2, B1, or A's position in B2, A1). The order of the outcomes for joint defection (D, D) joint co-operation (C, C), victim (C, D) or temptation (D, C) is as follows, D, C > C, C > D, D > C, D.

It is essentially a situation of conflict—either to go ahead and be tempted by the higher payoff; to be competitive and to exploit the co-operative move of the other *or* to co-operate by taking a minimal but joint payoff. However, the person who makes a co-operative move risks being exploited by the other who may defect, leaving only the "victim" option. If both parties give way to the temptation of a higher competitive payoff they may find themselves in the joint punishment option (D, D) with a low outcome.

The motivational problems of the Prisoner's Dilemma game are discussed by Kelley (1965) who points to the effects of different instruc-tions, permitted forms of communication, and the possibilities of arti-facts which might contribute to the general finding of cumulative competition in the game. For instance, it may be the restricted form of the game, the individualized instructions, or the absence of communi-cation between the partners that produces the competitive "lock-in" or bind, so often observed.

The collusive solution represented by C, C, as Luce and Raiffa (1957, p. 97) have mentioned, can be seen as a point of equilibrium but the prediction that this solution will be followed by the players has not been supported by the experimental results. What distinguishes this matrix from others is that the point of equilibrium is minimal where it is maximal in others (see Plon, 1967). For game theorists the C, C cell provides the rational solution, although this depends also on the cell values presented in the matrix. The Prisoner's Dilemma has no totally dominant strategy. In choosing D one can obtain more points than a maximum produced by C. Or, one could obtain a minimum with D which is more than the minimum from strategy C. If temptation (D, C) and punishment (D, D) values are made sufficiently favourable it might become a rational strategy to defect. Rapoport and Chammah (1965, p. 29) allow the point that the D strategy is rationally defensible but would cause a player to lose heavily if this cell were chosen repeatedly because of the counter-action of the other player. Rapoport's (1970) researches have demonstrated beyond doubt the influence of the struc-ture of payoffs used in a particular matrix. While there are many ver-sions of the Prisoner's Dilemma matrix, if we take it in its classic form with joint cooperation (C, C) as the assumed rational strategy we also find that empirically this is not the most frequently chosen outcome. In fact, Scodel, Minas, Ratoosh and Lipetz (1959) show that even when the values in the co-operative cells are augmented, co-operation does not increase.

The explanation of this empirical rejection of "economic" rationality may lie in the defensive reactions of players, or their distrust of one another. In the classic Prisoner's Dilemma without verbal communication, it is easy to see how conditions for trust do not develop. Another possibility is suggested by Erika Apfelbaum (1967) who seeks to qualify the assumption that each individual tries to maximize his gains, by introducing the concept of social motivation. If we now accept that the participants attempt to maximize not the strictly personal values of gains but the difference between their own gains and those of others, then we will have a more adequate basis for understanding what happens, as McClintock and McNeel (1966) and others have demonstrated. Results failing to confirm the rational prediction might be an artifact of instructions to the player that he should work only for himself, or of preventing communication between players.

Plon (1967) asks: what does the Prisoner's Dilemma *represent* for its participants? Little is known of this aspect. He refers to Pruitt (1967) as the first investigator to provide an experimental test of this question. Pruitt's experiment (for other similar attempts see Chapter 11) presented the matrix in separate parts to each player in a "decomposed" Prisoner's Dilemma game. By changing the sheer physical arrangement of the game, by dividing the matrix into three graphic presentations instead of one, Pruitt demonstrates that this change, in the way alternative choices are presented, gives a different pattern of results with fewer competitive moves; thus, the *classic presentation* tends to produce some responses before others and this casts a doubt on the value of the design. Pruitt's analysis of the game exposes artifacts which derive simply from the formal presentation and it could be that this presentation corresponds imperfectly with the way in which persons usually perceive a conflict.

Another example of this effect is found in the experiment by Evans and Crumbaugh (1966) who compare two presentations of the Prisoner's Dilemma, one by matrix the other by alternative instructions. They are able to show that the latter presentation leads to more co-operation between players. Plon (1968) also describes an experiment where he does not use the matrix presentation at all; he asks his volunteers to imagine themselves in various real-life situations where their choices have to be expressed between courses of action such as might occur in a particular situational context. Plon advocates this form of simulation or role-playing after criticizing the matrix design because it leaves too many unresolved questions about what the choices mean for the participants. While acknowledging the elegance and ease of using matrices, Plon concludes that formalizing the game in this way leaves an open question about what it is that has been formalized. Nemeth (1972) makes similar criticisms of the abstraction and ambiguity of motives and goals in the Prisoner's Dilemma design, commenting that the design leaves out parameters likely to be of particular importance in bargaining such as regard for the other person.

Communication in the P.D. design

Thus the subjective preferences (utilities) under different social conditions have become a research topic for psychologists using the game matrix. The game theorists had emphasized effects of structure of gains and losses, whereas psychologists found that it could be quite as effective to manipulate strategies and conditions of context by varying the instructions, by simulating the other player or by increasing opportunities to communicate. Deutsch (1958, 1960) shows how co-operation occurs much more with unrestricted communication than with no communication. Loomis (1959), Daniels (1967), and Terhune (1968) all report similar results. However, as McGrath (1966) points out, "communication, per se, is not a *sufficient* condition for successful resolution of conflict" (p. 105). Pilisuk and Skolnick (1968) demonstrate that an opposite effect can occur if players are suspicious and if they communicate to deceive an opponent. Boyle and Bonacich (1970) emphasize that communication can act "as a catalyst which facilitates the way which *other* factors operate on the role-taking process, rather than as a purely independent source of effects" (p. 127). Modifications of the Prisoner's Dilemma design may introduce information on the other player (for example, see Swingle and Gillis, 1968) and restrictions on visual communication in the classic form of the game have been dropped to provide a richer environment (see Kelley and Stahelski, 1970a).

The Prisoner's Dilemma format has been recently modified to include questionnaires testing personal values, offering opportunities for players to exchange information and showing the virtue of a paradigm which is responsive to criticism. As we have seen, social psychologists have recently added to the evidence establishing the important effects of social comparisons, of *relative* gains and of increasing as well as decreasing the other person's outcomes (for example, see Wyer, 1969). It is demonstrated in these instances that there is no proclivity to concentrate on the economic maximizing of gains.

Plon's (1967) main criticisms of this paradigm concern the confusion entailed by using an economic structure of payoffs, and, secondly, the *ad hoc* treatment of results. Let us consider first his criticism of the economic framework of the game. Here he especially criticizes the payoff matrix of Thibaut and Kelley. In the previous chapter (Chapter 3, pp. 51–52) I discussed how they tried to avoid assuming a maximizing or optimizing model. They do not postulate, for social behaviour, that there is always egocentric, deliberate optimizing of rewards—even if an individual has enough accurate information for an optimal decision, which frequently may not be the case. All the same, it is doubtful whether Thibaut and Kelley succeed completely in throwing off a calculative bias.

We also saw in the previous chapter that Thibaut and Kelley caution about the limits that exist in the similarity between their model and that of game theory. There are some obvious differences. For instance, we have just mentioned that they do not require that a person has complete knowledge of the possible outcomes, nor do they assume the fixity of values in the matrix cells, even over short periods of time. In actual social situations the parties in a relationship will not know of all the alternatives available; Thibaut and Kelley draw attention to numerous factors which may intervene continually, altering the consequences which will attach to a given choice of action. Thus, in their adaptation of the game theory matrix they do not incorporate the utilitarian assumptions which produced the game model. Plon grants that they do not entirely accept utilitarian assumptions and that they have made some important reservations, but he is critical of their use of economic terms. He argues that introducing the game matrix within social psychology presents a major source of weakness because it avoids the formulation of a theory and he stresses that the theoretical position of Thibaut and Kelley, as a result of their adopting economic premises, is largely weakened by ambiguity.

Plon does not discuss the model of Thibaut and Kelley directly; his attack is a general one against the experimental game paradigm for its theoretical sterility and their model draws his critical attention because they alone among the exchange theorists employ the gain-loss matrix as their central stratagem. Thus, he does not consider the accumulation of studies influenced by Thibaut and Kelley (1959). Although the model has the faults discussed in Chapter 3, we should recognize that it has certainly provided a theme and framework for many recent studies.

Arguments in favour of the Prisoner's Dilemma

The arguments put forward by Kelley and Stahelski (1970a, 1970b) give perhaps the clearest statement of what the Prisoner's Dilemma design is intended to achieve in social psychology. They also make an outright claim for the *generality of inference* from this design as a situation of convergent and divergent choices. Kelley and Stahelski (1970b) mention that the Prisoner's Dilemma involves, even in its restricted form, communicating and diagnosing intentions at the same time as gaining rewards or reducing costs. Kelley's view is that there is a great similarity between the Prisoner's Dilemma and *social situations rich in information* about other persons. This is a conviction to be respected although many others do not share it, as we have seen. It should be noted that Kelley and Stahelski are not uncritical about the Prisoner's Dilemma game, for instance, they consider it to be ambiguous about the *relative risks* a person runs in taking the cooperative option. Kelley and Stahelski (1970b) discuss the risks for the person making a cooperative choice: principally, that he may be exploited by the competitive choice of the other player. However, the fact that a player seeks to know the intentions of the other; that there are both potential gains and dangers which can influence a player's decision, lead Kelley and Stahelski (1970b) to restate their belief that "The mixed-motive game poses for its players many of the difficult decisions that men face in their everyday life" (p. 379).

Although the classic Prisoner's Dilemma presents a relatively uninformative environment simply because the players cannot communicate, Kelley and Stahelski (1970a) see the restrictive nature of the game from a rather different angle from its critics, believing that this is a definite advantage because it allows the simulation of social interaction in which players seek information about each other "rather than merely about social roles and structures" (p. 77).* Secondly, they argue that the aims a person has in this game should *reflect his general social orientation*, and not the demands of a particular situation, assuming that an individual will approach the experimental task with the same orientation that he tends to adopt in all such relationships and not in an *ad hoc* or arbitrary way. This permits them to generalize from their results and "draw the inference . . . about the nature of the general relationship between the person's orientations and his expectations about others' orientations" (p. 78). More particularly, they wish to discover if a competitive person sees others as competitive too. It is assumed that there is a psychological continuity between the game and social relationships in real life, wherever the individual has to decide to co-operate or to compete. They are interested in the way a person perceives the intention of the other and argue that a player is continually seeking to know the other's intentions and especially to know if he is likely to reciprocate. Thus, a given action may reflect long range intentions or may be merely a defensive move against the other player's next move. A choice may be active or reactive in its meaning.

Considering these studies by Kelley and Stahelski, a difficult question arises immediately for their claim to test a stable general orientation, either to competitive or to co-operative strategies. Even over the brief periods of the experimental games there are switches from co-operative to competitive behaviour, and vice versa. Kelley and Stahelski (1970b) recognize that a change from co-operative to competitive decisions may mean a person is forced into competitive action by the structure of the Prisoner's Dilemma game—his competitive response is now a defence against a competitive partner. Kelley and Stahelski (1970a, 1970b) can only conjecture this, in the form of questions which raise more fundamental issues than their adaptation of the Prisoner's Dilemma can possibly elucidate. They encounter interpretative difficulties familiar to investigators of natural situations. The data are vague enough to allow several alternative explanations, all equally plausible. In short, Kelley and Stahelski raise questions which their data cannot satisfy. This in itself suggests that resolving them will involve designs other than the Prisoner's Dilemma.

* It is doubtful that these informational components can be separated in the way Kelley and Stahelski suggest.

Is the two-choice game a complex situation?

A familiar criticism of the payoff matrix is that it is an over-simplified representation of situations of conflicting choices. The usual answer to this criticism suggests that extreme simplification is nevertheless necessary. For instance, Wilson and Bixenstine (1962) justify the two-choice game as a *necessity* in face of the obscurity of issues in natural situations. This counter-argument is frequently extended to many forms of the controlled experiment. What if we now reverse the criticism and argue that the matrix is too complex? The design *seems* to offer a simple two-way choice to each of the players seeking a share of the joint payoff, but when the issues are formalized, the relative gains and losses spelled out, it becomes much more than a simulation of everyday decisions—as a symbolic representation of a conflict situation, it may be far too sophisticated. Recently there has been support for this view, as we shall see in a moment. Yet previously, the experimental game had been regarded as providing an over-simple task, a boring and repetitive series of choices. It seems that the actors in the game face an austere environment, devoid of cues, but that the decisions they have to make are symbolized in an over-complex way. Solomon (1960) argues that an array of alternative values such as is found even in a two-by-two matrix could be visualized only very rarely in day-to-day decisions. Gumpert, Deutsch and Epstein (1969) suggest this when they comment that the participants in the Prisoner's Dilemma game may be pushed into a competitive pattern of choices without understanding fully the structure of the game. Moscovici (1971) describes the difficulties an experimenter faces in conveying to students the reasoning which underlies the payoff matrix. This certainly implies complexity in the game. Thus, Plon (1968) asks "can a person in an actual situation extract from it a representation such as one would have in a matrix?" (p. 211). So, it appears that, while the two-choice repetition is apparently an over-simplification, the presentation of relative values in the matrix cells consists of a quantification which is altogether too elaborate. The degree of calculative thinking required of the player seems too great for plausibility as a simulation of actual everyday decisions in social relationships.*

---

* This can be related to the criticism against assuming calculative behaviour in social situations which was discussed in Chapter 3, p. 52.

The two-choice design as an economic exchange, not a social game

Kelley (1965) drew attention to the weakness of the payoff matrix as a simulation of conflicting motives because only very small or imaginary money incentives were offered. This criticism has, to some extent, since been met by Gallo (1966), Kelley (1966) and McClintock and McNeel (1966) who either increased the money rewards or awarded class points in student courses as a payoff (and providing evidence that cooperation is sought more strongly with a money incentive). Nevertheless, the criticism has not been completely overcome. Gumpert, Deutsch and Epstein (1969) suggest that with repeated presentations of the matrix, the participants become bored and hence more competitive in order to make the game more challenging. Kelley *et al.* (1970) see money as a means of increasing the magnitude of incentives to secure improved joint outcomes but one which, at the same time, may produce a qualitative change in the situation, a change from a social game to an economic exchange.

Probably the most frequent criticism of the matrix design is made against its restriction of communication to written messages or, as in the Prisoner's Dilemma, "communication" consists only of the actual choice of options. That the latter does not permit any communication between players, over and above their decisions, has led some investigators to consider the decisions themselves as ways of communicating future intentions or warnings to the player (see pp. 81, 110). Schelling (1963) makes a point of emphasizing the *tacit communication* which constitutes a choice of options and the process of mutual influence which can result. As noted above, several researchers have introduced communication into the Prisoner's Dilemma design, observing its influence; when written messages can be exchanged there is a well-confirmed result that more co-operative choices occur.

It should be noted that, in earlier experimental games the players were placed in separate booths or separated by screens; this was originally seen as an advantage, so that the uncontrolled influences of gesture and facial expressions could be ruled out. Usually there was no face-to-face interaction between the players (for instance, in the experiment by Kelley (1966) they sit back-to-back!). However, this visual restriction has now been accepted as a severe flaw in the plausibility of results if these are to be extrapolated to social behaviour *in other situa-*

tions and in the recent work by Kelley *et al.* (1970) and Kelley and Stahelski (1970a), players sit facing each other, only their score cards and instructions being hidden by low screens. This seems to be an attempt to increase the veridical nature of the social relationship and contrasts with the earlier controls of the "minimal" social situation. It may also be in response to criticisms of previous designs that Kelley and Stahelski (1970a) have allowed written messages to be exchanged.

Even in designs which allow for some communication in experimental bargaining there is still the caution made by Wilson and Bixenstine (1962) that experiments will focus on immediate choices and will lack many of the subtle and implicit elements found in social interaction. Even though the experimental game offers a tightly controlled view of interpersonal behaviour, there are a number of variables which have not been controlled, as Kelley *et al.* (1970) point out. For instance, little attention has been given to possible effects of cultural or personal values, nor has there been until recently any effort to estimate their influence. Eiser and Tajfel (1972) bring this into open discussion (see pp. 113–115 below) when they confirm that students classified by pre-game questionnaires as competitive tend to anticipate competitive behaviour from the other player.

Additionally, it is worth mentioning an exceptional approach from the game theory side by Pilisuk, Kiritz and Clampitt (1971) who discuss the differences obtained with the Prisoner's Dilemma design between the performance of Berkeley students and Army cadets—in the expected direction, the former group being less competitive, more cooperative than the latter. This illustrates our point; and the experiment is notable as a controlled design to measure the performance of groups known to hold different values.

In their report on experiments in eight locations, described earlier in this chapter, Kelley *et al.* (1970) are so much aware of these influences that they especially aim at an analysis of the influence of possible cultural effects. They advocate a greater richness in experimental studies than has been conventionally the case, for instance bargaining experiments should use "complex miniature social situations which subjects are likely to associate with their everyday social system" (p. 413). Thus, they expect that this *miniature situation* should reflect the influence of norms from the wider society rather than a motivational response simply generated by the experiment. In this instance, the same experiment was carried out at universities in four countries, precisely in order to discover such influences. The results reveal variations between locations which do not divide neatly by countries, rather these appeared to reflect "different types of subject populations available" from site to site. Especially interesting is the comparison in the meaning of "co-operation" and "competition" among the sites. A pre-game questionnaire distribution was carried out using Osgood's semantic differential rating scales, each participant being asked to choose between pairs of adjectives describing himself and "a typical player". Factor analysis of ratings suggests that at Columbia University (New York) and North Carolina co-operation has a "weak, passive" connotation: at Paris, Leuven and Dartmouth College, New Hampshire, it tends to mean "moral, good". Type of incentive was varied across sites, by presenting outcomes either in money or points; this variation also influenced the meaning given to competition or co-operation. When the investigators observed the process of negotiation itself they found that players with money incentives tended to reach agreements more rapidly, with less interpersonal bargaining. In their discussion of the negotiation process, Kelley *et al.* conclude that the players under the points incentive appear to have laboured at greater length over a moral position, between co-operation as "good" and competition as "bad"; they comment that "exploration of the implied interplay between type of orientation to the relationship and type of incentive is clearly an important agenda item for future research" (p. 435).

Competition

Much of the research in two-person bargaining tends to focus on whether "co-operative" or "competitive" options are chosen, yet, as Apfelbaum (1966) comments, the meaning of these terms is unclear. In the Prisoner's Dilemma game how does a student, who is new to the situation, see the important issues? Will he aim at maximizing his absolute gains, maximizing joint gains, or at increasing his gain relative to those of his partner? Will he prefer to have a substantial lead over the other player, even though his total score is less than it could be with a near-equal joint outcome for both? McNeel, McClintock and Nuttin (1972) re-emphasize that most studies cannot pretend to clarify the meaning of behaviour labelled "co-operative" and "competitive", partly because the Prisoner's Dilemma, which they call "the most intensively researched game paradigm", confounds an individual's own gain with his relative gain, under the one competitive choice. They seek a separate measure of *relative gain* as the true competitive choice expressing rivalry, following the definition that rivalry occurs when there is some noncorrespondence of outcomes and here they quote Thibaut and Kelley: that "each one seeks not only to improve his outcomes but to defeat the other person" (1959, p. 228). McNeel, McClintock and Nuttin continue with the Maximizing Difference design introduced by McClintock and McNeel (1967) where the experimenter can specify whether an individual is seeking his own gain or his gain relative to the other person.* This game presents a measure of the player's relative gain that is not confounded by individualistic maximizing irrespective of what his partner gains, nor by the co-operative maximizing of joint gains.

In their recent work, Thibaut and Kelley are very largely occupied with the study of competitive and co-operative behaviour but without developing further the theoretical discussion of their *Social Psychology of Groups* (1959, pp. 227–229). Nor have they yet detached themselves from the work of implementing experiments to a point where they consider implications of new evidence.

Competition, as a problem area, is central to social exchange because of the questions involved in whether persons reciprocate, retaliate, reward others, or try to gain greater rewards by defeating them, or by securing more at their expense. For instance, the prevalence of competitive behaviour in the Prisoner's Dilemma suggests it is useful in providing evidence, or counter-evidence, about the reciprocity principle generally assumed. If competition reflects the exploitation of one person by another then this may not involve reciprocal behaviour; here there is no exchange, unless there is retaliation. But as we have seen we cannot be sure that the choice "competition" is a retaliatory one—it may also be a defensive reaction. For instance, if a D choice is played with the expectation of a C from the other, then it is exploitation. If a D choice is played with the expectation of a D from the other, it is defensive. Even a C choice is exploitative if it is taken as a means to establishing trust which can then be exploited.

When Michel Plon (1970) states that the underlying assumptions in experimental games have been passed over by researchers, with the result that there is no coherent system of theory, he gives as an example

---

* Later, in Chapter 11, I discuss a version of this game adapted to the possibility of *minimizing differences*: where the aim is to maintain equity or equality. In this case too rational behaviour is not related to the strictly economic model of maximizing profit.

the terms "co-operation" and "competition" which, he argues, are introduced, "in the abstract" without ever being defined except by their relationship to a particular game. Thus, "in the abstract" means that they are not connected to any conceptual system. Next, he attempts to identify the underlying ideas in the implicit use of these terms. He cites Deutsch and Krauss (1960), Deutsch (1962) for whom *competition* derives from the existence of threats which a person sees as an attack on his prestige, his self-esteem. Here competition is a reaction to conserve prestige, to save face; a reaction supported by the social norm that one should never allow oneself to be intimidated, under penalty of losing status. Plon comments that this idea lies behind Deutsch's notion of interpersonal trust which can develop only in the absence of actions aimed at diminishing prestige; but Plon identifies this as an ideological and not a scientific definition, implying that Deustch wishes to encourage co-operation within an established social or power structure. In a similar vein, Moscovici (1972) refers critically to "the liberal tendency, represented by Deutsch, with its stress on dialogue and the development of trust" (p. 25). Moscovici, however, contrasts Deutsch's position with that of Kelley who prefers an "option of realpolitik, that is a strategy of negotiation supported by the realities of power" (p. 25). Kelley does not separate co-operation and competition by a qualitative distinction but sets them at either end of a continuum of actions among which an individual may choose. In Kelley's (1965) own commentary on Deutsch's experimental results he maintains that here "competition" has its origins merely in the design of the trucking game (see *The Kelley-Deutsch Polemic*, p. 125 below). More precisely, the existence of an alternative, an escape route, in this simulation design means that there is no necessity to co-operate: it is too easy to avoid co-operation and instead to "compete", as the term is here defined.

Erika Apfelbaum (1966) refers to the ambiguity present in interpreting the meaning behind what are termed competitive or co-operative choices in experimental games: it is unavoidably a matter of inference *both* by the experimenter, *and* by the opposing player. In the game situation a player may feel uncertain of the meaning of his partner's choice or, if he is certain, he may be in error; there is no way of controlling either possibility. Apfelbaum notes that the definition Deutsch gives to the term "competition" is only operational in the immediate context of his experimental game. In general, she continues, most authors take care to emphasize the absence of explanatory value in the terms themselves; nevertheless, they interpret the results of their research as if these notions had a definite meaning. This criticism is echoed by McNeel, McClintock and Nuttin (1972) when they reaffirm that the goals underlying co-operative or competitive behaviour have been ignored in most experimental studies of game playing. They seek an empirical answer to this through the paradigm of their Maximizing Difference game, where they separate competitive choices (maximizing relative gain) from either of two remaining goals (own gain, joint gain). We have already mentioned the advantage of this design, comparing it to the Prisoner's Dilemma (see p. 85 above). Most of the evidence collected by experimenters using the Prisoner's Dilemma simply proceeds from the assumption that it provides a situation of choice between co-operation and competition, and from there to an inferential discussion of choice sequences. For instance, in their research, Kelley and Stahelski (1970a, 1970b) concentrate on the changes they observe from co-operative to competitive behaviour or the reverse; they focus our attention on patterns of interdependent choices and try to show the influence of dispositional tendencies in players, as revealed by answers to a pre-game questionnaire.

Kelley and Stahelski refer to several reports of experimental games showing irregularities in co-operative and competitive choices. Some of these are worth summarizing here very briefly. Conventionally, game theorists have focused their attention on the effects of varying the structure of gains. For example, Rapoport and Chammah (1965) confirm that co-operative choices increase when the payoff for them is greater, although these investigators also demonstrate how co-operation depends not only on the co-operative (C) or competitive (D) scores taken individually, but on the relationship of their difference. But we have noted also that psychologists using the experimental game have examined the influences of communication: as it increases, so co-operative choices between players become more frequent. Another interesting line of research is that taken by Sermat (1962, 1964) suggesting the possibility that totally co-operative behaviour by one person may *not* lead to mutual co-operation, but to exploitation by the other.

Apfelbaum (1967) advances this hypothesis further in a Prisoner's Dilemma design. Here, student volunteers are divided into three categories after being asked their preferences between *either* (A) egalitarian sharing of gains (unconditional co-operation) *or* (B) maximizing personal gains (competition) *or* (C) a reciprocal approach, showing responsiveness to the gains and losses of the other person (conditional co-operation). Their (simulated) partner is represented by verbal descriptions corresponding to the above categories, and showing him as *either* (A) egalitarian *or* (B) seeking only his personal profit *or* (C) prepared to consider his partner's profit to the extent that this concern is reciprocal. These descriptions were given after the first five preliminary trials in the experiment and before 50 subsequent ones. Subsequently, from analysis of choices, Apfelbaum cross-tabulated percentages of co-operative choices of players with different "partners". Table 1 indicates more co-operation in pairs where they are *conditional* players or partners.

TABLE 1

Percentages of co-operative choices as a function of player's orientation and description of partner

Player	Partner: A (egalitarian)		B (personal gain)		C (conditional)	
A (egalitarian)	*47·3*	66	*46·6*	36	*76*	71·3
B (personal gain)	*45·3*	30	*30·3*	34·3	*44·6*	56·6
C (conditional)	*72·6*	68	*35·3*	52	*63*	63

In each case the percentages of co-operative choices are presented separately for the first and last 25 trials (the first 25 are in italics). Adapted from Apfelbaum (1967).

B players confronted with partners of the conditional disposition show a further interesting tendency: their co-operative choices, initially low, tend to increase as the experiment proceeds. Apfelbaum remarks that the reciprocating partner "draws the other person progressively more into co-operation by the image he presents of his own attitude but also by the fact that he responds to co-operative advances" (p. 293). On the other hand, if the simulated partner is *unconditionally* egalitarian, players tend to augment their outcomes by competitive choices. Discussing the implications, Apfelbaum notes that co-operation will develop only if there is "interpersonal reactivity"—an assurance that the other person will be sensitive to a player's choices. She concludes that when a partner shows this element of reactivity, players are capable of learning to co-operate whatever their initial orientation. Thus, the notion of "reactivity" places an emphasis on the dynamic aspects of the interaction.

We should add that this effect might be explained by the operation of a reciprocity norm which is adhered to if the partner's behaviour is clearly flexible. The temptation to "exploit" must always be strong, by the very nature of the payoff structure in the Prisoner's Dilemma; it must be even stronger when a partner's choice does not appear as contingent on what has happened in previous joint options.

Wilson and Bixenstine (1962) formulate game situations in terms of interpersonal control and refer to the framework of Thibaut and Kelley in order to elaborate on the prototypes of fate control and behaviour control (see below p. 121). Bixenstine and Wilson (1966) use a pre-arranged strategy on the part of a simulated partner in the Prisoner's Dilemma. They vary the number of co-operative moves of the simulated partner, recording the sequences in the game and observing the influence on co-operative or competitive choices. Thus, they are able to show that programmed runs beginning and ending competitively but with a co-operative middle, produce most co-operative choices. Changes of strategy give rise to a response on the part of the other player and focus on the reciprocal influence in the immediate context of the game. This conclusion is confirmed by Apfelbaum (1966) who shows that a competitive partner produces the counter-action of a competitive response.

The identity of a person's partner in the two choice game is yet another possible source of influence on the pattern of co-operative or competitive behaviour. For instance, Sermat (1964) shows that a competitive strategy varies as a function of the partner's identity and such a strategy can be interpreted as defensive when the "partner" is thought to be a machine programmed simulation but may be considered an offensive option when the partner is known to be another student. Faucheux and Moscovici (1968) demonstrate that the understanding of a matrix varies quite neatly with the way the "partner" is identified. They asked male medical students to make their choices between red and black playing cards and a payoff matrix was displayed; the points outcomes were as given in Table 2. As part of this design, half the students were told they would play against "chance" half that they would play against "nature". It was expected that the chance condition would "offer some of the features of an interpersonal relationship to the extent that the subject will see himself confronted with a challenging adverse agent in a risky situation over which he may expect to have little control". The "nature" condition was expected to provide "a rather neutral non-malevolent situation over which he may have some control". Faucheux and Moscovici excluded contingency from the relationship: the students made

TABLE 2

Students matched against "Chance"
(or "Nature") as opponents

| | | Simulated Partner | |
		Red	Black
Student	Red	1, 1	0, 2
	Black	2, 0	0, 0

their choice and then turned over the top card of a deck in front of them in order to reveal the "opponent's" choice for each trial. The latter strategy was programmed to give only 38 per cent exploitative or competitive choices. In each condition it would therefore have been possible for the student to realize quickly (within the first twenty trials) that the opponent was playing equitable or co-operative choices much more often than exploitative ones. After the experiment a check was made on students' comprehension of the payoff matrix: this showed that, of those told they were playing against nature, 33 out of 40 had a good comprehension and perceived they could maximize their gains by always playing black. Among those told they were playing against chance, only 12 out of 40 comprehended this point well. Faucheux and Moscovici comment that this suggests "that people will actively attempt to explore the resources of their situation only to the extent to which they think they can partially control it". In the condition where the simulated player's identity was seen as predictable then the experimental task was understood without difficulty. In the case of uncertainty, where this identity had something erratic, capricious about it, then this appears to have had a distracting effect and there was difficulty in mastering the task.

Kelley and Stahelski (1970a, 1970b) mention that if there is some assurance that the other person is to be co-operative it seems preferable to be competitive—at least in the short term, presumably. This illustrates something of the *realpolitik* of the experimental situation and it also reveals the individualistic bias of the authors. There is some inconsistency in the conclusion drawn by Kelley and Stahelski that a competitive person sees other people as competitive. If this is the case, how can he anticipate that the choice of the other person will be a co-operative one? However, by observing the course of co-operative and competitive strategies and drawing inferences from them, these and other studies that we have mentioned, offer possibilities for stating limiting conditions to the reciprocal rule. When is exchange likely to occur, when is it not? What are the exceptions to the hypotheses drawn from Homans' Propositions 2 and 3 which state the tendency, in general, to seek frequency and value in *reciprocal* rewards (see Chapter 8, pp. 159–166).

Although the model of Thibaut and Kelley and the explanations or concepts offered by Homans and Blau appear as references in most of the research reports and reviews which I discuss in this chapter, there is little recognition of any overall explanatory scheme to which the testing of hypotheses should contribute. Usually the investigators, including Thibaut and Kelley, elaborate only on the immediate implications of the experimental conditions; sometimes exchange concepts are noted as general introductory references, or else some fairly isolated exchange notion is given a brief mention. Michel Plon's (1967, 1968, 1970) attack on experimental games for presenting *ad hoc* results without supporting theory therefore finds some support. Certainly the references to sources as "exchange theory" become apparent only very recently in the literature. And this may account for the number of errors made by experimenters in their use of theoretical concepts (see Chapter 11, pp. 245, 246, 250).

The accumulation of research meanwhile awaits a systematic set of explanations. If there were a more explicit use of exchange explanations, this would avoid undue emphasis on individual strategies at the expense of the social relationship. Kelley's (1973) development of attribution theory does not ignore interpersonal factors in social behaviour, but neither does this approach focus on reciprocal relations and process. More clearly, in Kelley and Stahelski (1970a, 1970b) individual personality factors are emphasized to the neglect of the *interdependency* which, as Thibaut and Kelley have stated, should form the main subject matter of their model, in game playing as in other empirical situations (see Chapter 3, p. 25). Furthermore, although Thibaut and Kelley themselves have not chosen, or used, the term "exchange theory", their model does form part, *de facto*, of this collection of explanatory statements, and is most frequently referred to in conjunction with them.*

It is, perhaps, useful to ask if research results from the payoff design can add to our understanding of social exchange. Hypotheses concerning the frequency of reciprocal activities under difference conditions of concerning the return of value for value, or even the influence of satiation effects, could all be applied within this experimental paradigm.†

The tendency to exploit may well be exaggerated in the Prisoner's Dilemma design either directly by the instructions as Deutsch (1949a) showed in his early experiments; or by the short-term, somewhat asocial, form of the game where there is no accountability to relationships in any way approximating to those existing over long periods of time. However, if exploitation appears to be a preferred strategy over the short term, this is itself of some interest as a statement of predisposing conditions. All the same, it is doubtful that this design is rich enough to sustain very many exchange hypotheses.

* Social exchange explanations share a similar basis in learning theory, reinforcement theories, and elementary economics; this basis is elaborated in the chapters to follow.

† Homans is no exponent of the classic Prisoner's Dilemma design because of its restrictions on communication (see Chapter 1, pp. 6–9) yet the design has been used to test his hypotheses particularly those derived from notions of distributive justice.

5

The Comparison Level

Introduction

In this chapter I shall discuss first the meaning of the concepts *comparison level* and *comparison level for alternatives* as developed by Thibaut and Kelley and, more recently, by other researchers. I shall consider the use of the concepts as aids to the explanation of social behaviour, as well as the criticisms of their individualistic bias. Thirdly, I will examine the attempts to establish the comparison level explanation by empirical tests of hypotheses derived from it.

The pervasive tendency of individuals to compare themselves with others is formalized in the Thibaut and Kelley model, by their use of the concepts of *comparison level* and *comparison level for alternatives*. In their version of the payoff matrix they drop the maximizing conventions accepted in the theory of games by focusing on the notion of relative gains as an influence of greater importance than sheer maximization of outcomes. The psychological dimension of game-playing is given an emphasis, in place of the strict economic model of rationality. Their use of the comparison level concept especially demonstrates the separation between economic and psychological views of rationality since it is a means to showing why maximizing absolute gains is not the only rational choice. In this respect, we need not exaggerate the contribution of Thibaut and Kelley over other authors in social psychology. Much work has appeared on interpersonal comparisons (influenced by Festinger, 1957) and reference group theory; recently, discussions of equity and equitable exchange have focused on social comparisons (for example, Walster, *et al.* 1973). Thibaut and Kelley themselves acknowledge their great debt to Heider (1958). Explicit links are made with

individual psychology in their derivation of comparison level concepts
from Helson's (1948) adaptation level theory. There are similarities
with Bevan's (1963) postulate of an internal standard against which an
individual makes his assessment of the relative value of a reward.*
Thibaut and Kelley utilize the concept of adaptation, emphazising the
influences of past experience, in order to outline this explanation of how
a preference scale is established for an individual's goals. But they argue
that it is established *socially* because the individual refers to standards
of justice and to the prevailing norms of a group or society. As we saw
in Chapter 4, the comparison level (CL) provides an explanation of
how a person evaluates a social relationship; it is a mid-point on a
preference scale of outcomes, with the neutral point occurring where
the relationship is neither satisfying or dissatisfying. The comparison
level for alternatives ($CL_{alt.}$) presents the lowest level of outcomes that
a person will accept in the light of available alternatives. Referring to
the latter may lead a person to break off a relationship, should present
outcomes fall below what is available elsewhere. Are these concepts no
more than a form of expressing that the distributive justice principle
should hold?† Or does the precise formulation which Thibaut and Kelley
suggest, achieve more than this? We could seek an answer by looking
for evidence of how the CL and $CL_{alt.}$ have fared as measurement
scales. The evidence itself is quite sparse, but it is important to make the
point that the CL is not only a conjectural notion, it implies an attempt
at measurement and must be discussed as such.

Several investigators make references to the comparison level as a
scale, although it is doubtful that they have implemented it as Thibaut
and Kelley intend, as we shall see in a moment. According to
Wyer (1968), the magnitude of outcomes in a social exchange is
assessed from the comparison level as a point of neutrality on a continuum of positive and negative outcomes. Smith (1968) equates the
comparison level with what he calls "outcome expectancy", giving its
definition as the point of indifference on a subjective scale of goodness
of outcomes. Thus an outcome will be increasingly satisfying as its
judged distance above the comparison level increases. The comparison
level itself is determined by the average of outcomes known to be avail-

* See Messick and Thorngate (1967) for a discussion of the similarity between
Bevan's ideas and the comparison level.

† See Chapter 3 (p. 45) for a reference to common ground between notions of
distributive justice and the comparison level.

able from the relationship, but a person's past experience of outcomes will also be influential.

Smith and Emmons (1969) discuss the comparison level in the context of competitive behaviour and emphasize the influence that knowledge of another's outcomes may have in placing the neutral point. Forty-eight pairs of women students each played 16 trials of a trucking game—those without information about their partner's gains consistently produced higher joint outcomes and were less likely to use the gates blocking the movement of their partner's truck. These results support an explanation for competitive behaviour derived from the comparison level—simply by the evidence that players without knowledge of their partner's outcomes are less competitive. Smith and Emmons note that their explanation is consistent with observations by McClintock and McNeel (1966) in a game situation showing that behaviour becomes more competitive when participants have knowledge of the other person's payoffs. They suggest that there are many situations where a person's comparison level will depend on the perceived relative gains and losses of others.

Thibaut and Kelley themselves have not developed, since 1959, the concepts of the CL and the $CL_{alt.}$; with the exception of Kelley's (1966) discussion of the $CL_{alt.}$ (see Chapter 6, *Negotiating Behaviour*, p. 119). In their model the empirical possibilities of support either for the CL or the $CL_{alt.}$ are stated only briefly (see Chapter 3, p. 19) and they avoid the question of measurement for these scales. One somewhat adverse indicator for the use of these concepts as a means of under-standing the *interdependency* between persons (which they see as a major aim of social psychology*) is that the CL and $CL_{alt.}$ necessarily require analysis at the individual level. For example, to understand the conditions of group survival, Thibaut and Kelley propose to examine the comparisons which individuals make between themselves and other group members and between what is offered by their own group as compared with other groups (see Chapter 3, p. 47).† However, in recent studies, the CL has been presented as a mechanism internal to the individual, dissociated from social context and there has been no

---

* See Chapter 3, p. 25.

† This is consistent with Blau's interpretation of why people may leave one group to join another, but he also includes the structural phenomena in groups in his hypotheses—for instance, a person's status position in his group is a major factor in these decisions (Chapter 12, pp. 325–327).

rigorous testing of the notion in social situations. Faucheux and Thibaut (1964) use the CL only as an *ex post facto* explanation when they discuss the formation of social norms. Thibaut and Ross (1969) examine Helson's adaptation level theory, from which the CL was derived but, far from developing the CL and the $CL_{alt.}$ in their social applications, they make the analysis in an individual-perceptual framework, a retrograde step if the aim is to describe the interdependency. This tends to affirm Moscovici's (1972) criticism of the "profoundly individualistic" view of social reality found in the CL which he sees as part of an attempt to construct explanations of collective processes from an individualistic basis and which he links with an economic interpretation of social relations:

> As is well known, Thibaut and Kelley assume that each individual has at his disposal a sort of internal "clock" or scale which determines the comparison level (CL) which indicates the profit which he might obtain if he engaged in a relationship alternative to the one in which he is engaged at present. If this profit is greater, he abandons the current relationship; if not, he stays with it. Thus, all social relations are capable of being translated in terms of supply and demand. The possibility that a demand which reflects the needs of an individual, or which he feels is his due, can be satisfied elsewhere on better terms defines the limits of the power than an offer may have. It is from this nucleus of ideas that Thibaut and Kelley proceed to the definitions of norms in work groups, of power etc. What appears to me significant is the attempt to construct a theory of collective processes on the basis of an individualistic theory; and this seems to be done through the assimilation of these processes into the functioning of a market economy. The market is a special social institution characteristic of a certain historical period, nevertheless a general sociopsychological theory is founded on the principles of its functioning (p. 26).

Moscovici's criticisms are part of his general attack against exchange notions which foster, he argues, an "economic conception" of social psychology with everything explained by individual decisions. As we shall see later, this general criticism cannot be made, strictly speaking, against the body of exchange explanations and empirical work, which currently form only the rudimentary outline of a theory. This outline at present consists of numerous statements about reciprocal activities and about equity, justice and normative rules. The criticism is also well-represented by Plon (1972) when he argues, at its most basic, "exchange theory" involves a utilitarian view of man as "homo economicus" or as a risk-taking rational actor, "homo aleator", and that both views are

unreal abstractions of individual behaviour. Considering the criticism
technically, as emphasizing that exchange notions are based on notions
of economic rationality, it can be counter-argued that considerable
limits are placed on this form of rationality by exchange theorists themselves as we shall see.

Moreover, Moscovici does under-emphasize the fact that the CL
requires a definition of rationality which is psychological, not economic; involving factors such as perceived status and relative social
advantage. While Moscovici's broader criticisms can be contested, his
specific criticism against the CL as individualistic seems to be a fair one
by our criterion in this book, which is its subsequent empirical influence. When we look at the development of the concept since 1959, we
find that its influence is still confined to the discussion of individual
motives. Nevertheless, the concept has many protagonists even among
sociologists. Atack (1973) had noted that it approximates to a "satisficing" interpretation of social behaviour (see Chapter 7 below).
Singelmann (1972) emphasizes that the instructive quality of the CL
concept lies in the recognition of "mind" as intervening between
"stimulus" and "response" and, for him, the CL is an instance of
current exchange theory consisting of much more than a behaviouristic
approach. Thus, both CL and $CL_{alt.}$ "imply a capacity for subjective
understandings, evaluations, feelings, and decision-making that enables
man to construct his world activity within the structure of his environment" (Singelmann, 1972, p. 417). Thus, the two concepts seem to be
of value mainly for the general orientation and insight which they
provide. It is clear from the empirical studies to be discussed in this
section, that the explanation afforded to researchers by the CL is
invariably a very broad speculative one—that *something like* the CL
could give certain results. In fact, the CL has not been refined in the
more ambitious form of a preference scale, although strictly speaking
this was its definition put forward by Thibaut and Kelley in their
Social Psychology of Groups. It must be a fair comment, therefore, that
unless future work is done on the comparison level *as a scale* it promises
no greater advantage for research than would any broad concept of
expectancy—relative to past experience, present opportunity and norms
of social justice.

Further empirical work on the CL

In the recent experiments described below, the design is either a two-by-two game or, if the design does not involve a game, it is a laboratory task providing observations of contrasting pairs of conditions suitable for the analysis of variance technique. Thus, when the comparison level is introduced it is in one of two conditions: *high* or *low*, and other variables have also to be in contrasting pairs. For example, in the experiment by Ross, Thibaut and Evenbeck (1971) the comparison level introduced by the experimental procedure is either high or low (condition 1); secondly, outcome control is either present or not present* (condition 2); thirdly, outcomes are equitable or inequitable (condition 3). The investigators principally aim at introducing feelings of inequity, which, it is argued, would stem from a discrepancy between the CL and actual outcomes. In this experiment, schoolboys undertook a task in pairs, pulling a rope to match a specified target force. "Competence" was manipulated through feedback evaluation of their performance from the experimenter. It was expected that the CL (high or low) would depend on this evaluation. Points allocated to the boys (outcomes) and the division of points between each member of a pair were varied to provide an equitable or inequitable share. The major dependent variable, *intensity of protest*, was measured by allowing the boys to choose between sending neutral signals or painful white noise to a (fictitious) group of "managers", whom they were told were the distributors of points. Results show that boys who had been told they were competent and whose inferred CL was highest, responded more actively in protest at their failure to receive sufficient points, than those in the low CL condition. The extrapolation of these results to real life situations is typically ambitious: in their discussion, the authors describe the sociological prediction (Davies, 1962) that revolutions are most likely to occur when long periods of economic prosperity are followed by an abrupt slump. They reinterpret this phenomenon by referring it to individual conduct: economic prosperity leads to a gradual rise in the CL—the more an individual receives the more he feels he deserves and a sudden economic decline, set against the individual's high CL produces acute discontent. Thus, they speculate that if this happens to many people there is an increased potential for violence and social protest. A further extrapolation to the wider society

* See Smith (1968, p. 43) below.

is suggested by their hypothesis that aggression will be directed against the distributors of wealth (in the experiment, the allocators of points).

If we consider the comparison level, not as involving a scale but as a plausible source of explanation, then it is found to be an extremely successful background concept. We have described reports of experimental games and other designs where the investigators examine the importance of relative gains in the social context, how this consideration influences their choice of alternatives, with the comparison level concept as a frequent point of reference.

Let us consider again our statement that the comparison level should receive greater attention as a preference scale. Even Wyer (1969) who discusses the CL thoroughly, does not refer to a CL scale. He gives attention to mathematical assumptions but these are expressed as probability equations stating forward estimates of utility. In other respects, several experiments by Wyer and his associates are of interest, notably because they examine exchange formulations* together with alternative explanations, simultaneously putting each explanation to the test. In these experiments, as I shall describe in a moment, there is evidence supporting the hypothetical CL as a more convincing explanation than alternative hypotheses derived from other theories.

The method used by Wyer and Bednar (1967) and Wyer (1968) is characterized by a careful approach to measurement; they aim to establish the CL with a high or low neutral point. This they do by arranging for nursery school children to complete simple tasks successfully, or to fail, by means of an apparatus requiring choices to be made between pressing either of two buttons, after which the experimenter signals a correct or incorrect choice. Wyer assumes that the comparison level is established by the preliminary run of "success" or "misses"; the CL is thought to evolve from task performance and from the child's view of his own competence. Next, after manipulating the comparison level, Wyer sets out to test predictions of the ways in which high or low comparison levels will influence later performance on other tasks (a rope-pulling game and a puzzle). For example, an individual who has

---

* Emphasis on the cognitive is illustrated when Wyer (1968) defines exchange theory as proposing that "persons attempt to maximise the outcomes they anticipate to result from available behavioural alternatives. The magnitude of these outcomes is defined in terms of positive and negative discrepancies from one's comparison level (CL) . . ." Wyer (1968, p. 270).

failed may want particularly to succeed in future trials (and will therefore try harder on difficult tasks) while one who has succeeded, having a
high comparison level, will expect success but will try to avoid failure
(and will try harder on easy tasks). A person with a low CL would
value success highly as a reward but attach a low cost to failure; someone with a high CL would have relatively little to gain from further
success but would have much to lose by failing. This prediction is
contrasted with alternative hypotheses taken from *achievement-motivation
theory* (Atkinson, 1957) and there is some evidence that the comparison
level is a more convincing explanation of motives to persevere in the
task. Before we examine these results and at the risk of digression, let
us consider Atkinson's explanation: he assumes that incentive to
success is greater in difficult tasks, while incentive of avoiding failure is
greater on very easy ones. However, after failure, the probability of
success decreases; after success it increases. So on an easy task after a
prior failure the motivation to persevere will be greater than after
success. And on a difficult task a person will persevere more after prior
success than after failure. The value of this explanation for Wyer is that
it can be opposed to his CL hypotheses—what he now has to do is
manipulate experimental conditions of success and failure and the ease
and difficulty of subsequent tasks and to note the differences in performance which result.

Success and failure were manipulated as already mentioned, and
subsequent tasks were arranged as easy (rope-pulling) or difficult (a
puzzle; fitting wooden shapes together). Duration of time spent on the
tasks (perseverance) was generally greater on a difficult task although
this may have been because of its content or interest. However, data
revealed a significant interaction of actual task difficulty and level of
previous success: the children persevered longer in the difficult task
following failure than they did following success, but persevered longer
on the easy task following success than they did following failure. As
well as manipulating actual task difficulty, Wyer introduced two conditions in the experimenter's instructions to the children whereby each
task was said to be either easy or difficult. This variation is not important
to the main hypothesis and need not concern us here, but it did lead to
some ambiguities which are left unresolved. A further unresolved
question concerns the possible effects of personal histories of success and
failure antecedent to the experiment. Despite some unexplained effects
Wyer and Bednar are able to conclude: "These data are consistent with

hypotheses based upon exchange theory, but contradict the relation-ships predicted by achievement motivation theory" (p. 262).

Wyer and Schwartz (1969) arranged that messages be passed to students in the form of statements about racial and other social issues; in two experimental conditions students were told *either* that the messages came from the same *or* from different persons, and they were next to rank the statements by their degree of positive or negative content. Wyer and Schwartz present several alternative hypotheses to explain the effect of the source conditions on these rankings. They assume that the CL can be manipulated and that this will have certain effects. For instance, if initial messages are highly positive a high CL is established and any subsequent message which is only moderately positive will be valued less highly than in the case of a relatively low CL, established by starting with a series of negative messages: here a moderately positive message should now be ranked highly. Thus, following the CL explanation, previous positive messages should result in a lower evaluation of succeeding positive ones. Similarly, previous negative messages should establish a low CL and thus produce the effect of higher evaluations of an equivalent positive message subse-quently. According to Wyer and Schwartz the opposite tendency would be predicted by *congruity theory* (Osgood and Tannenbaum, 1955) because messages from a negative source would tend to be assimilated towards a negative value, while those from a previously positive source would be rated relatively highly. The authors do allow that both processes, as postulated by congruity and comparison level notions, may operate and for this reason their aim is to explore some of the factors influencing the relative dominance of one or the other process rather than to test the theoretical validity of either approach. In the case of messages coming from the same source, resolving incongruity between different messages may be a much stronger influence than would be found as between messages from different persons. Whether or not the congruity effect will occur when there are evaluative differ-ences in degree between statements, rather than outright contradictions in meaning is a question which is raised but is left unresolved. Much of the discussion of the results concerns technicalities of the experimental method and we need not deal with them further. In each of the reports of Wyer and his colleagues we are left with the curious result that although "exchange theory" is a major point of reference, the CL concept has not in fact been applied to a *social exchange* nor has there been an attempt to simulate exchange process. The CL has been applied as a general explanation for personal reactions or motives. And in all these cases the CL is used as an explanatory statement rather than, as Thibaut and Kelley originally suggested, requiring a scale to be refined by observations made in social situations.

Let us examine one or two further examples. Walster, Aronson and Brown (1966) refer to the CL in order to provide some *ex post facto* speculations about the results of their experiment in which they used electric shock as a test condition—a fashionable method in the 1960s. In brief, student volunteers were told that they would have to eat either pleasant or unpleasant foods as part of a medical study of blood pressure changes. They were also asked to apply some mild or severe shocks to themselves to assist an investigation of pleasure-pain stimuli. Analysis of the subsequent behaviour showed that those who thought they would have to eat the unpleasant food voluntarily administered most shock. The experimenters argue that a person who anticipates an unpleasant experience would have a lower CL than someone who is either unsure about what to expect, or who is expecting future benefits. This leads them to the hypothesis that "any given magnitude of shock should seem less unpleasant to those lower CL subjects than to others" (p. 406). Among a number of conjectures which are put forward is also the suggestion that perhaps these students were consciously *lowering* their CL as a preparation for the future negative experience of unpleasant food.

In the next example we come closer to applying the CL in social situations. Teger (1970) refers to the comparison level concept as one of a number of explanations which could explain why early co-operation may increase retaliation to a subsequent hostile act.* Teger cites Heider (1958) in order to argue for the influence of past behaviour on how a person interprets a hostile act; he refers to Berkowitz (1960) for suggesting that a negative event if compared to an initial positive expectation will appear, in contrast, even worse than it actually is. Teger also discusses the possibility that the extent of the hostility is of significance, for example, the sheer number of consecutive competitive choices in an experimental game might determine the retaliation. Thus, past co-operation may have built up a credit of goodwill which reduces retaliation when the hostile act is small, but when the hostile act is large

* Note the contrary effect on another person of a player's change from competitive to co-operative choices in an experimental game. (See above p. 90.)

past co-operation may increase retaliation due to frustration or contrast. The experimental task was a modified form of an earlier game devised by Deutsch (1967) which simulated international relations and where students, playing against a confederate of the experimenter, had to allocate points to alternative courses of action such as "investments", "trade" or "arms". Money amounts were offered for different choices, if they were matched by the choice of the other person. Thus, each "trade" choice, if it was chosen jointly earned a money reward; an unmatched trade choice earned nothing. "Investment" brought a money amount regardless of the other's choice; "arms" involved losses to the other person as well as gains to the user. Each person was also provided with a fund of units which he could distribute over the options and in the arms option this allowed him to incur different amounts of loss on the other person. After ten practice trials in which the confederate gradually increased his trade options, runs of 14 further trials followed in which the confederate took the arms option either early or late and there were two further conditions in which he used the arms option either heavily or lightly. In summary, the results showed a markedly larger retaliation against the use of the arms option incurring a heavy loss to the victim; this effect appeared both when this option was used earlier or later in the sequence but the retaliation was greater when the hostile option was used late—after co-operative trade choices. Teger does not claim to test any of the theories to which he refers but he does conclude that the frustration and contrast explanations are upheld and so presumably is the CL interpretation although he gives no detailed attention to this concept.

William P. Smith (1968) explores the influence on the comparison level of the degree of control a person can exercise over outcomes in an experimental task (see Chapter 4, p. 18). Briefly, he reasons that with little control over outcomes a person will not expect much from a relationship; if he has considerable control he will expect to obtain all that he merits. Smith, whose research supervisor was John Thibaut, discusses the case where someone else controls the better outcomes; if this happens a person may believe there is only a small chance he can attain them. Consequently, the CL will move downwards. Or it might happen that the other person's capacity to direct outcomes is ineffective, with a similar result for the CL. This leads Smith to consider a triadic relationship in which a person (A) is allocated rewards from another (C) through an intermediary (B). If B only has what Smith calls "imprecise" power (to grant "all" or "nothing"), A's comparison level will be low, if B has more precise control (over a range of allocations) A's comparison level will be higher. In the first instance A would be more satisfied with a given outcome than in the latter and therefore less likely to retaliate against the intermediary by seeking an alternative relationship. Working in isolation, students representing person (A) passed counters (each one worth one cent) through a slot to a supposed person (B) whose job it was to supervise a worker (C) in a task which would provide outcomes for A. Both B and C were fictitious persons, and the contrived nature of this arrangement does raise some doubts. However, the results support the CL hypothesis as far as those with imprecise control (simulated by having power to grant all-or-nothing money rewards) differ, as follows, from those who have precise control (over rewards on a finely graded money scale). In the imprecise control condition there was greater satisfaction with outcomes gained and those taking part requested less often that the "worker" be substituted than where there was precise control. As expected, if the intermediary had precise control there was less satisfaction with a given level of outcome (a higher CL) and people were more likely to seek an alternative intermediary.

It should be noted that Smith, in his presentation of an alternative relationship, refers also to the $CL_{alt.}$, omitted in the other experiments which I have described, despite the similarity of the CL and $CL_{alt.}$ which Thibaut and Kelley emphasized in their original model. It is to be expected that most emphasis should be placed on the CL in view of the fact that most of the experiments we have mentioned focus on individual motives rather than social process or group membership. Although Smith (1968) has shown the way for the inclusion of the $CL_{alt.}$ by providing the option of changing intermediaries under varying levels of outcome, there appear to be no instances of other attempts in experiments to demonstrate the operation of the $CL_{alt.}$. In natural situations there must be many opportunities to explore the CL_{alt} concept, which Vroom (1964) discusses in the context of occupational mobility—referring to it as "the standard used by participants in a social relationship in deciding whether to remain in or leave that relationship. The value of $CL_{alt.}$ is assumed to depend on the perceived quality of the best of the member's available alternatives" (p. 200). With occupational choices in mind, Vroom comments that the information required in order to predict conditions under which employees will leave an organization is "seldom, if ever, available"—we do not know sufficient about the alternatives and we know little about the process of comparing alternatives differing on several characteristics.

The nearest approach to treating the CL as a scale is found in two experimental reports, one by Kahan (1968), the other by Rubin and DiMatteo (1972). The first of these, a brief report of a research project supervised by Thibaut, starts by discussing the CL and the "level of aspiration" (Siegel, 1957). Kahan suggests the hypothesis that co-operation in two-person bargaining is maintained easily when joint rewards are above the comparison level and competitive choices are more likely when joint rewards are below it. In a rather complicated set of bargaining conditions (for points) with a matrix presentation (adapted from Thibaut and Faucheux, 1965); players discussed their terms of agreement, in face-to-face conversation, before each choice. CL levels, true to the definition that these are an average of what has been obtained in the past, were to be manipulated by instructions giving a target score supposedly based on the averages of previous players. It was found that, as targets were set higher relative to the joint outcomes available, so co-operation became less, suggesting support for the CL hypothesis as stated.

Another attempt to explore how a CL is established is made by Rubin and DiMatteo (1972) who set up a bargaining situation, a version of Siegel and Fouraker's (1960) bilateral monopoly game. Here, students are asked to imagine they are either sellers or buyers of television sets and they have to maximize their profits in imaginary money during the course of eighteen bids (offers or counter-offers) which each player is allowed. By means of a simulated partner, conditions are manipulated in this design so that a player receives high or low offers and available alternative agreements are similarly presented in two conditions, high or low. Although the players tended to reduce their bids over the course of the game and to ask for smaller profits in their final bid than in the initial one, those who received high (programmed) offers asked for greater profits than those in the low offer condition. Furthermore, those receiving the low offers dropped their bids far more during the course of bargaining. At the end of the experiment, players were asked to rate their satisfaction with obtained profits on a five-pont scale; those receiving higher offers were more satisfied. They were also asked (1) about the highest profit players would like to obtain in a future game, this was termed the aspiration level (AL);

(2) what would be the mid-point (CL) above which they would be satisfied and (3) what would be the lowest profit ($CL_{alt.}$) they would settle for. A main effect for the higher offer condition emerged, those receiving the highest offers aimed for much higher profit levels than those in the low offer condition on all three indices. The analysis confirms that the high offer condition has a significant effect on the level they set for AL, CL and $CL_{alt.}$. However, any relevance of this report for social behaviour is considerably weakened by the economic profit-and-loss form of the experiment. Moreover, there is a devastating flaw in trying to use a commercial exchange to elucidate a social psychological problem. We have already mentioned the possibility of qualitative changes in the experimental game by focusing too much on the economic structure of gains (see p. 83 above)—a possibility admitted by Kelley et al. (1970).

To summarize on the influence of the CL concept: it is useful as a general, plausible explanatory idea despite the fact that there has been little attempt to refine its application as a scale. Even if the earlier suggestions of Thibaut and Kelley for scaling a person's goals and outcomes have not been realized, the explanatory notion of a comparison level continues to attract research and is often used as a means to a general understanding of social behaviour, in many discussions of behaviour in natural and experimental situations as well as a theoretical anchorage in experimental reports. The CL is important also because the nature of social comparisons touches closely on the difficult but recurrent question of subjective preference (or utility). The concept was suggested by Thibaut and Kelley in order to clarify what a person may perceive as a reward or cost in a particular relationship and involves their definition of rationality. They assume that if one can discover the comparisons which are significant to individuals or groups it can thereby be discovered what is perceived as rational by the actors in a given situation. But this is largely a matter of conjecture and of future promise.

6

Negotiation and Bargaining

Introduction: negotiating behaviour

Most of the empirical contribution by Thibaut and Kelley to exchange theory occurs in their experimental studies of negotiation. Here they consider different aspects of the process of reaching an agreement and, to some extent, follow in the tradition of Deutsch (1949, 1949a). Negotiation, at its most basic, is the process of reaching an agreement. This process is of importance in exchange quite simply because persons must agree on the amount, quality and frequency of what is exchanged. Is negotiation the same process as bargaining? In fact, a clear distinction can be made because negotiation involves an *exchange of information* over and above bargaining, which may itself consist only of stating and accepting the actual terms of agreement. Less clearly, negotiation is usually overt and bargaining is often implicit, but this distinction may be difficult to maintain always. Both "bargaining" and "negotiation" refer to a process which is likely to (but may not) result in an agreement or bargain. So, negotiation as a concept is applied to the overt process of bargaining, of communicating offers, bids, counter-offers, refusals or compromises: it involves information of these various kinds. An attempt to define negotiation in industrial bargaining is made by Stevens (1963) who gives a definition similar to the one I have just mentioned: negotiation is present only if there is an information exchange over and above conveying offers and accepting or rejecting them. He points out that:

in order to conclude any transaction, the parties must exchange minimal information—namely their terms and their subsequent acceptance or rejection of the other's terms. However, they may be said to negotiate if they exchange further information relevant to the transaction. An analysis of negotiation is in large part an analysis of the content and function of such additional information and of the tactical "moves", agreement problems, and so forth, reflected in it (p. 1).

Although his definition is obscure about the content of such additional information, it is helpful mainly because it makes the distinction between negotiation and bargaining. He states that in *all* exchange transactions, a bargain is struck about the terms. Thus, any exchange involves bargaining at least in some implicit sense, but only some situations involve explicitly negotiating the terms of an agreement and exchanging information in order to do so. Negotiation is particularly characteristic of economic bargaining where bids, counter-offers, or concessions can be made in precise amounts of money or goods, but is present in many other situations so long as there is information to be shared which may modify the eventual agreement. Now, to take the matter a step further than Stevens' definition—what is the nature of this information?

Information in bargaining

There is no doubt of the importance of negotiation in a bargaining situation between persons who disagree over the terms; it is a means to an agreement about who gets the greater or lesser share, how costs are allocated, or how much of one kind of activity is to be exchanged for another.* In experimental games the influence of the amount of information disclosed appears to be decisive, in so far as better payoffs are achieved and there are less differences between the payoffs of each partner (Siegel and Fouraker, 1960).

Daniels (1967) makes a highly competent summary of previous work and current problems touching on negotiation, presenting the results of his own research, supervised by Kelley. He states that, at present, we have sparse knowledge of the effects of different amounts and kinds of information; it is not even known if results from one set of experimental conditions apply to other situations, and he sets out to make a start at establishing some common ground. His own main experimental condition involves a contrast between a game played with no communication beyond actual decisions (as in the Prisoner's Dilemma) and one requiring communication of what each player proposes to give to the

---

* Variety in the content of social exchanges has been discussed in Chapter 2 and Chapter 7 (pp. 20–22, 137).

other—by means of a nonverbal presentation of tentative offers. In the latter case, they have to agree which of several counters are to be exchanged, each one carrying a points score for the recipient and a cost to the giver—although the players know these details only for themselves and not for the other player. There is a further condition of two incentive levels—low (playing for points) or high (playing for money). First, Daniels hypothesizes that joint outcomes will be greater when there is communication beyond simply making choices, that is, if players are allowed to make offers and counter-offers. He also tests the hypothesis that greater information leads to more equal payoffs. Eighty pairs of undergraduates exchanged coloured tokens, passing these through apertures in six-foot high screens. Each pair undertook forty trials. Daniels provides convincing evidence for the first hypothesis, although the data do not give any strong support for the second.

One of the interesting points which Daniels makes, in a very full discussion, concerns the importance of expressing *conditionality* in offers or counter-offers; he shows that lack of opportunity to make conditional proposals limits the eventual outcomes.* This he explains as an effect of a player not having the capacity to give selective rewards to those actions of the other which are most desirable to him. Daniels also mentions a problem inherent in the experimental design, where choices and outcomes are recorded and the experimenter afterwards makes interpretations about the players' motives. The chief weakness lies in "the inferential character of our knowledge about the amount of information that subjects in the various experimental conditions obtained" (p. 72) and he leaves us with the question, what were players' perceptions of one another's costs and values?

In this experiment, there was no free verbal communication in any of the four bargaining conditions. How much of the essence of negotiation did this exclude? In a natural situation much of negotiation consists of what is said, transmitted relatively freely, between the participants. On the other hand, negotiation in experiments may be conducted by non-verbal signals as several investigators have observed (see Kelley, 1965a, p. 87) and in the Prisoner's Dilemma game the actual choice made by a player can be considered as indicative of his next choice, giving notice of his future intentions. The choice itself can act as a warning, or a promise, and since no other forms of communication are allowed in this design it is quite likely that players give atten-

* See Apfelbaum on conditionality, above p. 89.

tion to the informational content of choices and counter-choices in the Prisoner's Dilemma (Kelley, *et al.* 1970). This effect is probably similar to that of the tacit communications, in the form of actions that convey feelings, mentioned by Kelley (1965) as occurring in some situations of bargaining where threats can be used as co-ordination devices in the absence of other means of communication. Kelley (1965) offers a helpful three-fold classification of different kinds of communication as explicit, tacit and implicit. Tacit communication may be behavioural, as we have just illustrated, or can take the form of verbal messages suggesting terms of agreement but couched in an indirect form—they are apparently about something else. Although these aspects of negotiation have yet to be closely studied, Kelley (1966) gives us a useful conceptual treatment of the process of information-exchange which we will describe in a moment.

A further distinction between negotiation and bargaining is added by Kelley (1965) when he notes that bargaining may take place in implicit forms where a person may not even recognize the problem of reaching agreement, nor that his words or actions are meant to influence others. In this case, negotiation cannot be said to occur. Implicit bargaining is a form of activity exemplified in family studies* where exchange concepts have been applied to explore this aspect of the relationships between parents and children and between pre-marital and marital partners. Scanzoni (1972) argues that "persons today bargain during courtship, during the decision to marry and furthermore they continue this bargaining all through the length of their marriage" (p. 53). He employs an exchange framework to explain the "dynamics of marriage formation and subsequent interaction". We shall discuss this topic later in the book after we have considered Peter Blau's analysis of love relationships in Chapter 12.

Information scarcity

We have described some attempts to focus on seeking and exchanging information as part of the bargaining process and these indicate at least a tentative approach to informational aspects by social psychologists which is quite different to the traditional game theory emphasis on strategies and outcomes. The following experiments now pursue this line of interest by more specific attention to experimental conditions

* See Chapter 13.

where information is lacking or incomplete as is usually found, in fact, in natural situations of negotiation.

Information scarcity is the focus of three bargaining experiments reported by Kelley, Beckman and Fischer (1967) in which each player was instructed to obtain a joint settlement with another player. He was told he had to obtain a "minimum necessary share" of the outcome with another player whose minimum he did not know. In short, the players were instructed to seek a profit above a given break-even score (varied between games) and observations were taken of their offers and counter-offers. Other communications coded by the experimenters included, concessions, threats or lies (for example, if a player indicated he had reached his break-even score even though he was some points above it).* Agreement had to be reached within brief time limits and players received dollar prizes at the end. The game was arranged as a simulation of common bargaining situations. At the outset, since there is flexibility about how the profits are to be divided, each person is expected to try for a maximum share of the outcome but without forcing too hard against the other. How do the players accommodate these partly conflicting, partly shared interests? In this case, Kelley, Beckman and Fischer suggest hypotheses which are game theoretical rather than psychological, referring to Harsanyi (1962) who suggests two mechanisms tending to produce agreement. The first is a "stereotype utility function" which is a player's expectation about the other person's priorities. A second mechanism involves mutual adjustment of these expectations during bargaining as a result of tentative offers and counter-offers, a process complicated by bluffing from either party. A further emphasis towards game theory appears in the importance which the experimenters give to an analysis of trends in the effects of varying levels of "minimum necessary share" between players over a number of trials of the game. Nevertheless, there are several points of psychological interest, notably that "full and honest communication" did not occur, instead, deception and absence of trust were evident.

If a person is dependent on another for information, what happens when the dependency is asymmetrical? Benton, Gelber, Kelley and Liebling (1969) report the results of a two-person game where one

---

* There were three different conditions for communication: (a) free conversation (b) communication with restriction of visual contact (c) visual contact without verbal communication. However, the effects of these conditions are not given in the experimental report.

person has the information and the other is dependent on him. They put this forward as typical of actual negotiations between labour and management, or between the buyer and seller of a house. In the latter instance, each wishes to make an agreement with the best possible deal for himself. Only the buyer knows his own alternatives, the time and money pressures on him; only the seller really knows the condition of the house, the disadvantages of the neighbourhood, how long he can afford to wait for the sale. To simplify this problem, where there is mutual dependence for information, the experimenters created an asymmetrical dependence. Students were asked to play a card game in which a player selects a card which is matched by the other player to a card *he* has selected. The latter, the "declarer" (a confederate of the experimenter) announces whether they are the same or different in colour. If they are the same the first player collects two points, if different the "declarer" gains two points. The first player can either accept or doubt the declaration—if the declaration is false he stands to gain, if not he is penalized for doubting. Over blocks of trials, different proportions of false declarations were made by the "declarer" following a previously determined programme. The experimenters' aim was to examine reactions of players to various degrees of untrustworthiness in their partner. Questionnaires were administered, before and after the experimental procedure, to test attitudes towards the partner. The experimenters showed that as the number of deceptions increased, doubting increased also, but in the upper range of deceptions there was no corresponding rise in doubting rates. Benton, Gelber, Kelley and Liebling conjecture whether the rate of doubting levelled off because there was little incentive to catch up with the other player, or because doubting was restrained by a desire not to make the other player more competitive. They conclude with the question: did doubting apparently level off as a function of the particular conditions—that is, the payoff incentives of this experiment "or is it a more general phenomenon holding over a wide range of situations?" (p. 178). As we have discussed in the section *Generalizing from Experiments*, the question of extrapolating from research results is one which Kelley and his colleagues frequently raise (and see pp. 69, 72, 80 above).

Concern with the kind of information that is sought by participants in a two-person bargaining situation is carried further by Eiser and Tajfel (1972) who refer briefly to the study by Kelley, Beckman and Fischer (1967) but propose to simulate a condition of *no information* in order to observe what information a participant will first seek, starting from this condition. The experimental task consisted of passing "messages", coloured cards each with a certain points score to the recipient and cost to the sender. Each student was shown the range of cards he could send to his partner: the score to the partner and the costs to him. But he was not shown the corresponding score and costs of the partner's cards. Participants were allowed to seek information about these from the experimenter, forfeiting a small number of points in doing so. Specifically, since no information was given about the other's costs or benefits, Eiser and Tajfel aimed to discover which of these two kinds of information would be seen as most useful by a player: information about the score value to the other of what he receives, or information about the cost to the other of what he gives.

They suggest as their first hypothesis that more information will be requested about the value to the other of what he receives than about the cost of what he gives. A second hypothesis states that if participants can be classified as "competitive" and "non-competitive", the former will make more requests for information about the other member's gains rather than his costs since they will be more likely to assume that their partners are also competitive and give most importance to sheer maximizing of gains. The experimenters manipulated the *target scores* for different pairs to test the hypothesis that those with higher targets perceive the task as more important and therefore will make more requests for information.

Among a number of inferences which are derived from the data, it was found that the first hypothesis on information-seeking was supported: many more "value to him" than "cost to him" items were requested. Moreover, as predicted by the second hypothesis, this tendency was more marked in those classified on their questionnaire replies as more competitive. Students who were competitive, who said they intended making higher scores than their partners, sought information on the value to the other of their messages, probably in order to avoid sending more points than they received in return. But non-competitive students sought wider information on their partner's choices; they wished to know about the points he scored *and* the costs he incurred. Eiser and Tajfel make the interpretation that the non-competitive student was interested in understanding the motives of the other player, either in order to influence him actively or to respond more appropriately. This suggests the further hypothesis that competitive persons are less likely to seek greater insight into the intentions and choices of the other, since they will have pre-empted the necessity for this by assuming their partner also is competitive and profit-seeking, a suggestion similar to that of Kelley and Stahelski (1970a).

Information about the other person

Discussing, as an aspect of information, why it is important to know another person's intentions, Kelley and Stahelski (1970a, 1970b, 1970c) reviewing the results of their Prisoner's Dilemma design, point out that co-operation will be successful only if it is reciprocated and that the success of a course of action is therefore conditional on the actions of the other. As they suggest, different strategies will emerge depending on conditional expectations. For instance, if a person intending to make co-operative choices knows too little about the other's intentions he will perceive a strong risk that his co-operation will not be reciprocated and he may therefore act defensibly (that is, competitively). On the other hand, a player who tends towards the competitive option may anticipate his partner's co-operative choices in order to exploit them. Although this view of the experimental game may seem to over-emphasize the *realpolitik* of social interaction, as we mentioned earlier (p. 87), Kelley and Stahelski do, in fact, raise at least two important issues. One is their confirmation of a tendency for co-operative players to be "assimilated" so that they reciprocate the competitive choices of a competitive partner; the other is their theoretical discussion concerning the stability of a player's intentions and, in particular, concerning the nature of an "assimilative" change. They attempt to answer the question whether such a change is likely to be temporary or permanent, taking their explanatory hypotheses from Heider (1958), Jones and Davis (1965) and Kelley (1967). They offer a definition of intention which locates its stability somewhere between the long-term personality dispositions and the immediate motives leading to actions in a given situation. There are interesting indications in these three experimental reports. As we have noted, players starting with a co-operative intention tend to switch, if they are faced with a competitive partner, to competitive choices as a defence (1970a). Competitive players project their own competitive orientations on to their partners, failing to see the partners' competitive choices as imitative (1970b, p. 414). In a broader discussion of these and other experiments

Kelley and Stahelski (1970c) draw our attention to the use by Sermat and Gregovich (1966) of experimental schedules of co-operative and competitive sequences in a simulated partner. They suggest that assimilative changes are temporary in nature and as soon as the competitive choices of a simulated partner are removed and a co-operative pattern substituted then mutual co-operation is quickly re-established. This is a rebound effect in the original co-operators who "are behaviourally assimilated to the competitive schedule, but they readily return to co-operative behaviour when the schedule becomes co-operative" Kelley and Stahelski (1970c, p. 72).

In the version of the Prisoner's Dilemma game presented by Kelley and Stahelski (1970a) mutual co-operation brought five points; one player co-operating and the other competing brought a loss of ten to the former and a gain of ten to the latter; mutual competition brought a loss of five.

TABLE 1

Payoff matrix (Kelley and Stahelski, 1970a)

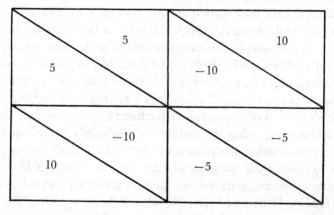

Participants in this experiment were allowed to choose which type of intention they would adopt for the entire game—co-operative or competitive—and they were then paired either with someone of the same or different intentions. Each was unaware of his partner's chosen intention. Over thirty trials, after each block of ten, questions were asked about the other's intentions. Further questions were asked at the end. "Assimilative" errors were found to occur, where competitive players perceived co-operative ones as having competitive intentions similar to their own (see above, Eiser and Tajfel, 1972). In the second report by Kelley and Stahelski (1970b) they describe a brilliantly arranged experiment in which participants judged the intentions of variant strategies of hypothetical players who are shown to follow all possible combinations of co-operative and competitive choices in a three-choice paradigm. Thus, a hypothetical player may have a first and second choice as follows: C-d, C (persistent co-operation in face of a partner's competitive response) or C-c, C (consistent correspondence of behaviour). Kelley and Stahelski discuss the informational effects of a person's agreement, disagreement, imitative or initiating choices and suggest hypotheses within the framework of attribution theory. As we have already mentioned, it might, in the future, be worthwhile to examine the effects of competitive or co-operative changes in a partner's strategies in order to elucidate tendencies in social process, testing for different conditions of interdependency. For instance, does a switch from co-operative to competitive, produce a stronger reaction than a change from competitive to co-operative? Could we interpret the results of different conditions of reciprocity as a modest contribution to exchange propositions? Whether the PD game is itself suitable or acceptable as a means to advancing exchange theory raises questions that have not been resolved, but there are still a number of hypotheses which might be tested in the most recent versions of this design.

Kelley and Stahelski have speculated about the meaning of empirical patterns of choices and of short-term strategies. When they consider the judgements and behaviour of the competitive players, the hypothesis is suggested that the latter may have personality characteristics producing lack of insight into the motives of others. However, as they stand, these experimental reports could easily be reinterpreted as a demonstration of the reciprocity principle. This interpretation would fit perfectly the behaviour switch observed in those students who were initially co-operative. We could apply, in future research, an exchange hypothesis stating the converse of Homans' Proposition 2 (see Chapter 8, p. 159): the less a person's behaviour rewards the action of another, the less frequently will the other take this action. Or we might look for evidence to support hypotheses covering different conditions of retaliation; they would have the advantage of focusing the explanation on the interdependency rather than on individual dispositions. Re-interpreting these reports by exchange propositions would be similar to the line argued by Bloch and Goodstein (1971) when they advocate that exchange propositions be substituted for self-disclosure theory because "the vigour of both the research and theoretical formulations of social exchange theory, or reciprocity, suggests . . . (it) is to be preferred" (p. 596). Their claim that Jourard and Jaffe's work on self-disclosure could be reinterpreted by the reciprocity rule could be made equally strongly for research data from two-person games.

Negotiating and bargaining as a process

Bargaining involves situations where no single outcome appeals to both parties and there have to be mutual adjustments in what each party sets out initially to obtain. There are several possible outcomes, which are likely to be asymmetrical, but a joint agreement has finally to be reached. Offers and counter-offers are made, each person trying to find an appropriate course of action, to discover information about the other's intentions and possibly to modify them. Kelley and Thibaut (1969) discuss the process of information exchange which accompanies bargaining: each party tries to acquire information about the preferences of the other while selectively disclosing information about his own.

Since negotiating and bargaining involve a process which settles the terms of exchange it seems important that researchers should develop descriptions of this process, rather than considering the end-results, the scores in a payoff matrix. Kelley (1965) gives credit to Fouraker and Siegel (1963) for doing more towards process analysis than most investigators of bargaining; and for presenting in an appendix every decision taken by each participant in their experimental games. Kelley inclines to the view that their work is a contribution to what he calls interdependence theory rather than to economic theory. He emphasizes thay they do not focus their work on a particular market or business situation and, taken out of its economic context, the research throws some light on the conditions under which persons in an interdependent relationship arrive at mutually good solutions.

Kelley (1966) describes the nature of the information, in two-person bargaining, which it is desirable to know about the other person's goals. To some extent the interests of the parties are opposed but there is also an area where solutions could be acceptable to both. This he represents in a diagram, using the $CL_{alt.}$ as the break-off score for each negotiator, although he notes that, in reality, it is often a vague zone rather than a definite point. The zone is illustrated in Fig. 7.

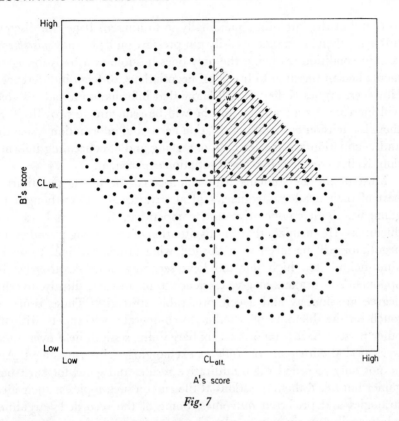

Fig. 7

The problem for person A is stated as follows:

Because of the incomplete nature of A's information, though he may know (or assume) that a region of the sort characterized by Z exists (i.e. that there are some contracts that are maximally desirable from his own viewpo nt and acceptable, though minimally so, from B's), *he does not know where it is*. He can judge that it lies somewhere between his highest score and his $CL_{alt.}$. As he considers contracts at higher and higher scores, he increases the probability of leaving the viable subset altogether by dropping below B's $CL_{alt.}$. On the other hand, as A moves downward toward his own $CL_{alt.}$ he increases the probability of getting into W-type contracts, which are fine for B but only barely adequate for himself. All of this means that A is greatly in need of more information about the situation if he is to find contracts in region Z and not in region W (or in region X, which is poorer than necessary for both) (p. 57).

Kelley discusses the information of most importance to person A, information about what kind of agreement will be minimally acceptable to B and at the same time maximally so to himself. If he can discover this zone, then he can more easily put pressure on B; he may *misrepresent* certain conditions as being the only ones possible as a basis for agreement; he can threaten to break off negotiations, or feign indifference.* However, argues Kelley, B will know that information about his goals will increase A's advantage and he will be reluctant to provide it. So there is a tension between information needs and information restraints, and negotiation is a matter both of seeking and of concealing information. Kelley now describes his negotiation experiment.

Most of the 22 students who volunteered for the negotiations as part of their academic course, said afterwards that they thought the game was both co-operative and competitive; Kelley analyses their dilemmas. He surmizes that in this situation of conflicting purposes, the negotiator will be faced with the following problems: first, to set his aims neither too high nor too low; secondly, how far to trust his opponent's assurances or give credence to his threats; thirdly, to what degree are honesty and deceit preferable strategies. These issues all touch on the dilemma of whether to co-operate or compete with the other person. Kelley reports on six bargaining sessions held over a ten-week period with pairs of students exchanging written messages. And he not only recorded the quantitative results and gains for each bargainer but asked them questions at the end on such topics as their ideal strategies and preferred outcomes. Some of the recorded bargaining solutions in the six games played are of interest. For instance, the typical bargainer started at a much higher demand level than his eventual agreement level. Kelley is able to show evidence supporting several broad premises as follows: (1) that the first general requirement of a negotiator is to avoid early commitments (2) that the other person be induced to make concessions (3) that the negotiator himself should make concessions and (4) that the negotiator should acquire information about what is considered a reasonable outcome for him to attain.

This study by Kelley (1966) has often been referred to in the literature and it is useful particularly because it states the problems common to many negotiating situations in a clear analytical form. Kelley concludes that because of the dilemmas which are present "successful negotiation can be viewed as a process of implicit collusion, the purpose of which is to make each party feel satisfied with the agreement"

---

* An example of Kelley's *realpolitik*. Plon (1967) and Moscovici (1972) discuss this aspect of the philosophy behind the Thibaut and Kelley model.

(p. 72). For a negotiation to achieve success as it is defined here, information has to be exchanged for each party to be able to achieve up to the limit of what is possible in view of the goals of the other. While the exchange of information can occur in the form of explicit assertions and requests, much of the negotiation may occur in the form of tacit offers and counter-offers; or it may consist of testing, probing and exaggerating demands. There is also much implicit exchange through what Kelley calls "action and reaction" as bargaining proceeds—each party learns more of the situation of the other and what may be satisfactory to both.

These explorations by Kelley of the negotiation process do have a face validity for actual situations although he himself does not on this occasion consider such implications. They easily suggest to us a similarity with bargaining between unions and management. Here we can find several "predictions" which might be tested against descriptive data on bargaining collected by observation in natural situations and we might expect these to corroborate the laboratory pattern. There have been no attempts to apply the hypotheses proposed by Kelley to field studies, even though some of them seem to be especially appropriate. For instance, the effects noted for concessions are particularly interesting. Kelley's conclusion that bids start high but concessions follow and Gruder's similar inference that small regular concessions are likely to be most successful, provide working hypotheses suitable for the study of bargaining in organizations or small groups. The effectiveness of concessions, and the acceptance by the parties of a positive exchange, brings us back again to the possibility of an underlying explanation by a reciprocity rule.

Threats, power and co-operation

One important feature of negotiation, the use of threats and promises, is discussed by Thibaut and Kelley (1959) when they examine how a person exerts influence on another, particularly in relationships where one person tries to control the other's outcomes from a position of power. In *fate control* one person has power to allocate rewards to himself, irrespective of the choice of action by the other person, but a limit to this kind of control is set by the weaker person's possibilities of escape from the relationship. Fate control may be implemented through formal authority, or threats directly from one person to the other. To some extent the weaker person exercises counter-power if he, in turn, threatens to leave. As we saw in Chapter 3, fate control becomes converted to *behaviour control* where the more powerful person allows an improvement in the weaker partner's outcomes, seeking an accommodation that can thus be understood as partially the result of mutual threats. Leading on from this discussion of basic stratagems Thibaut and Kelley discuss the process by which matching rules are conveyed verbally or by acting them out, with the end that one person's behaviour, desirable to the other, is matched by positive behaviour from the other (rewards given or promised). At the same time, it is made known that alternative behaviour may have a negative result (punishment, or threat of punishment). While Thibaut and Kelley present their exemplar of this process in a two-person relationship, they soon illustrate how, at the level of larger groups, the matching rules are embodied in social norms (see Chapter 3, p. 42). The process by which matching rules and norms emerge has been the subject of research by Faucheux and Thibaut (1964), Thibaut and Faucheux (1965) and by Thibaut (1968)—these studies will be discussed in a moment.

Kelley (1965a) defines threat as an intention to inflict harm unless the threatened person modifies his behaviour in a way indicated by the threatener. As we shall see, he states his concern with the psychological aspects of threat—its meaning for the threatened person as well as its intended result for the user. Baldwin (1971) distinguishes between these two aspects of threat when he comments that, while strategies and choices of the user are of interest to the theory of games, the meaning of the threat is a problem for psychology. For game theorists the results of a threat are thus a matter of strategy, the rewards and costs of expressing or implementing threats must be weighed up before the action is taken. For psychologists, the question consists more in the meaning of threats for the receiver. And as Kelley points out, this merges with a third area, because threats must also be considered as influencing the interdependency, the social relationship between two or more persons. Here especially there are a number of problems for social psychologists to analyse.

Thibaut (1968) refers to three main kinds of threat. First are those which are *contingent* on some action being taken by the other person, persuading him to desist from or to pursue an activity. Secondly, threats may be *non-contingent* on any action taken by the other person and these simply demonstrate the power which an individual has to affect another's situation. Thirdly, in pursuing his own goal regardless of the other, a person's action may constitute a threat by the sheer fact that attaining it will deprive the latter of an advantage. Thibaut suggests that a threat can be conveyed either verbally or by an action to demonstrate the intention; a threatening action may be made as an indication of worse things to follow. In experiments carried out on the influence of threats in game playing situations it is usually the latter kind which is observed. This has obviously to be the case in the Prisoner's Dilemma and similar designs where, in most instances, no communication is allowed between the participants other than their choices in the game. Difficulties arise in defining a threat in these circumstances either because it is tied to a particular set of experimental conditions, or else there is some doubt about what the actions (choices) mean for either party. The players themselves have to make their own inferences of just what the other person's actions indicate of his future intentions. The experimenter also has to make inferences about what player's reactions mean—to make inferences about inferences.

Smith and Leginski (1970) note that research on the effects of threat in bargaining usually involves, first, the presentation of capacity to threaten by one or both members of a dyad, and, second, a comparison with dyads without such capacity. Smith and Leginski contribute a refinement by examining how magnitude and precision of the capacity to threaten affects the strategy of the bargainers who possess that capacity. They use a negotiation game similar to that of Kelley (1966), which we have just discussed, this time with one partner simulated in a standard way by the experimenter. The game was arranged as a true bargaining situation where the parties had to accommodate to each other over their share of the total outcome: "the two parties must agree on the division between them of some finite quantity of reward to which they jointly have access by virtue of their relationship with each other" (p. 58). Smith and Leginski argue that it is clearly very important for the participant to persuade the other person to accept a settlement and that the essence of threats and punishments is that they are tools of persuasion. However, they point out that bargaining is not only a matter of persuasion; some agreements are out of the question. For instance, a person cannot be persuaded to accept poorer outcomes than those he can easily obtain elsewhere. In a case where both bargainers know exactly what outcomes are possible, an agreement with such poor relative outcomes will not be offered. On the other hand, in many situations bargainers will not have this knowledge. The authors conclude that a person must be careful not to overdo coercive strategies, taking into account that threats are potentially damaging to the relationship and that, where future outcomes are unclear, he should therefore incline towards leniency.

Cheney, Harford and Solomon (1972) examine the effect of communicating threats and promises which are either contingent or non-contingent upon co-operation. They adopt Schelling's (1963) definition of threat and promise: a threat is a warning of punishment contingent upon the other's behaviour; a promise offers contingent reward. In bargaining, both warnings and promises are designed to control, and can be viewed as different forms of social influence. But the context in which they are used is important—the context of power relationships, the relative utilities of the partners, and their previous experience in bargaining, as Heider (1958) has illustrated. Cheney, Harford and Solomon use a version of the trucking game as developed by Borah (1963) and by Shomer, Davis and Kelley (1966) in order to differentiate threat or warning from actual punishment, and promise from actual reward. This leads them to discuss the positive influences for co-operation, of promises rather than threats, and to seek an explanation for this in Heider's suggestion that promises, although they are made by someone else, enable a person still to take a choice and, at the same time, follow his own volition; to keep a control which cannot be present under the coercion of a threat.

On a similar theme, Tedeschi *et al.* (1971) see a promise as something which is perceived as helpful, if there is a normative rule to "help those who help you". In the bargaining situation they describe, the participants preferred exerting influence by promise of exchange and offers of reward rather than by threats; they seemed to follow a tacit social norm for friendly behaviour. Horai and Tedeschi (1969) examine the influence of what they call "threat credibility" on subsequent compliance. They criticize previous studies for their ambiguity, because there was no *verbal* communication of threats in these experiments. As an illustration, they quote Kelley (1965a) in support of this criticism, particularly emphasizing the variety of meaning which could be attached to the use of the gates in the Deutsch and Krauss (1960) trucking game. Shomer *et al.* (1966), Borah (1963) and Gallo (1966) are mentioned for showing further contradictory aspects of the Deutsch and Krauss design.

The Kelley-Deutsch polemic

The problem of inferring the meaning of implicit threats gave Kelley his major criticism of the classic transport game constructed by Deutsch and Krauss (1960, 1962) where threats took the form of one player closing a gate to prevent access by the other to the shortest route. Here there was no threat in the sense of an expressed intention, merely enactment of threat and the experiment took the form of a study of these actions and of similar counter-actions taken by the other partner. A difficulty arising from this definition of threat is that it leaves considerable looseness in the interpretation of just what the actions mean for either party. Much of the discussion and argument about this classic game concerns just this issue.

Kelley's main point of dispute with the conclusions of Deutsch and Krauss is over the meaning of closing the gates; more specifically, of their use when the option is coupled with that of a longer alternative route. The well-known conclusion of Deutsch and Krauss is that use of "threats" (closing the gates) leads to escalation of conflicts. Kelley suggests that Deutsch and Krauss's results are to some extent an artifact of having the longer route available as an escape, so that failure to co-ordinate may occur because of the escape possibility rather than because of any increase in competitive behaviour. In his own experiment Kelley (1965), using an adaptation of the trucking game without escape routes, demonstrated that a show of force is necessary to resolve conflict, to force the parties into reaching agreement. Moscovici points to the underlying philosophies in this debate which, in his view, reflect

> two dominant political options: on the one hand, the liberal tendency, represented by Deutsch, with its stress on dialogue and the development of trust; on the other, Kelley's option of *realpolitik*, that is a strategy of negotiations supported by the realities of power (p. 25).

But there is also a methodological aspect which has to be emphasized so that the difference between the protagonists turns out to be at once technical, methodological and "political". There may be a greater separation between Deutsch and Kelley than Plon (1967) allows when he also points to their mutual failure to question the conventions of the experimental game. In the course of his criticism of the trucking game, Kelley turns to the essentially psychological problem of the meaning of behaviour in experimental games and in order to do this he also has to explore what the game symbolizes for each player. We see, in the studies, that he depends for evidence on replies to questionnaires administered to the players as they finish the experiments. In relying on percentages of opinions towards various possibilities he declines to rely only on observations of choice behaviour, even in the carefully varied conditions of the laboratory game, since these cannot supply the answers which he seeks; instead he relies on opinion polls and questionnaires and has to face the usual problems about the validity of replies. At least on one occasion, we find Kelley raising the conjecture that the respondents might be answering according to their preconceptions of what might have been the experimenter's aims. Kelley now faces the same problems as are encountered by social psychologists whatever their area of study, where limitations of method curtail what can be achieved. But this is not the main point. It is important to recognize that whatever the defects of methods used to test attitudes and however inferior these may be to the strict quantification of behaviour in game-playing, by admitting the evidence of attitudes, Kelley has made a substantial approach towards a social psychology of bargaining.

In this debate, Kelley (1965) claims that it is rather arbitrary to refer to closing the gates as a threat: "in view of the wide range of 'messages' subjects might try to send with the gates . . ." (p. 81). He goes on to mention that a person might use the gate to assert his priority to pass through first; to punish the other, to gain revenge; to enforce a particular pattern of sharing the quickest route. Moreover, the other person may infer a variety of intentions and react not merely to being threatened but to being exploited, tricked, or unjustly punished. Kelley cites Borah's (1963) remark that intentions can quite as easily be communicated by decisions in the game as by such threats as closure of the gates, or by electric shocks introduced by Borah (1961, 1963) as part of a repertoire of actions available to participants. Borah's contribution lies in the importance he demonstrates for initial attitudes between the players: the attitudes attributed to the other, positive or negative, had a marked effect upon the degree (higher or lower) of subsequent co-operation. The method of elucidating the meaning of shocks, gates or choices comes largely from questionnaires given at the end of the experiments to the students participating.

Kelley (1965) describes how in a further experiment by Shomer, a game-board was substituted for the Deutsch and Krauss apparatus. Now, participants had to move their trucks from a starting position to a goal, along paths with a one-way central section where they could not both proceed at the same time. Thus the situation involved conflict and the need to co-ordinate. The participants proceeded along their separate game-boards until the experimenter sounded a buzzer to indicate jamming on the central section. The influence of threat was given special attention by providing participants with a threat button making a yellow light appear for the other player and signifying the intention to levy a fine; a second button operated a red light showing that he actually had been fined. Each time a player's truck reached the goal he was credited with a small fee, from which was substracted a time penalty. Questionnaires administered at the end of the experimental game gave some clues about the meaning of the threat to fine—what the user intended it to mean and its interpretation by the other. The partners in this game who were most successful were those who understood the yellow light to mean a signal aiding them to co-ordinate their use of the common path.

As I noted earlier, in every instance where Kelley describes evidence touching on this issue as well as on the meaning of threats in general; when he cites from Shomer, Gallo, Siegel and Fouraker, he depends for his support on the replies to questionnaires administered to the participants. Methodologically this is a very different position to that of Deutsch, but it is similar to that of researchers in the uncontrolled conditions of field studies in that he now has to face similar problems about the validity of data. He is not now relying on the carefully varied conditions of the laboratory game but on an opinion poll of his questionnaire sample.

Lastly, as a result of examining these experiments involving the use of threats, Kelley notes that there are some interesting ambiguities. For instance, in Shomer's study a threatening act had primarily a positive effect, while in Borah's experiments threats had no apparent effect at all. Furthermore, the meaning of a threat to the other person seems to depend very much on the circumstances of a particular game. For example, in a bargaining game between buyers and sellers the pressures towards co-operation probably over-ride tendencies to compete or withdraw, which seem to be encouraged in the trucking game. Thus, Kelley emphasizes that some efforts will need to be made in the future at classifying different negotiating situations in order to make more clear with conditions influence competition, co-operation and the use of threat. Kelley's conclusions are consistent with his general view of experimental games as a means to discovering the psychological meaning of different conditions of threat or negotiation.

Threats and norm formation: "spokesmen" as representatives in negotiation

The emergence of interpersonal agreements to reduce the disruptive possibilities of threats has been studied by Faucheux and Thibaut (1964) and Thibaut and Faucheux (1965). They argue from the simple situation of a dyad with completely convergent interests but with one member having greater power. In this case, he cannot use his power against the other without also hurting his own interests. Complicating the example, the authors next point out that where a conflict of interests develops, if the more powerful partner threatens to use his power against the other, then the low-power member may appeal to a norm of fairness or equity. Conflict may arise also if there are attractive alternative relationships and this time it is the low-power member who is more likely to threaten the relationship by seeking these alternatives; faced with this threat the high-power member may appeal to a norm of loyalty.

Thibaut and Faucheux (1965) argue that if both these conditions hold and there is power and counter-power, then adaptive norms will surely emerge. I would like to give some details of the experiment they carried out. In a face-to-face bargaining task with open discussion, players were assigned at random to positions of high or low power in dyads. "Power" involves control over the allocation of points. The powerful players competed for points with players in the same position in other dyads. Payoff matrices were presented to participants with instructions on the agreements or alternatives to be chosen. The experimenters manipulated four conditions combining high or low attractiveness of an alternative and high or low conflict of outcomes in the payoff cells (high-low, high-high, low-high, low-low). Players were given opportunities to form contractual agreements—this was the dependent variable to be measured by frequency of their recourse to it. 48 dyads, 12 for each treatment, were recruited from two schools in Paris. Results showed that under high conflict of interest the more powerful partner took the lion's share of points. Also as expected, the weaker partner, under the high attractiveness condition, sought the alternative—a favourable points option outside the matrix. The high attractiveness-high conflict pairs (the "double disruption" possibility) showed a much greater tendency to set up rules either prohibiting seeking the alternative or maintaining an agreed share of points. And these pairs fixed heavier deductions of points for violating contracts. Dyads with low alternatives and low conflict of interests showed least recourse to contracts. So, the experimenters argue that such norms of equity and loyalty are least likely to be "generated from within the group in the absence of temptations to violate them" (p. 101).

Thibaut (1968) elaborates on this rationale by enquiring into the advantages of a normative solution. He refers to Thibaut and Kelley (1959, pp. 130–142), suggesting that a person with superior power in the relationship may find social norms useful as a stabilizing influence, reducing the costs of personal surveillance and eliminating the "ostentation of . . . power usage". Moreover when a person has the power to exploit another, the latter may be tempted to transfer himself to an alternative situation. For someone who has little power a norm provides protection from the arbitrary personal use of power by others. Thus, there are strong mutual threats which may lead to an appeal to rules forbidding their implementation; these rules are likely to be embodied in norms of equity and loyalty. A relationship of interdependence now develops where each party's acceptance of the rule is compensated by the removal of threat.

For his experiments Thibaut (1968) replicated the 2×2 design we have just described (high v. low conflict of interests; high v. low attractiveness of alternatives) this time with male undergraduates but, in addition, he arranged for dyads to play against dyads with one member of each as spokesman.* The results show a similar significant effect in higher frequencies of contractual agreements in the high conflict, high alternative conditions, but even in high conflict, low alternative conditions, contracts tended to be sought. We shall discuss this in a moment. In further experiments high stress from mutual threats (a. high conflict, or b. high alternative) was introduced by simply telling participants that their partner was (a) "exploitative" or (b) "disloyal" and again a pattern of contracts emerged with most occurring

* See below p. 134. Negotiation may be defined with or without "representation" in bargaining.

in the high-high condition. Lastly, a variation producing increased threats from high alternatives yielded some confirming indications. In this last variation opportunity was given for the weaker player to use counter-power by delaying the negotiation and possibly reducing the other's score. The additional option of a norm fixing shorter time limits was also offered to the players; post-experimental analysis of players' preferences showed that this norm was favoured most by the powerful partner and least favoured by the weaker one (preferences were reversed for the norm prohibiting seeking an alternative). In his discussion Thibaut emphasized the role of the weaker partner's counter-power as a threat to the powerful member's outcomes although he acknowledges that this "is to an extent inhibited in its use by its radical and subversive character . . . his power may be too revolutionary to be fully effective" (pp. 110–111).

Thibaut mentions at the end of his discussion that one major factor in the norm formation must be a degree of common interest which in many situations would not be attained either because of the extremely high aspirations of participants, or because of the privacy of their alternative resources, tending to destroy the possibility of agreement. Furthermore, he raises a doubt about the general applicability of the results when he mentions that the experimenter has been all along an active third party to the negotiations by formulating and putting forward the contractual options.

Subsequently Thibaut and Gruder (1969) explore the tactics available to the weaker partner by introducing two conditions (high, low) for (a) the attractiveness of an alternative, (b) the legitimacy of the power differential, (c) the availability of another bargainer to act in coalition with the weaker partner. The experiment was arranged as an international bargaining game in which students were asked to negotiate trade agreements on behalf of two nations, one very wealthy, the other undeveloped. They were to receive small money amounts in direct ratio to the totals they earned for their nation. Although the game was explained verbally and matrices were not shown, the experimenters worked from a matrix of trade outcomes, allocation of which was vested in the stronger partner; either party might choose to take an alternative (high, low) leaving the other with nothing, but this was the weaker partner's sole threat. Of the 80 bargaining groups in this experiment, half were dyads and half double dyads (a "spokesman" and a "constituent"). The pattern of contractual agreements in the dyads of this study did not confirm the earlier results for the high alternative condition to induce more contractual agreements. Again, as in the Thibaut (1968) study, double dyads showed a tendency to form contracts even in the low alternative condition. Thibaut and Gruder now discuss the actual tactics of the tape-recorded negotiations. Their analysis suggests that, in the low alternative condition, weaker partners were able to emphasize the positive advantage of a package deal with outcomes to the other party above his break-off level. The experimenters had gathered information on break-off levels by questionnaire after preliminary bargaining sessions but before sessions with opportunity of forming contracts. They recognize that it may have been the questionnaire itself which focused the attention of weaker partners on the possibility of promoting a package agreement. They also mention that, in double dyads, discussion between fellow bargainers may be especially productive of tactical ideas, referring to the study of Pylyshyn, Agnew and Illingworth (1966) for the suggestion that dyadic bargaining parties are more co-operative and, in that sense, rational, than are individuals in a Prisoner's Dilemma design.

Some aspects of the differences just noted in bargaining between individuals and between opposing pairs are studied in more detail by Gruder (1971), whose research was supervised by John Thibaut, this time to explore the relationships of a spokesman both with his adversary and his constituency. The game was presented to its participants as a negotiation between the spokesmen of two industrial companies over their financial share from a joint enterprise; their constituent was to be an employee representative. Students were paid small amounts of money in proportion to their gains for the company. By manipulating the spokesman's accountability to his constituent and to his opponent Gruder hoped to determine effects on bargaining of the extent of accountability to each. More precisely, in the experiment, either the constituent and the opponent were anonymous and future acquaintance with them was not to be anticipated or else the negotiator was told he would meet them after bargaining. In addition, the negotiator's perception of his opponent's intentions was varied—players were informed either that their opponent would be fair or that he would be exploitative. Gruder suggests that in the former condition, with a fair opponent, accountability would produce reciprocal behaviour; nonaccountability would encourage his exploitation. In the other condition, where the opponent is seen already as exploitative, accountability would make little difference. Gruder recognizes the stress operating on a spokesman from conflicting role demands—to reach an agreement with the other spokesman and simultaneously to satisfy the more self-centred demands of his partner. In this experiment negotiators who were made accountable to their partner were expected to feel some degree of stress and, furthermore, they might be less inclined to grant concessions to their opponents. Students were paired together so that there was simulated bargaining between dyads, a spokesman for each dyad exchanging written offers with another "spokesman" in a different room (actually programmed by the experimenter). They attended in groups of four and although they were told that they each had a different role, in fact they were independent participants in the same role of spokesman. Thus, the "partner" in the dyad was also represented by programmed messages. In the bargaining sessions, apart from outright offers, brief messages could be passed on cards to and from the spokesman. For each participant, measures were derived from the proportion of offers made which were concessions from the immediately preceding offer, plus the average size of concessions. At the end of negotiations a questionnaire was administered to assess reactions to the accountability condition and to the experiment itself.

The results of this experiment supported the initial hypotheses in one aspect: they indicated that in the condition where spokesmen expect their adversary to be fair and where they were told they would meet him afterwards, they then made more concessions than spokesmen who were not accountable in this way. On the other hand, where they were told to expect an exploitative adversary, accountability seemed to have an adverse effect since these spokesmen made a lower proportion of concessions than those who were non-accountable, a result for which no immediate explanation was available. Furthermore the manipulation of the spokesman's accountability to his constituent did not reveal any evidence of differences in bargaining behaviour under the two conditions. Apart from doubts that arise about the effectiveness of these experimental manipulations, the major fault of this study, and it is a fundamental one, is that its subject matter is a purely commercial exchange with negotiation about large hypothetical quantities of dollars. I mentioned earlier (p. 83) some criticism concerning the use of money incentives, an issue raised by Kelley *et al.* (1970) and it has to be underlined that the approach via economic bargaining cannot be a sound means to understanding social exchange *which is non-economic by definition.*

This is probably an obvious criticism and perhaps does less than justice to the many issues which have been raised in research influenced by Thibaut and Faucheux (1965). We can now discuss more of these experiments but first I would like to refer to a very useful summary of negotiation experiments of this "school". Gruder (1970) in his comprehensive review uses an interpretative framework based on the construct "social power" as defined by Thibaut and Kelley (1959) and discussed by Kelley and Thibaut (1969). He discusses empirical studies in negotiation which have focused on the influences of such factors as the effects of anticipated future interaction, of friendship outside the game situation, of knowledge of an observer's reactions to the decisions taken and so on. Working from a definition of power (Thibaut and Kelley, 1959, p. 101) as the ability to alter the outcomes of others, Gruder now asks: how, when and why is such power used? He notes that an uncompromising position is more difficult to sustain when there is communication, that negotiators are more competitive when there is to be no subsequent meeting with opponents. He mentions commitment as an important, influential factor if it can be conveyed to the opponent, as in the game of "chicken"; when it is played with motors approaching each other along the centre-line, commitment is shown by taking off the steering wheel (see Schelling, 1963). Next, he looks at the effect of lies, for instance in misrepresenting the attractiveness of an alternative. Where only the negotiator knows his own outcomes he can argue that an agreement is just not profitable enough. This was possible in some instances in the studies by Fouraker and Siegel (1963), Kelley (1966) and Kelley, Beckman and Fischer (1967). The latter noted lies were at a maximum when the offer yielded the negotiator a *small* profit (if less than this, he was not lying when he said that the outcome was unreasonable!). Gruder conjectures about the meaning of lies in this experiment and concludes that information about an opponent's $CL_{alt.}$ will be distinctly advantageous; if a person can, at the same time, withhold the same information about his position then he may effect a unilateral gain. Gruder gives a passing reference to long-standing conflicts and the resolutions which hold over the long term, say, in a business partnership or in a family. He has here indicated a topic to which we will return in Chapter 13 when we discuss the studies, influenced by exchange theorists, that explore bargaining as a process over time and focus on the duration of time between an act and its reciprocation.

With the exception of Thibaut (1968), Gruder (1968) and Thibaut and Gruder (1969), studies to date have primarily considered *inter-personal negotiation*. Gruder draws attention to the importance of investigating *inter-group* negotiation, giving attention to the effects of power relationships among members of a party on bargaining between parties. He recalls how, in his study, he arranged for one person to represent his dyad with a (programmed) representative of another. The independent variable was the spokesman's relationship with his (programmed) constituent. Spokesmen either felt accountable to their constituent or not; this was manipulated by introducing another person as the constituent and leading the spokesman to believe he would have to defend his bargaining to his constituent following negotiations. It was thought that accountable spokesmen would see the constituent as having power over them and as desiring a very profitable agreement; that they would therefore take a firmer bargaining stand. In fact, the only difference that eventually appeared was in the size of the first concession—accountable spokesmen made smaller ones. Gruder argues that the negotiator's problem in dealing simultaneously with partners and opponents "is central to a truly general account of bargaining in the mixed-motive situation" (p. 150). He notes that research will be required on the effects of the correspondence of outcomes of members of the same group; the composition of the group, whether homogeneous or not. He also mentions the private view of a representative about his own group's bargaining position: "He may deviate from his own group's position and agree with the opposition, or he may be a loyal representative" (p. 150).

The important message of Gruder's discussion is that there is a line of research which began with Thibaut and Faucheux (1965) and which may lead to an improved basis for generalization. And he has hinted that a wider perspective is needed for future work.

Murdoch (1967) presents a report on research supervised by Thibaut in which he postulates norm formation as a process of establishing extrapersonal control of disruptive forces in groups. He argues that if both members of a dyad can wield threats against the other they will eventually seek agreements to refrain jointly from reducing each other's outcomes. The experimental design was basically the same as the one used by Thibaut and Faucheux (1965) in that one partner is given power to allocate division of rewards but the weaker partner may opt out of the relationship if his own allocation is too low. Murdoch hypothesizes that norms develop stating the importance of fairness (providing against abuse by the powerful partner) and loyalty (preventing the weaker partner from leaving). To test this, he varied both the fairness of the reward-divider (A) in two conditions fair v. unfair and the loyalty of the weaker partner (B) who was represented to A as either loyal or disloyal. He also proposed to vary the precision of A's control over allocations since imprecision would be likely to produce overuse of power (exploitation, as seen by B) which might, in fact, be unintentional and as such would make A apprehensive about the possible withdrawal of B. Thus, a condition of imprecise control should lead more quickly to norm formation than a condition of precise control. In the experiment, this was manipulated by having A make any division he wished of the joint rewards (precise control) or allowing him only four possibilities of division (imprecise control). These conditions were tested in a $2 \times 2 \times 2$ factorial design. Results showed, first, that there was a more frequent use of contracts and more stringency in their enforcement where both partners had power to threaten; person A might make unfair allocations, B might seek an alternative. However, differences between precise and imprecise control conditions did not form a clear pattern.

Murdoch and Rosen (1970) in another study of two-person bargaining, again discuss the influence on norm formation of each partner having high disruptive power. These authors refer to Thibaut and Kelley (1959) for the suggestion that players recognize that overuse of power can be self defeating and that they will try to accommodate to each other's interests (see also Kelley, 1968). Murdoch and Rosen ask the interesting question: to what extent does agreement to a contract specified by an experimenter constitute "emergence of a norm"? They also question whether the results of the bargaining game can be generalized to non-gaming situations. Murdoch and Rosen suggest that, because the experimenter calls the attention of participants to various options, these may act as cues to forming contracts. For these reasons, they substitute a work task for the bargaining game, thus attempting to find support for hypotheses about norms in a different situation. In this experiment it was hypothesized that, if power to disrupt is varied in two conditions (high, low) then (a) more power use occurs when both partners have high disruptive power, or (b) more interpersonal accommodation occurs when both have this power, or (c) more norms develop when both have disruptive power. With an impressive design, a conflict situation was created for student volunteers, participating as a course requirement. The high power (HP) partner was to complete a visual search task for which he was paid according to accuracy. The individual with low power had only to distribute task sheets and to time the other's performance. He was subsequently paid according to the speed of the HP member—the faster HP worked the more points LP would receive. In fact, the number of errors HP was told he made varied inversely with his time so that if he worked very fast he scored low irrespective of his actual accuracy. HP might try working slowly in order to secure high outcomes but this would deliver poor outcomes to LP; at the same time, the latter was given the alternative option of a fixed outcome for each trial and in this case HP would receive relatively little. Conflict of interest was manipulated by allowing HP extra time to correct errors (at LP's expense) and alternatives were also varied in high or low conditions. Dependent measures were taken from task performance, discussions in the dyad, and post-experimental questionnaires. Results showed that there was a tendency to agree on adaptive norms, appearing as promises to curb disruption on the part of both members, and these were recorded most frequently in the extreme disruptive condition (high conflict, high alternative). More efforts at inter-personal accommodation (promises to speed up, or not to use the alternative) were also observed to occur more under high disruption possibilities. However, the first hypothesis was not sufficiently supported to give strong support for the view that power use is an antecedent to norm development. The experimenters offer the explanation that overuse of power might have been seen as self defeating; they suggest that future research might focus on more subtle power strategies including nonverbal ones. Murdoch and Rosen end by suggesting that these findings might be "applied" to other situations but they do not develop this point at all, leaving us with some very brief conjectures concerning norm formation between husbands and wives. Here, they think conflict may be lessened by appeals to general norms stipulating roles of either partner, or norms may emerge similar to those observed in the work task where "one member yields his ability to disrupt only if there is a reciprocal yielding by the other member" (p. 272).

7

Rationality in the Payoff Model

Introduction

In discussing the payoff matrix we have seen that attempts have been made with some success in recent research to incorporate additional assumptions of maximizing or minimizing differences rather than sheer maximizing of gains (see pp. 77–78 above and Chapter 11, p. 257). If we try to adapt the payoff matrix to social situations, one considerable obstacle will be the operation of rewards and costs other than those "amounts" presented in the matrix. For instance, payoffs assumed by the experimenter might not be similarly understood by the actors. We have such an instance in experiments which have not taken account of the influence of social comparisons and we have discussed situations where an actor may prefer to reduce his gain if by so doing he can reduce another person's gains still more (see above p. 88 and Chapter 11). This kind of result does not require the surrender of the notion of maximizing *per se*, it merely draws attention to the breadth of meaning which is involved in the concept of rewards and costs, whether these be material or non-material. On the matter of altruism and whether it is possible to draw a clear dividing line between another person's welfare and one's own (see Chapter 3, p. 50) there has been little progress although we shall discuss some recent research on this in the section *Equity* in Chapter 11. The greatest problem for exchange propositions is how to deal with non-material or altruistic rewards and, for the Thibaut and Kelley model, how to represent qualitatively different rewards in the same matrix—problems which Turner, Foa and Foa (1971) have sketched in outline. Difficulties occur in comparing the utilities of different persons and these are discussed in Chapter 2 (p. 20) and Chapter 8 (p. 175): subjective values are shown to be impossible to classify unless one refers to their relative meaning in a particular context, to group norms and cultural influences. It also has to be accepted that persons differ in the *effectiveness* with which they strive to attain a particular goal, some being more rational (efficient) than others in attaining it. The existence of varying degrees and approximations to this latter kind of effectiveness (or rationality) is the concern of game theory and economics, when prescriptive solutions are sought to improve payoffs by a choice of strategies. Economists such as H. A. Simon (see below) are concerned with the "bounded rationality" of behaviour in complex situations, with finding good enough solutions rather than optimal ones.

In the classic game theory the player is perfectly rational, able to calculate his optimal choice from knowledge of the payoffs ranged on an interval scale. Luce and Raiffa (1957) add to this view of rational behaviour when they say it has to be assumed both that material payoffs will be maximized *and* whatever it is that is maximized must be quantifiable. So the game theory model admits only outcomes which can be expressed in points or money amounts on an interval scale. Thus far, Thibaut and Kelley adopt the game theory model but considerable ambiguity occurs because there are further assumptions in the classic model which these authors do not accept, as was discussed in the previous chapters.

It is important to differentiate between the use of the term rational by the narrower definition in game theory and the general use of the term for behaviour which is *reasonable* with the meaning of Aristotle's practical rationality. In the latter sense, presumably, behaviour may always be reasonable to the person doing it and certainly it is reasonable to have aims that are justifiable to others in a given group or society. "Rationality" is a highly subjective matter; as is commonly observed, what is a reward for one person may not be valued particularly highly by another. Whether a person or act is judged as rational or irrational depends on who or what provides the criterion for judging. One person's "rational" behaviour may appear "irrational" to others, just as behaviour can appear irrational if it is based on faulty calculation or misunderstanding of a situation. Thus Wiberg (1972) draws attention to rationality as a property of (a) a world picture (b) a value system (c) the relation between (a) and (b) and a decision. I discuss this kind of practical rationality as it appears in Homans' theory in the next chapter (Chapter 8, p. 173). Obviously it is imperative to drop the ideal model of the game theorists. The model has not been verified empirically; there have been many instances where observations made of experimental games do not confirm game theory predictions. Instead, preferences change over time or participants appear not to optimize (see Wiberg, 1972, pp. 325–340). For Kelley and Thibaut (1969) rational (reasonable) behaviour seems to involve mainly reduction of costs and social routines or norms are useful as "a rapid, low-cost method of resolving potentially difficult problems of outcome distribution" (p. 48). While they do not argue that there must be rational analysis of information in the game theory sense, they are still committed to a broad assumption that persons are "motivated to maximize their reward-cost positions" (Thibaut and Kelley, 1959, p. 136). The ambiguity in their approach results from their denial of the stricter game theory postulates while at the same time they accept a general maximizing assumption from which logically the stricter postulates could in the end be derived. Even so, the maximizing proposition serves as a means to collecting research evidence which may qualify or extend this broad starting assumption. It could be said that it is a useful research stratagem to postulate maximizing in social relations, if it is seen as largely a matter of raising questions to be answered by empirical work.

Maximizing and exchange

Homans and Blau (see Chapter 8, p. 168, Chapter 11, p. 248 and Chapter 12, p. 280) do not assume without qualification that actors strive to maximize rewards. The maximizing assumption is heavily qualified by considerations of distributive justice. Blau, very early on in his exposition, rejects the economic rationalistic model. His assumption that men choose and evaluate between alternative social relationships or actions, selecting their preferences, "does not imply that they always choose the one that yields them the greatest material profits" (Blau, 1964, p. 19). Homans rejects the economic notion of maximizing utilities, arguing that it cannot be applied to social exchange. As an illustration of this he takes the economic notion that a person, to maximize his utility, will make the marginal utilities of two activities equal. He then says, first, that it will never be possible to measure value precisely enough to discover whether utilities are maximized in these terms. Secondly, he states, we cannot say that two persons in an exchange ever maximize their rewards. This would mean the relationship would have to be terminated at an exact point, and this point may be satisfactory to one of them but not to the other. There is another issue which makes maximization, he says, somewhat irrelevant. Two persons in interaction must strike two sorts of bargain. One is over "the momentary rate of exchange"—how much of an activity to give to another person in exchange for the other's activity. The other, must be a bargain over the total amount of activity over a longer period of time. Into both of these conditions, how much of a given activity at a particular moment and how much in total over a longer period, intrudes the problem of not just a profitable exchange but of fair exchange.

Atack (1973) makes some useful distinctions between notions of maximizing, optimizing and satisficing—the three models of rational-adaptive behaviour. He describes the assumptions required for maximizing explanations of behaviour, particularly the assumptions about information: "that the actor will have all socially available relevant information for forming expectations" (p. 221). These assumptions, far from supplying a simplifying model of behaviour make it "highly complicated". For instance, the maximizing model assumes that an actor uses all relevant information and as the number of different aspects of situations to be taken into account increases arithmetically, the number of conjoint alternatives to be considered increases exponentially. The concept of optimizing is often used as if it were an improved form of maximizing, but it merely assumes subjective maximization and is the more realistic since optimization does not require us to apply the stringent rules of maximizing and allows for relativity, depending on the social situation, of both rules and information. The optimizing model is still a complicated one and for this reason Atack suggests that we use a satisficing model which assumes only that a person's behaviour will follow heuristic rules in scanning for a satisfactory solution—here the actor is not attracted to a solution through calculated expectations of payoffs but is forced into a search for alternatives because his present situation is unsatisfactory. It is interesting that Atack draws attention to the similarity of the $CL_{alt.}$ concept of Thibaut and Kelley and the satisficing concept of Simon, which we will discuss in a moment.

Exchange theory and game theory

Despite the flaws in game theory definitions of rationality, some social psychologists continue with the assumption of some form of rationality in two-person games. For instance, Messick and Thorngate (1967) who pursue a mathematical approach to gain maximization, refer to the probability of choosing a particular alternative as a non-decreasing function of the expected payoff, which they term "a minimal statement of rationality".

Again, the assumption of *economic* rationality is clearly the basis of an experiment by Kelley and Grzelak (1972) who examine decisions in a market context. Here an individual is expected to weigh his alternative outcomes from the point of view of maximizing his cash profit. The authors are interested in the common situation where an individual's own immediate advantage conflicts with that of the totality of individuals as, for example, in avoidance of taxes. In order to simulate this type of conflict Kelley and Grzelak arranged for groups of ten to fifteen student volunteers to sit round a table facing each other. Each was given a choice of two coloured cards and asked to hold up one of them in view of the group. They were told that one colour would always give a higher score but the more that group members held up this colour, the lower both scores would be. Thus, the choice given to each student was "whether to hold up the colour that gives yourself the highest score, or to hold up the colour that keeps everyone's scores high (including your own)". In a 2×2 design, two conditions (high, low) of individual interest (II) and two conditions (high, low) of common interest (CI) were introduced by varying the instructions. Observations were made of the numbers of "competitive" (II) and co-operative (CI) responses. The hypothesis that co-operative responses would decrease with heightened individual interest was borne out by the relatively low rate of co-operative responses even in the high CI condition (32 per cent). This drew the authors' comment that the students may have misunderstood the experimental situation, an interpretation supported by the increase of co-operative choices over successive games in the different conditions. This experiment leaves many queries unanswered although perhaps its most questionable aspect is an assumption of generalizability from behaviour in face-to-face groups to the larger social collectivity; from the individual's accountability in small groups to his accountability in the community at large. In this, as in other experimental procedures we have discussed, the outcomes are precisely and numerically presented, thus fulfilling one game theory convention. But there is no bridge between this convention and conditions existing in most natural situations where probable outcomes are often unclear or unknown to the person himself, nor will he know the preferences of others.

There are further confusions in the "simulation" by Kelley and Grzelak. They fail to recognize that there are three possible effects from an individual's decision in a social context. First, there are the consequences for the person himself. Second, there are consequences for his immediate group. Third, there are consequences for the larger collectivity of society as a whole. In this experiment it is postulated that the individual may act in deference to his immediate group lowering his individual payoff in the interest of all members of his group. This is thought to represent a situation similar to the one in everyday life where a person may forgo his immediate personal returns assuming that others do the same and that the eventual effect of such individual curtailment is to increase the wellbeing of all. But Kelley and Grzelak commit two errors. One we have already mentioned concerns the degree to which a face-to-face laboratory group can simulate "society". The other error is that they overlook that there are three levels of decision effects. In other words, outside the laboratory if a person defers to his group such a group may be acting counter to the general wellbeing of society. Kelley and Grzelak therefore cannot establish in a small group experiment a result which can be taken as implying a general collective trend in society—far from it, because the actions of individuals or of groups may clash with the interests of society as a whole. So there is a basic confusion in the conception of this experiment and therefore in the interpretations which are made from it.

In his earlier discussion of the applications of game theory to social behaviour, Plon (1967) warns against attempting to accept the postulate of rationality in its game theory meaning, reminding us that the game theorists have economic rationality in mind, and have never sought to argue beyond this to social behaviour. He suggests that, rather than raising questions about rational or non-rational alternatives we should distinguish between several types of rationality, psychological as well as economic, and that the former requires discarding the economic notion of maximizing gains. At first sight, this would seem to place Thibaut and Kelley (and other exchange theorists) in a difficulty by the sheer fact that they accept the economic postulate, suitably translated, as providing a basic proposition for social behaviour. However, in their defence, we could argue that, if they do accept it, they accept it in a tentative form as a starting point to which qualifying conditions must be added, as evidence accumulates and specific hypotheses are stated. There need be no absolute assumption of a *homo economicus* in a theoretical approach which uses economic analogies only as a point of departure, at the level of its general premises. From this point onwards, the theoretical derivation proceeds to less general explanations, adding and qualifying the starting propositions to account for empirical data. Irrespective of what was borrowed, by analogy, at the level of basic propositions it is now what is *added* to explain social situations which becomes predominant. This is certainly so in the theoretical approaches developed by Homans and Blau (for instance, see Chapter 8, *Transferring Terms from Economics*). However, for the Thibaut and Kelley model there is a greater ambiguity and more problems are present simply because they have not confined their borrowing from economics to general analogies (as Homans and Blau have done*) and the payoff matrix is central to their model.

In his attack on economic rationality as a common assumption in two-person games, Plon draws attention, above all, to the individual's understanding of the situation of choice. He reminds us that even before games were adopted into social psychology Simon (1956) suggested a psychological model, in opposition to the economic one, substituting the concept of "satisficing" for that of maximizing. In Simon's argument an individual's adaptation appears to fall well short of the ideal of maximizing as proposed in economic theory. Moreover, in any situation, there can only be degrees of approximate "rationality" because there is limited information about consequences and limited capacity in the actor to utilize it. Simon speculates from laboratory observations of an animal seeking a single goal (food). However, his conjectures can be carried through to human situations such as those where human actors apparently do not seek to maximize their gains, even though they might easily do so. (See Faucheux and Moscovici, 1968.) These are considerations which bring Plon to his insistence on

* Blau largely follows Homans in the use of economic analogies except in one instance where he attempts a direct "application" of the economic model of indifference curves. However the end result is still a general analogy (see Chapter 12, pp. 307, 312).

the importance of defining the meaning of payoffs for the participants in experimental games, of clarifying the question of how the game is perceived by the actor. These topics have already received some attention in recent researches such as those by Kelley *et al.* (1970) and others discussed in previous chapters. Plon (1972) attacks the game-theoretical influence for reducing social psychological problems to the level of *homo economicus* and for encouraging an assumptive bias towards regarding social problems as a matter of faulty individual perceptions. He criticizes Thibaut and Kelley for expressing these tendencies. For our purposes here we must note that, as in his earlier criticisms Plon refers to Thibaut and Kelley as exponents of an experimental paradigm, not as exchange theorists. So we should consider the criticism as appropriate in this context of one form of empirical research, rather than in relation to exchange theory. We should recall that for us this area of theory is also represented by the work of Homans and Blau. As it will be unfolded extensively in the later chapters, social exchange is not a matter only of one model, or of one set of research methods, and we must therefore reserve our appraisal of the totality of "exchange theory", since it involves several different perspectives, until later.

The rational assumption as a research strategy

In this spirit Meeker (1971) discusses some of the assumptions found in the three main exchange contributions—by Homans, Blau and Thibaut and Kelley. Although he takes a blatantly optimistic view that individual values can be measured in the same way as perceptual responses, he also asks a more fundamental question: granted that we are able to measure what a person values, can we say that his actions are "strictly determined by an effort to maximize his values"? (p. 486). In this sense, is behaviour "rational"? Meeker sees this as a persistent question in social science, citing Weber's (1947) proposal that people do not always pay attention to the expected consequences. For illustration, Meeker describes the exchange of goods in primitive societies and the controversy over what such an exchange implies—does it optimize gain or fulfil a reciprocal rule? In the latter case, "the criterion for decision is the *balance* of exchange rather than the amount gained for one or the other party" (p. 486). Meeker here opposes reciprocity to a strictly economic goal. Furthermore, he notes that the model of rational behaviour could easily become tautological: if we predict that people choose what they value and then find out what they value by observing what they choose, nothing much has been accomplished, he says. On the other hand, he favours assuming some form of rationality because this can be useful as a simplifying proposition to be applied to a variety of situations. He comments that "This is the reverse aspect of the tautological property of a universal assumption; if we assume that all behaviour is rational in the sense of maximizing values we are equipped with a way of finding out what people value" (p. 486). In fact, it might be found that alternative assumptions function quite as well. Meeker considers the principles of reciprocity and, similar to it of equity, as alternatives to assuming rationality; other concepts found in exchange theory include competition or rivalry; yet others are altruism and social responsibility (discussed in Chapter 11, pp. 248–252). Meeker argues that these several concepts and propositions containing them, should be applied as ordering principles, either to systematize confirming evidence or to state exceptions. It is clearly impossible to fit all social behaviour under any one of them, and Meeker's suggestion is therefore nothing more than the broad strategy of collecting evidence about the special conditions when each of the principles, including rationality, can be expected to apply, and when not to apply. Meeker advocates that these statements be applied as *decision rules* and *alternative rules* to be tested empirically, but here again we have returned to the cataloguing approach which was discussed in Chapter 2.

In Chapter 3 (p. 53) I described how Thibaut and Kelley are influenced by the conventions of the classical S–R experiments. In experiments on human perception, the experimenter can examine discrepancies between the objective phenomenon and the subjective response. Similarly, Thibaut and Kelley state that they will proceed by comparing actual social behaviour with the outcomes predicted by objective criteria (of the optimum). In setting up an optimizing model, there is a danger that such a model considers the non-rational elements of behaviour negatively in relation to those things which they are not; thus, co-operation is rational and then conflict will be seen as non-rational and deviant. This was Parsons' criticism of Max Weber's "ideal type". Weber (see Parsons, 1964) argued that we should first establish what a rational course of action might be and then treat the irrational elements of behaviour as "factors of deviation from a conceptually pure type of rational action" and thus "it is possible to understand the ways in which actual action is influenced by irrational factors of all sorts, such as affects and errors, in that they account for the deviation from the line of conduct which would be expected on the hypothesis that the action was purely rational" (p. 92). Weber's view is that non-rational behaviour is deviation, whereas Parsons attacks this dichotomy with the counter-argument that there is definitely an "integration of affective and rationally cognitive elements in the same action" (p. 27), in that irrationality presents a problem which is much more complex than a deviation from what he calls "an isolated ideal type" (p. 17). He thinks the "abstract dichotomy" ignores the mixture of rational and irrational elements to be found in human behaviour and he illustrates this point by citing a range of empirical influences which might have some bearing on a given act. It is possible to distill from Parsons' arguments that there is much in social situations that cannot be easily classified either as "rational" or "irrational". Moreover, he is critical of Weber's definition of rational acts as (a) oriented to a clearly formulated, unambiguous goal, and (b) the means chosen are, according to the best available knowledge, adapted to the realization of the goal. Parsons comments that these criteria do not give an adequate description of any concrete act, nor do they specify the content of a goal but only the way it might be formulated. Weber himself gives as one precedent of this theoretical strategy, the principles of pure economic theory which indicate "what course a given type of human action would take it if was strictly rational, unaffected by errors or emotional factors and if, furthermore, it will completely and unequivocally direct it to a single end, maximisation of economic advantage" (p. 96). Weber adds that this state of affairs is hardly ever found but is valid as a methodological device "by throwing the discrepancy between the actual course of events and the ideal type into relief, the analysis of the non-economic motives actually involved is facilitated" (p. 111). It seems to me that this is the nearest that could be found to the expression by Thibaut and Kelley of their own theoretical strategy as we have discussed it in Chapter 3.

A thorough summary of definitions of rational behaviour is to be found in Wiberg (1972) and here I propose to consider only one or two further points strictly within the context of exchange theory. All through the discussion of social exchange notions we have encountered references to what Homans (1972) has termed "the vexed question of rationality". Homans says no more than that some form of rational calculation, conscious or unconscious,* frequently occurs. Thibaut and Kelley, however, go so far as to predicate what the rational objectives for a given person in a given situation will be. They seem to have fallen into a well known trap in even thinking that we can know what, in a given situation, rational decision would be. Let us take this further. Hempel (1965) touches on some of the very difficult questions which we meet in postulating a rational course of action. The notion that a person may act rationally implies his complete intellectual grasp of a situation, access to all relevant information and a clear set of objectives. Now, to discover whether a person acts optimally in this sense turns out to present a self-defeating and obscure question. Hempel remarks that in the physical sciences "the conditions of near-ideal behaviour can be stated with considerable precision in terms of just a few quantitative parameters" but it is quite a different matter in a social situation where "the conditions under which a given individual will come very close to acting with conscious rationality can be indicated only vaguely and by means of a long, and open-ended, list of items which includes environmental as well as physiological and psychological factors" (p. 482). If we think of a person as behaving in a consciously rational way and wish to establish that this is so in a given situation then we will only be able to do so when the solution is a relatively simple one. The highly quantitative character of the model limits its application to decisions of a simple type which permit strict experimental control. Thibaut and Kelley have a similar strategy: they postulate a rational-based choice and propose to study the deviations from it. They put forward a precisely quantitative estimate of the alternatives available, but in doing so they also restrict their model to relatively simple experimental situations. Criticism of this restriction appeared as a theme in our discussion of the model in Chapter 3. Now, more than a decade after the publication of their *Social Psychology of Groups* it remains a persistent criticism. In other words, the payoff model is restrictive in its assump-

---

* We do not need to discuss here questions of whether the rational decision is conscious or unconscious (but see Chapter 8). Note that Davidson, Suppes and Siegel (1957) were able to show in their experiment, that persons may take rational decisions but without awareness of their subjective probabilities and utilities. Commenting on this experiment Hempel remarks about those who took part in the experiment: "They act rationally in the sense of acting *as if* they were trying to maximise expected utilities. Here, then, we seem to have a type of conscious decision which is *nonconsciously rational* with quantitative precision" (Hempel, 1965, p. 483).

tions, in its genre of empirical tests and therefore in its subsequent influence on research. Although this influence has been very strong, as we have seen in Chapters 4 and 6, it is usually tied to one kind of method and to one kind of design, the two-person experimental paradigm.

Plon (1972) from a Marxist position also attacks this restriction in methods, referring to the limited nature of the problems investigated in the two-person game. Plon and others such as Pecheux (1970) and Bruno *et al.* (1973) are critical of the Thibaut and Kelley model because they regard it as the most "behaviouristic" of social psychological models and because they think the game theoretical view of social behaviour is too abstract, reflecting only the experimenters' ideas of strategies and counter-strategies. These critics claim that ideological influences in social psychology have produced the effect in current experimental models of diverting attention from significant social questions; furthermore, they may be nothing more than a means to improving control techniques in the service of an established order. By these arguments the experimental game is attacked on two fronts, both as a flight from reality, a diversion of attention to trivial topics and (or because of the diversion) a sinister control technique. We can do no more here than note the ideological debate; it does not, strictly speaking, touch on social exchange theory for reasons I will now state. Their criticisms of the Thibaut and Kelley model are made precisely because it represents the most ambitious use of a game theory matrix in social psychology. Furthermore, the model exemplifies the restrictiveness of such matrices and, not only that, but it is over-ambitious in its quantification of outcomes. In social psychological research dealing with motives, attitudes or evaluations it is only possible to use ordinal scales for measuring and comparing degrees of difference. However, Thibaut and Kelley require a cardinal scale for the payoff outcomes, a requirement which Plon (1970) rightly attacks. His technical criticism is a fair one and I have put forward similar arguments in the discussion on numbers in the payoff cells in Chapter 3.

Plon's technical criticism is sound but we cannot easily dismiss the Thibaut and Kelley model, despite its flaws, if we consider it as part of an exposition of exchange notions which includes the work of Homans and Blau and the many others whose research and theoretical efforts are discussed in this book. Now we see that the model is one among many research designs and approaches which take exchange propositions as their common point of reference. Even the payoff matrix itself cannot be comprehended only as a utilitarian model. For instance, Berkowitz and Friedman (1967) and Foa (1971) refer to the non-utilitarian aspects in exchange (see Chapter 11, p. 250). The qualifying conditions which have now been attached on to the original statement of the payoff matrix and its inclusion into an explanatory framework of much greater breadth has not been the result of work by Thibaut and Kelley so much as of those who have been influenced both by them and by the other exchange theorists. On its own, the payoff matrix would seem to portend a relatively sterile future development, as well as appearing unattractive to many researchers because it does seem to express with some naivety that social behaviour follows a general maximizing or optimizing rule. In comparison with Homans' elaboration, in contingent hypotheses, of the principles of justice and equity in exchange and in comparison with Blau's treatment of social conflict hypotheses the starting position of Thibaut and Kelley might express something akin to naivety. Yet, taking the exposition in *Social Psychology of Groups* in its entirety as we discussed it in Chapter 3, and with all the recent development of exchange explanations, we can see that there is more to it than the ideological critics allow. But, as I said before, these critics have not touched on exchange theory as it exists empirically.

A more important question for the payoff model is whether it has, in fact, been able to comprehend the interdependence between persons which was, after all, the aim of Thibaut and Kelley in setting up their model in the first place. The extent to which the model has achieved success in this, is still problematical. So much so that it has been criticized as "individualistic" by Moscovici (1972), a criticism which was mentioned in Chapter 5 (pp. 97–98). There is no doubt that when Thibaut and Kelley discuss the comparison level concept they concentrate on individual perceptions, evaluations or aspirations and factors other than sheer maximizing of rewards. However, we shall discuss later, in Chapter 12, a structure of variables such as group memberships and status rankings which enter into social comparisons—and Blau has especially called our attention to these. Nor do exchange explanations avoid historical and situational influences and these figure largely in the theoretical exposition described in later chapters. By their fundamental nature exchange propositions cannot abstract an individual from his social environment. At the same time, there is also an assumption of freedom of choice, of freedom of options. In this aspect, exchange assumptions are consistent with the epistemological arguments that assert freedom of choice: "even though we know that all is determined yet we can proceed on the assumption that a man is free to decide and we can assume that he is, with complete assurance, if for no other reason than that in believing he is free, in disbelieving determinism, he has in actuality become free" (see Koestler, 1967, pp. 247–250).

8

Homans: Social Behaviour: Its Elementary Forms

In his book, *Social Behaviour: Its Elementary Forms,** George Homans expounds a theory for which he states the basic structure in the form of general propositions or corollaries, and descriptive propositions (specific hypotheses). Given conditions (parameters, boundary terms) and variables constitute the terms of the descriptive propositions, allowing measurement of the empirical results. Homans presents five propositions and from these deduces a larger number of other propositions and their corollaries. Homans thus follows the rule of parsimony in restricting explanation to as small a number of representative terms or relationships as is possible. He is also following a procedure well known in psychological theories, for example, in learning theory where a very few general propositions are used to state the basic terms. The five axiomatic propositions are presented with the aim of explaining relationships between dependent and independent variables, the relationships being stated in the many lower-order propositions which are descriptive of the research evidence. The magnitude and direction of the relationships discovered at this level are influenced by the special circumstances or given conditions of the particular case. Homans makes no claim for predicting the degree of relationship between variables as a specific function, one or the other, and no logarithmic terms are sought or offered, as will be seen when the theory is discussed in full, but the direction of relationships (as a probabilistic statement) and their strength (as an approximate, numerical statement) are expressed in the propositions of the theory.

* Throughout this chapter I refer to the first edition (1961) of *Social Behaviour*. The second edition (1974) has some additions which are discussed in Chapter 9.

S.E.T.—6

The influence of different given conditions is a central issue which is worked out very fully in his book. For example, the interaction-liking proposition—that social interaction leads to positive sentiment and liking between persons—which was stated in his earlier book *The Human Group* and has been a target for critics, is now shown to be influenced by different given conditions to the point where there are several propositions and corollaries in place of the single one. This proposition caught the imagination of commentators rather more than others and has been discussed by Zetterberg (1965), Collins and Raven (1969) and in its algebraic expressions by Bartos (1967), Coleman (1964) and Simon (1957), as will be seen later in this chapter.

In *Social Behaviour* Homans makes an explicit and persistent attempt to apply one body of terms and propositions to the available empirical findings and to make explicit also the internal structure of the explanatory statements and their derivation. The latter aspect is the most important advance on Homans' previous book *The Human Group* (1951), where he presented concepts and working hypotheses without building these further into an explanatory scheme. The main emphasis here was on the operation of three social variables on each other; proceeding inductively from the findings of several field studies by psychologists, sociologists and anthropologists, Homans demonstrated an explanatory approach using the concepts of interaction (social communication), sentiment (attitudes) and shared activities (tasks, roles), using these three elements he was able to explain each of the social situations described in the field studies.

The theoretical discussion in *Social Behaviour* builds from the inductive approach of *The Human Group* to a deductive theory taking the explanation of behaviour further by its emphasis on the psychological aspects of motive, perception, decision—the evaluation and expectation of rewards and costs. It is no longer a matter of explaining behaviour from the interdependent variables of interaction, sentiment and activity, although the mathematical expression of their interdependence has been taken to a degree of refinement by Coleman (1964) Goodman (1964) and White (1972). The explanation now goes beyond the operation of these variables on each other in order to include further variables and given conditions which place the theory much closer to individual psychology. The reductionist argument has no stronger advocate than Homans.

The resulting theoretical analysis is a more comprehensive attempt and while something of the original concepts and hypotheses of the earlier work are retained, they are incorporated into a structure of propositions, starting with a small number of general propositions,* and moving by deduction to predict for interpersonal behaviour in a variety of applications—with more than sixty field and experimental studies (carried out principally by social psychologists) brought in as empirical support. Sprott (1958) was one of the few psychologists to give due credit to The Human Group as "without doubt the most illuminating book on group psychology published in the last few years" and "important for its contribution to social psychological theory" (p. 51), continuing with a brief but fair appraisal and summary of Homans' thinking, in this earlier work. Since the publication of Social Behaviour there has been considerably more discussion, largely by American sociologists, of specific aspects of Homans' theory. An idea of the pervasiveness of this discussion can be gained from the paper by Cloyd and Bates (1964), a review of the references to Homans' ideas in the sociological literature between 1951 and 1962. The paper itself occurs in an issue of Sociological Inquiry devoted entirely to "Research and Commentary on the Theorems and Perspectives of George C. Homans".

Shaw and Costanzo (1970) consider Homans' recent work as a contribution to social psychology but their appraisal is made with reference only to laboratory studies—a crippling disadvantage in assessing a theory which is based equally on research in experimental and natural situations, a coverage which is perhaps its foremost advantage. While their treatment is fuller than any other currently available it is obscured by a heavy and turgid style where Homans' own presentation is elegant. Mulkay (1971) gives Homans' theory a central place in a comparative discussion of concepts and theoretical strategies from a sociological point of view. He discusses theoretical structure and the meaning of concepts, yet he largely leaves out the direct relationships in dyads and primary groups to which Homans gives all of his attention in applying his explanatory scheme to numerous empirical examples. Mulkay considers questions of definition, changes in the use of terms between Homans' early and later publications, and whether the theory has provided "a firm reference point for the investigation of

---

* They are not axioms in the Euclidean or Newtonian sense, they are empirical not axiomatic statements and they are contingent statements, modifiable by the test of evidence.

more complex, institutionalized social structures . . . a comprehensive sociological theory" (p. 177). Unfortunately, Mulkay has not accepted the theory as it is, in the light of its contribution to social psychology. Instead he assesses the theory by goals which its author does not set himself, and nowhere does Homans claim to set up a "comprehensive sociological theory". On the contrary, he expresses strong misgivings about extrapolation from small groups to the wider society. It seems likely that Mulkay's criticism is invalidated by the nature of Homans' theoretical aims which are to explain such regularities as are observed in primary groups. Social behaviour is the province of several disciplines and perhaps the title of Homans' book is therefore a little misleading, but there should be no doubt about its content. The fact that there have been a number of misinterpretations of the theory is discussed by Cloyd and Bates (1964) who say that there has been "some disjuncture" between commentaries on the work, partly the result of the rich insights which the theory supplies: "These contradictions suggest, not so much that there are internal contradictions in Homans' own thinking, as that there is a process in academic discourse comparable to the sharpening process which Allport and Postman describe for rumour. A man's simple statements are inevitably both more quotable and didactic than his more complex explanations" (p. 125).

The definition of social behaviour

Homans begins with a statement on his subject matter. His object is to "try to explain behaviour and not just describe it" (p. 2). The behaviour to be explained has the characteristic that it is social "which means that when a person acts in a certain way he is at least rewarded or punished by the behaviour of another *person*". Thus, in a sense Homans begs the question by defining social behaviour from the beginning as behaviour which is followed by reward or punishment from another person. He states this as a necessary condition, and repeats later in the book that elementary social behaviour "is an exchange of rewards (and costs) between persons" (p. 317), and again "an exchange of rewards (or punishments) between at least two persons" (p. 378).

An additional characteristic of social behaviour as defined by Homans is that acts directed by one person towards another must "at least be rewarded or punished by *that* person and not just by some third party". Therefore, direct social relationships, "the actual social behaviour of individuals in direct contact with one another" (p. 3), are his interest. Thus subject matter consists of observable and external acts in "current, face to face, social behaviour and its changes within rather short spans of time" (p. 48). He goes on to say, in effect, that the same explanations will serve for cognitive subject matter (e.g. social norms) although the explanations will thereby have to cope with greater complexities. Homans has called his subject matter *elementary* social behaviour because direct social behaviour is "relatively easier to explain" (p. 3) than behaviour in the formal organizations of society. Thus, Homans does not attempt to explain established patterns or norms where these involve the structural, institutionalized aspects of social behaviour, these aspects may be taken into account as given conditions but they are not to be a focus of explanation in themselves.* A main point of contrast between Homans' explanations and those offered by Blau is that, while the former takes as granted the structural aspects of organization, Blau treats as constant anything that concerns psychological aspects of behaviour, the motives and evaluations of persons—he avoids what Homans regards as the fundamentals, the psychological propositions.

An advantage of studying social behaviour at the "elementary" level is that it is general to all societies: "given the difference in rewards, the propositions describing the behaviour of individuals realizing rewards of some kind through face-to-face transactions are probably much the same . . ." (p. 6). The claim might also be made for the theory that it should apply to a wide range of situations within any society. There is a methodological point worth noting when Homans refers to the method of "continuous, direct observations" (p. 7) as providing the evidence for an analysis of elementary social behaviour. Homans makes only one empirical condition: that the evidence be collected by continuous, direct observation. He asks for no other convention of research design, so that there is no restriction of data collection to experimental or laboratory methods. In fact many of the studies undertaken in natural situations, demonstrate that his propositions hold good. Very much to the advantage of Homans' theory, is the fact that it can be demonstrated by reference to studies of quite different methodological approach. He points out that observation cannot be made of large numbers at one time and that it is convenient to study

---

* Acceptance of a variable as a given condition does not mean that it is not measurable as one of the terms in a theoretical proposition, see pages 190–192 below.

behaviour in the small group, the closed network, where each member is in contact with others. In *Social Behaviour* the empirical evidence used is about equally divided between experimental and field studies, with slightly more of the latter; since the book was written, the general propositions have been followed through in a variety of theoretical papers and empirical studies, including some by computer simulation which are discussed in Chapter 10.

The basic propositions

Homans refers to the theoretical statements used in his previous book *The Human Group* as "empirical generalizations", that is, propositions which describe the conclusions of research studies but which do not have an explicit theoretical derivation. He now contrasts this with his present attempt to explain the empirical statements about observed effects by deduction from more general propositions. The fundamental propositions are the result of borrowing from one main source: from experimental studies of animals "usually in nonsocial situations" (p. 12). Some of the concepts are taken from classical economics dealing with "the behaviour of men exchanging material goods for money in a so-called perfect market" but the propositions themselves come from experimental psychology and Homans believes that classical economics itself can be derived from experimental psychology. Homans is careful to emphasize that social exchange, which is often of intangible services, does not have the impersonality of the economic market and he demonstrates this in his discussion of what is considered as fair exchange by participants who share a standard of "distributive justice". It is clear that Homans recognizes that lifting terms from economics in order to fit them to the data of social behaviour can only be approximate and that there is some slippage in the translation. In doing so, he largely anticipates any objections which might otherwise be made to the borrowing terms from these sources; his theoretical strategy is to formulate basic propositions by analogy and the limitations to the strategy are quite clearly recognized by him.

Experimental psychology and economics have in common that they deal with "behaviour as a function if its pay-off" (p. 13) and these propositions state that amounts and kinds of behaviour vary with the rewards and costs which follow as a consequence of that behaviour. Although many individual terms are borrowed from economics, the propositions themselves, in the form they take, owe more to experimental psychology. Homans devoted a whole chapter to an outline of the research on animal behaviour by B. F. Skinner (1938, 1953, 1959), describing something of the laboratory techniques used for reinforcing the operant or spontaneous behaviour emitted by animals. Although the precise measurement and control of the laboratory cannot be applied to many aspects of human social behaviour, Homans seeks propositions similar to those of Skinner where variables are expressed as measured frequencies—of behaviour and of reinforcers. Such propositions as these, for social behaviour, would relate frequency of behaviour to frequency of reinforcement "roughly and approximately" (p. 21).

Thus, a general explanatory approach is adopted as follows: that behaviour is a result of its consequences and is strengthened and maintained because of the reinforcers which follow it. By the same rule, behaviour is weakened by consequent punishment or incurred costs.

A hedonistic theory?

As has been mentioned, there is some slippage in Homans' transfer of terms by analogy from the animal laboratory or economics, to human social behaviour and there has, inevitably, to be some redefinition of terms. For example, the term *reward* is now to be used instead of *reinforcer*, thus appearing to add a hedonistic meaning to the original term. In fact, examination of his theory reveals simply that he has taken the term *reinforcement* from experimental psychology, but in using *reward* as its equivalent he departs from the strictly, empirical, descriptive use of reinforcement (positive or negative) as an event influencing prior behaviour. By putting "motive into the system" he has at once moved away from the parsimony of Skinner's original concept and invited attacks on the philosophy of "reward" as a behavioural determinant.

Homans need not have used Skinner's research to derive his propositions, he could have taken his choice in adapting explanations from several reinforcement theories in psychology. Whichever one he might have used he still would not have escaped the generic criticism, against hedonistic theories. Let us examine this a little further. The hedonistic implication of Homans' theory has drawn the attack of sociologists who, in the same breath, attack both Bentham and Homans (Abrahamsson 1970, Buckley 1967). The hedonist issue is discussed critically, in more general form, in Solomon Asch's (1959) superb essay. Asch argues against the over-emphasis of the biological needs of self-centred individuals, what he calls "the egocentric formulation" which decrees even that "it is egotistic to enjoy one's unegotistic action" (p. 371). Asch comments on "the capacity of individuals under some cir-cumstances to transcend their own particular interest and to act in the interest of their group" (p. 37) and he concludes: "One may safely say that if social psychology is to make progress, it must take into account the vectors that make it possible for persons to think and care and work for others" (p. 372). Homans would accept that his is a hedonistic theory—if hedonism is defined broadly enough—"I've seen too many altruists getting absolute personal pleasure out of altruism" (personal communication). Homans shows that he is aware of the difficulties which arise because there is no simple dichotomy between altruism and hedonism and, as was pointed out above, in Chapter 3, they are difficulties which constitute the general problem of reinforcement theories; they are not particular to any one. The fact that in his theoretical argument he recognizes these difficulties without resolving them (see *The Reward Scale* below) means that the theory as it stands, far from being the last word, is only at its conjectural beginning.

Homans' use of the analogy to existing theories as a basis for deriving explanatory terms creates several further problems. If he uses the same terminology it may give a spurious impression of identity with the original;* if he adopts an equivalent term such as reward he encounters the problem of additional meanings. I suggest that the answer to this dilemma is as follows. As a beginning, the theory may be derived by analogy but it has also to start from scratch in establishing terms which have to be carefully redefined against the empirical evidence of its own subject matter, complex human social behaviour. An example of how confusion could arise is supplied by Homans' use of the descriptive term *emit* which is borrowed from Skinner and used in the first four of Homans' propositions, each of which predicts for different frequencies of activity *emitted* by persons in a social relationship with each other. The term *emit* was introduced by Skinner to refer to spontaneous behaviour *emitted* as distinct to behaviour *elicited* in response to a stimulus, as in classical conditioning experiments. Thus the terms *emit* and *operant* behaviour are used by Skinner (1938) in order to elucidate

* The "homynyms" referred to in Chomsky's (1959) critique of Skinnerian explana-tion of human behaviour.

their connection with posterior events,* the reinforcers. But Skinner was particularly concerned with the conditions for learning and it is difficult to see why Homans should insist, in this case, on using the term *emit* when his concern is with performance rather than the learning process itself.† Nevertheless, Homans avoids further confusion by using *activity* instead of Skinner's *operant*, and in this instance when he prefers the former, because it is close to everyday language, he is probably also granting implicitly that *activity* is less artificial and does not exploit or strain the analogy too far.

His adaptation of Skinner's mode of explanation is consistent with his own position as a reductionist. Apart from this, Homans has other reasons for finding particular value in borrowing by analogy from experimental psychology. He criticizes anthropologists who tend to find explanation for social behaviour in the existing structures of a society, arguing that "they cannot fully explain their own findings unless they make certain assumptions about what men find rewarding" (p. 383). Homans plainly states that it is not enough to say that behaviour is rewarding because it is repeated, or that it is repeated because it is rewarding. Specific assumptions have to be made about the nature of rewards and so Homans really goes beyond the empirical description of rewards, beyond Skinner's "reinforcement contingencies", to the underlying mechanisms of behaviour, to motives, which he holds are present or at least implied, in his five propositions.‡

Propositions 1, 2, 3 and 4

The first proposition can be paraphrased as follows: if, in a particular situation activity has been rewarded in the past, then the more similar is a present stimulus-situation the more likely is the activity to recur. This is an abbreviation of Homans' proposition which in effect seems to be a statement of the general conditions for learning, of stimulus generalization, and would be representative of the starting position of any of the reinforcement learning theories. The proposition, as a very simple

* Although it was also accepted that an *operant* usually does acquire a relation to prior stimulation (Skinner, p. 21).

† In his revision of *Social Behaviour* (1974) Homans has dropped the term *emit* and he uses the term *action* instead of *activity*. In this revision he starts with fundamental propositions stating the relationship not between two persons but between action and what follows it. See also Chapter 9 below.

‡ Homans says he is "anxious to get motive into the system" (p. 13).

and general statement about learning, would be equally in the tradition of Thorndike, Hull, Spence, Miller or Tolman: even the "two factor" theorists, those who would admit of both contiguity and reinforcement as factors in learning would go part of the way with such a proposition. In other words, it would be acceptable to all except the contiguity theorists, led by Guthrie, who hold that the association only of stimulus and response is sufficient for learning.

The next three propositions state the relation between frequency of reward and frequency of behaviour—the more frequent the reward from another . . . the more frequent will be the activity that obtains it (Proposition 2); between value of a reward and frequency of behaviour (Proposition 3); lastly, frequency is related to satiation in the individual the more frequent a recent reward . . . the less value it will have (Proposition 4).

Proposition 2 thus states that the more frequently an activity is followed by a reward from another person, the more frequently will that activity tend to recur and Proposition 3 is very similar to this; stated in full it gives the flavour of Homans' terms: "the more valuable to a man the unit of an activity another gives him, the more often he will emit activity rewarded by the activity of the other" (p. 55). Proposition 4 embodies the satiation principle, namely that the more often an activity is followed by reward from another, the less valuable it will become.

Corollaries

As mentioned earlier (Chapter 2) the starting propositions of a theory should be comprehensive but couched in a very general form and several stages removed from the empirical data. They should allow deduction of empirical propositions which predict effects in particular situations. Thus, Homans' next step from the basic propositions is to present a number of associated propositions and corollaries and from these he sets out to demonstrate the empirical application of descriptive propositions—as large a number of these as is required by the range of different "givens" (the particular conditions present in the behaviour under observation, the given characteristics of persons, groups and environments). The descriptive propositions incorporate the different characteristics of individuals and groups which are encountered in empirical situations. And because these descriptive propositions also refer to different kinds of rewards and activities they may elaborate considerably on the simple "x varies as y" proposition in its most general, least detailed, form.

In the basic propositions and the many corollaries derived from them there are two variables: the frequency of rewards or costs, and the degree of value attaching to them. According to Homans' definition, social activity is itself a reward or cost exchanged between persons. "Activity" is merely a descriptive term for *any* behaviour inducing rewards or costs; and while it gives a necessary identification only *frequency* and *value* are the units which are measured.

Homans' view on method can be summarized as follows. The first variable of *frequency* as a matter of counting incidents (almost like counting heads) presents no conceptual difficulties. However, care has to be taken to carry out observation by standard methods, to control observer bias or changes in an observer's attention. The second variable —*degree of value*, presents difficulties both in the assessment of the value of a reward or a cost, and because there may be fluctuations in value over time; the satiation proposition (4) does allow for this. Nowhere does he resolve (but nor has anyone else) the question of whether an objective, standard value scale can be presented for the rewards or costs of different persons, but he would consider it possible to present alternatives at a particular moment of decision on a single scale. For instance, if it were possible to examine the past decisions of a person, it would be discovered which rewards were valued most on a simple rank-order scale. On the problem of value—measurement, Homans moves away from the behaviourist approach. The notion of a *fair* value also has to be settled, since this becomes an important factor in exchange, and here he is not a behaviourist at all.

Proposition 5

Now Homans introduces the concept of *distributive justice* which refers to a person's expectations of the rewards due to him and costs which he may incur—the proportion of his rewards to his costs: that these should be seen to be distributed in a *fair* ratio to each other. This rule of justice is found to hold in many situations and often it is therefore not only what ought to be, but what is—the person who contributes much also receives much. Justice is thus a third variable and is included in the fifth basic proposition. This proposition states the relationship between

failure in "the rule of distributive justice" and the consequent probability that the person who experiences this failure "will display the
emotional behaviour we call anger" (p. 75). One person in a relationship may drive a hard bargain, the expectations of the other person
will be proportional to his investments and, as Proposition 5 states: the
more to a man's disadvantage the rule of distributive justice fails, the
more likely he is to display anger.* In this proposition the quality of
emotional behaviour enters as a characteristic varying with the degree
of justice attained in a social relationship. Thus, the empirical, behaviourist model which provides Homans with a starting point and an
analogy for the other four propositions is dropped.

The failure of an expected reward leads to anger or resentment; this
is in itself a punishment "and its avoidance is accordingly a reward"
(p. 77). Men therefore learn to pursue activities which are rewarded by
the attainment of justice and to avoid those that involve unjust exchanges. In this way justice becomes a value itself exchanged and
efforts will be made by the participants in a social exchange to maintain
a standard of distributive justice. No new proposition, Homans writes,
is required to express this but it must be recognized that establishing
fair exchange directly influences the degree of reward. However,
Homans touches on the important problem of value-measurement
which has just been mentioned, when he states that two men seeking to
establish such an exchange may make use of different scales of values
in appraising rewards, costs and investments and, while they agree on
the rule of distributive justice, they may not agree on what components should count and what weight they should have, in applying
it. So Homans acknowledges the difficulty of differing and subjective
scales of value.

Difficulties with the concept of value: classical economics and the use of empirical measures

In discussing frequency as his first variable Homans is on safe empirical
ground. For the second variable, value, propositions from classical
economics are brought into the explanatory scheme, but even so, per-

---

* Homans (1974) revises his explanation, substituting a frustration-aggression
hypothesis for Proposition 5 and then following with general propositions on expectations and distributive justice, the latter being a general (and Aristotelian) rule even
though there may not be agreement between individuals on which rewards should
count most.

sonal and subjective values continue to present a great deal of difficulty for the theory. It will be interesting to see, later on, how Homans deals with motives and the cognitive aspects of value.

In his discussion of how value should be measured, Homans makes his first incursion into elementary economics. He has already defined value as the degree of reinforcement adhering to each unit of activity. Proposition 3 states that with more value per unit, the more frequent will be an activity. He argues that it would be a tautology to say, now, that value is equivalent to or can be expressed as the amount or frequency of activity. In this tautology, the only measure of value would be the quantity of activity put out. This would be nothing more than a definition of value similar to that once used in economics called *value in exchange*, but quantity and value are separate variables and there has to be an independent measure of each. Homans mentions that the economic term for the degree of reward is utility,* and that the term marginal utility has a similar meaning as value per unit-activity in social behaviour—the value one obtains for additional amounts of activity.

Moreover, value is more than the degree of reward achieved or of costs incurred in exchange, it is also value perceived by the person, the equivalent of state-of-the-organism variables in experimental psychology. Homans notes that "our knowledge of values will always be imperfect, and the predictions we make from it will be gross and statistical, based on a few obvious similarities and differences, bound to go wrong in detail" (p. 47). The research methods used in measuring values are not likely to be anything as precise as those for counting frequencies, although in Homans' view research is no less useful because its methods are not the most sophisticated. Measurements of value will always tend to be imprecise and of the "more or less" variety, says Homans, but the general notion of value does have the advantage of parsimony. A person requires more or less of a particular activity depending on his circumstances, his experience, his characteristics; or values it more at some time than he does at others. There is something other than the influence of a person's previous *success* that influences the amount of an activity he requires, and this factor Homans terms *value*. There are two kinds of value: the value of an activity in a scale of comparison with other activities, and, secondly, the value of an activity

* Note, however, that economists define utility as a psychological entity (see Samuelson, 1955, p. 414).

over a period of time, fluctuating with the amount recently received or given. This latter kind of value will show increases because of deprivation or will decrease because of satiation. Since Homans distrusts verbal methods, he would prefer that the value of an activity to a particular person or persons is inferred from individual or group characteristics such as level of skill or recent history. Again, he does not maintain a consistent position on this, because later he is willing to use empirical findings in the form of verbal expressions of value perceived. The limitations of analogies to laboratory observations on non-human subjects are nowhere more clear than in this instance.

Another doubt arises over the operation of the satiation proposition (4)—the more often in the recent past a man has received a rewarding activity from another, the less valuable is any further unit of that activity. Satiation, a concept established for physiological variables is of little use in understanding abstract human values. In effect, Homans asks: How does the value accorded to personal conscience become satiated? Clearly Proposition 4 will operate only for certain rewards, and will not apply to others. An answer to the question of what an individual still desires, over and above what he has, or is already receiving, cannot be the simple one of satiation, writes Homans, when it comes to values like autonomy or variety.

Homans now turns to empirical studies in social psychology for evidence to support his concept of value. The first six empirical studies described by Homans are used to illustrate the experimental manipulation of the amount and value of interpersonal activities such as expressions of liking or approval (Homans uses the terms *interchangeably**) and expression of agreement or disagreement with the opinions of others. In all six studies the conditions of communication in pairs and groups of 6–14 members were controlled by the experimenters. In the case of experiments on consensus of opinions as a reward exchanged, notably those by Festinger *et al.* (1952) and Gerard (1954), one of the hypotheses tested concerned the effect of liking, induced experimentally by telling subjects that they would find other group members congenial, on the degree of agreement between them measured on a simple three-point scale.

In particular, this experimental result supports Proposition 3—that the more valuable is an activity which a person receives from another,

---

* In *Social Behaviour*, *liking* and *approval* are terms for an identical reward, the value of which is measured by only one method, the sociometric test.

the more often he will behave in ways which bring him this reward. The corollary of this proposition is also supported: if a person's activity is unrewarded by another then this activity will become less frequent.

The exchange of value for value: reciprocity

Homans adds what appears to be another corollary of Proposition 3 when he states that the more valuable to a person is the activity or sentiment he gets from another, the more valuable to the other is the activity that person gives him.* This is similar to what sociologists refer to as the norm of reciprocity. It is worth noting that Homans does provide an underlying explanation to this rule, by his proposition of distributive justice which introduces expectation and motive into the theory. Reciprocity of value is already implied in Propositions 2 and 3: in the first of these the reciprocal exchange is expressed in equivalent frequencies of behaviour; and in the second, value, is exchanged for frequency. Now, in this corollary Homans states the exchange of value for value.

Homans' method in *Social Behaviour* is first to state the basic explanatory propositions, making explicit their derivation in experimental psychology and secondly to suggest the application of these propositions and their corollaries to a large number of the descriptive statements yielded by over 60 empirical studies, mainly of the 1950s. Subsequently most of the book consists of a description of the empirical findings and the interpretation of them by means of the propositions and corollaries. Homans' discussion of the propositions concerning value is a good example of this technique, where the empirical findings are shown at least to be consistent with the propositions or to support them directly. Homans discusses the results of the classic field studies reported by Moreno (1934) and Jennings (1950) at the State Training School, Hudson, New York. The principal research method used was the

* This can be stated in converse form as "the more valuable to the other . . . an activity he gives the other, the more valuable to him . . . an activity the other gives him" (p. 75). Maris (1970) considers that this *is* the rule of distributive justice (and therefore connects it indirectly to Proposition 5) but he overlooks that it has already been implicitly stated in Homans' discussion of Proposition 3: "The more Person needs help, the more often he will ask for it and *the more thanks he will give when he gets it*" (p. 55) (my italics). Furthermore, the term distributive justice involves more complex variables than are included in this particular corollary; among other things, it refers to the accepted expectations within a group of what constitutes justice in the allocation of rewards and costs between persons.

sociometric test, measuring choices and rejection among over one hundred girls. The results are interpreted by Homans as suggesting that friendship choices are influenced by services received; that is, persons give more approval to those whose activities are most valuable to them. Some further evidence is taken from an experimental study by Israel (1956), establishing that an individual's choice goes to those who actually reward him personally.

After extensive discussion of value and behaviour, Homans presents a combination of Proposition 3 with the corollary concerning reciprocity of value: the more valuable to a person is the activity of another, the more valuable is the approval he gives in return *and* the more often he directs activity towards the other. This is expressed in a shortened if-then form, with Homans' characteristic pronouns Person and Other: "if Other does Person a service, Person is apt to like him and to interact with him often" (p. 182).*

The negative form of Proposition 3 has been mentioned—the less the value the less frequent will be activity expended in obtaining it. Proposition 4 explains a similar effect as a result of satiation with receiving a reward on successive occasions, it becomes less valuable, and therefore by the negative of Proposition 3 the activity to obtain it will be less frequent. The effect of decrement in value with repeated rewards is illustrated in the case of a person's association with someone of superior occupational status: as more rewards are obtained from him "the less their value becomes and the higher their cost" (p. 327). Homans gives several illustrations to show that although the company of superiors is sought after, costs may accumulate to the point where the highest status person is avoided.

In his discussion of value, Homans refers to the profit of an activity as "the difference in value between its reward and its cost, cost being defined as the reward of some alternative activity forgone in emitting the first" (p. 266). Thus Proposition 3 can now express the relationship between profit and frequency of an activity: the greater the profit of an activity, the more often will a person do it.

Value and satisfaction

Homans also uses the concept of value to clarify the relationship between a person's assessment of profit and his feelings of satisfaction.

* The relationship of liking to interaction is discussed below.

The more valuable is a reward the more often will a person expend activity in obtaining it, but the less likely is he to be satisfied with what he has received so far—satisfaction is low where profit is still high. However, the value of an activity will decrease merely by the number of times the activity is given in a social exchange, the relative costs rise and so profit decreases. Thus satisfaction will rise with the attainment of valuable behaviour, even as profit is diminishing. While greater profit will encourage more frequent activity, it is not the case that higher satisfaction will do so. To explicate the connection between a man's satisfaction with a reward and the amount of behaviour he will put out to get it, Homans has distinguished between value, satisfaction and profit-per-unit of activity. The relationship of satisfaction to profit obtained is a subtle one, mediated by value, and there is a further complication. Homans emphasizes that an explanatory solution to an individual's expectation of reward cannot be the simple one of satiation by repeated administration of rewards as Proposition 4 states. While there may be many situations where this proposition will be sufficient there will be others where consideration of distributive justice (Proposition 5) has to be introduced. What a person still desires, after having received a reward is then the amount by which the reward falls short of his investments according to the rule of distributive justice. The amount required to match expectations is called the "satisfaction quantity", which like the value scale is assumed by Homans to be constant for an individual at least over the short term. But investments change and increase—a man tends to put more of his seniority or skill into a particular job, and so his level of aspiration rises. What he desires will therefore tend to increase and therefore his satisfaction will decrease unless there is a corresponding rise in rewards.

Thus, Homans explains the dynamic changes in expectations which have proved so troublesome in studies of occupational behaviour: for example, where an increase in the responsibility attached to a job brings more interest and status but leads consequently to dissatisfaction with the available promotion and pay opportunities. Homans concludes "Any satisfied desire creates an unsatisfied one" (p. 276). In the course of his discussion, Proposition 4 (the satiation proposition) and Proposition 5 (the failure of the rule of distributive justice) are both applied to empirical findings on work satisfaction.* It is worth noting

* The majority of Homans' references to field studies in *Social Behaviour* are taken from research in business and industrial organizations.

too that Propositions 2, 3 and 4 have to be qualified by the operation of variables contained in Proposition 5 which is thus given primacy over the others. As has been mentioned, this proposition is an exception to the other basic propositions in that it is not derived from behavioural psychology and later on the full implications of this fact for Homans' theory will be considered.

The value-scale

Throughout his book Homans chooses to use as his illustrative example of social exchange the relationship between two federal civil service agents described by Peter Blau in *Dynamics of Bureaucracy* (1955). The problems which arise in applying the notion of profit per unit-activity to social relations are also exemplified in this situation. Here one man seeks help from a colleague in carrying out a task at the cost of acknowledging his inferiority in return for, on the other side of the bargain, the esteem he is able to give to the other—whose costs are the interruption of his own work. The possibilities of assessing the total profits (reward minus cost) of each person or even their total rewards are largely conjectural. How are the values of units of activity varying over time, and alternating with other activities, to be measured? Homans writes that:

> Economics says that each would maximise utility if he so divided his day that the last unit of activity he exchanged with the other got him a reward just equal in value to the last unit he spent on his own work. In the language of economics, to maximise utility, he should make the marginal utilities of his two activities equal. But we shall never be able to measure value precisely enough to discover whether a man maximises his utility in these terms (p. 72).

The conditions of social exchange make it very unlikely that either person can break off relations at the moment when he has maximized his rewards. A fatal weakness in the economic analogy occurs when Homans emphasizes that, more important than considerations of profitable exchange are those of fair exchange—as has been made explicit in the rule of distributive justice.

Discussing the notion of fair exchange, Homans mentions that while men may agree on the rule of distributive justice they may not agree in the appraisal of rewards, costs and investments. A man will compare his own situation with that of other persons of similar characteristics to himself (age, skills, seniority, experience) but there may not be a general consensus on what constitutes a fair exchange. Two men in similar situations may not agree on the values which they attach to the time and effort taken in their activities. In other words, they each have a different scale of values.

Although Homans makes much of the analogy of economics in the estimation of social profit, he does not suggest that it is to be taken literally nor that in social interaction there is profit-seeking only in the materialistic, or hedonistic sense—"So long as men's values are altruistic, they can take a profit in altruism too" (p. 79). Homans' view is similar to that encountered in the theory of games (see Bartos, 1967) where such motives as concern for others is incorporated into the player's "utility" which describes the preferences resulting from all motives, whatever they may be.

Non-verbal and verbal behaviour

In his discussion of satisfaction and profit, as in discussing values, Homans expresses a preference for data on activities rather than information about internal feelings of the actor. He is apparently striving to keep to the behaviourist tradition, and is "more interested in what men do than in what they say about what they do" (p. 266); more interested in profit than in satisfaction, and critical of verbal report and its ambiguities. But he cannot be quite consistent about it. Much of his argument focuses on motives, the intervening connections between behaviour and its payoff. Homans admits that he cannot give his full attention to perception or to decision making. All the same, much of his discussion deals with cognitive aspects, with perceptions, values and evaluation of rewards, because these aspects lead to actual behaviour. Justice and status are both treated as matters of perceived stimuli, each influencing different forms of behaviour. The importance of stimuli is stated explicitly in Proposition 1, but the effects in observed behaviour between one person and another are always emphasized. Status is entirely a matter of stimuli and where a status factor is incongruent with another, it is costly to the person because of the effects it may have on the future behaviour of others towards him. Activities are still to be given primacy; always Homans underlines the importance of what a person may do over what he may perceive or think; he makes the interesting remark "behaviour and not mere thinking is always the payoff" (p. 250).

Homans' departure from the behaviourist position

Homans has stated right at the outset that a theory of social behaviour has to be tested against observation of what he refers to as "actual behaviour". But in fact he continually discusses and interprets the cognitive influences on behaviour—the person's assessment of rewards and costs; the perception of stimuli; their manipulation and recognition. His arguments show behaviour such as help, advice, or guidance being exchanged usually for a cognitive result—approval or esteem. From this, further behaviour may follow such as obedience, task completion, co-ordinated activities, but the explanations are still S–O–R rather than S–R in approach. Although he uses Skinner's "hard" descriptive-type proposition as a beginning, soon he is drawing a number of inferences about emotional and cognitive states which might be better served by propositions from psychological research other than that of Skinner, and possibly from Tolman's work on cognitive purpose and problem-solving.

The fact is that Homans' propositions do not leave, as Skinner's have, a gap in the middle between the social stimulus and the behaviour subsequently observed. There is provision for the cognitive decisions made by individuals during social interaction: in choosing between one of two courses of action, in deciding to change from one kind of behaviour to another, in offering or demanding help, esteem, obedience, loyalty, pleasure or sacrifice. Derivatives of propositions 1, 2, 3 and 4 are used to explain the results of many of the experimental and field studies which are cited, but Homans also gives a good deal of space, in between, to discussion of the cognitive. Cognitive and emotional processes are not given a central place in these propositions, except for what is implied in a person's assessment of the value of other persons and activities, and in his choice between alternatives. In contrast, so much of Homans' discussion, when he argues that the propositions fit empirical data from research or confirm common experience, consists of examining the plausible interpretations of the cognitive and emotional process underlying them. There is much attention to how the individual balances his rewards and costs, makes comparisons with the reward and costs of others relative to their investments, and Homans seems to encounter the dilemma of the "tender-minded behaviourist", who is concerned with explaining what happens between S and R,* between the social stimulus and the behaviour subsequently observed. Arguing for the plausibility of his propositions in a variety of social situations from common experience, or finding support for them in research findings, he seems occasionally to be explaining the descriptive statements not by reference to terms and propositions of his theory but by additional concepts which are not present in them. This is only apparently so because the notion of distributive justice and the concepts of frustration or aggression are included in the theory. Here I am referring to the formal propositions of the theory. Only in Proposition 5 does he formally introduce concepts which go beyond those adapted from Skinner. There is no direct reference to the cognitive in the other fundamental propositions beyond the effects of recency, frequency and value of behaviour.

In view of the current uncertainties of cognitive theory, this restriction might seem to be almost an advantage. To take only a single instance. It might be proposed, in order to explain conforming behaviour, that a cognitive explanation be adopted such as Festinger's well-known explanation that behaviour is directed towards reducing dissonance between stimuli or acts. But the notion of some mechanism within the individual resolving inconsistency between beliefs or acts would in its turn have to be explained. One could ask: why is such a mechanism activated? Does inconsistency generate tension? and so on. Tedeschi, Schlenker and Bonoma (1971) suggest an alternative to the cognitive dissonance explanation, in the individual's attempts to maintain his self-esteem, or to maintain his credibility with others because he wishes to be trusted by them, to have influence over them. They argue that the dissonance explanation does not apply when the contradictory attitudes or acts exist by constraint (are manded) and do not arise from a source internal to the individual (when they *tacted*). If, as Tedeschi and his colleagues argue, inconsistency of behaviour is to be avoided because of the impression it might make on others, the further question is also raised of why the individual desires to exert such influence or to be trusted by others. Homans avoids this kind of regressive exercise by limiting his explanations: interpretation of attitudes is limited to measures of sociometric choices, of ranking of values and to

* The dilemmas of an S-R approach and the tender-minded view, that of S-R mediation theory are outlined in John P. Seward (1965).

comparisons with others. This is a limitation of method in the theory as it stands at the moment, there is no intended restriction in Homans' exposition. Help, admiration, and guidance—these are part of the cognitive as much as esteem or liking and they are central to his discussion.

The focus of the theory on these methods may be justified where social behaviour is concerned because of the very great advantage of applying the same measures both in the laboratory and in a variety of natural settings rarely utilized for studies of the cognitive (see McGuire, 1969). What appears to be a limitation thus frees the theory for very wide applications; a theory which can include experimental and natural groups, social acts and their evaluation by the participants is an extremely comprehensive one.* The descriptive propositions based on measures of frequency, recency and the value of behaviour, do refer to a variety of social phenomena: the behaviour of deviants; the effects of status, the influence of friendship choice and reciprocal actions; the interdependence of interaction and liking, of authority and esteem, of authority and interaction, the attraction of a group for its members, and hostility between groups.

Limited as the propositions are† they have an advantage in requiring the isolation of what can be observed in a variety of situations: they they are suitable for application both to experimental and to field studies. Although Homans' theory does not include formal interpretations of the cognitive, neither is the cognitive excluded. Homans would be reluctant to draw a sharp line between cognitive and behavioural theory. The propositions do suggest plausible interpretations of cognitive influence on social choice and decision. If the propositions hold repeatedly for stated conditions then it would appear that Homans has good grounds for making inferences about the cognitive meaning of such behaviour.

---

* I therefore disagree with the view of Morton Deutsch (1964, p. 165) that this is in any sense a small theory.

† Early in his book Homans states: "I must confess that I shall be so anxious to emphasize the connection between a particular kind of behaviour and its payoff, so anxious to get motive into the system, that I shall have little to say about how the connection got established in the first place . . . In this field, which may include some of the most complicated processes of thought, I shall have to take many things for granted without explanation. This book pretends to be a complete psychology no more than it pretends to be a complete sociology" (p. 13).

Calculative decisions: the theory of games

Homans' theory does require that the individual chooses between alternatives in social interaction. It is assumed by the economic analogy, that an individual will choose the alternative which brings more profit, and even after this choice has been made he may again change to another alternative when the rewards of his present activity decrease and costs increase to the point of zero profit. This is really the psychological principle of satiation, as expressed in Proposition 4 (the more often . . . the less value . . .). The notion of profit has also been connected by Homans to Proposition 3 (the more value . . . the more often . . .) and thus to the corollary which predicts that the more profitable is the average value of what each party to an exchange gives the other, the more time they will spend together. There seems to be a definite rational assumption when Homans says that "each distributes his time among alternative activities in such a way that he achieves a greater total profit than he would have achieved by some other distribution" (p. 71). In his most recent publications Homans states this assumption in what he calls the *rationality proposition*, as follows: "every man, in choosing between alternative actions, is likely to take that one for which, as perceived by him at the time, the value (v) of the result, multiplied by the probability (p) of getting the result, is greater; and the larger the excess of $p \times v$ for the one action over the alternative, the more likely he is to take the former action" (Homans, 1970, p. 318; 1974, p. 43). This proposition has to be qualified by the operation of different given conditions which provide answers to the question of why one activity has more value for a person than alternative activities, and to the question of what his evaluations or perceptions are likely to be; why one man's rational decision is different from another's.

In *Social Behaviour* calculation is introduced when Homans contrasts a true "leader" with an "operator". The true leader will have purposes which are other than selfish, whereas an operator tries to manipulate others into a position of obligation towards him—a position of indebtedness in order to secure something in return "for selfish reasons". But "to admit that the favour was only done in order that it should be returned; and to lay bare your calculation in this way is to destroy your moral superiority" (p. 299). The manipulation of stimuli is described where an individual shows an awareness of status stimuli and through this awareness attempts to turn the behaviour to his own account: he associates with those of higher status level in order to raise his own status with others. This is an instance of the *secondary mechanisms* which Homans points to, as not necessarily providing immediate rewards, but as leading to other rewards indirectly and in the longer term.

Another example of calculation given by Homans is that of the high status person who decides to resist the majority opinion in his group, to choose a solution unpopular with the others for the possibility that he will turn out to be right, the other wrong. Homans refers to the calculative decision to be made: if he goes against the opinion of the group but turns out to be correct then he will have gained considerably; if he turns out to be wrong he has plenty of esteem to spare. He may estimate his chances as follows "When the ratio between the values of two rewards is greater than the ratio between the probabilities of attaining them it is wiser to go for the greater value than the greater probability" (p. 350)—but Homans does not claim that the calculation has to be a conscious one. And despite these possibilities and insights, Homans is careful to add that men do not necessarily take the decision that is good for them, nor do they take the most rational decision, the best in the long term.

It should be noted that neither is this assumption made in the theory of games. In the theory of games, it is assumed that men have freedom of choice even to choose what is *not* best for them. Otherwise it would not be possible to show ways of improving decision making. Quite rightly, Homans argues that social behaviour may turn out to be aimed at the immediate reward rather than the greater long term profit. In his view, the theory of games in providing the calculation of probabilities for optimal outcomes may be good advice but a poor description of social behaviour. It is therefore not necessary, Homans says, for calculation to be included in the propositions.

The theory of games is a normative and not a descriptive theory, and Homans is justified in making this distinction between it and his own deductive system tied to descriptive propositions. Nevertheless the theory of games does offer interesting concepts and has useful similarities for any effort which may be made to explain social behaviour; some of these similarities are suggested in this section and the next. The closest links between the explanatory schemes of Homans and Thibaut and Kelley are found in the probabilities and strategies of social exchange. Homans might have made more of them although he says that fuller treatment of the theory of games is not required in his task of deriving the body of descriptive statements from basic propositions. Nevertheless let us be clear that although the probabilities for choice between alternatives, and the advantages of one outcome rather than another are of interest to him, Homans is more concerned with *why* the choice is made, and *why* one alternative has more advantage than another. Homans is concerned with the explanation of decisions at one stage back from the decision-making model which accepts motives as given. Motive is what really interests him, even though at the present stage of the theory he has not been able to take the explanation very far.

The Reward-scale

Homans' propositions have been criticized by Deutsch (1964) for the implication that there is a single dimension along which values exchanged can be ordered, suggesting that the value of one "unit" can be compared with the value of another. In fact, transformation of value scores into standard units is not argued by Homans and he makes no claim either for a standard scale expressing the values of different rewards, or for a mutually agreed scale, between two persons, or the same reward. When Homans says that two persons may make different evaluation of the same reward he makes a point similar to the postulate of the subjective utility function in the theory of games, which recognizes that there is a gap between the objective material payoff and its subjective utility to the person. Thus there is a problem in comparing the utilities of different persons.*

Moreover, in view of the cautions which Homans states for the profit-seeking analogy, the criticisms which could be made against it have largely been anticipated. Deutsch's criticism misses the point, unless it is made as a general criticism of *all* reinforcement theories, which encounter difficulties in dealing with values such as altruism, self-respect or investment of the self in others—values which may not be amenable to measurement—as Asch (1959) has indicated.

Homans acknowledges that the rewards which are influential in social exchange are varied and may not be comprised in a hedonist

---

* One way of solving this problem in the theory of games is by the use of a *transformation coefficient* whereby the payoff value is multiplied by the value assigned to its subjective utility.

interpretation, which has to be abandoned to admit such rewards as inhere to an individual's self-respect and, as Homans mentions, his pride, altruism or aggression. However, in applying the theory to empirical data some, even if approximate, measurement must be made and this has the effect of limiting Homans' theory to the explanation of such rewards as liking (sociometric choice) or help (activities observed) —that is, to forms of reward that can be expressed clearly by rank order or frequencies. When Homans discusses how much of the change in one variable is associated with change in another he is also accepting the principle of correlation. Homans therefore has to accept restriction of the theory to the explanation of descriptive statements dealing with such data as can be treated statistically, and data must be confined to a restricted list of rewards, that is, to rewards which can be scaled, albeit only roughly. All Homans does claim for the *reward scale* is a very modest ordinal ranking, which it may only be possible to quantify in relatively limited situations.

Homans emphasizes that rewards and costs are not to be measured on a cardinal scale, only by ordinal ranking of the sort that is possible in a social exchange where individuals compare their own rewards and costs with those obtained by others. Homans warns against assuming that in social interaction there is a quantitative assessment of ordinal differences. There are probably many situations where there is disagreement "not only on what the rule of distributive justice is but also on what particular investments, rewards, and costs should fairly be placed in the scales and at what weights" (p. 247). In order to make a rule of justice workable there must be assessment of others on the *same* scale and often this may not be attained. Homans' recognition of limitations on the degree of consensus which may be possible between individuals or between groups, and his outright statement that cardinal measurements of reward and costs are not appropriate to social exchange, provide a large contrast with the assumptions in Thibaut and Kelley's model (see Chapter 3).

The comparisons involved in assessing rewards and costs are given extended discussion by Homans, although the comparisons, again, are more modest in their quantitative implications than those of the Thibaut and Kelley model. Homans does not commit himself to numerical values except briefly to illustrate such points as the proportionality of reward to costs: a person with high rewards and high costs will have equal profits to those of a person with low rewards but even lower costs.

Comparisons are important, for instance, in the assessment of status and, as Homans writes, "anything that can be perceived about a man may become a status factor" (p. 249). For there to be consistency, if the stimuli presented by a person's own characteristics and behaviour are compared to those belonging to someone else, they should be perceived as forming a rank-order; one of the two persons should come out better on all, or they should be about equal. There is inconsistency if one person is better on some but not on others, now the stimuli are "incongruent" with each other. This is a source of social costs because where stimuli are conflicting a person's status is thrown into doubt, becomes ambiguous and the behaviour of others towards him will also be unsure (see also page 254). However, the point to be emphasized is that some process of rank-ordering takes place in the person's perceptions of others.

It has been shown that Homans takes a modest view of the possibilities of ranking rewards as a matter for "more or less" comparisons, and he recognizes the diversity of values which prevent the application of one standard kind of assessment. But, practically, a test of his theoretical propositions requires several kinds of measure. Inferences about values may be tied to such empirical data as can be provided by questionnaires or interviews, or some form of observational record. Observations of behaviour may be made by counting frequencies and here the definition of a unit of activity is a necessary procedure and does not present any serious obstacle. Approximations to a reward scale are dealt with by Homans under the notions of longer-term or constant personal value, and shorter-term variation in value as a result of frequency and recency of rewards. In assessing the values of rewards and costs, I do not think Homans intends anything more than relatively broad gauge comparisons of the kind which common knowledge suggests an individual may make between one kind of reward (or cost) and another.

Transferring terms from economics

The introduction of economic terms such as cost and profit into the propositions has already been mentioned. Homans' definition of punishment or costs (he uses these terms as equivalents) is a very good illustration of his skill in blending the propositions of psychology with those of economics. Cost is first defined, with examples from Skinner's experiments on pigeons, as punishment which cannot be avoided in the course of activities achieving reward. In addition, the costs of any one activity tend to increase either through satiation or fatigue, making more likely a change to some alternative activity. The fact that the new activity leads to avoidance of current costs is a reward in itself. Homans argues that punishment lies as much in the withdrawal of a positive reinforcer as in the application of negative reinforcers; therefore a person's decision to forgo one activity in favour of another contributes to his costs by the withdrawal of the alternative rewards. Thus, as in economics, "a cost may be conceived of as a value forgone" (p. 58), and Homans elaborates on this with an historical illustration: "Unless a real alternative is open to a man, and so forgoable by him, his activity costs him nothing. Thus economists argue that the reasons why in most circumstances the air a man breathes costs him nothing is that he cannot forgo it if he would. And great captains try to arrange that their soldiers have no alternative to fighting the enemy, as Cortez did burning his ships behind him. . . . By this token we shall consider as costs only those forgone rewards that remain available . . ." (p. 59).

The formal definition of cost is now presented in a more refined form: "The *cost*, then, of a unit of a given activity is the value of the reward obtainable through a unit of alternative activity, forgone in emitting the given one" (p. 60). Applying the notion of costs to Proposition 3 gives the corollary statement that the more costly is an activity the less often will it be undertaken.

Among the "costs of interaction" (p. 226) are those to persons of lower status in communicating with superiors. Acknowledgement of inferiority is one such cost, for example, where a person who seeks help of another gives esteem in return and so forgoes esteem that he might otherwise have retained for himself. Thus, in the case of two persons of near-status, each may hesitate to endanger his equality by asking help of the other. Homans refers to Goffman (1959) to make the point that for a status-conscious person, to ask a service of an equal might be to place his own status at risk, to incur costs in lowered esteem, forgoing the esteem to himself and giving it to another. Homans gives further references to support this descriptive proposition. The status-conscious person is probably the one whose status is also most uncertain, and he implies that this kind of behaviour is quite general.* Another sort of cost is illustrated by an instance Homans

* Note that Treiman (1966) presents survey evidence to suggest that two-thirds of heads of U.S. households show discrepancies of status rankings.

takes from primitive societies where the economic conventions concern gift exchange rather than buying and selling: providing a set of rules about gift exchange, "we have institutionalised the market, they have institutionalised the gift" (p. 319). If a gift is not returned this is seen as a sign of inferiority and loss of status follows—the cost of not returning a gift is social inferiority. Inferiority is a cost because as has been mentioned "esteem he gives the other he forgoes himself" (p. 320). A secondary mechanism may develop where someone gives to others gifts which they cannot repay as a means to asserting his superiority over them.

Another instance of costs is found in the exercise of authority where control tends to incur costs on those who are controlled, and compliance to authority may involve forgoing other rewards. The rewards of compliance may arrive only in the long term while, in the meantime, costs accumulate "even though the reward does come in the end, a man who incurs you costs is still a man to be avoided . . ." (p. 300). For this reason a son may find his relationship with his father less comfortable than with his grandfather, who is much less of an authority figure. Next, Homans discusses authority and the possibility of punishment which may not always be intentional, coming sometimes from the mistakes of the person in authority. Lippitt's (1948) study of group meetings is cited as showing that members tend to choose their equals in esteem as leisure time companions and as meetings progressed this trend became clearer. Task leaders make their followers incur some costs and the direction of choice moves away from them. An observational study by Bales (1956) of undergraduate discussion groups similarly showed that the most frequent initiators of interaction are not the highest-chosen on a sociometric test, and they attract more expressions of dislike. Further evidence is produced to show that persons with authority and control incur two kinds of costs for their followers—punishment and the forgoing of alternative activities—but these costs may be counterbalanced if the rewards eventually attained are sufficiently high. Thus interaction between equals is advantageous both as a means to mutual rewards and as avoidance of the costs which are present in relations with those in authority. The Hudson study is referred to again in some detail for what it shows in the girls' choice for leisure companions: the more nearly equal was the number of choices they received from others to be living and working companions, the more likely they were to choose each other as leisure companions. Those who had received an equal number of living-and-working choices "were apt to be similar in other ways as well, and similars are apt to reward each other" (p. 322). But there was another factor, best expressed as where a girl felt under constraint with some people and in interacting with them incurred costs. For example, such costs would be incurred in interacting with people of higher esteem or authority. Homans discusses how the price to be paid by the girls for the services of superiors was "a tacit confession of their own inferiority" (p. 314). Moreover, the high esteem girls tended to be critical and this again would show up inadequacies of the other girls who in their leisure would want to escape, to be free of "judging or being judged" and to "exchange rewards on even terms and thus escape the costs of inferiority" (p. 324). The leisure companions provided "the small coin of sociability" and this, it is argued, is another instance of the balancing of rewards against costs, "even if one's reward is low, one still has a profit if its cost is even lower" (p. 325).

Homans and Blau

Throughout *Social Behaviour* Homans uses the "excellent field study" by Blau (1955) in order to illustrate a number of arguments and especially what Blau "has to say about the social economics of consultation" (p. 363). This is the situation where a man seeks advice from a colleague, paying a price in acceding his inferiority, while the other gains prestige in return for permitting disruption of his own work. Blau is quoted as describing the deflation in value which occurs after many consultations—the price paid in frequent interruptions becomes inflated. Seeking advice also has its costs, the self-confidence of the seeker may suffer and, if the consultant is in the least discouraging, or postpones discussion, these costs can become prohibitive. In Blau's example the costs of inferiority were greater in that the two persons involved were of the same Civil Service grade and started, at the beginning of exchange, as equals. By the rule of distributive justice, according to Homans, seeking help unavoidably means conceding superiority to the other. By this rule, those giving advice must have costs proportional to their rewards. Blau's findings illustrate much of Homans' arguments: experts provide real services and receive esteem, thus establishing their social rank. Costs are incurred by both parties; they increase and rewards decline with the number of exchanges, as

Proposition 4 predicts. In this situation, alternative sources of help may be sought at lower cost.

Profits in social exchange

Homans comes close to Blau's theory in discussing the economic analogies and in particular the question of costs. Homans defines "psychic profit" as reward less cost and argues that no social exchange continues unless the parties to it are making a profit. The influence of economics comes out strongly in references to profit per unit activity— the less is a man's profit per unit-activity, compared to that of an alternative activity, the more likely he is to change his next unit to the alternative. Thus the point of zero profit lies where the probability of this change is greatest. It is now quite natural for Homans to refer to a *rate of exchange* in social behaviour, where relative profits settle at a mutually acceptable level. Thus, when a person gives social approval to another in exchange for this help in carrying out a task, the rate of exchange between approval and help "should equal the proportion that profit per-unit approval bears to profit per unit-help" (p. 68).

Homans gives a good deal of attention to the economics of price. He is concerned "to show that the principles of elementary economics are perfectly reconcilable with those of elementary social behaviour, once the special conditions in which each applies are taken into account" (p. 68). Economics tends to treat with physical goods, many units of which can be simultaneously exchanged; only one unit of social activity can be undertaken at a time. Furthermore, social activities may change rapidly, unlike economic commodities, from one kind to another "from one grade of approval, for instance, to a warmer one" (p. 68). He recognizes that economics has independent measures of value—this is not so for social activities. In addition, economists assume a perfect market where the behaviour of any single buyer or seller has negligible effects; in the perfect market it is assumed that no one of the many buyers and sellers need enter into more than one transaction. He contrasts the conditions in social interaction where each person's action may have a marked effect on the rate of exchange, and one transaction will lead to others so that a sequence of social activity will develop. In general, Homans is more interested in emphasizing similarities rather than contrasts in conditions. He compares the Law of Supply in economics to Proposition 3 which states "the more valuable . . . the more often . . .—which is very similar to the economic law that the higher the price of a commodity the more of it a supplier will sell, so long as it is remembered that the price of a commodity is equivalent to reward in the social relationship. The Law of Demand is similar to the cost version, the converse of this same Proposition 3—the higher the price of something, the less of it a consumer will buy. The meaning of costs as an alternative forgone is thus re-emphasized because in the Law of Demand the price of a commodity prevents the spending of money on an alternative one. Proposition 3 and its converse can be clearly understood by the single statement that "the greater the profit (reward less cost) of a unit-activity, the more often it will be emitted" (p. 69).

However, Homans has not yet finished with economic metaphors, for example, he compares individual behaviour in competitive social groups to the policies adopted by business firms: competitors tend to undertake similar activities, since they are after the same goal. This is similar to the commercial rule that where "a competitor is selling two lines of goods, the firm must sell goods in the same two lines . . . and thus the goods sold by the two firms tend to get more alike" (p. 135). The results of an experimental study on groups of students by Deutsch (1953) is used to demonstrate that members of competitive groups are more alike in their activities than co-operative groups where activities are more specialized.

Homans adduces economic principles to the five basic propositions and their corollaries. Economic principles are applied so that they appear to explain social exchange, the services exchanged between persons. Occasionally Homans translates social relations into economic terms. Thus, someone who can supply a rare service which is also much in demand, one that is valued by many, can command a high price (in social approval). The analogy is carried to the point where several persons are said to be bidding against one another for this man's services, running the price up: "over a period of time, the men supplying the (rare) activity would receive a greater total reward, in terms of number of units of approval times the value per unit, than members providing an activity in ample supply" (p. 148). A man gains approval or esteem in the "open social market" by giving services valuable to others which are in short supply: "In elementary social behaviour there is no unearned income" (p. 152).

What has Homans achieved by these incursions into economic terminology? He is stating that the different forms of exchange, economic and social, have similar laws. He does not overlook that conditions and givens of social behaviour are very different from those of the impersonal economic market. Homans' exposition can be criticized, however, for not making it sufficiently clear that the similarity exists only on the most general level. The similarity does lend plausibility to the basic propositions of his theory—they are shown to accord with existing knowledge in economics—but it adds little to the work of theory construction from that point on. The economic analogy is left behind when the theory is developed to the point of explaining the empirical evidence by means of specific hypotheses and descriptive propositions. Now the specification of given conditions and corollaries introduces additional meanings so that the terms of Homans' theory became less and less similar to the general propositions of economics. The basic propositions of Homans' theory at their most general level do resemble propositions at an equivalent level of human economic behaviour. But at other equivalent levels of abstraction, whenever there are general axioms these tend to resemble each other and one may encounter an apparent family resemblance. For instance, in neurophysiology, "fatigue" in firing nerve cells could be explained in terms similar to those of a corollary of Proposition 3 (cost-effects) or Proposition 4 (satiation effects).

The Thibaut and Kelley comparison level

Homans draws attention to the similarity of the distinction between satisfaction and profit and the distinction drawn by Thibaut and Kelley between comparison level and comparison level for alternatives (see Chapter 3, p. 45). The comparison level involves the evaluation of the rewards and costs by the individual's own criteria of what he deserves, and the comparison level for alternatives represents the lowest level of rewards he will accept in a particular relationship, in view of available alternatives. The similarity lies in the explanation of withdrawal from a relationship: as soon as rewards drop below the comparison level for alternatives the individual will leave the relationship and similarly, the point of zero profit is where the likelihood of a change to an alternative is greatest. Since Homans has defined cost as equivalent to alternatives forgone, the notions of profit and cost are always tied to the presence of alternative opportunities.

In yet another corollary to his propositions Homans makes explicit mention of the presence of alternative activities, which tend to increase the costs of a person's current behaviour so that the less his current profit (the less the excess value over cost) the more likely is a person to change to an alternative, increasing his profit. In the first six experiments cited, those by Gerard (1954) and Festinger and Thibaut (1951) demonstrate the importance of other persons or sub-groups as alternative sources of reward, replacing the majority of the group in which an individual is currently a member. Conformity to the majority opinion is less likely if the formation of sub-groups is possible.

There is, however, a large difference between the two analytical frameworks of Homans and Thibaut and Kelley, which it is probably more important to recognize than the mere fact that both tend to agree on an explanation for changes from one behaviour to another. As has been described, satisfaction may rise independently of profit per unit-activity and while the latter may be decreasing satisfaction may be on the increase. Homans' explanation thus allows for a more complex situation than does the Thibaut and Kelley model where comparison level and comparison level for alternatives tend to vary together. Following the latter analysis, a man changes to an alternative because his satisfactions are low; by the former, his satisfactions may be high but he may still move on to an alternative activity because he is in search of different satisfactions.

The interaction-liking-interaction hypothesis

I shall attempt to give an adequate idea of the applications and derivations of the propositions stating the relationship between social interaction and the sentiment of liking; of the empirical studies which Homans cites in their support and the different measures which are used for the sentiment of liking or approval. Some indication will be given of the shortcomings in the present state of the theory.

One of the major propositions of Homans' earlier book *The Human Group* and perhaps the most controversial, was the interaction-liking hypothesis: "if the interactions between the members of a group are frequent . . . sentiments of liking will grow up between them, and these sentiments will lead in turn to further interactions . . ." (p. 112). The amount of discussion which this earlier hypothesis attracted, and its incorporation since then into the propositions and corollaries of Homans' later theory, justifies some detailed consideration of it. He now brings the interaction-liking hypothesis more clearly into focus by deriving it from the basic propositions and by stating different forms of it as corollaries. The original hypothesis is converted into two separate propositions.* Changing the position of the independent and dependent variables, one states that interaction leads to liking, the other that liking leads to interaction. These propositions are demonstrated by the empirical results which Homans cites from recent experiments or field studies and they are each in turn explained as deductions from one or more of the basic propositions and their corollaries. Homans warms to this discussion, stating that, of the propositions in his earlier book, "none was more often attacked" (p. 186).

Liking-interaction

In *Social Behaviour* (p. 90) the relationship of liking to interaction is collated to Proposition 1, when Homans says that liking another person constitutes a condition under which in the past the individual has found that his social activities have been rewarded—hence liking is followed by interaction. In support of this, he cites an experiment by Kurt Back (1951) on pairs of undergraduates, showing that subjects who were told that their partners were congenial were subsequently more active, and more likely to be influenced by them than those who were told their partners were *not* congenial. In effect, liking (awareness that partners are congenial) leads to more frequent interaction. Secondly, he refers to an experiment by Potashin (1946) on pairs of primary school children where the behaviour of pairs who had chosen each other on a sociometric test was compared to pairs who had not chosen one another. In the Potashin study the independent variable was "favourable sentiment" or friendship. Uninterrupted discussion was greater in pairs of friends than in pairs of non-friends and the friends tended to talk and to initiate talk in equivalent amounts, in contrast to the non-friends where the differences were greater between members of pairs.

Interaction-liking

Changing the position of variables, Homans finds support for the statement that interaction leads to liking in an experiment by Thibaut

* Zetterberg (1965), refers to this kind of hypothesis as expressing a reversible relation: if x, then y; and if y, then x.

(1950) on teams of ten to twelve boys engaged in a series of competitive games. This provides the descriptive statement that liking (expressed as sociometric choice) increased among those "in whose company they had won . . . rewards" (p. 142). This condition, where frequency of interaction itself is treated as the independent variable, is also found in situations of proximity in a neighbourhood or occupational situation. Two closely situated persons will tend to interact more often than with others; the chances are increased of there being some value in the activities exchanged "if only because they may be obtained at less cost . . . than from a third party at a greater distance" (p. 134). Again, in an experimental study of student discussion groups by Bovard (1951) frequency of interaction was treated as the independent variable. It was found that the number of choices mutually given was less in the condition of "leader-centred" discussion than in the "group centred" discussion. To achieve these two conditions, Bovard had trained group chairmen either to monopolize a discussion, or to turn it back to the group. In the latter case Homans suggests that the chairman "gave them an opportunity to reward one another, and the reward produced the liking" (p. 184). Note that liking is defined again as sociometric choice, and so this result might otherwise be expressed as: reward from another person produced the intention to continue relationships with that same person.*

Homans says that "practically speaking, one of the ways of getting people to like one another is to make them interact with one another. It is a method that works—other things equal. It is also one that Americans believe in without benefit of psychology . . ." (p. 185). Another study described by Homans, the field experiment in a boys' summer camp by Sherif and Sherif (1953) used sociometric tests to demonstrate that increased interaction led to increased liking or choices between group members; decreased interaction was followed by a decrease in choice. Finally Homans mentions Newcomb (1956) in support of the interaction-liking hypothesis, quoting Newcomb's conclusion that "Actuarially speaking the evidence is altogether overwhelming that *ignoring other variables*, the proposition is correct in a wide range of circumstances" (p. 106). And he now proposes to examine given conditions that might make for exceptions. Homans lays par-

---

* Homans defines liking in terms of *one* choice—the result of asking the question "Do I like him?" But when such choices are summed, then what is measured is esteem or status.

ticular emphasis on the cautionary statement—"other things being equal". Certain given conditions such as agreement between persons in their values and expectations, their similarity in age or background, will affect costs or the availability of rewards. Another given condition, if the interaction-liking proposition is to hold, is that there should be freedom to leave the relationship should the interaction fail to yield results. If this condition is not present and interaction continues under constraint of circumstances then liking will decrease.

Note that Homans does not discuss the possibility of a relationship in which liking is largely irrelevant, where people will associate together because of other rewards. Homans has chosen to make his paradigm of social exchange a relationship where help is provided in return for approval. Perhaps he does not give enough attention to relationships which are socially profitable and where interaction is maintained or increased because of rewards other than approval or liking. He does refer briefly to the possibility that interaction may continue despite the fact that liking is not one of the rewards exchanged, but this is in the negative sense of two persons who are forced into interaction, failing more profitable alternatives in which case "a man will go on interacting with another even though he finds the other's activity punishing" (p. 187). However, there is no difficulty in accepting Homans' view that in many situations reward in the form of liking or social approval is paramount. It is a form of reward that is in general currency, the reader has to accept this.

Let us try to make explicit what is only implicit in Homans' argument. The connection of corollaries for interaction and liking to the basic propositions can be summarized as follows. (i) The cumulative effects of social exchanges are stated in Propositions 2 and 3. (ii) Liking is a reward in general currency, a "generalized reinforcer" possibly as important as money in economic exchange. (iii) Therefore the effects of continued interaction include the probability of increased liking. (iv) A further corollary states the reciprocity of value for value: the more valuable to the person is the activity of another, the more valuable is the activity he gives him in return. This is related to the rule of distributive justice. (v) Since one of the activities a person may give to another is approval or liking, the further corollary holds that: the more valuable to the person is the activity of another, the more valuable is the approval he gives him in return. (vi) Other corollaries can now be stated expressing the relationship between rewards such as conformity to a group norm, which is exchanged for approval from others.

There could be some confusion about the relationship between liking and interaction if it is not borne in mind that there are different degrees of liking and that it is measured in different ways in the studies to which Homans refers for empirical support. Homans uses the terms liking and approval to represent identical behaviour, but if this is so, there can be no different degrees of the behaviour and different measures of it. There is little doubt, that this part of his explanatory effort will require greater refinement in future developments of the theory. For example, why should Homans use two terms for the same thing? When he says, about a person's sentiment towards a non-conforming member of a group that he "will not simply disapprove of him but positively dislike him" (p. 118) this refers to different degrees of disliking, but why use "disapprove" and "dislike" in the same sentence, without further elucidation? Liking/approval is usually measured by the expression of choice for work or leisure companions. Liking has also been introduced into an experimental situation by telling the subject that other persons "are congenial" as in Back's (1951) study, mentioned above. Approval, mixed with respect, can become *esteem* without implying the warmer values of friendship. Homans recognizes that the research findings he uses "may lump together liking of different degrees . . ." but he adds that, even with these disadvantages, "grossly and statistically we should expect the relationship to hold good . . ." (p. 119).*

Corollaries for groups larger than dyads: esteem-interaction

Next, Homans turns to groups which are larger than dyads. For instance, discussing the effect of liking on continued interaction, Homans writes: "as usual we began with a proposition stated in terms of the relation between only two men. We shall next . . . show what the proposition implies about a larger number of persons . . . On the assumption that a group consists of a number of pairs . . ." (p. 188). Some interesting corollaries emerge, to state the special conditions existing in larger groups. Where interaction is frequent one of the

---

* Zetterberg (p. 67) notes that the interaction-liking proposition "was a good start, even though later theorizing makes it plain that two additional variates have to be introduced—viz. cost of avoiding interaction, and availability of alternative rewards".

rewards exchanged may well be conformity to a group norm—hence the corollary which states that "the larger the number of members that conform to a group norm, the larger is the number that express social approval for other members" (p. 119).* Homans finds support for this in the study by Festinger, Schachter and Back (1950) which showed that the more friendship choices there are within a social group, the more is the conformity to the majority opinion. An industrial study by Seashore (1954) who correlated group productivity figures with employees' scores on a measure of attraction to their work group, is shown by Homans to support the same corollary. The groups with the strongest attraction for their members were also those which tended to have least dispersion of individual productivity figures. It is therefore concluded that there is a strong association between the positive choices expressed for a particular group and conformity of its members to a group norm. These empirical findings are explained by the corollary expressing the relationship between conformity and approval, and are quite easily derived from basic propositions concerning two-persons relationships—either from the proposition stating reciprocity of rewards or from Propositions 2 and 3.

Another corollary extends the liking-interaction proposition to the degree of esteem (liking plus respect) as the independent variable influencing interaction. The distinction between liking and esteem is elucidated when Homans points out that in Bales' (1953) analysis of discussion in six-man groups high interactors did receive "social approval of a certain kind, but they were not particularly well 'liked'. We may have to distinguish between different kinds of social approval instead of lumping them all together . . . to distinguish between a principal ingredient of esteem . . . 'respect' and another kind of social approval . . . 'liking' " (p. 197). The corollary is stated as follows: the higher the esteem in which a person is held, the more frequent is the interaction from others, or as Homans writes "the larger the amount of social approval received by a single member from other members (that is, the higher his esteem) the more frequent the interaction he receives from other members" (p. 188). A field study carried out by

---

* Homans lists the rewards of conforming. Some people "are rewarded by the result that the norm itself, if obeyed, will bring" (p. 116)—such as mutual assistance or protection. Secondly, conformity to a norm is a reward to other persons who value that particular form of behaviour. Thirdly, conformity may be sought for the sake of the approval received from others.

Homans (1954) in a large public utility demonstrates this corollary. A frequency count was made by checking the social contacts in a group of clerks every fifteen minutes of their working day, and the clerks were interviewed. A question "Who are your close friends in here?" yielded a rank order of sociometric scores; the rank orders obtained in frequency of interaction were then correlated with the rank orders of friendship choices. A high positive correlation was found, confirming the corollary.

Proximity, interaction and liking

The interaction-liking proposition is a good example of a proposition derived from more general ones, under specified given conditions. By a more general proposition is meant one from which other propositions also can be deduced, allowing for specified and different given conditions. The latter, which are taken as constant for the period of time under consideration, do not have to be explained in themselves: "the scientist is not called upon to explain all things in the course of explaining one" (p. 206). Homans makes some illustrations of given conditions, such as have been included above, suggesting that under different conditions the same basic propositions will predict different actual behaviour. He warns that it is not possible to cover all the kinds of givens that may from time to time be important in determining social phenomena and he concentrates on three classes of givens that are very frequently found in field studies. These are: physical or functional proximity; the past histories or backgrounds that make men likely to hold similar values; the positions that men hold outside the group in question, which makes them well able to reward other members of the group. There are many other possible givens including those conditions established in an experiment which "must always be taken as givens in explaining its results" (p. 108). One example of conditions to be taken as given is found in the relationship between geographical location in the Festinger (1950) study of neighbourhood contacts in an apartment block, and referring also to Gullahorn (1952), Homans starts with the descriptive propositions concerning the pattern of contacts. The givens are the physical lay-out and the past experience of a number of students of similar age and background. Under these given conditions, the nearer the occupants are to each other the more likely they are to become friends. But proximity has this effect only with other things being equal, and liking need not follow unless the persons involved reward each other—as they often do "if only because near rewards are purchased at less cost than distant onces . . ." (p. 214). Homans draws attention to the possibilities of other givens which could counteract the proximity effect, among which values and background differences might clearly be important factors: "People who are thrown together do not like one another unless they reward one another."

Some industrial examples of the effects of functional proximity of jobs illustrate that proximity leads to interaction and liking. In industry, taking into account environmental givens, it is possible to deduce from general propositions that certain descriptive propositions will hold good. Again, if they are supported by the evidence, the general propositions are confirmed, the descriptive ones explained. Thus Homans returns to the assertions which he made right at the beginning of *Social Behaviour* about his theoretical aims and here again he makes clear what he expects a theory to do and what form it should take.

Values and liking: deductions from general propositions

The previously mentioned point on similarity of values, as given conditions for liking between persons, is now pursued further—similarity makes them likely to reward and ultimately like each other.* A study by Precker (1952) demonstrates the correlation between friendship and similarity in values (value-homophily). The comparison of results from a questionnaire on values—what factors were considered most important in education—is drawn between students who chose each other on a sociometric test, and those who did not. The students' values tend to resemble those chosen rather than the values of others whom they did not choose.

Sometimes the values of persons in a social exchange are different but complementary. More often it is the similarity of their values that makes them likely to reward and ultimately to like each other. The proposition is stated: the more similar the values, the more the liking. For instance, observation may support the descriptive proposition that A likes B more than he does C. If there is no other apparent explanation, but if there is independent evidence that the values of A resemble those of B more than they do those of C, then the descriptive proposi-

---

* A statistic summarizing how similarity predicts choice is the homophily coefficient (Coleman, 1958).

tion is explained because it can be deduced from the general proposition—with similarity of values as givens, explanation is achieved. In effect, Homans is here demonstrating a successful explanation requiring given conditions, together with propositions of three different kinds: descriptive, general and fundamental. This approach has been referred to earlier but it is worth a reminder here, because Homans has demonstrated the connection very effectively in this case. The givens provide the independent variable in a proposition which also states the degree (a measure of the "more or less" variety) of some dependent variable. The latter constitutes the content of a descriptive statement such as rank-order in sociometric choice or frequency of communications. Observations made of actual behaviour, by one of these methods, constitute the descriptive propositions; these are explained by a general proposition or corollary which is, in its turn, explained by a more general, higher-order proposition. Homans notes that this latter proposition may itself remain unexplained.

An interesting point is made later about variation in the givens. Under conditions different from those so far assumed, the same propositions may predict and explain different behaviour. By conceding this point Homans intends to avoid the confusion that might come from assuming mistakenly that only one pattern of behaviour should go with one set of propositions. On the contrary, if there are differences in the givens, one set of propositions can predict and explain a large variety of different patterns. As an example of this, Homans presents a "model matrix" of sociometric choices, showing the frequencies which would follow a given rank-order of similarity in values. Next, this model is compared with an actual matrix which deviates in the distributions of choices, and the question is asked; under what given conditions it might be derived from the same propositions. The actual matrix is taken from a sociometric study of Lemann and Solomon (1952) of three residential houses in a women's college. The big difference between the findings here and the model matrix, is that the lower status members tend to choose each other on a sociometric test rather than directing their choices towards those of high esteem or status. Why should this have happened? In the absence of further data from the study, writes Homans, it is possible to conjecture that there may have been different given conditions, for example geographical location of rooms, similarity of values—or perceived injustice on the part of the lower status members in relation to those of higher status. The latter possibility was confirmed by the number of sociometric rejections from lower to high status and vice versa. Thus, the point is made that with different givens, even findings which at first sight seem contradictory do not require a change in the basic propositions in order for them to be explained.

The proposition stating the relationship between interaction and increased liking is accompanied by the proviso "other things equal". As soon as this proviso is dropped then the propositions can take corollary forms to allow for such conditions as *constraint* where one of the parties in exchange has authority or control over the other and social approval *as liking* now changes to social approval *as esteem*. The corollaries in Homans' theory which treat with frequency of interaction and value per unit-activity are still appropriate for these conditions of constraint. Furthermore the corollaries can be expressed to allow precise measurement of the variables of constraint: for example, different kinds of leadership behaviour are identified by the ratios of initiation to receipt of interaction; esteem and expectations of leaders as introducing rewards, punishments or costs for followers and incorporating measures for variation in task performance and acceptance or rejection of leaders. They systematize the special conditions of authority in social relations. There is a possibility that in future research they can be applied to such problems as that of "psychological" (perceived distance) or "social" distance (i.e. distance as a function of actual contacts) between leaders and subinates which, up to now, has been a matter of empirical generalizations but is still an issue which lends itself to some vagueness. Now, Homans' propositions require that the variables of interaction as well as those of attitudes, be measured. Whereas research in this area has usually been limited to the attitude measures and to a single measure of behaviour (usually group productivity), Homans gives more attention to social process by the observational study of interaction. The result is an improved empirical base for explanation. An investigator applying an interaction-esteem corollary would be able to deal with social distance (attitudes towards leaders, perceived and actual forms of communication) rather than psychological distance (attitudes towards leaders and perceived communication). Fiedler's (1958, 1967) classic accounts of leadership research raise a number of possibilities for the effects of psychological distance but unless further measures of behaviour can be included there seems to be little hope of satisfactory explanations.* Homans' theory offers a solution for the weakness

* For a recent summary of research on "psychological distance", see Gibb, 1969.

inherent in studies of psychological distance as mentioned by Vroom (1965)—who was unable to assess the significance of findings "without knowing more about the behavioural correlates (of attitude scores) . . . in actual leadership situations" (Vroom, 1964, p. 219). Homans' theory has a great deal of practical potential if prediction for actual leadership situations is sought.*

A difficulty in producing empirical evidence to support the descriptive propositions of interaction-liking is that the investigations use quite diverse methods, the meaning of "liking" changes from study to study, and as Homans admits, he has had to "lump together" degrees and kinds of liking. Besides this variety of measures, there is the further complication when "social approval", an equivalent term for "liking", is subsequently used as equivalent to "esteem". Sometimes the distinction between interaction and liking itself becomes blurred as in the Festinger study of neighbourhood groups where a measure of "seeing others socially"—which is strictly speaking an interaction measure— was also held to reflect friendship choice. Homans has had to fit different meanings and degrees of liking to his propositions. Nevertheless he has put into the terms of formal theory a hypothesis (and its alternative hypotheses) which, as Sprott writes "fits in with common sense" (1958, p. 53) and he has spelled out its propositions, corollaries, special conditions and exceptions. It can be concluded from Homans' discussion that it is highly probable that interaction will lead to liking, with exceptions under certain given conditions.

Homans' discussion of the interaction-liking relationships has in at least a couple of instances stimulated further thought on formal theory in sociology and psychology. Zetterberg (1965) presents the proposition as an instance of how observed events conform to and are thus explained by an established general proposition; he gives it the weight of a law. He also points out that it is an instance of a reversible relation —if X, then Y and if Y, then X. As has been pointed out above, the proposition contains two separate ideas and therefore requires separate testing of each. Bartos (1967) has provided a mathematical translation for the relationship. Instead of the clumsy verbal statement that, starting with a given degree of liking, as interaction increases liking also increases but at an ever decreasing rate, Bartos proposes the simple mathematical expression (X is interaction, Y is liking, A is the starting level of liking), $Y = A + \sqrt{X}$. The equation is graphed in Fig. 8 below

---

* Bearing out Homans' dictum that there is nothing so practical as a good theory.

showing how the square root function is utilized to represent longer terms and the stability of the relationship.

Schwartz (1968) qualifies the interaction-liking hypothesis with the statement that there is "a threshold beyond which interaction is

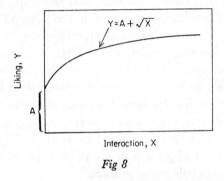

Fig 8

unendurable for both parties. It is because people frequently take leave of one another that the interaction-liking proposition maintains itself" (p. 742). This qualification is consistent with Bartos' expression of the square-root function and the Y plateau—but it does not add more to the explanation already afforded by Proposition 4 and its corollaries.

Homans and the dyad

Just after Homans has stated the first four basic propositions, he raises the possibility of analysing interaction among more than two persons. He gives the instance of a third member entering a relationship and does this to show its complicating effect on his archetypal example of the dyad taken from Blau (1955). This is the exchange of favours between colleagues in an office situation, specifically an exchange of social approval in return for the provision of help in carrying out a task. Now, if two persons are seen to offer approval instead of one, the third person, offering help, moves to a greatly improved bargaining position. Much of Homans' discussion in *Social Behaviour* deals with the dyadic relationship rather than with groups of larger numbers, an emphasis which seems to be acceptable for its illustrative advantages. He justifies it by saying that the dyad is the nucleus of all social relationships and that the larger groups consist basically of a number of dyads, of two-person relationships multiplied.* Even where the relationship is between one person and simultaneously a number of others, as when an individual addresses the others collectively, the basic relationship of a dyad still holds—there is now one person and the "generalized other".

But there is an interesting inconsistency between Homans' illustrative examples of social interaction, and the empirical studies which he cites. Homans emphasizes the dyad in the form he gives to his basic propositions, in his illustrations of social exchanges, in the exemplars he presents of interpersonal relationships. He does not maintain this emphasis when it comes to testing the propositions against empirical evidence, nor does he seek empirical support solely from research on two-person relationships. In *Social Behaviour*, when he uses the results of more than sixty experimental and field studies to confirm propositions and corollaries, a very small minority are studies of dyads; the rest are observational studies of groups of six to nine members, or studies of larger groups such as colleges or schools.

This distribution of references seems rather surprising and it suggests the inadequacy of the dyad in content, as a factual source for generalizations. In other words, it suggests that relationships which are of interest to the social psychologist cannot be tested in the simplified conditions of the dyad. Although Homans' propositions dealing with frequency and recency of rewards or costs are exemplified in the dyad, a person's assessment of value tends not to be. Nor can concepts of authority, justice or status be fully demonstrated in the dyad. As value is treated in Proposition 3 and as a person's expectations of fair treatment are stated in Proposition 5, each of these propositions introduces more complex relationships than those found in the dyad. Even the awareness of costs, as a matter of alternative rewards forgone, involves a wider range of social relationships. For example, where person A seeks interaction with another B, this may be because the rewards attained through their association (such as esteem) are relative to A's position in a larger group, i.e. his status relative to persons C, D, and E.

Conformity behaviour, collusion between several persons, deviance, the effects of esteem and leadership influence, specialization of activities—these topics are among the most interesting in social psychology and they are outside the terms of reference of the dyad. Since many

* Priest and Sawyer (1967) discuss the difficulties in obtaining data on all pairs in a group because even a small sample of persons involves a large number of pairs. Computers have given a way out of this difficulty.

group events are not demonstrated in dyads, Homans has to introduce corollaries referring to larger groups, to the conditions which pertain in them. Of course, the basic propositions apply equally to those groups and the descriptive corollaries follow without requiring additional assumptions. Even though there are corollaries to explain group events which are not present in the two-person relationship, nevertheless the dyad does exemplify the social relationship in its simplest and also its clearest form, so it is to be expected that the basic propositions should be expressed in the convention of the dyad.*

Extrapolation to the larger society

Propositions based on the dyad can be extended to explain the multiple relationships when larger numbers of individuals are present, by the use of corollaries derived from these propositions. Are there limits to this extension? Can further extrapolation now take place to larger entities, collectivities or formal organizations? The theory is already quite versatile in that it applies to groups of any size where the members are in direct contact with each other but Homans thinks it will not stand further extrapolation to the wider society—"Let us not be in a hurry" he writes "to generalise from what happens in the small group to what happens in the society at large" (p. 152). The additional conditions present in the larger society are revealed in the comparison Homans makes between the concepts of esteem and status. The former refers to approval earned through a person's activities in the primary group; the latter to formalized rank, possibly inherited, and ascribed to a position rather than to a person. In the primary group, esteem, approval and status (the latter is the formal recognition of the first two) may be earned by what a man is able to do, through his qualities and skills. This is contrasted to the situation in larger social structures where status can be inherited or attached to positions rather than to persons. Thus, status in the larger society cannot be explained by the same propositions that predict the level of esteem. Elementary social be-

* Blau (1964) cites Simmel's (1908) distinction between dyads and any group of more than two and emphasizes that power strategies such as dividing the opposition, or forming coalitions are outside the scope of the dyad. In a review of studies of small groups, DeLamater, McClintock and Becker (1965) point out that only 25 of 166 variables included in these studies required observation of exactly two persons; 66 could be obtained from single individuals; 75 required observing 3 or more.

haviour may have determined the status position in the first place, but when status becomes part of an institution it is perpetuated in a different way.

Status in formally organized groups, as might be found in studies of the leadership behaviour of those invested with formal authority in occupational groups may be a phenomenon which is "beyond the boundaries of elementary social behaviour" (p. 313) yet Homans does make the point that esteem in the primary group is often proportional to status in the larger society, in the organization of which the group is a part. Thus, formal status may place a person in an advantageous position for receiving esteem from others although clearly this is not necessarily so. This is really no more than a peripheral matter of the givens influencing the small group. Homans maintains that the primary or informal group should never be seen as "a microcosm of society at large" (p. 357) and it would be dangerous, he says, to generalize from the sub-institutional to the institutional. It is true that there are many similarities but there is also one major difference in that in the informal group both rewards and costs occur through direct exchange whereas in the larger society they may derive from a man's position in some institutional scheme. He concedes that institutional behaviour is not basically dissimilar from that observed in the primary group, indeed it has probably developed out of direct exchange at an earlier point of time. Homans allows that there is a continuity between the small group and the larger institution but it is the complexity of connections between the act and its reward which keeps institutional behaviour separate.

This is similar to the situation where a mathematical model is suitable for application to small groups but not for larger collectivities. For instance, an assumption which has to be made in order to apply the theory of Markov chains to group process, and more precisely to dominance relationships, is that each member either dominates or is dominated by every other. This implies a limitation of the theory to groups where two-person dominance relationships can be identified. Again, graph theory which is suitable for representation of relationships in the small group loses the advantage of direct representation when applied to large social structures of complicated multiple relationships.

Testing the theory by experimental or field studies

The view is sometimes encountered (for example in Shaw and Costanzo, 1970) that theories of social behaviour can be tested only by reference to strictly controlled experimental studies, where the effects of an independent variable can be measured precisely in the form of attitude measures, performance of prescribed tasks, choices between alternatives, or by measures of physiological indicators of emotion. In the laboratory a clear definition of the problem is achieved which is not often found in naturalistic settings. The laboratory study tends to be carried out on the dyad, for the practical reason that this is the most manageable unit as well as providing a simple exemplar of social behaviour. But there are good reasons for studying behaviour outside the laboratory. In field studies group processes can be observed which are not represented in the two-person relationship. When a researcher observes naturalistic groups he tends to find that the individual is involved in multiple relationships. The observational unit becomes larger than the dyad, to include a group with at least several members associated together with shared interests or purposes.

It is perhaps not surprising that, of the empirical investigations which Homans uses to test, confirm or qualify his explanatory statements, more are field studies in natural situations than are laboratory studies. In *Social Behaviour* he cites some 60 investigations of which under half are of dyads or small groups in the laboratory.

What are Homans' reasons for selecting this distribution of empirical supports? When recurrent or regular relationships in groups are to be described, when esteem given to others settles into a rank-order, when rates of interaction form into a recognizable pattern of rewards and costs, then reference needs to be made to field studies over a longer period of time than is possible in the laboratory. Homans calls this settled condition "practical equilibrium" (p. 114) and argues that to elucidate this condition as well as the changes which occur in group patterns, field studies are clearly more relevant. Moreover, Homans has much to say about the "secondary mechanisms" of social behaviour, such as the use of established status in order to consolidate an individual's influence over others; and the effects of established status on the extent to which a person becomes an innovator, a conformer, an initiator of interaction with others. Lastly, when he discusses the rules of distributive justice, situations where a man attempts to attain justice or to avoid injustice, it is interesting that he notes that the evidence has to be taken from field studies and he remarks: "no laboratory experiments on justice have yet been carried out" (p. 233).*

However, the great value of Homans' exposition is that he combines experimental and field studies, he is no methodological snob.† In discussing status and conformity he takes field research first and then, at great length he examines the experimental evidence taking the analysis further. For example, field research suggests that men of both higher and lower status show a tendency towards nonconformity and experimental results are then called in to support these findings, to answer the question of how far those of middle status tend to conform and to seek their possible motives for doing so. One of these results is an experimental analysis by Kelley and Shapiro (1954) of a tendency suggested in field studies—that a group withholding approval from a member, loses its control over that member's behaviour. It is important that Homans does not deny the advantages experimental studies have over natural groups although he says that he likes "to examine research on both real-life groups and artificial ones" (p. 170). His use of experimental studies such as that by Israel (1956) is another instance of an effective argument combining both field evidence and experimental results. Homans starts from the hypothesis suggested by field studies: that actual rewards received from others influence the approval given in return. Israel's work clarifies this so that the reasons for giving approval (sociometric choice) are shown to depend not only on actual value received (contribution to joint task performance) but to depend also on notions of justice. This style of argument utilizes the advantages of experimental method, where it is most effective for stating a relationship with greater clarity than is possible in naturalistic observation.

* This was true at the time. Since then there have been a number of experiments by J. Stacey Adams (1963, 1965) and other investigations, which are discussed in a later chapter (see *Distributive Justice*, Chapter 11).

† Unfortunately many psychologists are: they are social-science climbers and must only be seen in the company of the "right" methods.

Research investigations used by George Homans in support of theoretical propositions and cited in this chapter

Adams, J. Stacey (1963). Toward an understanding of inequity. *Journal of Abnormal and Social Psychology*, **67**, pp. 422–436.

Bales, R. F. (1953). The equilibrium problem in small groups. *In:* T. Parsons, R. F. Bales and E. A. Shils, *Working Papers in the Theory of Action*. Free Press, Glencoe, Illinois, pp. 116–161.

Bales, R. F. (1956). Task status and likeability as a function of talking and listening in decision-making groups. *In* L. D. White (ed.) *The State of the Social Sciences*. University of Chicago Press, Chicago, pp. 148–161.

Bovard, E. W. (1951). The experimental production of interpersonal affect. *Journal of Abnormal and Social Psychology*, **46**, pp. 521–528.

Deutsch, Morton (1953). The effects of co-operation and competition upon group process. *In* D. Cartwright and A. Zander (eds) *Group Dynamics: Research and Theory*, Row Peterson, Evanstown, Ill., pp. 319–353.

Festinger, L., Back, K. W., Schachter, S., Kelley, H. H. and Thibaut, J. (1950). *Theory and Experiment in Social Communication*, University of Michigan, Ann Arbor, 21–36.

Festinger, L., Gerard, H. B., Hymovitch, B., Kelley, H. H. and Raven, B. (1952). The influence process in the presence of extreme deviates. *Human Relations*, **5**, pp. 327–346.

Festinger, L., Schachter, S. and Back, K. W. (1950). *Social Pressures in Informal Groups*. Harper, New York, pp. 33–59.

Festinger, L. and Thibaut, J. (1951). Interpersonal communication in small groups. *Journal of Abnormal and Social Psychology*, **46**, pp. 92–99.

Fiedler, F. E. (1958). *Leader Attitudes and Group Effectiveness*. University of Illinois Press, Urbana, Illinois.

Gerard, H. P. (1954). The anchorage of opinions in face-to-face groups. *Human Relations*, **7**, pp. 313–325.

Goffman, Irving (1959). *The Presentation of Self in Everyday Life*. New York, Doubleday.

Gullahorn, J. T. (1952). Distance and friendship as factors in the gross interaction matrix. *Sociometry*, **15**, pp. 123–134.

Homans, G. C. (1954). The cash posters. *American Sociological Review*, **19**, pp. 729–733.

Israel, J. (1956). Self-evaluation and rejection in groups. *Stockholm Studies in Sociology*, **1**, Almqvist and Wiksell, Stockholm.

Jennings, H. H. (1950). *Leadership and Isolation*. Second Edn, Longmans, Green, New York.

Kelley, H. H. and Shapiro, M. M. (1954). An experiment on conformity to group norms where conformity is detrimental to group achievement. *American Sociological Review*, **19**, pp. 667–677.

Lemann, T. B. and Solomon, R. L. (1952). Group characteristics as revealed in sociometric patterns and personality ratings. *Sociometry*, **15**, pp. 7–90.

Lippitt, R. (1948). A program of experimentation on group functioning and group productivity. *In* W. Dennis, R. Lippit, *et al. Current Trends in Social Psychology*, University of Pittsburg Press, Pittsburg, pp. 14–49.

Moreno, J. L. (1934). *Who Shall Survive?* Nervous Mental Disease Publishing Co., Washington D.C.

Newcomb, T. M. (1956). The prediction of interpersonal attraction. *American Psychologist*, 11, pp. 575–586.

Potashin, R. (1946). A sociometric study of children's friendships. *Sociometry*, 9, pp. 48–70.

Precker, J. A. (1952). Similarity in valuings as a factor in the selection of peers and near-authority figures. *Journal of Abnormal and Social Psychology*, 47, pp. 406–414.

Seashore, Stanley E. (1954). *Group Cohesiveness in the Industrial Work Group*. University of Michigan, Ann Arbor.

Sherif, Muzafer and Sherif, Carolyn W. (1953). *Groups in Harmony and Tension*. Harper and Row, New York, pp. 229–295.

Skinner, B. F. (1938). *The Behaviour of Organisms*. Appleton-Century-Crofts, New York.

Skinner, B. F. (1953). *Science and Human Behaviour*. Macmillan, New York.

Skinner, B. F. (1959). *Cumulative Record*. Appleton-Century-Crofts, New York.

Thibaut, J. (1950). An experimental study of the cohesiveness of under-privileged groups. *Human Relations*, 3, pp. 251–278.

9

Recent Developments of a Theoretical Structure

Introduction

As we have seen, there are a number of weaknesses in the theory as stated in *Social Behaviour*. For example, the measurement of value, the reward scales for different persons, the relationship of social interaction and degree of liking, raise major problems which have still to be resolved. Moreover, it would be quite unrealistic to think that here is a theory consisting of a Euclidean structure amenable to disproof. It is better described as a theory-sketch, the term used by Dumont and Wilson (1967) because the structure has yet to be developed. While there are gaps and tautologies, these have not constituted a strong limitation on subsequent work. George Homans has, characteristically, continued to refine his theoretical statements and they have been elaborated, criticized and discussed by many psychologists and sociologists. Even where there has been no direct testing of his propositions they have influenced the directions of research and provided, at the least, alternative hypotheses. There has been no restriction in applying the propositions in studies using quite different methods. For instance, Homans' propositions provide working hypotheses in a participant-observer study in the Dutch navy (Lammers, 1967); in a study by observation and interviews of steel workers and managers (Chadwick-Jones, 1969) and in studies of young children by classroom observation and experimental teaching methods (Hamblin, Buckholdt, Ferritor, Kozloff and Blackwell, 1971). Later in the chapter the applications of the theory to computer models and other attempts to build its internal logical structure will be discussed. Furthermore, Homans' notions have been applied to the experimental paradigm of game theory and to factorial designs, so that the theory is perhaps unique in its extremely wide influence.

Homans' recent exposition has led him closer to the model of Thibaut and Kelley and further from sociological explanations. In his discussion of the five basic propositions in Smelser (1967) he uses the payoff matrix introduced by Thibaut and Kelley to illustrate his own propositions. Again, Homans (1970) moves towards psychological explanations, and towards the viewpoint of Thibaut and Kelley on calculative decisions, when he presents what he calls *a rationality proposition* to explain individual choice, arguing that choice is a result of *perceived value* multiplied by the *probability* of gaining a particular outcome. This tendency is currently found in Homans' (1974) revision of his theory to include frustration-aggression explanations, which he regards as basic. His capacity for continual rethinking and explicit restatement allows us to clarify the similarities and dissimilarities with other exchange theories: the former in his treatment of the Thibaut and Kelley matrix (Homans, 1967, 1974) and the latter in his counter-argument to Blau (Homans, 1970, 1974).

Homans and Thibaut and Kelley

Kelley (1972) acknowledges that he and Thibaut were influenced by Homans' *Human Group* in writing their *Social Psychology of Groups* and Homans has since returned the compliment. In Chapters 4 and 6 I drew attention to the cross-references they made to each other's work. Thibaut and Kelley attempted a translation of Homans' propositions on interaction and liking. Homans commented on the similarity of his distinction between satisfaction and profit and the distinction made by Thibaut and Kelley between the comparison level (CL) and the comparison level for alternatives ($CL_{alt.}$). This similarity lies especially in the explanation of withdrawal from a relationship where, it is assumed, rewards have dropped below the $CL_{alt.}$ and the individual tries to find an alternative. In Homans' terminology this occurs at the point of zero profit where costs rise to an equivalent level with reward and, since costs are always assessed as alternatives forgone, we are now very near to the notion of $CL_{alt.}$. However, as I mentioned in Chapter 8 that there was an interesting difference between the two explanations of the withdrawal point. Homans does allow for a situation where perceived rewards (in Thibaut and Kelley's terms, the CL) may be high but the person's costs are also high and the pressure to move to alternatives is great, notwithstanding the high level of rewards.

At its most fundamental, Homans' theory emphasizes the influence of past differential reinforcement on present action and on the evaluation of likely outcomes: how an action is evaluated may often depend on whether it has been rewarded in the past. Thibaut and Kelley give a more general reference to past learning which influences the values assigned to rewards. Both have similar derivations in learning theory when they give importance to this evaluative process which as Bandura (1969) has suggested "becomes relatively independent of external reinforcement and the specific contingencies of the original training situation . . ." (Bandura, 1969, p. 34). However, while Thibaut and Kelley attach significance to this long term influence on the values assigned by an actor to a particular outcome in their matrix, the arbitrary nature of the matrix representation appears clearly if we attempt to apply it to a continuous process of interaction (see Chapter 3, p. 43). *Now* in the immediate situation the matrix does not represent the influence of repeated rewards, of satiation and fatigue. These "sequential" effects are undoubtedly important, comment Thibaut and Kelley (p. 19), but they have to disregard them: and so the influence of differential reinforcements during the interaction process is not captivated in the matrix. There is no equivalent here to Homans' Proposition 4 (the more often a rewarding activity is received . . . the less valuable any further unit becomes).

While there is common ground at a very general level, Homans (1967a, 1974) has taken up some interesting adaptations of the payoff matrices from the Thibaut and Kelley model. In Fig. 9 he illustrates a co-operative exchange: by co-operating both parties gain equally over the remaining alternative of not entering the exchange at all. An explanation derived from Proposition 3, stating the return of *value* for *value*, would predict that the participants are each likely to take such action as is represented in the maximum outcome cells of the matrix.

From this simple illustration, Homans (1967a, 1974) continues with a discussion of power where he uses the matrix to illustrate more complex effects. Again, the two theories are seen to approach each other when Homans takes up the possibilities of *alternative* ways of getting rewards as well as *alternative rewards* and he discusses the change from one form of behaviour to another, the change to an alternative. Now,

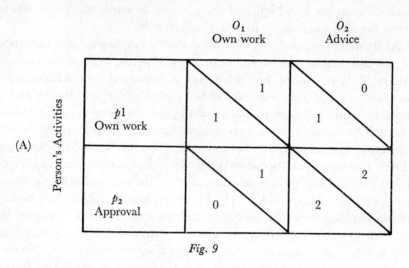

Fig. 9

instead of an equal outcome out of co-operation between two persons, Homans presents a matrix, shown in Fig. 10, where Person A has more to gain than Person B, by entering into an exchange. For B doing his own work brings just as much reward as giving advice to A, whereas the

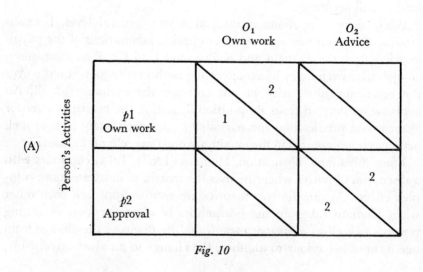

Fig. 10

latter stands to gain by persuading B to give his advice in return for deference or approval.

He next suggests that Person A will decide to change and to increase the value of his approval so that the value proposition ("the more valuable the reward of an activity is to a person, the more likely he is to perform the activity") operates for Person B, as in Fig. 11.

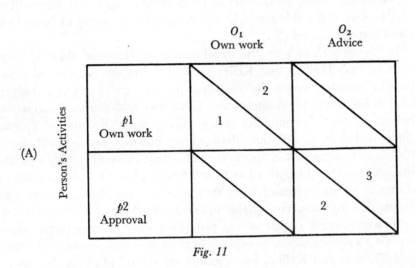

Fig. 11

Person A has had to change his behaviour to get the same advice as before from Person B who now gives it on better terms. Homans concludes that B is the person with more power. This is similar to the *behaviour control* option described by Thibaut and Kelley (see Chapter 3, pp. 37–42). In *behaviour control*, however, there may be no exchange since behaviour may be the kind of pseudo-contingency where each party pursues his personal aims and the other's activity is of minor importance to him. (This was discussed in Chapter 4, p. 13) Homans claims he takes a further step than Thibaut and Kelley by considering the relative advantages of *both* parties. He discusses the relative gain for each in changing from *own work* to *advice* or to *approval*, and he considers also how the relationship might settle over time into a stable transaction.

Homans states a general condition for differences in power; referring to the change made by one party to improve the grade of approval he gives to the other: "the party to the exchange who gets the lesser net reward from it is less likely to change his behaviour than is the other party" (Homans, 1967a, p. 53). Later, he elaborates on this and refers to it as *the principle of perceived least interest*, citing Thibaut and Kelley who make this identical point when they say that a person can "dictate the conditions of association whose interest in the continuation of the affair is least" (Thibaut and Kelley, 1959, p. 103). Again the convergence of the three social exchange theories is apparent when Blau (1964) argues for this effect in his discussion of courtship behaviour (see Chapters 12 and 13).

It becomes clear with the development of Homans' thinking that both he and Thibaut and Kelley set high importance on the alternatives in exchange and in the conditions producing changes from a given kind of behaviour to an alternative. Changes could happen because the behaviour itself becomes less attractive, possibly because of fatigue (increased costs) or satiation (diminishing returns) as stated in Proposition 4; or because of the appearance of a new, more attractive alternative. A tendency in both cases to attempt explanation of the point of change,* or to recognize it as an unresolved problem, leads one to expect that in future research this aspect of behaviour will be emphasized.

In summary, a review of the published work during recent years reveals a convergence between the explanatory statements of Homans and Thibaut and Kelley; investigators are often influenced by one or the other, but often they give references to both. In Chapters 5, 6 and 11 recent publications are discussed which give joint reference to Homans, Thibaut and Kelley.

Homans has also drawn closer to other theories in social psychology. In his chapter in Smelser (1967) he recognizes that much of reciprocal behaviour could be predicted by assumptions of balance in social relationships and of consonance in attitudes. He points out that, if a relationship is rewarding or if it is punishing, it tends to be consistently so. Persons who reward each other tend in further communications to add rewards and there is "a certain strain toward consistency" since "it is rather difficult, although not impossible, to keep on interacting with a person who rewards in one way and punishes in another"

---

* See Chapter 3, pp. 29–33, for the views of Thibaut and Kelley on the decision or choice points of game theory and the difficulty in applying such concepts to social behaviour.

CHANGES IN THE CONTENT OF HOMANS' THEORY

(Homans, 1967a, p. 46). In this respect, his position is seen to be closely allied with the general approach of balance theory (Heider, 1958) and its cognitive dissonance branch (Festinger, 1957). Later on, we will see in some detail how many investigations refer both to balance theory and to exchange theory as providing equivalent explanations.

Changes in the content of Homans' theory

Homans has made modifications in the propositions since the publication of *Social Behavior* (1961). He has elaborated and added to them and in his revision (1974) he has incorporated the frustration-aggression hypothesis into the general propositions. Let us take some instances of the modifications to date. Homans (1967a, 1967, 1974) changes the order of Propositions 1 and 2, calling them the *success proposition* (originally Proposition 2) and the *stimulus proposition* (originally Proposition 1). The wording of the propositions is also slightly altered, particularly in the success proposition where he substitutes for frequency of activity, its greater likelihood. Thus, in place of the original proposition "the more often within a given period of time a man's activity rewards the activity of another the more often the other will emit the activity" he prefers the abbreviated proposition: "the more often a person's activity is rewarded, the more likely he is to perform the activity" (Homans, 1967a, p. 33).

As I mentioned at the start of this chapter, Homans (1970, 1974) introduces a *rationality proposition* which carries the meaning that an individual's choice between alternative actions is likely to be the one for which he perceives the value of the result multiplied by the probability of getting it, is the greater. If follows that the larger is the excess of probability $\times$ value for one action over another the more likely he is to take it. The assumption of rationality appeared in a fairly explicit statement in *Social Behaviour* (p. 71) and was discussed in the previous chapter (Chapter 8, p. 173) where the implications of calculative decisions were fully considered. Although the rationality proposition refers to estimates of value and probability, Homans recognizes that a man's decision may not be made in his own long-term best interest. A person's choice will thus be for the alternative with greater value and probability "as perceived by him at the time" and he may not choose what is apparently the optimal, or what is best for him by somebody else's standard. The recent and explicit references to a rationality proposition do not therefore add to the earlier development of the theory, so much as they elaborate on what was already present in it.

Criticism of Homans' theory

During the period since 1961 there have been a number of criticisms of the theory which it may be profitable to consider. One of them is the constructive point that the effects of partial or variable rewards were not incorporated by Homans into his propositions. As he had taken other reinforcement notions from learning theory, why not this one? Deutsch and Krauss (1965) mention this in their sharp critique of Homans' theory which pre-empts much of the criticism made subsequently. They refer to the missed opportunity of including one of the most effective of the Skinnerian notions, that of intermittent reinforcement schedules. Recently, Singer (1971) takes this up again, commenting on Proposition 3 (the more value . . . the more often) and Proposition 4 (the more often . . . the less value) and considering at the same time the principle originally postulated by Skinner that responses learned under partial reinforcement are more difficult to extinguish than behaviour reinforced continually. Singer implies that Homans should have added a proposition intermediate to Propositions 3 and 4 and indeed this is the criticism of Deutsch and Krauss: that Homans has not allowed for the strong effects of intermittent rewards.

Suggesting an example, Singer argues from such a general proposition through to the descriptive hypothesis that in families of several children "maternal warmth and approval, given less often to the first child as he reaches the age of three or so, are more valuable to him, and, in turn, lead him more often to behave in ways that will elicit warmth and approval" (p. 33). This is the kind of hypothesis, derived from an intermittent-reward proposition, that could well be confirmed by observational studies: Singer leaves the possibility there, but the hypothesis has already been tested in school situations by Hamblin *et al.* (1971) using an exchange theory approach to learning, and in several other studies (see p. 275 below).

Some criticism has been very sweeping. For instance, Wilson (1970) has doubts about the entire enterprise of deductive explanatory schemes such as those of Homans or Blau, because the data that the deductive theory must explain are not objective in the sense that the word is used to describe data in the natural sciences. The meaning of what is done by the actors in a social situation cannot be captured in a similar objective way, argues Wilson, the description has to be interpretative and tentative; for instance, the data are not what the actor perceives but what the observer infers of the actor's perceptions. Literal description is not possible. Wilson mentions the difficulties in interpreting measures, and in establishing the unequivocal meaning of a social process. He urges more attention to choice and purpose in the actor, but warns that the work of interpreting overt appearances will not yield an adequate description compatible with the logic of deductive explanations. A weakness in Wilson's argument is that he does not give a lead to an alternative approach to replace what he attacks. He merely proposes that more careful methods be used in data collection. Wilson's attack is thus drawn to familiar methodological difficulties and does not carry against the theory itself. Furthermore, there is no reason why a deductive attempt may not encourage precise statement of hypotheses and an orderly effort to test them.

In the mid-sixties Homans (1964) and Zetterberg (1965) discussed the merits and problems of deductive theory, as did Costner and Leik (1964). This discussion suggests that pursuing the general principles of a formal deductive system does not give an immediately satisfactory structure. Liska (1969) follows on from this earlier work to show how tautologies are present in Homans' theory. Liska argues that tautologies (admittedly he defines them in a special sense) have definite advantages; yet their presence affirms that the construction of deductive explanation is not so inflexible or impeccable a matter as Wilson assumes. Maris (1970) is extremely critical of the internal structure of Homans' theory, while he concedes that its present incomplete stage of development still marks a considerable advance. I shall discuss the views of Liska and Maris in some detail in this chapter.

A general criticism of social exchange theory is made by Stanley (1968), in the course of which he argues that both Homans and Blau assume that prestige or status is a scarce resource "capable of functioning as an all-purpose medium of exchange equivalent to money in a material economy" (p. 859). Homans does not say this. The statement is more extreme than can justifiably be adduced from Homans' discussion, and it is difficult to assess Stanley's further criticism that there is no intensive analysis in Blau's, and therefore in Homans', treatment without knowing what he has in mind in using the term "intensive". Certainly Homans has treated several aspects of status quite thoroughly.

When Stanley points out that exchange theory is useful only if one wants a theory to mirror the social organization of "a market society", he over-emphasizes the dependence of Homans' theory on economics. Homans does use a number of analogies with economics and shows how economic concepts can be applied so that they appear to explain psychological transactions, such as the degree of approval given to someone who provides a reward in scarce supply (see Chapter 8, pp. 181–3). However, value, frequency and justice which are his basic concepts are not deducible from economics, even if there are similarities between the explanations of elementary economics and elementary social behaviour. A frequent criticism of exchange theory is that it is based on an economic model, as if this involves a strictly economic qua materialistic interpretation. But Homans and the other exchange theorists do not exclude non-material values, such as (for example) self-denial and there is no reason why the influence of self-denial on individual choice should not be observed in experimental or natural situations (see *Altruistic Behaviour* below). Homans argues that the influences on social interaction are not comprehended by a narrow hedonist interpretation, which he himself does not accept (see Chapter 8, pp. 158, 169).*

The restriction of the theory to explaining social relations as an exchange of certain rewards—approval, liking, or conformity—results from a methodological constraint. Homans' explanatory propositions are contingent on empirical measures, and on values which can be scaled in an ordinal ranking. The theory must ultimately rely on descriptive statements with some statistical treatment of observations and its content is confined by this requirement. Nevertheless, Homans does offer starting propositions which touch on the values of equity and altruism and they have provoked lively and controversial research in recent years, which I shall discuss later.

Another general comment on social exchange theories is made by Weinstein, DeVaughan and Wiley (1969) who cite Homans, Blau and Thibaut and Kelley. They mention that exchange theory is not explicit "in specifying parameters" affecting rewards and costs. Their criticism is less valid because Weinstein *et al.* refer, not to *Social Behaviour*, but to the earlier *Human Group*. In this earlier book, the theoretical development stopped at empirical generalizations. Deutsch (1964) has said of these generalizations "there would be no difficulty in citing excep-

---

* The point that altruism is by no means excluded from exchange theory has also been made, with reference to the Thibaut and Kelley model, in Chapter 3, p. 50.

tions and counterevidence to them" (p. 157) and he comments that they merely refer to frequently observed relationships with "the contingent conditions determining the occurrence or non-occurrence of the expected relationship being unspecified" (p. 157). Thus, the criticism by Weinstein *et al.* repeats this, although Deutsch's views could lead to the further possibility that, if the contingent conditions are specified, a more reputable theory will develop.

Weinstein *et al.* attempted to create experimental conditions of one creditor and one debtor in dyads in order to explore the consequences of imbalance in exchange (we can note the affinity with balance theory) and the obligations upon the person who is beneficiary to restore parity. Those who cannot do so incur inferiority as a cost. Weinstein *et al.* now emphasize that the cost of deferring to another is a function of the person's own esteem. Thus, their first hypothesis is that a person's self-esteem and the degree of deference he grants to another, will be positively related. Their second hypothesis refers to a contrast between the forms of return of obligations, to friends and to strangers. In the case of friends they suggest that the "payment" may be put off until some later time but, for strangers, deference will be expressed straight away. The method of content analysis which they used for rating deference, from tape recordings, is not clearly described. This obscures the meaning of the results although they do show the opposite of the prediction by the second hypothesis—friends immediately express gratitude. A number of alternative hypotheses, contradictory but equally plausible, are considered. Next comes the point of main importance. Weinstein *et al.* illustrate the divergent interpretations that can be made under the framework of exchange theory and conclude that the theory "is not sufficiently articulated to provide firm guidelines for specific deductions", complaining that it is always possible to posit exchange after the fact. However, it must be said that, in this experiment, there was little control over the content of the exchange (if it is exchange). Weinstein *et al.* have a worthwhile aim in attempting to reveal evidence for the exchange of psychological rewards in return for material ones, a relatively unexplored topic. They blame exchange theory for not providing a firm prediction of specific outcomes, but perhaps the solution lies in further attempts on the empirical problem.

A matter of tautology

In a similar vein of criticism, but more pointedly, Doreian and Stockman (1969) take Homans' treatment of distributive justice, a notion to which they (questionably) attribute relative autonomy from the rest of his theoretical work, and they express criticisms of the principle that a person expects a just return, mainly by arguing that provision is lacking for "independent criteria of the equivalence between investment and reward, other than the presence or absence of the dependent variable" (p. 55). Although they do not refer to it, they are repeating the criticism made by Deutsch (1964) and Deutsch and Krauss (1965) who state: "Homans is in the position of defining a value as that which is valued, paralleling the Skinnerian circularity of a reinforcer as that which reinforces" (Deutsch, 1964, p. 161; Deutsch and Krauss, 1965, p. 115).

Doreian and Stockman claim that Homans' "theory is either tautologous, with exchange effectively defined as interaction, or it is empirically false" (p. 55). They seem to misunderstand the functions of Homans' theoretical terms and the approach advocated by Braithwaite (1953) which Homans largely follows. We have seen in Chapter 2, that the question of independent measurement of variables *is* a point which is *usually* made concerning tautologies, but it should also be mentioned that both Braithwaite (1953) and Liska (1969) have argued for the opposing viewpoint that "empty" variables may be an advantage, at a particular stage of theory construction. This seems a good point at which to discuss the meaning of tautologies and their place in theoretical development, with special reference to exchange theory.

Let us consider the criticism that Homans' theory is tautologous. It is sometimes assumed that by merely stating this criticism, the theory is shown to be faulty. Liska has considered the criticism very carefully and he concludes that there are two kinds of tautology. In the first, the empirical content of the two main terms of a proposition is the same, and the tautology is merely an exercise in relabelling. This is the usual meaning of a *logical* tautology. But Liska shows that there is another class of statement which he calls a *relational* tautology.

He illustrates this by taking Skinner's first proposition: "If the occurrence of an operant is followed by the presence of a reinforcement, the strength is increased" (Skinner, 1938, p. 62). If, for the term *rein-*

forcement, its definition is substituted in the brackets, it will now read: "if the occurrence of an operant is followed by the presence of (a stimulus which produces the resulting change in strength), the strength is increased". Liska continues with an illustration of the tautological property of Homans' Proposition 2, pointing out that it has been admitted by Homans (1964, pp. 953–955) that the antecedent condition (value) is not defined independently of the consequent condition (frequency of activity). But Homans claims that tautologies are useful and refers to the example of force in mechanics "as it appears in the equation: $f = ma$. In the interpretation of this equation, force is not defined independently of mass (m) and acceleration (a)" (Homans, 1964, pp. 953–954 and Homans, 1974, p. 34). Nevertheless, it is possible to substitute for f a number of different force functions, such as that of gravitation, and the work of explanation is advanced. Force is therefore an open concept, an empty variable which allows the accumulation of empirical knowledge.

Thus, the general proposition is tautological on the theoretical but not on the operational level. The antecedent term is not theoretically defined independently of the consequent one, but neither is the antecedent defined by the *same* operations as the consequent term. Still, the only way the antecedent can be validated is by correlating it with the consequent term, and so the tautology remains (different in kind from relabelling, it is true). Thus the first term is what Liska calls an open concept, or empty variable. Liska emphasizes that tautologies are often made the grounds for criticism, yet, if they are regarded in the relational sense, they are basic to successful theories.

Liska sees a paradox in criticizing the presence of tautologies in social psychology while, say, in economics they are frequently employed. He considers that at an early stage of theoretical development it may be most important to aim for definition of content in the concepts used; it is more appropriate, at the moment, in social psychology to use open concepts. By leaving the concept open it is possible to incorporate into the theory a variety of empirical findings. He points out that Homans' argument is quite clear on this. The higher-order propositions may be tautological in the relational sense, but the open concept can be filled empirically, and this would "leave the various conditions that create differences in value in particular circumstances to be described by lower-order propositions. . . ." (Homans, 1964, p. 954). Such a concept is said to be implicitly defined (see Braithwaite, 1953, p. 77).

s.e.t.—8

It will be helpful to examine Homans' (1964, 1974) treatment of this problem. He relies to a large extent on Braithwaite's (1953) fuller discussion of tautologies, and on the view that explicit definition would prevent the empirical extension of a theory. Braithwaite shows that, in the case of a theory starting from rather loose, tautological general statements, such extension easily occurs. He argues that, if a theory is to explain, in the future, more generalizations than was originally possible, then it must have freedom in its theoretical terms, more than would be the case were they to be logical constructions, strictly defined, out of observable entities. Homans (1964) now emphasizes the importance of implicit rather than explicit definition. This is also the issue of *nominal* versus *real* definitions, which has concerned some sociologists (Zetterberg, 1965). Homans gives an illustration from social psychology: group cohesiveness is a term which has a part in some theories similar to the one which value has in Proposition 2. Cohesiveness is defined nominally in the higher-order proposition—the more cohesive a group the more its members will take part in its activities. The simiarity of this to the term value in Proposition 2 is that there is no single measure of group cohesiveness independent of the participation of the members. Various lower-order propositions are brought into the theory, each stating what makes for cohesiveness under particular circumstances: the number of friendship choices within a group, the value of rewards obtained from group activities and so on.

Now we can return to Liska's argument. In relational tautologies, one term is an open concept and is only evaluated by the extent to which it correlates with measures of the second term, which it is employed to explain. This has the consequence that if a hypothesized index of the first term does not correlate with a measure of the second, then rather than reject the theory, *the hypothesis that the index is valid* is rejected. The empirical testing of a hypothesis involves only the index and not the theory. For example, in the case of Skinner's reinforcement proposition referred to earlier, the concept of reinforcement serves to integrate the many conditions which produce reinforcing effects; those conditions which do not increase the strength or frequency of response, will simply not be conceptualized as reinforcers and so Skinner's general proposition is not itself shown to be invalid. The two terms are related to each other in a proposition which is "tautological"* but, because of this very fact, growth and extension of the theory may be achieved (or

* In the special sense of a relational tautology.

at least a cataloguing of contemporary rewards or costs). Lastly, Liska suggests that the proposition can be evaluated by the degree to which it generates descriptive hypotheses in a parsimonious system without too many special conditions for anomalous findings; although a tautological proposition cannot be directly disconfirmed, it is subject to the rule of parsimony so well enunciated by Kuhn (1970).

If we take the point of these views, as they have been expressed by Braithwaite, Homans and Liska, a frequently cited criticism (see, for instance, Abrahamsson, 1970) of exchange theory loses its edge. The view that exchange theory is so loose and tautological that it cannot be disconfirmed, is now answered by the use of relational tautologies as a stratagem.

The sociologists Burgess and Akers (1966) discuss the tautological aspects of Skinner's reinforcement proposition and one of their comments is worth noting. They take the more conventional view that a statement is not a tautology if it can be tested empirically and exceptions found. They continue:

> One exception does not falsify the theory; a number (as yet unspecified) must be found. If the empirical exceptions accumulate to such an extent that they render the theory useless for explaining a large range of behaviour, then we conclude that the theory is wrong in too many cases, and hence falsified (p. 308).

This is a view which has long been familiar in the psychological literature. A very similar argument was stated by Meehl (1950) under what he called the *Weak Law of Effect** which asserts that all reinforcers are effective irrespective of the particular situation. A failure of this law to hold in given instances would mean that the investigator could

> specify the exceptions and would hope to be able to generalize about them, that is, to discover empirically what are the kinds of reinforcers, or kinds of differences among situations, which reveal its invalidity (Meehl, 1950, p. 62).

In more recent discussions of reinforcement and the law of effect, the approach by "cataloguing" reinforcers or non-reinforcers is regarded pessimistically. Premack (1965) remarks that it has never been implemented because "the claim of two classes was never seen to be a claim of any empirical consequence. The fact was too trivial to merit test"

---

* Meehl also gives the *Strong Law of Effect* as "Every learned increment in response strength requires the operation of a trans-situational reinforcer" (Meehl, 1950, p. 64).

(p. 131). Discussing animal experiments, Premack mentions that no list has ever been drawn up of a class of events that have been shown not to be reinforcing. He adds that it is easy to recognize some reinforcers, like food, as general or trans-situational without the effort of cataloguing and he concludes that because this was so self-evident "probably not even a master's thesis was devoted to it" (p. 131). Voss (1971) points out that support for the law of effect comes from experiments in highly restrictive situations and that "the frequency with which animals and men in non-laboratory situations repeat punished actions and fail to repeat rewarded ones is so great that, as a statistical generalization, an empirical law of effect is all but vacuous" (p. 26). While these were criticisms expressed about reinforcement theory in S–R experiments, they are relevant to Homans' basic assumptions because his starting propositions largely state reinforcement effects. Nevertheless, the counter-argument resting on the use of relational tautologies is a productive one and favours the kind of research in actual situations described by Opsahl and Dunnette (1966). They focus their attention on the likely effects of pay on work behaviour, examining the role of money, for instance, as a generalized reinforcer because of its repeated pairing with primary reinforcers. While they show that the evidence in occupational studies is inconclusive, they discuss several theories including Adams' (1963, 1965) applications of Homans' propositions, particularly as these two authors examine rewards in the context of notions of equity and inequity. They note Adams' interesting demonstration of the tendency for overpaid workers to increase the amount of work performed. (See also below, pp. 242–248.)

Logical structure

Homans (1961) aims at building up a deductive structure, and has given a consistent set of explanations with at least a sketch of what the theory may become. Dumont and Wilson (1967) suggested the term "theory sketch" for several theories including that of Homans in the positive sense that an outline sketch gives direction, despite its vagueness and its "imprecision of definitions and empirical indicators" (p. 988). Homans has since re-emphasized (1964, 1967a, 1970, 1974) his intention to derive hypotheses explaining observed behaviour, from a small number of general explanatory statements; and he has held to it despite the criticisms I have summarized in the preceding section. And despite others, which I will now discuss, focusing on the internal content and structure of the theory itself.

There have been two main attempts to discuss the logical structure of the theory, by Maris (1970) and Blain (1971).* Maris approaches the theory as a philosopher of science and aims at refining the theory by applying the rules of symbolic logic. The main fault in his attempt is that he fails to refer the logical structure of higher-order propositions to the contingent hypotheses and social observations they are meant to explain. It is no exaggeration to say that concern only with structural relations has led Maris into a somewhat perverse diminution of the aims of the original theory, as we shall see in a moment. Nevertheless, what he has done should be taken seriously as part of the very necessary discussion of form and derivation of explanatory statements. I shall comment on the most useful parts of Maris' critical discussion and the counter-criticisms which have followed, by Gray (1971), Price (1971) and Turner (1971). Afterwards it may be possible to assess the present logical status of the theory. In the remainder of the chapter we will turn to the most recent empirical work which the theory has influenced.

Maris (1970) makes a formal examination of the logical adequacy of the theory. What difference to scholarship or empirical investigation, he asks, would an adequate theory make? He gives the answer that it would integrate many apparently unrelated propositions; it would be the means of discovering new empirical associations. Maris lists 23 of Homans' theorems,† and attempts to deduce others which are not specified by Homans. According to Maris these suggest empirical associations which are neither obvious nor trivial.‡ Thus, Maris considers Homans' theory to be useful "even if it is logically, operationally and empirically inadequate ... the attempt is as important as the result" (p. 1070) because it has begun an analytical procedure which can be developed further. Also, Maris grants that Homans offers at least a system to reject, encouraging argument and counter-formulation

---

* Blain's critique deals mainly with the view stated by Homans that there are no sociological general propositions which cannot be derived from psychological propositions and is discussed in Chapter 14 under the Reduction question.

† By "theorem" Maris means a proposition deduced logically.

‡ Maris suggests theorems on social approval, esteem, rank, and authority. For example, he states $(+O \text{ e } P) \rightarrow (+O \text{ sa } P)$, $(+O \text{ sa } P) \rightarrow (+P \text{ rk } O)$: "Having a disproportionate share of social approval, P tends to be esteemed by Other. In the latter case the more O esteems P, the more P ranks above O and, thus, has more authority over O" (p. 1079).

to take place. He makes the criticism that Homans has not followed through his aim for the construction of theory, he has not expressed the propositions and their inter-relationships as a formal logical structure.

Maris argues that the theoretical structure which Homans puts forward in *Social Behaviour* is no advance on the point reached in *The Human Group* where there are only two levels of structure—descriptive statements and the empirical generalizations derived from them. Maris points out that deduction "implies premises manipulated in accordance with the rule of inference. At best, Homans is setting up equivalences, at worst tautologies" (p. 1075). Maris mentions that Homans' explanations have only two kinds of proposition, giving as an instance Proposition 1. This states the influence of similar past situations associated with rewards (see Chapter 8, p. 159). He claims that the descriptive proposition immediately follows: "the presence of congenial persons encourages conformity to the social norms valued by those persons"— with no other proposition between the two. But Maris is mistaken in referring to this as a descriptive proposition: it is not a descriptive statement, it is a corollary of the general propositions. However, Maris has omitted other propositions in the deductive chain. For instance, there are the corollaries that conformity to a norm is rewarding to others, that approval is a reward in general usage, that others will, in return for conformity, tend to render approval.

But Maris' attack can be considered in a further example, which he himself supplies when he cites Homans' statement that

> People who compete with one another are in a position to deprive one another of rewards, and the withdrawal of a reward stimulates the emotional reactions of hostility and aggression (*Social Behaviour*, p. 144).

Maris holds that it is subsumed under Proposition 5 which states the emotional response as a consequence of injustice, and therefore he indicates that only two levels of deduction are involved. In fact, Maris does less than justice to Homans' efforts because, as I shall show, there are at least three levels in this instance. Usually, the theoretical argument of *Social Behaviour* starts from the basic propositions, then presents corollaries which introduce specific given conditions and ends with descriptive or operational statements. Maris has said that only two kinds of propositions are required in the above example, which he has chosen as illustrative of Homans' explanations. Actually, there are three. Maris claims that the two propositions are as follows: The first is Proposition

5, "The more to a man's disadvantage the rule of distributive justice fails of realisation, the more likely he is to display the emotional behaviour we call anger", and the second is the further explanatory proposition: "People who compete with one another are in a position to deprive one another of rewards, and the withdrawal of a reward stimulates the emotional reactions of hostility and aggression."

I would like to demonstrate more fully what I have already mentioned in the instance of conforming behaviour. While Homans has not set up a formal structure of logical steps, other assumptions, corollaries and general statements are certainly to be found in his exposition. If they were to be stated as corollaries they would probably be as follows:

Withdrawal of rewards is, by the rule of distributive justice, perceived as the withdrawal of something due to a person from another.

In competition between persons, where attainment of a desired object by one person involves its withdrawal from another the conditions of perceived injustice will prevail.

It follows that in competition between persons then the emotional reaction of hostility on the part of one or other of the parties is likely to occur.

And only at this point is it appropriate to introduce a descriptive statement of an actual situation of competition, where conditions for perceived injustice hold. This might, in an experiment, take the form of the description that: "Person A expresses rejection, on a sociometric test, for his competitor, Person B", or in a natural situation it might be observed that: "Person A declines to offer congratulations to his competitor, Person B, after the latter has achieved a scientific award."

This seems to defeat Maris' contention that Homans has used only two levels of logical structure. It is significant that Maris does not introduce a true descriptive statement at the level of empirical observation. As we shall see, his attempt to elaborate on the logical structure of the theory and to apply logical rules founders because of this same mistake. He forgets that ultimately the theory is contingent on its meaning in specific contexts of social observation. I will consider Maris' applications of structural rules, in a moment.

To summarize, the extent of Maris' criticism of Homans goes no further than an attack on Homans for not having spelled out the deductive steps formally. Maris claims that all Homans has done is to recognize that a particular relationship is an instance of some general proposition. But, in *Social Behaviour*, as was illustrated in Chapter 8 (see p. 192) a chain of inferences must, and can, be found between these propositions and the relationships represented by empirical description, if the empirical findings are to be explained. All the same, Maris has a sound point when he concludes that the logical structure is not made clear in *Social Behaviour* and there are "suppressed premises" and "incomplete arguments, which is not to say they cannot be supplied" (p. 1075).

More than this, what has Maris really achieved? He has made an examination of Homans' propositions by applying rules of elementary logic: he has used the following syllogistic procedures: for example, *conversion, transposition* and *material equivalence*, as defined by Copi (1961).

Let us examine one or two instances of these. *Transposition* is made from the statement $-V \rightarrow +A$ (as value diminishes, anger increases) to the statement $-A \rightarrow +V$ (the less anger the more value) or, again, from $-r \rightarrow -L$ (the less reward the less liking) to $+L \rightarrow +r$ (the more liking the more reward). Apart from the truncated nature of these symbolic statements, the question soon arises of whether it is appropriate to apply syllogistic rules to propositions referring to events which, at the descriptive level, are expressed as statistical probabilities.

The disparity now appears between the logical rules and the empirical meaning. For example, Maris argues that the rule of distributive justice is equivalent to a *universal affirmative*. According to Maris the rule of distributive justice can be stated as follows: $(+PvO) \rightarrow (+OvP)$—in ordinary language, the more valuable to Other the activity he gets or expects from Person, the more valuable to Person the activity Other gives to him.* This affirmative, Maris argues, is a proposition of the same kind as the universal statement "all dogs are animals". The converse statement of such a universal affirmative proposition is only possible by limitation, so that in this instance the universal is *converted (by limitation)* to "some animals are dogs". Similarly, by this limitation rule it would be incorrect to state $(+OvP) \rightarrow (+PvO)$ because "all that can be *logically* inferred from the rule of distributive justice is that some OvP is PvO" (Maris, 1970, p. 1075). Maris uses Venn diagrams to illustrate the point that while one may say that everything in the class PvO is also in the class OvP, it cannot be said that all OvP is PvO.

---

* However, it would be correct to say that the rule of distributive justice is not concerned with subjective value but with the relative amounts of a particular good two persons get, as perceived by them.

Maris concludes that as Homans' propositions become particularistic, by the limitation rule, the converse proposition cannot therefore be used for further inference.

Although this is an interesting exercise, it can be quite easily objected that general propositions, stating probabilities, can hardly be universal affirmatives. The propositions of the theory must connect up with empirical relations. *In an empirical sense* the converse of the proposition discussed above is the *same proposition* seen from the point of view of the other person in a reciprocal relationship; it is merely a reiteration of the proposition from the second person's point of view. Translating this social relationship into Venn diagrams for classes and sets seems to place too much burden on the empirical meaning. It is also inappropriate because the empirical relationship of Person to Other is lost in the translation. Empirically, this proposition and its "converse" turn out to be the same proposition when taken, necessarily, to hold for each of the parties in a relationship. I have suggested that there can be no claim for such a proposition to be a universal affirmative—it is a matter of statistical probabilities. In a later note, Maris (1971) has now accepted this conclusion, arriving by means of a somewhat devious logical statement at a conclusion which is so obvious in an empirical sense.

To begin with, let us assume that there is a collection of people denoted by the symbols $Q_1 \ldots Q_m$, where $M \geqslant 2$ and that "P" and "O" are used as generic names for individuals from that collection. In a given line of proof (unless quantified universally) each use of "P" refers to the same specific individual in the collection (likewise for "O"). When "P" and "O" appear in the same line, they refer to different people. With this convention we can interchange "P" and "O" in any proposition . . . (Maris, 1971, p. 714).

Several counter-arguments to the proof which Maris attempted, have since appeared. Gray (1971) has made the criticism that the logical calculus which Maris uses does not permit an interpretation in time-order, yet the propositions do incorporate a time sequence of actions. Including a time dimension should considerably restrict the use of the logical rules which Maris applied since they were not developed for time-order conditions. An instance is the rule of *transposition* which can be used when time-order is not involved, but not when it is, for the following reason. In transposition $+A +B$ is transposed to $-B -A$, the term on the left-hand side of the sentence must precede in time the term on the right-hand side, as in the examples mentioned above. Gray suggests that one cannot have transpositions of terms without violating the time-order and he concludes that Maris has not faced up to the dilemma of preserving *either* a time interpretation *or* the logical rules of inference that he uses. Only in one rule, the Hypothetical Syllogism, does the time-order criticism not apply, in this instance where $P \supset Q$, $Q \supset R$, and therefore $P \supset R$, for the rest, Maris' logical representation of the original five propositions and their corollaries cannot be reconciled with time conditions.

Turner (1971) criticizes Maris's rules of inference on the grounds that they are adaptations of formal logical rules, but Maris does not state what are the new rules; there are no clear criteria for judging their adequacy. Furthermore, by the introduction of symbols the syntactical meaning of the original propositions is lost in a number of instances. Turner is a severe critic of Maris' logical translations: "His symbolisation of Homans' theory is no more than the transformation of an argument in ordinary language to a symbolic pidgin English" (p. 711). One disquieting result mentioned by Turner, is that, applying his logical formulations, Maris arrives at the inconsistency of $+OrP \rightarrow -OrP$ (Maris, 1970, p. 1080)—"the more Person is rewarded by another, the less he is rewarded". He extricates himself only by referring to the temporal sequence "the more rewarding an activity in the past, the less rewarding is future activity" (p. 1080). In a further critical note Price (1971) draws attention to this instance because it shows that Maris allows for temporal sequence to avoid contradiction in his propositions. Price repeats the criticism made by Gray, that the consequence of allowing a temporal sequence is that all inferences depending on logical steps such as transposition are invalidated.

In summary, all three critics agree that Maris does not state which calculus or set of logical rules he is using; that his symbolic statements are not an adequate translation of the propositions; that he confuses the issue by allowing for temporal conditions in an attempt to escape logical inconsistencies. As Price (1971) comments, the deductive procedures which Maris introduces are valid in themselves but "are invalid for the uses he makes of them" (p. 711). The great weakness in applying rules or elementary logic or of Venn diagrams, apart from the inconsistencies which have already been discussed, is that these procedures could be pursued without reference to the empirical aims of the theory and therefore without a constructive outcome. Lastly, I think it worth noting that there is one curious lapse, where Maris represents social approval and liking as different terms in the same sentence, yet Homans uses these terms as equivalent. Here again, we seem to lose touch with empirical referents and this emphasizes the weakness of the translation to symbols. A more effective strategy may be to continue with an informal deduction in ordinary language, from the original propositions. It now seems that Maris' presentation of a list of theorems may be most useful, not so much as a logical structure, but as additions to Homans' propositions leading to further empirical testing.

I have suggested that applying logical rules may be less helpful in theory building, at the moment, than testing the descriptive hypotheses which are derived informally from general propositions. There seems to be a danger that the pursuit of an internal, logical structure can be relatively sterile for systematizing the description of social behaviour. This criticism has been upheld against Maris' translation of probabilistic general statements into the logic of classes and it could also be made against the attempt to translate Homans' theory into mathematical terms. Several mathematical expressions of parts of Homans' theory share the disadvantage that they are scarcely grounded on social measures, which is one reason why they have not been utilized by researchers working with empirical data. As was mentioned in the previous chapter, this is the case of Bartos' (1967) expression of the interaction-liking proposition as a square root function—it remains an arbitrary translation unconnected with data. Coleman (1964) again taking the interaction-liking hypothesis from *The Human Group* is concerned mainly with the possible application of mathematical conventions and with the procedures required for deriving objective values for differential equations. He doubts that such procedures can be applied in social research, but takes the discussion only as far as stating the problems. Simon (1953, 1957) makes a similar internal examination of the mathematical formulae which might clarify the structure of Homans' explanations, and Doreian (1970, p. 150) is fairly cautious about this development. White (1972) discusses the formulations of Simon and Coleman and gives tentative indications of empirical tests which might show whether the mathematical assumptions can be justified.

Simon, Coleman, Bartos and White give their attention to simple, isolated hypotheses, usually the interaction-liking proposition and the translation of periodic changes in the measures representing each term into differential equations. They do not refer to a general theoretical structure, partly because their efforts are based on Homans' early work in *The Human Group* where the explanatory scheme was limited to empirical generalizations. Even now, after publication of *Social Behaviour* and subsequent work, Homans' theory is still at a largely informal stage. Coleman makes the point that until there is a theory with a clear logical structure, mathematical expression will go no further and he remarks that: "It is only when the logical structure of relations between concepts becomes clear and precise that the shift to a formal structure of mathematics is possible" (Coleman, 1964, p. 9).

It is in the nature of mathematical development to abstract from a situation a small number of attributes and to explore the relationships between them (these attributes may be highly influential ones). It is appropriate for mathematicians to do this and for social researchers subsequently to utilize the mathematical expressions for analysis of empirical data. On the whole, the use of algebraic and differential equations by Simon, Coleman and others leaves an open question until such time as empirical work can be undertaken to a point of greater refinement. One cannot be particularly optimistic about this in the short term since it is noticeable that little work has followed the lead which these authors offered.

Other individual efforts have been made at mathematical translations of different kinds. Hamblin and Smith (1966) borrow from psychophysics the S–R law which expresses as a power function the effect of magnitude of stimulus on magnitude of response. They apply this formula in order to analyse status characteristics which operate as stimuli and the subsequent response of esteem, approval. They hope by this mathematical treatment to clarify the inter-relationships between different elements of status, although here again we can note the requirement for improved descriptive analysis. Hamblin (1971) discusses the power function equations and other possibilities referring to exchange theory; he illustrates the shortcomings of some statistics traditionally used in social psychology, where the level of variance accounted for is usually low. He points to what might be done in the future if mathematical procedures are applied to precise experimental measures, emphasizing the rigorous methodology which would satisfy mathematical criteria.

10

Computer Simulation: Homunculus

Introduction

As described in Chapter 8, the methods usually applied to verifying Homans' propositions are the sociometric test, questionnaires with ordinal scales, or counting of frequencies in social communication. In the next chapter, further evidence is presented of more recent work with experimental procedures using the game theory paradigm, and factorial designs devised to test hypotheses derived from the theory, such as those stating different conditions of distributive justice and status. Other hypotheses have appeared as mathematical expressions, especially for degrees of liking as a function of interaction (see Coleman, 1964a). However, there has been one completely novel approach which merits special attention—the attempt by John and Jeanne Gullahorn to translate the theory into computer language. There is a large difference between this computer program and the other methods mentioned. The latter have led to tests of particular hypotheses, whereas the computer simulation is an attempt at a comprehensive model taking in all five of Homans' basic propositions. This work is therefore, potentially, a much more ambitious enterprise; but it is one that has encountered difficulties and more recently has been modified until it approximates more to the hypothesis-testing approach. In order to appreciate its careful development we should consider the computer model from the initial program of 1963 through to its recent modifications.

For John and Jeanne Gullahorn (1963) the work of George Homans as presented in *Social Behaviour* "represents one of the most provocative explanations of human response in interpersonal situations yet published" (p. 375). Applying the major propositions of the theory, they have constructed a program which imitates interpersonal exchange of rewards or costs. Their original programme, called Homunculus, in Information Processing Language, Version V. (see Newell and Simon, 1959) was designed to simulate a simple social interaction sequence representing a dyad. One person gives reward (help) to another in exchange for reward (esteem) from the other; then, as the exchange continues, costs are allocated as degrees of effort or time expended, interruptions or forfeiture of alternative activities. The content of the sequence is taken from the study of office workers by Peter Blau (1955) which plays such a large part, as we have seen in Chapter 8, in Homans' discussion of exchange, especially of *fair* exchange. The Gullahorns present a flow chart as their interpretation of the decisions to be taken by the person with greater skills, whose help is sought by a colleague. Two-person and three-person interaction is programmed to follow a sequence determined by considerations of rewards and costs as predicted from the basic propositions, and thus "the consequences of hooking-up hypothetical process into complex sequences can be observed directly" (Gullahorn and Gullahorn, 1965a, p. 444). At this stage they express the hope that the model "will ultimately contribute to the goal of naturalistic prediction of behaviour in small groups" (Gullahorn and Gullahorn, 1963, p. 376).

Before going into more detail let us consider some of the arguments for or against computer simulation in general. Feigenbaum and Feldman (1963) refer to computer models of social behaviour as an improvement on the few mathematical models which are available. It may be preferable to construct a computer program instead of applying existing mathematical formulations such as the Markov chains theory because such formulations have quite restricted applications and may not be suitable to the problem in question, whereas the computer will allow a tailor-made approach. In addition, Abelson (1968) considers that computer simulations are especially useful when many variables are simultaneously in operation and other methods fail. It is true that computers have especially been used to model behaviour as it might exist in natural settings where large numbers of variables require an orchestrational approach. It is usually assumed that the attempt will be made, subsequently, to match the computer results with observed social behaviour, but this can only be done where there are clear measures in the field situations such as voting behaviour, and there may be relatively few situations which provide suitable measures. A further disadvantage, mentioned by Abelson, is that applications of computers are extremely time-consuming. However, the simulation possibilities are more optimistic if certain features are present. Firstly, what is modelled must be a dynamic process, happening over time, and secondly, there must be well-specified and explicit contingencies. Furthermore, the success of a computer translation, as seen by Abelson, depends on how far the following features are incorporated—units, properties, inputs, processes, phasing, consequences. The units and properties are stored in computer memory, the inputs are presented from punch cards or magnetic tape, the processes are actuated within the computer as "sub routines" under the phasing specified by the "executive routine" or program; the consequences are output by the computer, in card, tape or printed form.

It can easily be appreciated that John and Jeanne Gullahorn in constructing a model of social interaction over time, even where the relationship is restricted to a dyad or triad, have undertaken a difficult task. They write in a number of interchanges where rewards and costs are evaluated and behaviour is influenced by the operation of the five propositions. Does the model contribute to the theory? They suggest, particularly in their earlier papers (1963, 1965a) that if the computer model is valid, so is the theory. In order to be valid, the program run must be shown to match research observations made in natural social sequences. In this way the starting propositions of the program, which are also those of the theory, would be confirmed.

Thus, the Gullahorns aim at an eventual empirical validation. Without wanting the reader to pre-judge their program and its results, which are described in a moment, it is reasonable to point out that there are several obstacles to establishing the validity of this program against research observations. First, difficulties will occur in describing social sequence, transition points or "terminal" measures in natural situations. Exactly how would one take out a sequence from naturalistic observation in order to match it to the program? Secondly, there are the methodological problems of how similar the match has to be for validity to be established. Thirdly, there is an even more serious obstacle—the chief difficulty with Homunculus is that it is programmed for the most general of Homans' propositions, which are not in themselves situation-specific. *Help* (stated in its generic form) is exchanged for *esteem*, again without further specification, except by the use of simple three- or five-point scales. At this level it cannot be validated against situational results, unless these results are themselves fairly abstract. Of course there are problems which arise "because of . . . complexity and because generally accepted conventions and methods for . . . validation have not yet been developed . . ." (Gullahorn and Gullahorn, 1969, p. 57) but the main difficulty in using the program to refine the theory lies in its over-general content. It is written at too general a level to be suitable for empirical tests. In the end the program in its present form appears to be a test of the logical extensions of the five propositions and some corollaries and therefore the question of validation against data should not really be raised.

I should elaborate on this point that the Homunculus program has been written on too general a level. It is comprised of two kinds of proposition, the first of which are the five fundamental premises and the second kind are general descriptive statements referring to the two rewards (help and esteem) which are exchanged for each other, at a range of cost values. Although it is often not possible to see, from the published results, what may be the content of the rank-orders which are used for scaling reward and cost values, the resulting descriptions are still relatively remote when compared with a description of actual context in a natural situation. What is now missing is the specific working hypothesis predicting behaviour of the office workers; including statements expressing the technical and immediate activities of the situation. Otherwise, it is not surprising that one should get the somewhat monotonic exchanges which were found in the earlier runs of the model:

Ted: Asks for help
George: Gives help
Ted: Gives social approval
Ted: Asks for help
George: Gives help
Ted: Asks for help
George: Refers to another worker
Ted: Gives social approval
George: Gives reassurance, exits.

           (Gullahorn and Gullahorn, 1972, p. 194)

Really, in order to simulate the office situation observed by Blau, we should incorporate the detail of the activities exchanged and the structure of the theoretical statements should consist of more than two levels

—that is, they should be more than premises and general descriptive statements. While there are intervening logical statements to be added, of the sort discussed already in the previous chapter, it is the descriptive and specific hypotheses which have to be included before the program can predict for behaviour in natural groups.

Basically, the program represents an exchange between two work colleagues, of a small number of rewards and costs. Thus, the man who seeks help only receives it at the assumed cost of acknowledging the superiority of his colleague. The latter's costs are his effort, time, and the forgoing of alternative activities in order to give help to the other. In the program, each simulated member of the dyad receives, stores and discriminates between stimuli and responds with activities which maximize reward and minimize cost or, to put it another way, minimize maximum costs (the minimax solution of game theory). We will now consider the simulation in some detail as a possible forerunner of a novel method of theory testing. First, the program itself can be described and secondly, some examples can be given of the simulation routines which translate Homans' propositions and allow for their operation in a somewhat abstracted form of interaction. But it is a simulation process, nevertheless. The interaction sequence is started by a symbol representing a request for assistance from one person to another, in this case from Ted to George. The request is treated as an instance of Proposition 1 and is to be evaluated by a search through the lists for its similarity to previously rewarded activity (see Fig. 12, below) and eventually after a number of steps which will now be described, it results in an appropriate response from George. AR is "activity received", AE is "activity emitted".

Following Homans' propositions the routines are the same for both the simulated persons Ted and George but the information retrieved from the list structures describing the participants, determines the sequence of routines and which subroutines will be executed. In writing their program with reference to Proposition 1 certain ambiguities were found which John and Jeanne Gullahorn tried to clarify. For example, stimulus situations had to be divided into two aspects, a general and a specific. They state that, in future work, assessment of degrees of similarity between stimulus situations, past and present, might be made. A list of attributes could be built, one attribute list might have scaled values indicating energy expenditure, another such attribute might have scales denoting time expended on an activity. With these description lists a routine could compare the two activities, determining the number of attributes in common and for each attribute the degree of similarity in value.

In Fig. 12 at Box 1, a subroutine searches a memory list of rewarded stimulus situations in order to discover if the present input (a request

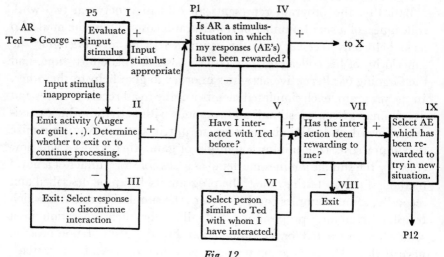

Fig. 12

for help) is among them. This is the general aspect of a request for help. Following on the positive branch from Box IV (i.e. a response to a request for help has been rewarded in the past) the next step is to proceed to the specific question of whether such a response has been rewarded *by Ted* in the past? Here a subroutine, in Fig. 13 this is represented in Box X, locates George's image lists of office colleagues and in particular the sub-list describing Ted in order to discover if Ted has asked for help and has rewarded responses to the request, in the past. If so, then George is programmed to retrieve the types of responses which he has made to Ted and which Ted rewarded (Box XXII).

At this point George selects up to three activities from a memory list of responses which Ted has rewarded. From then on in the *positive* branch the program processes further information about these possible responses in order, finally, to select a response which will yield a social profit. Proposition 2 (frequency and recency), Proposition 3 (value), and Proposition 4 (satiation) are applied to the calculation of making a decision between alternative responses. This calculation will be considered in a moment and is illustrated in Fig. 14 below.

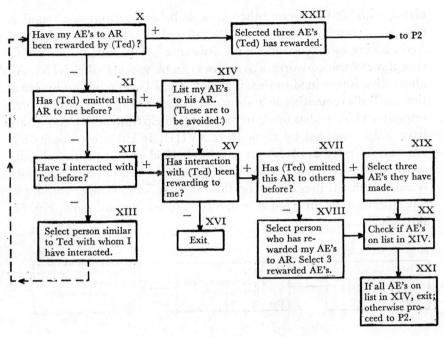

Fig. 13

Most of the items in the flow diagrams in Figs. 12 and 13 accommodate the *negative* branches of the program. In Fig. 12, after Box IV the negative branch proceeds with the question: Has there been any other kinds of interaction with Ted in the past (Box V) and if so have they been rewarded? (Box VII). If they have, a response which has been rewarded by Ted may again be tried (Box IX). However, if at Box VII it is found that previous interaction with Ted has not been rewarding withdrawal follows (Box VIII). Alternatively, if at Box V it is found that there has been no previous interaction of any kind with Ted the program may search the image lists for some person similar to Ted on such attributes as sex, age, position in the group, and this person's list will be used as a reference source for determining subsequent action (Box VI). Another negative branch proceeds in Fig. 13 Box X. Here, if George's response to a request for help from Ted has not been rewarded (Box XI) then George will not repeat the response (Box XIV) and the program can proceed to a general, and possibly final, evaluation of interaction with Ted as rewarding or otherwise (Box XV). This may lead to exit (Box XVI). On the other hand, if George has been asso-

ciated with Ted in some other area of behaviour and has found it
rewarding (Box XV) he may now "try to recall whether he has observed
Ted's asking other co-workers for assistance" (Box XVII) and in this
case three of the co-workers' responses can be selected (Box XIX). An
alternative is provided to this, if at Box XVII George has no information on Ted's requesting help from others then George may select three
responses which he has made to requests for help from others and which
have been rewarded by them (Box XVIII). In either eventuality the
responses selected as likely will now be checked against the list, already
mentioned, of responses to be avoided (because Ted did not previously
reward them). If they are all on this list (Box XIV) George withdraws
but otherwise the program now moves on to test Proposition 2, Fig. 14,
Box XXIII.

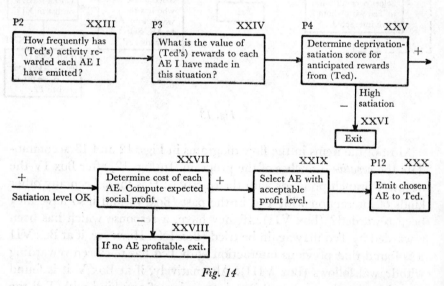

Fig. 14

There were a number of problems, mentioned by Gullahorn and
Gullahorn (1963, 1965b), in reformulating Proposition 2 for computer
simulation. If would have been possible to set a counter for each time a
response was rewarded and therefore to retrieve the information on
reward frequency, but this was rejected as an inadequate simulation.
Instead, a five-point ordinal scale was devised to evaluate frequency,
ranging from "nearly always rewarded" to the mid-point "about half
the time" and then ending with "almost never". Another method of
estimating frequency, considered by the authors of the program,

involved increasing the ordinal scale values after three rewards but this was dropped because it did not resolve the possible influence on estimates of frequency of "the emotional salience of the reinforcement" (Gullahorn and Gullahorn, 1965b, p. 57).

In addition to frequency of rewards, their values are also incorporated into the program. Value has two components, one constant in the long term the other variable over short periods of time. Proposition 3 (the more valuable . . . the more often) expresses the first meaning, while Proposition 4 (the more often . . . the less valuable . . . any further unit of activity . . .) expresses the second. The value component of Proposition 3 is represented in the IPL program by a rank-ordering of activities. For example, warm social approval involving Ted's complimenting George in front of colleagues will be ranked higher than a half hearted response of "hmm, thanks" or an annoyed retort, "well, sorry I bothered you". The program now allows for assessment of value of the three alternative rewards for which an estimate of frequency has already been provided (Fig. 14, Box XXIV). The routine executing Proposition 3 retrieves Ted's previous responses, estimates which he is likely to make now and searches description lists to find the reward value, by rank order. Next, to provide for Proposition 4 a deprivation-to-satiation score on an ordinal scale is stored as the value of a special attribute on the description list of each activity. Routines update this score whenever an activity is received (Box XXV).

As shown in Fig. 14, the program computes three measures for each possible response: frequency, value as a constant (rank-order) and value over the possible short-term (deprivation/satiation score) and "George can rank his contemplated responses in terms of their expected payoff".

But *cost* still has to be estimated. A routine was devised to compare the combined measures of frequency and value of one activity with another. Thus, the anticipated outcome for George in continuing his own work is compared with the anticipated outcome of responding to Ted's request for help. The alternatives forgone (continuing with his own work) can now be subtracted as a cost from the positive outcome of the anticipated response to Ted and so reward minus cost equals profit for this particular social activity. One possibility is that a loss may result. In this case, are there other alternatives, is there a third option for George between helping Ted and doing his own work? The program provides for such an alternative: by referring Ted to another person, George will still receive some approval and although the value of this is much lower than if he had offered direct help, the cost in time lost from his own work is also very small.

Proposition 5 posed "one of the more difficult problems for computer routines" and "in effect the list structures of our agents had to be programmed to have consciences and they had to include a repertoire of appropriate anger responses" (Gullahorn and Gullahorn, 1965a, p. 59); there was also the possibility of receiving rewards beyond those a man may consider he deserves (Fig. 12, Box II, "anger and guilt").

In short, these various instances illustrate that Homunculus is an attempt to clarify the course of social interaction by simulating the evaluation of different behaviour; the retrieval of information in order to project alternative strategies; and the discrimination of conditions under which one activity would be followed rather than another.

The investigators set out to represent each participant by a list structure consisting of several lists as follows: an *Identity List* consisting of name, sex, ability, education, verbal skill, activity rate, position in certain groups; an *Activities List* which contains stimuli received, activities initiated and activities witnessed. There are also *Image Lists* specifying membership and reference groups, the position of the individual in certain groups and the image of himself and other members. Lists also contain elements of his past history and his resulting values and needs. These lists accumulate as the program runs, adding more items to the list structure representing an individual.

Thus, at the beginning of a run, he may be represented by a list structure of as little as 200 words. By the end of some 50 or 100 interactions, he may require a thousand or more IPL words to describe him. In effect the individual learns from his experiences and keeps in memory information that will enable him to behave more appropriately in future interactions (Gullahorn and Gullahorn, 1965b, p. 52).

The simulation is such that each programmed individual receives, discriminates and stores information and is able to

differentiate reward and punishment, associate a stimulus situation with a response and associate a response with a reinforcement: and, on the basis of past experience, he has to be able to predict the consequences of each contemplated response (Gullahorn and Gullahorn, 1965b, p. 52).

Computer simulation and theory

The Gullahorns have not yet confronted the problem of testing the simulation against actual human behaviour although they have planned to check differences where a sequence of group interaction between human participants can be compared to a sequence between computer-programmed participants, using a form of Turing test. They have experienced difficulty with the Homunculus model because there are too many qualitative choices and the number of possibilities becomes overwhelming. Gullahorn and Gullahorn (1972) explain that:

> Trying to make program provision for an extensive repertoire of qualitatively different activities proved extremely difficult, especially when we expanded our model to include three simulated individuals. Initially we programmed each person with a limited repertoire of characteristics and allowed him to develop others on the basis of experiences. After 100 interactions, therefore, there could be a fivefold increase in each participant's memory structure—say from 200 to 1,000 computer words. Even for the dyads, tracing such sprouting trees proved unwieldy. . . . (p. 195).

Further limitation of choice would reduce this problem but the simulation would become even more abstract. The results of their simulation cannot be stated in conventionally verifiable forms and this may be partly because there is no suitable way of summarizing them and partly because it would hardly be possible to find formal empirical comparisons, *at this level*. The simulation has the great advantage of plausibility, but then the theory itself is plausible, so it can easily be seen that the attainment of some form of empirical test, eventually, is of great importance.

To conclude, this computer simulation can present results of a series of binary choices between alternative rewards; it allows evaluation on 3-point ordinal scales and it has plausibility in corresponding to common experience in the ways in which individuals pursue social activities. Its principal feature is what Gullahorn and Gullahorn (1965a) describe as "verisimilitude" with the behaviour observed in Blau's (1955) observational study of office workers and to that extent it achieves its starting aim. The Gullahorns have not achieved their further aims, as originally stated, of refining the evaluation measures of the program or of making a formal empirical test on Homunculus. But the program as it stands does suggest important possibilities (and because of this one hopes that more material will be published).

The routines allow for a behavioural pattern to develop through cumulative rewards; for the choice of one reward rather than another; for behaviour which is not rewarded and is therefore discontinued; and for punitive behaviour. In this way, different behaviour effects can be identified and classified as the result of varying prior conditions. The simulation therefore invites predictions, given certain defined rewards, of the behaviour which follows them. A contrasting example of a program where vagueness of theory has, in fact, precluded simulation is mentioned by Gullahorn and Gullahorn (1969)—this is the case of the Levi-Strauss functionalist explanation in sociology. Here, the explanation that a certain form of collective behaviour has greater functional value for social organization has not provided for independent measures and a program cannot therefore be written with measurable outputs.

Because of the problems encountered in this program, Gullahorn and Gullahorn have subsequently continued with more restricted models. Interaction has been simulated for three-person groups using the twelve categories suggested by Bales (1953) for the analysis of discussion groups. Instead of a small number of individual acts such as help, approval, or reassurance, the behaviour exchange now belongs to one or other of these categories: for instance, giving or requesting information; agreeing or dissenting with opinions; expressing group solidarity and tension release. The results are both interesting and notable for having provided a close approach to an empirical test. In the majority of cases the simulated triads developed into a friendly pair and an isolate. That is, a coalition of two persons resulted from cumulative rewarding episodes between them and tending gradually to leave the other simulated individual out of the interaction.

Each time this pair's interaction proves rewarding, information is stored in their image lists which lessens the cost of finding rewarding acts to emit to each other and increases the expectation of a rewarding response. Thus the rate of interaction between them increases . . . The third man does not have the opportunity to let the other know how rewarding he might be and remains an enigma (Gullahorn and Gullahorn, 1965b, p. 60).

Another conclusion from this program is that this result is especially likely when none of the members of the triad know the other two: if the three persons are already acquainted (each already has the others in an image list) then interaction is shared between the three. This finding corresponds with those of completely independent simulations of three-person interactions, which are also referred to by the authors. Gullahorn and Gullahorn (1972) point out further theoretical implications from this development:

These findings indicate that our formalisation of Homans' social reinforcement theory is sufficient to produce and explain coalition formation in a triad of unacquainted individuals, and more complicated mechanisms need not necessarily be invoked to account for this classical group phenomena (p. 197).

This could be expressed rather differently by saying that these results were predicted by the interaction-liking proposition, in turn underpinned by explicit reward-cost assumptions. Certainly, the validation possibilities are demonstrated in a more promising way here, for a specific hypothesis, than was the case for the more general formulation of Homunculus.

Gullahorn and Gullahorn (1965c, 1972) have also simulated individual choices between alternative courses of social action, in this case empirical matching was found in an earlier questionnaire distribution to a sample of trade union officials by John Gullahorn. This study of role conflict among union leaders is a particularly interesting attempt at a more formal test although in achieving it they have had to discard the complexities of interaction as a process in time. The questionnaire had been administered to union men, presenting a choice between taking office in the union (Chief Stewardship) and other activities (office in the employees' club). They translated into the computer program what they supposed were the influences operating in an actual situation, allocating weights to variables as these were thought likely to influence decisions. In effect, what they now did was to test a descriptive, situational hypothesis against the findings of the questionnaire distribution. Using the technique called "modular programming" by which routines for different hypotheses can be inserted or extracted, they found some agreement with the actual response distribution of the questionnaire study. Assumptions underlying the strategies written into the program are taken from similar social exchange notions as are found in Homunculus, where selection of choices should optimize outcomes. In some strategies other values are also included, for instance, weightings were allocated for "personal integrity". Even though the focus for matching with the questionnaire results is well specified, the program still becomes complex; its positive significance is that some data coincide with the union officials' questionnaire responses. The comment made by Abelson about this empirical test is relevant:

In this attempt they invented so many special rules to cover a single narrow empirical situation that in the opinion of the present author the resulting model was not useful either as an extension of Homunculus or as an independent general model. However, the goal of this effort is laudable, and further attempts should be made (Abelson, 1968, p. 326).

Another general criticism of computer simulation could be applied to its exchange theory applications. Moore and Anderson (1962) argue that there is "something disappointing about the possibility of predicting *how* people will solve problems" (p. 245), implying that if one can predict the results there is the feeling that such problems are trivial. The interesting problems are those "that neither we nor others know the answer to". Simulation is most worthwhile when it is capable of producing consequences unanticipated by the investigator, what Abelson (1968) calls "potential surprise". The question therefore is raised of whether the computer program trivializes the social situation and, in the cases we have presented, by taking a very limited range of rewards it may depart from the verisimilitude which is sought. There is the feeling that there must be more to it than this. On the other hand, even with such a limited number of strategies, the program can become too complex to handle.

The work is attractive for its potential and there has been an attempt to move from the face-validity of program inputs to more formal comparisons. The nature of this work so far is, however, tentative and still at the stage of preliminary trials. In the case of Homunculus the results of differential inputs in the values of rewards measured by ordinal scales have yet to be shown. For instance, it is easy to see that a negative ordinal value will lead to discontinuation of an interaction sequence; it is less easy to see how a low ordinal value leads to less frequent interaction, and at what level does it settle? It would be of interest to see results showing that a high ordinal value leads to more frequent interaction or that distinct and alternative settled rates of interaction will be found. Since an important feature of Homunculus is that it should simulate interaction over time then it should also have been possible to present some evaluation at different points of the computer run. As it is, the presentation in Gullahorn and Gullahorn (1963, 1965b) of the initial starting position of the flow chart is no more than a logically consistent statement of the likely alternatives which may be sought in a social relationship. The program should establish the results of different reward and cost values in the interaction sequence but we have not as yet been shown this; perhaps in a future publication John and Jeanne Gullahorn will present these kinds of data. Their use of more specialized programs subsequently to Homunculus confirms that they are very aware of this aspect of testing.

Have these attempts achieved the effect which Abelson (1968, p. 11) claimed for computer simulation, that it "sharpens theory"? It may seem that the attempt to give ordinal scale values to rewards does not introduce any greater precision than is already attained by the sociometric test and the conventional scales used in questionnaires or interviews. In the logical structure some clarification may yet be attained, a degree of precision is involved and there remains the possibility of greater precision in the future. The extent to which this possibility will be realized may depend on the influence of Homunculus and its related programs and on the next wave of investigations, if exchange theory is taken into the computer for further trials.

11

Distributive Justice, Injustice and Reciprocity

Introduction

I have already mentioned that Homans' theory has been most discussed in that aspect of it which is least behaviouristic. Proposition 5—stating the expectation of distributive justice and the emotional reactions to injustice—has attracted more interest than any other. This is a development which has escaped the attention of even the most recent critics or assessors of the theory, such as Shaw and Costanzo (1970). Often the derivations of Proposition 5 provide hypotheses for testing, or it is used as a source of alternative hypotheses. The notion of distributive justice has been influential to the extent that it has even been given an apparent autonomy from the rest of Homans' work by several authors, including Karpik (1967), Kimberly (1967), Doreian and Stockman (1969) and Box and Ford (1969), all of whom refer to "the theory of distributive justice". If its autonomy is to be taken seriously, it is especially because of the work of Adams (1963, 1965). Adams postulates that a great deal of behaviour can be interpreted as a means to attaining equity, reciprocity or justice and he has listed several propositions which focus on the attainment of justice and avoidance of injustice. In effect, when Adams claims the status of a theory for propositions dealing with distributive justice (and here he recognizes how close he stands to Homans' theory), he is really saying that there are a sufficient number of propositions derived from the concepts of equity or inequity; and sufficient empirical observations to support the descriptive hypotheses subtending from them. Adams cautions that this is not a new theory—"there are already too many 'little' theories in social psychology" (Adams, 1965, p. 276).

His arguments and the experimental tests which he presents are
developed from Homans' Proposition 5; from the hypotheses generated
by the field studies of Jaques (1961) and Patchen (1959) and from the
theoretical notion of cognitive dissonance (Festinger, 1957). Adams
notes that in a vast number of social relations "reciprocity is a functional element of the relation" (Adams, 1965, p. 278), and he defines
reciprocity as *equality* of exchange between persons (although it should
be noted that equality is not essential to distributive justice). His
definition of inequity is expressed as a ratio of investments to rewards,
where the former outweigh the latter. When Adams describes the ratio
formula, he refers to the sums of inputs and outcomes. There is a similar
difficulty here to that encountered in game theory where a given material
utility may have different subjective utilities to the participants.* Adams
mentions that Zaleznik, Christensen and Roethlisberger (1958), in a
field study by interviews with industrial employees, were unable to
sustain their hypotheses that expectations of justice were associated
with job satisfaction, and he attributes this result to the investigators'
weighting of inputs (such as age, seniority, education) equally when
their respondents may not in fact have done so.

A conclusion to be drawn from this discussion is that *equity, distributive
justice* and *reciprocity* are almost identical terms. Of course they are not
identical. The norm of reciprocity expresses the mutual returns which
are expected in interpersonal relations, generally in a positive sense.
Homans has given a thorough treatment to the derivations from the
expectation of distributive justice leading to reciprocal norms. Reciprocity is a special case of distributive justice. Thus, it is clear that the
principle of distributive justice underlies the norm of reciprocity.
Moreover, distributive justice involves more than the reciprocal return
of outcomes, it involves the evaluation of investments and rewards by a
variety of criteria and it involves assessing one's own returns against
those of another without necessarily implying an exchange with that
particular person.

In fact, most of the examples of distributive justice discussed by
Homans touch on reciprocal behaviour. The influences towards reciprocal exchange are expressed in Propositions 2 and 3, which state that
there will tend to be an equivalence of reciprocal rate or value of
behaviour between persons. In further corollaries Homans states the

* See Chapters 3 and 8 for discussion of the problems this presents for exchange
theory.

return of value for value, or possibly value *and* frequency may be reciprocated. An interesting extension of Homans' discussion is found in Schwartz (1967) who illustrates the reciprocity norm by the mutual obligations of gift-giving. As he emphasizes, explanations from this source are not always the obvious ones. One instance is the giving of undeserved gifts in order to produce shame, even as a form of punishment. Especially interesting is Schwartz's postulate of a balance of debt in social relations where reciprocal gifts or services must be a little unequal if a residue of gratitude is to be maintained between persons.

Explanation of the effects of injustice, such as Adams proposes, introduces speculation on psychological mechanisms very similar to those of cognitive dissonance theory. Thus, Adams (1965, p. 290) comments that "it has been postulated that the experience of inequity is equivalent to the experience of dissonance, (and) it is reasonable to believe that cognitive distortion may be adopted as a means of reducing inequity", but he adds that the existing evidence "is not very impressive". More recently, Greenberg and Shapiro (1971) discuss the operation of the distributive justice principle when a person becomes indebted to another. They consider that indebtedness is a state of tension which has "motivational properties such that the greater its magnitude, the greater will be the efforts to reduce it" (p. 290). They assume that this involves the feelings of guilt which accompany distributive injustice (see Homans, 1961) or inequity (Adams, 1963) because it disturbs the sense of "ought" (Heider, 1958). They also present the alternative argument that indebtedness may be a threat to status (Homans, 1961) or to power (Blau, 1964). For these reasons a person may hesitate to accept help if he sees the likelihood of his not being able to reciprocate. Greenberg and Shapiro manipulate the possibility of reciprocating help in an experiment where the partners of a dyad have each to work alternately on a difficult and an easy task. Results showed that where the subjects knew they could not return the favour, the incidence of asking for help was lowered, and the amounts of time elapsing before such requests were made were longer than under conditions where it was likely they would be able to reciprocate. These investigators add an interesting discussion of alternative hypotheses. For instance, anticipated reciprocity might have given the subjects greater confidence in asking for help when they encountered difficulty; or similarity of circumstances between the partners where reciprocal behaviour was anticipated, may have increased liking, leading to exchange of favours.

Greenberg and Shapiro note that the results confirm Blau's (1955) finding that equals in competence tend to seek help from each other rather than from a superior and affirm Homans' argument that exchange between equals avoids the costs of acknowledging inferiority.

Ellis (1971) in a speculative discussion of the "starting mechanisms" which lie behind the prevalent expectations of distributive justice, gives an emphasis, similar to that of Greenberg and Shapiro, on motivational properties. Ellis is critical of Gouldner (1960) for leaving unanswered the question of where the norm of reciprocity came from in the first place. He regards Gouldner's position as resulting from a decision "not to depart from the axiomatic basis of a normatively oriented sociology" (Ellis, 1971, p. 699)—in other words, where existing norms are taken as the explanatory starting point. According to Ellis, Gouldner has missed an opportunity to explore the starting mechanism variables. The same criticism can be made, Ellis states, against Homans (1961) for not explicating further the notion of distributive justice, but he notes that Blau (1964) gives a fuller critical evaluation of this concept. Ellis mounts a general attack on the closure of explanation at the level of norms and remarks that only Blau "among contemporary sociologically orientated exchange theorists" seeks to explain norms which restrain egotistic behaviour by postulating individual motives and "the existential conditions of exchange" (Blau, 1964) before the emergence of a norm of reciprocity.

In view of this criticism, it is surprising to see that Rosenhan and White (1967) interpret altruistic behaviour as reflecting an internalized norm, confusing altruism with a norm of reciprocity acquired from observation of others. They refer to Gouldner and, incorrectly, to Homans in support of this position. In fact, it would be more accurate to claim, as Blain (1971) has done that Homans' attempts "to explain reciprocation in terms of stimulus-response learning theory" (p. 19), and not in terms of a social norm—which would develop later, as a special case. Rosenhan and White mention what they consider to be unsatisfactory psychological approaches to altruistic behaviour. For example, psychoanalytic interpretations have emphasized neurotic guilt or anxiety feelings as a source of altruism. Some learning theories offer interpretations tied to egocentric motives of need or drive reduction. Rosenhan and White conducted an experiment with school children playing a bowling game for gift vouchers as prizes. The children were provided with an opportunity to donate part of their winnings—none of those who had not seen an adult giving, subsequently did so, although 48 per cent of those who first observed an adult giving, did follow suit. The result suggested the hypothesis that altruism is an internalized norm learned from others, but possible explanations from other sources, such as the children's prior expectations, could be further explored.

Blumstein and Weinstein (1969) not only discuss the starting mechanism possibilities but attempt an experimental test of conditions leading to redress of injustice. They suggest, following Homans, that distributive injustice is perceived by the individual when his rewards and investments are out of balance and he may seek to reduce the disparity. Blumstein and Weinstein draw attention to a number of possible explanations of this tendency to seek redress: some investigators see its motivational source in the attempt to reduce cognitive dissonance; similarly, in balance theory it is assumed there is a tendency to strive for orderliness in social relations. These authors introduce some confusion when they refer to distributive justice as a special case of the reciprocity norm. This is erroneous since the relation is vice versa but they go on to take up Homans' point, quite correctly, that justice can become a value and fair exchange becomes rewarding in itself.*

Blumstein and Weinstein present two types of injustice situation. In the one the person is victim and in the other he is beneficiary: in both cases the person involved either as victim or beneficiary will try to redress injustice. They suggest that either the victim will try to lower the rewards of the other or the beneficiary will attempt to raise rewards for the victim. The victim may try to deny esteem to the other, the beneficiary may grant more esteem. Their second hypothesis states that there will be a differential redress (Homans, 1961, p. 76), that is, the victim will be more active in his attempt than the beneficiary. In this experiment subjects were asked to complete a task together with a partner (a confederate of the experimenter) who, as part of the design, either did a large or a small portion of the work. A further experimental condition was introduced when the confederate claimed either one-third of the work contribution or two-thirds of it. There were two conditions in the experimental groups, in one the confederate partner made a high contribution with a low claim (the beneficiary condition), in the other he made a low contribution but a high claim (the victim

---

* Note also Blau's (1964) argument that in any exchange situation fairness is expected in exchange for esteem.

condition). In the control groups there were two conditions, in one group the claims and work conditions were both low, and in the other they were both high. The groups were counter-balanced with regard to sex, Machiavellianism scores and the order of experimental conditions. Unfortunately, the findings of this experiment are inconclusive but raise some questions for further work, possibly with improved designs.

Weinstein, DeVaughan and Wiley (1969) who discuss equality of exchange as a postulate of Thibaut and Kelley, Homans and Blau, explore the consequences of imbalance in exchange and discuss the obligations which the beneficiary incurs to restore parity. Those who cannot do so have to accept inferiority as a cost. This is quite clear, but Weinstein, DeVaughan and Wiley argue that exchange theory "is not very explicit in specifying parameters that affect this cost" (p. 2). These authors carried out an experiment on dyads, where they created conditions of one creditor and one debtor in each dyad, in an exchange of help in carrying out tasks set by the experimenter. In noting the degree of one person's deference to another, they used a (somewhat obscurely described) method of content analysis of tape recordings. They discuss a number of alternative, contradictory and all quite plausible, hypotheses and they conclude pessimistically that exchange theory "is not sufficiently articulated to provide firm guidelines for specific deductions" (p. 11), complaining that it will always be possible to posit exchange after the fact, although in this case it could be that the experimental method may have been at fault.

Abelson and Miller (1967) in a discussion of interpersonal antagonisms, mention the boomerang effect from personal insults where the recipient adopts a more extreme attitude. Referring to Homans (1961) they argue that if social equity is violated by gratuitous insults from one party, the other may attempt to redress the inequity by adopting a more antagonistic position. They accept that this is a much less formal derivation than that of Adams (1965) but intend their experiment as a tentative exploration. Wilke and Lanzetta (1970) cite Homans and Adams on distributive justice and comment that this seems to be more than just a vague prescription to help others who have helped one and involves some estimate of an exact return. In a role-playing experiment where students received requests for help apparently from another participant, the experimenters spread the range of values of offers to help already received from the other. They show that reciprocated help is a monotonic increasing function of amounts of prior help. While noting that this is consistent with prediction from "social exchange theories", they also mention that the experimental situation might have created strong demands for exact reciprocity and that help was easily scalable in this experiment which it may well not be in other situations.

The general tendency to reciprocate value, as discussed by Homans, is briefly mentioned by Mehrabian and Ksionzky (1970) in a review of recent studies of affiliative behaviour. Hollander and Julian (1969) in a review of leadership studies take up a position close to exchange theory when they suggest that leadership should be interpreted as "a *transaction* between leaders and followers in which the leader both gives something and gets something. The leader provides a *resource* . . . and in return receives greater influence associated with status, recognition and esteem" (Hollander and Julian, 1969, p. 388). They also use Homans' interpretation of the exchange of influence between leader and follower: "influence over other is purchased at the price of allowing oneself to be influenced by others" (Homans, 1961, p. 286).

The principle of distributive justice seems to have become one of the liveliest influences of Homans' theory (and to some extent of the theories of Thibaut and Kelley and Blau), a development which has escaped the attention of even the most recent critics or assessors of the theory, such as Shaw and Costanzo (1970); although the distributive justice principle and Proposition 5 have always been neglected in criticisms of the theory as behaviouristic. But Homans does not recognize a line drawn between emotion, cognition and behaviour and in Proposition 5 and its hypotheses the cognitive and affective components of social relationships make up a large part of his theory, as we have already seen in some detail (Chapter 8, pp. 161–172).

Altruism and reciprocity

The notion of distributive justice has been identified with the norm of reciprocity by many writers. All agree that the principle of distributive justice and the norm of reciprocity are congruent and closely related. However, it has been suggested, notably by Berkowitz (for a summary of his publications, see Krebs, 1970), that there is a norm of social responsibility which holds that, in certain circumstances, values should be given without return or anticipation of return. This is altruistic behaviour. Berkowitz and Daniels (1963, 1964) drew attention to the norm as an explanation for their experimental results showing that, contrary to exchange notions, college students offer help to companions even when return benefits cannot be foreseen. Postulating a norm of social responsibility, Berkowitz and several collaborators since 1963 suggest limitations to the resemblance of social interaction to an economic exchange. For instance, they argue that middle-class Americans attach importance to the norm that a person should help others who are dependent on him, regardless of return benefits (Berkowitz and Friedman, 1967). Their research confirms that students with this class background report feeling obliged to, and that other persons would expect them to, help dependent persons. What interests us is how they explain this finding.

Let us examine one or two of their experiments in order to see what explanations they offer. Berkowitz and Connor (1966) point out that people will help those who are in a position of dependency on them (see also Schopler and Bateson, 1965) and they report an experiment designed to elucidate the influence of the norm of social responsibility in persons who are relatively successful as against those who are relatively unsuccessful at an experimental task. It is hypothesized that the person who more easily gains his goals will be more liberal in his behaviour. Students were given a task to work on alone and were told that another person was engaged on the same task in an adjoining room. For the first experimental manipulation they were told that the other person would give supervisory instructions but whether or not he received a financial reward depended on the performance of the person receiving the instructions. Three different conditions of dependency were established in which 20 per cent, 50 per cent and 80 per cent of the assessment of the other's performance would depend on how the subject performed. A second experimental manipulation consisted of setting the subjects a jig-saw puzzle and arranging success or failure conditions. A control group was not given the jig-saw. Thus, nine experimental conditions formed a 3 × 3 factorial design. The results suggest that those who worked fastest were the successful subjects whose supervisors were in a greater degree of dependency on them.

The principle of distributive justice is mentioned by Berkowitz and Connor as one of several possible explanations, although they take the tendency to social responsibility or altruism as their basic hypothesis —simply stating that the successful completion of the puzzle increased the tendency to carry out obligations to a dependent person. The principle of distributive justice is used as a conjectural alternative hypothesis: subjects allowed to complete the jig-saw puzzle had received a monetary reward and so might wish to see their supervisors similarly rewarded. This is only a point for inferential discussion, and no test is made of the alternative hypothesis. What is theoretically interesting in Berkowitz's studies is the distinction which he draws between altruism and the principle of distributive justice. The major aim of his series of experiments, using variations of the same basic design, is to clarify or confirm the relationship between dependency in the recipient and altruistic behaviour. Yet, in the end, one is left with the idea that distributive justice, as much as altruism, might explain the observed effects and that the hypothesized influences have not been clearly separated.

For Berkowitz, Homans' principle of distributive justice is a significant illustration "that human beings have goals other than utilitarian" because this principle states that people seek to equalize ratios of rewards to investments both for themselves *and for others*. Berkowitz and Friedman (1967) point to the similar notion implied in Gouldner's norm of reciprocity which holds that a person should return help to another who has helped him. In emphasizing the non-utilitarian aspect of Homans' theory, Berkowitz and Friedman also distinguish, not quite correctly, between it and the exchange assumptions postulated by Thibaut and Kelley. In this paper, Berkowitz and Friedman align altruism with distributive justice against the view that social interaction is similar to a financial exchange, influenced by considerations of rewards and costs, which they identify with the Thibaut and Kelley model.*

Berkowitz and Friedman attempt a test of the possibility that class membership (as far as this could be reflected in parental occupations classified as middle or working class) influences college students' propensity to follow *either* the norm of reciprocity *or* the norm of social responsibility. They are not able to separate the two, or to discard the hypothesis that reciprocation of past benefits received is involved in a person's responsibility to others. They introduce the suggestion that

---

* Berkowitz and his colleagues have created a difficulty by calling Homans' theory "non-utilitarian" and the Thibaut and Kelley model "utilitarian". Goranson and Berkowitz (1966) refer to the assumption by Thibaut and Kelley "that a person behaves or interacts in a given way because he believes that it is *to his advantage* to do so" (p. 227). As I have argued in Chapter 3, Thibaut and Kelley state that both individual and social needs influence the value of outcomes; they do not assume an economic trading model for all relationships (see Chapter 3, p. 50).

altruistic behaviour will be augmented if it has been the person's previous experience that he has been helped in a similar situation, so now we see that in altruism there is at least an indirect kind of reciprocity. That a person follows the norm of social responsibility does not rule out reciprocal obligation nor that some form of return may be attached to altruistic behaviour.

In an experiment influenced by this research, Horowitz (1968), attempted to test the hypothesis that as costs increase, so the amount of help given to a dependent person decreases. Horowitz intended to introduce limiting conditions on the postulate that the norm of social responsibility has most influence when another person is perceived as highly dependent. Horowitz points out that in the Berkowitz experiments the costs of helping the other person were low *and he now introduces the exchange formulation as presented by Homans* that profit equals reward minus cost, in order to test the hypothesis that rising costs will diminish the amount of help to a dependent person. In the experiment itself where "social responsibility" was defined by the level of shock which subjects indicated they would be willing to endure on behalf of a dependent person in a proposed subsequent experiment (actually there was to be no further experiment) there seems to be at least a suspicion of effects from artifact. If we accept Horowitz's experimental definition of social responsibility and his conclusion that level of shock determines what is done on behalf of the other, then the distinction is blurred between social responsibility, rewards and costs. It seems that there is still a need to clarify the relationship between altruism and exchange; it is quite possible that each assumption should be included to introduce limiting or special qualifying conditions on the other. It is not so easy as it first appears to cite altruistic behaviour in opposition to exchange explanations and I am making the point that altruism need not run counter to exchange theory.

Exchange and altruism may seem to be opposing concepts; now we see that there are possibilities of drawing them together. Thus acts undertaken without hope of return benefits can be explained as following on from the benefits received in the past—the sort of indirect return mentioned by Berkowitz and Friedman. One may pass on to a dependent the benefits one has received from others when one was in a similar position of dependency. It is the sort of service that academics perform when they write references for junior colleagues. Furthermore, there is yet another possibility making it difficult to distinguish altruism from exchange. Sawyer (1966) reports on the use of an Altruism Scale to measure concern for others; he points out that the rewards of two individuals may not be clearly separable because the welfare of one person provides a reward to the other. Sawyer tries to demonstrate how different courses of action may be differentiated by the weight which is placed upon the welfare of the other. He asked a sample of students to fill in questionnaires where each indicated his preferences in academic grades and other rewards for himself and another person (either a friend, stranger or antagonist). Sawyer hoped in this way to differentiate between degrees of altruism, with co-opera-tion and competition at the extremes and individualism at the mid-point. He argues strongly that altruism is not necessarily opposed to egotism, one can be equally concerned with one's own and the other's welfare. His results confirm the influence of the type of relationship—much depends on *who* the person is "since reciprocation of friendship or antagonism forms the most basic kind of interpersonal balance" (Sawyer, 1966, p. 413) and they largely bear out the supposition that reciprocity and altruism are not to be easily separated in a given behaviour.

Tests of hypotheses

Many investigators have accepted as basic assumptions the individual's expectation of distributive justice and the norm of reciprocity—either or both—and have attempted tests of hypotheses derived from them. The most frequently used paradigm for experiment is the two-person game. There have also been a number of experiments using factorial designs with variables such as dependency, social class, indebtedness, and agreement, showing effects on reciprocal behaviour. In addition, success or failure has been manipulated in simple laboratory tasks in order to demonstrate something similar to the kind of magnanimity that one can observe in successful people in everyday experience.

Interpersonal exchange in the laboratory has to be easily measurable, usually in factorial or game-playing designs which will permit analysis of variance for main effects. As a result these experiments tend not to approximate to natural situations of interpersonal exchange where money is not involved. And there seems to be plenty of scope in some of the experiments for uncontrolled effects to occur either in the relation-ship between the experimenter and his participants or in the relationships between the participants themselves. For example, interpersonal liking may appear in conjectural hypotheses when the experimental results are discussed even though it was not included in the design; more explicitly references may be made to the effects of liking which the experimenter may have inadvertently failed to control. The substantive content of what is exchanged between persons, whether or not a game-playing paradigm is used, is very often expressed as points, or money vouchers, or points to be converted to money at the end of the experiment. But there have already been several notable attempts to examine social exchange with a more varied content. I have described how Berkowitz and his co-workers created different conditions of dependency of one person on another, and observed their effects. More directly concerned with exchange, reciprocation or equity are the experiments by Worthy, Gary and Kahn (1969) on self-disclosure and information exchange, adapted from the earlier work by Jourard (1958). There is the interesting experiment by Stephenson and Fielding (1971) which focuses on expectations of distributive justice in a situation where some group members get "one-up" on others by escaping from a boring laboratory task. Leon Mann (1969a) carried out observation of people queuing for football tickets, taking this situation as an illustration of the equity rule. Julian, Regula and Hollander (1968) tested an exchange effect by inducing a condition of prior agreement between persons as a likely influence on their subsequent conformity in the group. We shall discuss these results below.

Game-playing: the Prisoner's Dilemma

In recent years, game-playing designs appear as an active vein for research reports. The Prisoner's Dilemma game is encountered frequently; it is especially useful because it presents a general research paradigm for social interaction where conflicting choices exist between the alternative of mutual or divergent advantage—between mutual gain or personal gain, between co-operation or competition. As a mixed-motive game suitable for social psychology, the Prisoner's Dilemma was discussed by Solomon (1960) and Rapoport (1966) and there has been a steady supply of subsequent modifications and tests. Ost, Allison, Vance and Restle (1969) present some basic designs in their laboratory manual. The outcome matrix at its simplest is as follows, with each participant making the choice between co-operation

(C) or defection (D). Co-operation is equivalent to "not confess", defection to "confess" in the original anecdote of the Prisoner's Dilemma (see Chapter 4). The D.C. cell is sometimes termed the "temptation" option—temptation to defect. The implications of these options are discussed above in Chapter 4.

	C	D
C	C C	C D
D	D C	D D

Fig. 15 The Prisoner's Dilemma

Values in the cells can be varied, especially to increase the temptation to defect. Variations in the basic design mainly consist of changing the conditions immediately preceding an experiment—for example, by arranging for the participants to win or lose points in preliminary trials, or by changing the instructions. Secondly, the temptation to defect can be manipulated by raising or lowering the values of the CD or DC cells. This laboratory game therefore touches quite closely on the issues of reciprocal exchange and equity, even though the behaviour and rewards which can be included in the design are quite restricted, not only because the content of what is exchanged may be points or money but because in the usual form of the game there is no communication between the participants, except to see the results of the other person's decisions. The whole universe of conditions which lead to the development of co-operation in everyday life is left out. However, some researchers argue that results can be extrapolated widely enough, Pruitt (1968) considers that the allocation of money payments in the Prisoner's Dilemma game is "analogous to real-life situations in which people exchange favours" (p. 145).

In summary, the Prisoner's Dilemma game is well suited for confirming the tendency to reciprocate a given behaviour, usually but not always within the narrow context of a game for points or money payoffs. It has the further limitation that the partners, in the classic form of the game, are not in face-to-face contact with one another.* However, it

* Note that Kelley and other investigators have introduced some interesting possibilities for more open forms of communication in the game (see Chapter 4).

allows the experimenter to introduce co-operative or competitive behaviour purporting to come from one partner and to observe the subsequent action of the other.

Komorita, Sheposh and Braver (1968) mention Thibaut and Kelley and Homans as offering a systematic approach by emphasizing rewards and costs. In an adaptation of the Prisoner's Dilemma design the results are observed of programming to one partner the alleged non-cooperative decisions of the other. Previous studies have elaborated on the Prisoner's Dilemma by adding a third choice, for example Rapoport and Chammah (1965) proposed a "sanctuary choice" whereby either player could escape from the dilemma by playing his third choice. In the experiment which Komorita, Sheposh and Braver report, students were seated in front of control panels displaying a 3 × 3 game matrix representing three alternative choices for each of the pair. The control panels also held three push-button switches distinguished by colours corresponding to the rows and columns of the matrix. The experimenters could manipulate different power conditions by communicating any sequence of choices, allegedly from the other partner. The researchers point to the use, in many instances, of the third condition, a sanctuary choice with a lower payoff even though the other two strategies were to be preferred rationally as providing a greater outcome in payment. It is suggested that the sanctuary choice was a possible indicator of disapproval of the other partner's failure to co-operate. The principle of distributive justice provides one of the speculative interpretations of these results.

Pruitt (1968) uses a Prisoner's Dilemma design to test several hypotheses about reciprocal behaviour, for instance, that the level of reward provided to another person is a function of reward previously received from him or a reward expected from him in the future. The partner in this game was, in fact, a programmed set of responses passed into the cubicle by the experimenter. By arranging a sequence of conditions, two variables were manipulated: a person's past experience with the partner and the partner's future resources. A factorial design incorporated four conditions of past resources and two of future resources. In detail, the partner was shown to have given in the past either 80 per cent of one dollar, 20 per cent of one dollar, or 20 per cent of four dollars, and fourthly, there was a control condition involving no past experience with the partner. The future resources variable was presented in two conditions: either the partner's resources were going to be high (two dollars) or low (50 cents). The hypotheses tested were as follows (1) That the level of reward provided to another person is a positive function of reward previously received from him. (2) Holding level of reward constant a greater debt would be felt towards the other person whose resources, in the past, have been smaller. (3) The level of reward provided to another person is a positive function of the size of his future resources. This hypothesis rests on the postulate that reward may be provided in order to build up credit with another person, in the hope that he will reciprocate in the future. (4) The level of reward previously received from another person will interact with the size of that person's future resources to increase the level of reward given to him in return. The results show confirmation of the first, second and third hypotheses; no support was found for the fourth.

In explaining the result that more money is allocated to the person who has given 80 per cent of one dollar than the one who has given 20 per cent of one dollar, and more to the person who has given 20 per cent of one dollar than who has given 20 per cent of four dollars, Pruitt refers to Homans' principle of distributive justice. In each of these two instances more money is offered to the person giving a greater percentage of an equivalent amount or, where the amounts differ, to the person giving an equivalent percentage of the smaller amount. The principle of distributive justice, argues Pruitt, would suggest that people try to equalize the total value received by themselves and others and more return is therefore given to the person who retains less for himself.

Kershenbaum and Komorita (1970) manipulate the payoff values of the Prisoner's Dilemma game by varying the values of temptation to take the non-cooperative response: on some conditions this was symmetric (equal temptation for both partners), and in others it was asymmetric (unequal temptation). With the usual arrangements of cubicles, wooden partitions and pushbutton switches, students were told that their task was to accumulate as many points as possible and a conversion scale would be used to convert points to money at the end of the experiment. Although they believed they were playing a partner, they were in fact playing against the experimenter. There were four conditions in two of which temptation for self and other were equal, and unequal in the other two conditions (low, high; high, low). The results which concern us here, show that non-cooperative responses occurred sooner when temptation was unequal, and soonest when the other's temptation was higher. Kershenbaum and Komorita discuss the possibility that unequal temptation, with the likelihood that the other partner will be tempted to obtain more points, created a situation of inequity and they refer to the supposition that individuals strive for distributive justice or equity, following Homans and Adams, since this would explain why one would be less likely to co-operate if the other person was thought to be under a strong temptation not to. They conclude that when potential or actual outcomes are equitable each partner will think that the other is more willing to co-operate than when they are inequitable. These conjectural interpretations lead to a comment on nuclear test treaties, maintenance of which may depend on similar conditions. However, the result which is most worth emphasizing in this study is the fact that only very slight differences were found between the two unequal (high and low) temptation groups, a result which seems to run contrary to the earlier view of Rapoport and Chammah (1965) that co-operation varies inversely with the magnitude of temptation.

Marwell, Ratcliff and Schmitt (1969) draw attention to the motives which are emphasized in current work on game playing and are usually stated as some form of maximizing gain. They raise the possibility that there is also a motive to minimize differences between oneself and another—to make the exchange more equitable—and they set out to throw some light on this. Briefly, this was done by arranging the game so that one participant found his score well below that of the other; the former now tended to co-operate less than other participants whose scores were ahead of their partners, even though co-operation produces a higher absolute score. The experiment was based on the modified form of the Prisoner's Dilemma game as devised by McClintock and McNeel (1967). The major hypothesis was that, given a condition of inequity, "the person disfavoured will act so as to gain equity (make nonco-operative choices) and the person favoured will not retaliate with an equal level of nonco-operation" (p. 159).

To support their hypothesis, Marwell, Ratcliff and Schmitt refer to inequity and distributive justice as discussed by Adams, Homans and others. As is usual in game playing, separate cubicles and display panels were arranged for students who participated in two forms of the Prisoner's Dilemma game, the first of these was designed to introduce the initial conditions of equity and inequity and the second permitted observation of subsequent effects.

Figure 16 below shows (a) the inequity and (b) equity matrices with cell values representing payment in U.S. cents. To the right of the Fig. (c) is the modified Prisoner's Dilemma matrix used subsequently to the other two. Thus, the students participated in a two-stage experiment. (a) or (b) were the matrices used in the first stage, followed by (c) in the second stage of the experiment.

	(a) Inequity matrix		(b) Equity matrix		(c) Matrix for Modified Dilemma Game	
Player 1		Player 2			Player 1	Player 2
	B_1	B_2	B_1	B_2	B_1	B_2
	9	3	3	1	6	0
A_1					A_1	
	3	1	3	1	6	5
	3	0	1	0	5	0
A_2					A_2	
	1	0	1	0	0	0

Fig. 16 The outcome for Player 1 is in the upper left corner of each cell. (Adapted from Gerald Marwell, Kathryn Ratcliff and David R. Schmitt, 1969)

It is suggested that given conditions of inequity, action to minimize differences between partners (A_1B_2, A_2B_1) will be more probable than action merely to maximize the final total of actual gains (A_1B_1) and differences between partners will be minimized at the cost of sacrificing points which would raise the individual's absolute total. This experiment demonstrates at least the plausibility of the experimental hypothesis, although the presence also of a maximizing motive was not ruled out.

Exchange notions are present, if peripheral, in the discussion by Komorita and Brenner (1968) who suggest the principle of distributive justice as one plausible explanation of bargaining expectations, but without making any specific test for it in their two-person bargaining experiment. Organ (1971) in a version of the Prisoner's Dilemma attempts to arrange conditions similar to those where a "boundary person" bargains on behalf of the group. It is suggested very tentatively that one condition, where the group expresses high confidence in the bargainer, might have led the latter to exert particular efforts to optimize outcomes. The postulates of distributive justice and exchange, following Homans and Blau, are called in as possible explanations. Tedeschi, Burrill and Gahagan (1969) draw attention to the likelihood that influence over others is very much a matter of control over the rewards available to them, and state that this is consistent with the view of Homans and Thibaut and Kelley, among others. They use a Prisoner's Dilemma design as a test of social strategies where students play against a pre-planned "partner". However, this study focuses on the personality correlates of different responses to the exercise of power—the "partner" controlling the rewards of the other so as to gain his compliance. The experiments attempted to explore the correlates, on two personality scales, of strategies discernible in 100 trials with the "partner" in the stronger position.

The experiments which have been described give an idea of the current activity with game-playing designs and of its potential for social exchange theory. Although there is so much that is conjectural in the inferred motives and influences on game-playing behaviour, yet the value of this design shows most clearly in the variations, some of them quite subtle, which can be made in the experimental conditions. To an extent which has not yet been fully recognized the principle of distributive justice is used as a starting position, or its corollaries are tested. At the least, it provides alternative hypotheses for future investigation.

Distributive justice: other designs

Rothbart (1968) studied the use of financial incentives in two different experimental conditions, with students supervising others carrying out simple tasks. They were divided into two experimental groups, only one of which was offered a financial bonus if the performance of those they were to supervise reached a certain level. The others were offered no financial bonus although in both cases financial rewards or penalties could be given to those whose work they were to supervise. Homans' principle of distributive justice provided an explanation, *ex post facto*, of why the supervisors receiving the financial bonus should have tended to give more financial rewards, and why those not receiving the financial bonus reduced the financial benefits to those whom they supervised. Both trends could be explained as an attempt to restore equity. In a second experiment those who were supervised were to receive flat payment at the end, although supervision was to proceed as before with promises of financial increases or cuts. Some support was found for the equity explanation in that there was now, in the second experiment, little difference between the mean frequencies of penalties in the two groups.

Worthy, Gary and Kahn (1969) comment on the fact that the tests of the theories of Homans and Thibaut and Kelley have generally been confined to gains and losses of points or money, and they propose to extend the measurement of payoffs to *self-disclosure* defined as "that which occurs when A knowingly communicates to B information about A which is not generally known and is not otherwise available to B" (p. 59). Self-disclosure indicating trust or liking is thus a reward for B and mutual self-disclosure is a process of social exchange. Worthy, Gary and Kahn argue that if self-disclosure is a reward then the greater the self-disclosure the more the interpersonal attraction (liking) that will result. Their experiment tested three hypotheses: (a) that a person discloses more information to those for whom he has greater liking, and (b) more self-disclosure by a person increases the degree of liking expressed towards him. A third hypothesis utilizes Homans' principle of distributive justice, equated by the investigators with Gouldner's norm of reciprocity. (Actually, as we have seen, in page 243 above, the latter is a special case of distributive justice.) Thus, (c) it was hypothesized that a person would disclose more intimate information to those from whom he had received more.

A measure of degree of liking of other members was taken in each of twelve four-person groups before and after a procedure where group members exchanged their written answers to questionnaires reflecting varying degrees of self-disclosure. An analysis of co-variance for different effects demonstrated support for all three hypotheses. The investigators viewed their experiment as a step towards testing a wider variety of the outcomes in social exchange.

Experiments by Stephenson and Fielding (1971) were intended as a test of the effects of perceived injustice. Stephenson and Fielding discuss the principle of equity which, as they point out, is implicit in Thibaut and Kelley's approach and thoroughly explicit in Homans' discussion of distributive justice. Their procedure consisted of allocating a confederate of the experimenter, instructed to leave at a given time, to groups of students who volunteered to do a word-construction task. One person's leaving was considered to establish an inequitable advantage over the others still engaged on the task. Results were presented as (1) The average leaving times of different groups; relating these to the time of the first leaver's departure. (2) Average times stayed by different groups after the first person had left. (3) The comparison of subjects tested in groups with subjects tested in isolation. In one of the series of three experiments, the degree of equity was manipulated by giving some subjects a higher monetary reward than others; this allowed the comparison of the effects of confederate's leaving times relatively in "privileged" and "deprived" groups. The results suggest that the greater was the advantage of the initiator (that is, in the "deprived" groups) the more contagious was his early departure, thus supporting Homans' notion of distributive justice. It appeared (because, to some extent, this is speculative) that the experimenters had manipulated the conditions of equity and inequity by means of higher and lower monetary rewards. A person who left the group under conditions of lower reward thus procured inequity over those who stayed, since he had escaped from a relatively unrewarding task and they had not. In the case of the groups with higher reward the pressure to leave was counter-balanced by a greater obligation to carry out the task adequately. These experiments by Stephenson and Fielding suggest that the equity hypothesis might be applied in actual situations where there are similar phenomena. For instance, it might explain the phenomenon observed in corrective schools, where an escape by one boy may seem to trigger off a number of other escapes.

Mann (1969a) carried out a study of people queuing for tickets to a football game. He points out that the values of egalitarianism and distributive justice are invoked to help maintain a state of order in queues. The queue is defined as "a line of persons waiting in turn to be served, according to order of arrival" (p. 344) and "first come, first served, the fundamental concept of queuing, is a basic principle of the behaviour referred to as distributive justice" (p. 346). In queues there is a direct correspondence between time spent waiting and the right of priority, outcomes correspond to inputs, investment is clearly related to reward. The principle of distributive justice is extended to encompass leaves of absence in "marathon queues" and Mann comments that "it is reasonable to claim that rules regulating time spent in and out of the line are the essential core of the queue culture" (p. 346).

Status

Most recent studies focusing on the content of exchange have examined three kinds of valued behaviour: status, conformity, and liking, and for the remainder of the chapter we will be mainly concerned with these.

Several investigators have examined the effects of status on change of opinion, that is, where a person defers to the opinion of another who is of higher status. The higher is the status of the other, the more likely is a person to defer to him. This can be explained by the exchange theory notion of the return of reward value, for value received or potentially receivable from a higher status person. Some of these studies deal with the costs of deferring, the possible loss of one's self-esteem. I shall shortly attempt to answer the question of how far they have succeeded in defining these costs and in demonstrating conditions which influence them.

As I mentioned earlier, Weinstein, DeVaughan and Wiley (1969) make a brief reference to the individual's own self-esteem as a factor influencing the costs of deferring to others. This aspect is discussed more fully by Balkwell (1969) who examines the influence of the perceived competence of another person on an individual's agreement with that person's opinion when this contradicts his own previously-stated opinion. Following Homans' view, maintenance of one's self-esteem will be a reward for holding to the original opinion and loss of esteem is a cost of changing to the other's opinion; the value of self-esteem is not likely to be independent of the perceived competence of the other. Balkwell takes the problem as far as a well-documented but tentative exploration in algebraic form, the design consisting basically of repeated conditions of disagreement with others of high or low competence. Moore (1969) examines this identical topic by administering a questionnaire to a sample of girls allocated in pairs differing in educational attainment (for example, high school or university). The lowest status member was then presented with a conflict between her own and the other's judgement. Moore refers both to Homans and Blau on the cost incurred in deferring to someone else's opinion—admitting one's inferiority. This investigator finds the exchange interpretation adequate, although at this stage of his experimental manipulations, only conjectural possibilities are raised. Berger and Fisek (1970) undertook a similar manipulation of opinion disagreement in an experiment with pairs of supposedly different status; as in the experiment by Moore "status" is defined very narrowly. At the start of the experiment students were given two paper and pencil tests, sufficiently vague for the experimenter to present varying scores credibly. The manipulation of status was then carried out by reporting the supposed results of the tests. In a series of tasks between pairs of different status, an experimental assistant controlled information about the other person's decision, whether he agreed or disagreed. Given a disagreement with his partner, was a person influenced to change his own decisions? Although the influence of status was confirmed, the hypotheses tested were not of immediate concern to Homans' theory which was given only a brief reference, but were related more closely to the balance theories of Heider (1958) and Newcomb (1961). Berger and Fisek consider that Homans and others have been interested in diffuse status characteristics rather than in the kind of specific conditions introduced in this experiment. These results do not really advance the measurement of costs, although they point to some possible ways of doing so, and they do give strong support to the hypothesis that costs are lowered when deferring is a legitimate due to the person of high status.

Tedeschi, Bonoma and Brown (1971) in a review article draw attention to the promise of experiments where status can be introduced artificially by an experimenter appearing to give respect or approval to a member of a dyad, a confederate, in full view of the other partner. They suggest this as a means of testing Homans' postulate of the rather contagious effects of one's perceiving that a person receives esteem from a third party.

The influence of Homans' discussions of status is quite pervasive. Demarath and Thiessen (1966), discussing middle-class participation in a dissident group of free thinkers accept that "middle-class constraint has become a sociological cliché" (p. 683) and they note that their observations confirm Homans' comments on the licence allowed to high-status persons or groups. Kandel (1966) carried out a study of behaviour associated with status homophily (similarity) between persons, by observing the number of patients treated by doctors in a state mental hospital who were of similar social rank to themselves. She makes the point that status similarity may facilitate treatment in the special case of psychotherapy. Although the discussion refers only briefly to Homans' propositions concerning status congruence, Kandel suggests especially a tendency for high status doctors to treat high status patients.

There are several authors who introduce exchange theory into the discussion of status conditions or effects as an alternative theoretical source. Thus, in the interpretation of reactions to deviance on the part of high status members of a group, Wahrman (1970) suggests the cognitive consistency (balance) and exchange explanations. Wahrman argues that status is a measure of value or "goodness" in people; while norms represent shared judgements and value. Therefore, high status members of a group are expected to conform, as a matter of consistency. By the first (balance) hypothesis, high status members should live up to expectations of certain forms of behaviour which are of value to the group. By the second (exchange) hypothesis, there is an agreement, if only implicit, for the high status person to exchange valued behaviour for status. Wahrman's theoretical discussion is an example of how much balance and exchange explanations tend to converge, so that in this case they are barely separable.

Wahrman's experiment consisted of passing messages to students, seated in individual booths, about the supposed views of other participants concerning a delinquent child's case history and appropriate methods of treatment. The experimental test focused on the students' reaction to an unsympathetic view towards the child from a participant said to be a psychology graduate. The students tended to take negative sanctions against this view by saying they would be unwilling to have the graduate as a co-worker. However, given such a strong manipulation in this experiment, it is not surprising that these reactions took place.

Himmelfarb and Senn (1969) discuss the process of forming impressions of another person's social position as an averaging of individual characteristics. They examine the interaction of different status factors in forming judgements of social position. In two experiments, four levels of three variables (occupation, education and income) were included in a complex design yielding correlations and analysis of variance of each dimension. The experimenters explore the interaction of inconsistent high-low characteristics and the relative influence of each of the three dimensions of occupation, education and income. Homans' treatment of *status congruence** is influential in the discussion of results, together with work on cognitive consistency, by Sampson (1963). Himmelfarb and Senn stress that these writers were interested in the implications of status incongruity for a person and in the efforts made to avoid presenting incongruous impressions, while they focus on the

* See the discussion of this concept and distributive justice in Chapter 8.

ways in which a person may deal with the incongruous characteristics of another.

In a discursive treatment of the topic Runciman and Bagley (1969) point to the complexity of the definitions of status and hence of the notion of inconsistency. They challenge the explanations of attitudes and behaviour as resultants of status incongruence, as Runciman (1967) did in his earlier critique of Homans' views. They suggest that the useful question "is not how many of the person's multiplicity of status ranks are discrepant, but which out of the multiplicity of the available comparisons he makes between himself and others, and what are the consequences of this for his other social attitudes" (p. 364). Runciman and Bagley argue that a person's perception of his relative deprivation may be more important than the inconsistency of his different status attributes.

Runciman (1967) feels that "like most of the terms coined for social psychology, 'status congruence' is mainly a convenient name for a familiar truism" (p. 120) and it conceals much ambiguity about the aspects of status which may be most relevant in particular situations. It is a notion which has to be supplemented by so much further analysis that it is in itself only a weak form of explanation. To say that status congruence is important for a person and that his attributes be given consistent and due recognition, not less than to others', is, for Runciman, a covering hypothesis which is too vague and which leads to confusion with the notion of justice. More than this, Runciman attacks the fundamentals of Homans' theory in experimental psychology and economics: "It is no advance whatever to paraphrase the traditional preoccupations of a subject into a language which has yielded success in another field if that paraphrase will do no more than equate the traditional vocabulary with the 'scientific' by definition and therefore merely perpetuate the old difficulties in new, and perhaps more confusing, terms" (p. 124). Runciman offers reinterpretation of some of the studies discussed by Homans. For instance, he considers that Homans has read too much into the results, imputing too much influence to justice and congruence and not enough to the relevance of different attributes. Runciman discusses W. F. Whyte's (1943) field observations of group behaviour and Homan's (1954) own study of clerical workers in order to demonstrate this criticism. In a third instance, he disagrees with Homans' interpretations of the experimental study by Israel (1956) where students chose others of high ability as task colleagues although choosing colleagues of lower ability brought more financial reward. Homans summarized this as follows: "members had some slight tendency to give high choices to persons that got high scores and low choices to persons that got low ones, notwithstanding that this ran counter to their own monetary interests. When the investigator asked them about these choices, they said they were influenced by a sense of fair play: "a man who got a high score ought to get a high choice" (*Social Behaviour*, p. 175). Runciman reinterprets that the choice of high-ability members was not an effect of justice but of "esteem for ability" (Runciman, 1967, p. 119) but it is doubtful if this is itself a more basic explanation.

Kasl and Cobb (1967) refer to Homans' argument that uncertainty and incongruence of status positions may lead to attempts to align them better, but they do not test this particular hypothesis in the study which they report. In his theoretical paper Kimberly (1967) refers both to Homans' notion of distributive justice and Thibaut and Kelley's interpretation of rewards and costs. He discusses the complexity of status definitions and the problem of defining equality of rank, taking into consideration different status dimensions. He asks the question: how do different kinds of status phenomena come to be viewed as equal?

Alvarez (1968) suggests that a "rational" person who has to decide whether or not to conform to a majority, from a reward-cost estimate of the consequences, will be deviant if he is at the bottom of the hierarchy, and if he is at the top. He draws attention to the U-shaped relationship argued by Homans between deviation and status. The high status person may stand to gain by giving the lead in innovation, while the low status person has little to lose in the group, and may gain alternative rewards outside the group. In contrast, the middle status person cannot afford to deviate because he may lose esteem and he has little to spare. Alvarez sought to present data relevant to the contradictory predictions of two hypotheses: one stated by Homans, the other by Hollander (1958). Homans argued that both higher and lower status persons would lose relatively less for a given deviation and those of middle status relatively more. On the other hand, Hollander introduced into experimental groups the conditions of successful and unsuccessful performance by means of feedback from the experimenter; he found that higher status deviants lost more in esteem-ratings than the lower status ones, when the condition was that of an unsuccessful group. Alvarez used a factorial design, with students role-playing in hierarchical groups and he presents some evidence tending to fit the Hollander hypothesis, although not conclusively.

Conformity

Savell and Healey (1969) mention Adams, Homans, Thibaut and Kelley for their interpretations of the meaning of agreement or conformity with another's opinion. Essentially their experiment deals with the effects of prior agreement from another person on subsequent conformity with his opinion. Each of the students who participated was paired with an accomplice of the experimenter, so that different conditions of prior agreement, from this partner, could be arranged. In other words, it could be that conformity reflects an attempt "to restore balance to what was, until that point, unequal social exchange" (p. 316). Alternatively, a person who agrees with one's opinion will be rewarded with liking, and so conformity may represent a rewarding situation. These explanations are congruent with preferring balance with unbalanced states; again, this discussion demonstrates the closeness of exchange and balance theory and the connection between hypotheses concerning conformity of opinions and reciprocal liking. The investigators mention Jones and Jones (1964) who consider conformity as a strategy for eliciting liking from another person. However, Savell and Healey provide an interesting list of such possibilities commenting that "the list should serve to indicate something of our ignorance . . ." (p. 317). By introducing conditions of private or public statements of agreement, Savell and Healey hoped to show whether the evidence supported exchange and balance explanations or an internal, perhaps more fundamental attitude set, to agree or disagree, or "mediated generalization of affect" as suggested by congruity theory (Osgood and Tannenbaum, 1955; Tannenbaum, 1966). The latter explanation is summarized by Savell and Healey in their statement:

> when the other person endorses or rejects the subject's judgements this person becomes, respectively, more favourably or less favourably evaluated . . . and the other person's newly acquired value (positive or negative) is transferred to the stimulus objects with which this person then proceeds to associate himself—a process of mediated generalization of affect (p. 316).

In their factorial design, the analysis of variance did reveal a strong effect of prior agreement on conformity but did not show sufficient differences between the public or private conditions.

The effect of agreement from others on conformity is again examined by Julian, Regula and Hollander (1968) using six different degrees of agreement. They start with Homans' hypothesis of a "tendency to reciprocate support" and they state as a particular example of it, that "prior support or agreement from others should increase the likelihood of the individual's subsequent agreement or conformity to the group" (p. 171). Their study is aimed at refining this supposition by a factorial design to test the influence of different degrees of prior agreement with individual judgements, on subsequent occasions of conformity to majority behaviour. A Crutchfield apparatus was used to simulate five-member groups. As an experimental task each subject had to judge a sequence of flashing lights, presented to him as he sat in a cubicle on his own. The signalling panel also gave what purported to be decisions of the other group members. Results showed the expected effects of agreement, as arranged by the experimenters, on the incidence of conformity when the subjects had to respond after seeing the judgements of the other group members. But their interpretation of the results reveals a failure to simulate the social quality of reciprocal support and in this concluding discussion they consider the influence on the results of individual confidence, information and learning rather than conformity to a group norm.

Interaction-liking

Schwartz (1968) in a general discussion of privacy and its importance to the individual, argues the limiting case of the hypothesis that interaction leads to liking. He points out that privacy is essentially a relief from too much exposure to social surveillance and in his discursive treatment of this topic he quite clearly considers that there must be some qualification of the interaction-liking hypothesis. There is "a threshold beyond which interaction is unendurable for both parties. It is because people frequently take leave of one another that the interaction-liking proposition maintains itself" (p. 742). This argument suggests that both interaction-liking and the reverse liking-interaction effects could be made more precisely a matter of specifying rates of interaction and degree of liking. Is there a "steady state" of interaction appropriate to situations and persons? We do not know much about these possibilities. When does the satiation effect of Proposition 4 occur, when does intensity of liking bring its consequences in costs? It is surprising, in view of the controversy which the interaction-liking hypothesis has drawn (see Chapter 8, pp. 184–185), that more work has not been done in recent years, varying the conditions of liking. The qualification which Schwartz emphasizes is consistent with Bartos' (1967) notion of the square root function, the resulting curve allowing for an easing off in intensity and a stabilization of liking (see Chapter 8, p. 195). Even this attractive presentation of the limiting case has yet to be taken further by empirical studies.

Priest and Sawyer (1967) examine several aspects of the interaction-liking relationship. Although they mention the exchange theorists, they refer more explicitly to balance theory (Heider, 1958, Newcomb, 1961), and intend to explore balance as a phenomenon attaching to pairs of persons; such an analysis would be laborious because of the problem of obtaining data from each and every pair even in a moderately sized group. However, by means of computer analysis Priest and Sawyer were able to examine some 25,000 distinct pairs of persons. In this interesting study a sociometric test was administered in a student hall of residence, autumn and spring for four years, to 471 individuals in all. This provided information on which of the other members of the Hall each student recognized by name, talked to, liked, and who were his friends. The researchers expected to find a high degree of reciprocation of choice (Person likes Other, Other likes Person) as an indicator of balance in social relationships. Level of liking was scored from 1 for "recognized" to 5 for "best friend". Observations in this study were not carried out on individuals but on pair relations—the complete matrix being included in the computer analysis (see Priest, 1964, for details of this program). First, the effect of proximity was examined, by location of rooms; then of peership, by membership of college years; and lastly, through multiple regression analysis their combined effect was ascertained. Proximity was shown to be a major influence on degree of liking. Furthermore, tabulation of the percentages of students liking each other and who were members of the same or different college years, showed that peership also produced strong effects. Priest and Sawyer now went on to examine the joint effects of proximity and peership. In brief, peership was found to be a better predictor of liking than proximity. The investigators discuss a number of balance theory interpretations and they cite Homans and Blau, since their tests for the effects of proximity and peership are quite clearly tests of Homans' proposition that interaction leads to liking, with proximity and peership providing given conditions of differentiable importance. Priest and Sawyer add a useful refinement when they interpret the effects of proximity and peership in rewards and costs. They conclude that proximity reduces costs; peership, or similarity, increases rewards.

Darley and Berscheid (1967) discuss the nature of the processes which mediate the relationship between interpersonal interaction and liking. They refer to Heider (1958) for the suggestion that increased liking may be the result of a tendency for persons sharing a task or similar situation to assume sentiments in harmony with it. This tendency to harmonize the relationship should begin even before interaction starts, once a person knows that he is about to enter a task or situation with another. They offer this as an alternative to the explanations which have focused on mutual interests and values, as providing the basis for increased liking. Darley and Berscheid tested their hypothesis by asking women students "to talk about sexual standards for female college students" (p. 30) (in two-person discussion groups). Each subject made ratings of two other persons about whom she was given ambiguous personality information and one of whom she knew to be her future partner in the discussion. In a careful experiment, two sets of personality descriptions (A and B), one representing a future partner, the other a girl who was not to be a partner, were presented for rating. Half the subjects were told that the future partner was represented by description A: the other half that description B was of the future partner. The results showed a clear tendency to rate the future partner more favourably. The experimenters conclude that "simply the announcement of future meetings of the subject with another girl produces a greater liking for that girl" (p. 35). They suggest the possibility of reducing friction between groups—if the inevitability of their task contact were to be stressed then reciprocal acceptance should follow.

It is quite easy to explain this conclusion of Darley and Berscheid by Homans' propositions. The explanation would largely be in terms of Proposition 1 which states that if a particular stimulus situation has been the occasion on which a man's activity has been rewarded in the past, then the more similar is a present stimulus situation, the more likely he is to repeat that activity, or some similar activity. Sharing of task activities in the past will no doubt have been a condition where liking has developed between the persons involved, hence if task activities are to be shared with a person in the future it is consistent with his past experience that he now express liking for that person. This test of a hypothesis that anticipated interaction leads to liking complements the early findings of Kurt Back (1951) who showed that anticipated liking leads to interaction (see Chapter 8, p. 185). It is also consistent with the results of Bovard's (1951) study of discussion groups where reward from another person produced the intention to continue relationships with that same person. Although Darley and Berscheid have interpreted their results as showing a tendency towards harmony and especially to balance theory, this in no way diminishes the possibility of adducing the results to Proposition 1 and its corollaries. As I mentioned at the beginning of this chapter, Homans recognizes the strain towards balance in social relations, and therefore the closeness of his explanations with balance theory.

In Pruitt's (1968) experiment in two-person bargaining, the inter-action-liking proposition appears as an alternative hypothesis. One of the simulated partners sacrificed relatively more of his winnings to the participant in the experiment (see p. 255 above) and this had the effect of producing greater reciprocation of money rewards to this partner. The main hypothesis concerned the influence of the principle of distributive justice but one alternative explanation suggested that the partner "was perceived as more generous and hence better liked" (p. 147)— liking in this case leading to the strengthening of reciprocal behaviour, although no direct evidence of this was available. The experiment by Worthy, Gary and Kahn (1969) described earlier in this chapter, refers to liking exchanged for other social rewards. In this case, the other reward is disclosure of personal information by one individual to another. Self-disclosure is held to indicate trust or liking, and mutual self-disclosure is accompanied by mutual liking. If self-disclosure is a reward then the greater the self-disclosure the more interpersonal attraction (liking) that will result. These investigators draw attention to the relationship discussed by Thibaut and Kelley (1959, pp. 33–37) between sociometric choice and willingness to provide positive outcomes, as Homans also postulated. This experiment tested the hypotheses (a) that a person discloses more information to those for whom he has greater liking, and (b) more self-disclosure by a person increases the degree of liking expressed towards him. Measures of degree of liking for other members were taken in four-person groups, before and after a procedure where group members exchanged their written answers to questionnaires, reflecting varying degrees of self-disclosure. An analysis of co-variance for different effects demonstrated support for both these hypotheses.

One of the reasons for the paucity of studies designed to test the interaction-liking hypothesis may be the requirement of making observations over periods of time, although this pertains to many of the variables in social process. Another reason could be that despite its controversial nature the research evidence mostly supports the relationship and the exceptions to it are well known, such as in the conditions of differential status, or authority. As Homans says, "other things equal", the proposition is widely supported and the classic studies by the Sherifs (1953) and Bovard (1951) have not been much improved on.

Conclusion

Much of this chapter has been concerned with the classification and ordering of recent developments, in order to suggest which of these are of importance in advancing the theory. The substantial amount of research which has followed on from *Social Behaviour* cancels out the criticism by Sorokin (1966, pp. 532, 537) that Homans collected *ad hoc* a small body of findings to support his theory, because now we have a larger number of research reports which, at the least, take Homans' propositions as their starting position. We have seen some interesting moves towards greater logical clarity, attempts to formalize which have been only partially successful (e.g. Maris, 1970) and the mathematical and computer translations have been discussed, but again they show strong limitations. However, when these structural developments are placed alongside the body of experimental and observational studies influenced by Homans' theory, then a very remarkable diversity of efforts is revealed, stimulated by this one theory.

The criticisms of the theory have now all been considered; many of them, even the most recent, were pre-empted by Deutsch (1964) and Deutsch and Krauss (1965). Their view that Homans' propositions are tautologous has been fully discussed (pp. 214–218). Braithwaite, Homans and Liska argued that tautologies can be useful if defined in a special *relational* sense and, if one allows of propositions containing "open" concepts (p. 215). We may accept this as a stratagem, unless we wish to take up a positivist position and to demand, at the outset, a formal system of a kind not found in current theorizing. The theory (or theory sketch) drawn up by Homans is incomplete, modifiable and it remains relatively informal in structure. Furthermore, since Homans adapts several of his general propositions from reinforcement theory we have considered some of the general arguments and counter-arguments around the reinforcement notion (see Chapter 9, pp. 217–218 above, and Chapter 2). All the same, the critical attack against Skinnerian assumptions should not be transferred piecemeal to social exchange theory. Yet it has often been done. Homans' use of analogies from Skinner's observations on pigeons has provided a tempting target for this kind of selective criticism. Justified as it was in Chomsky's (1959) criticisms of extrapolations from animal studies in his review of *Verbal Behaviour*, the criticism becomes exaggerated when it is made against *Social Behaviour*, for instance, by Deutsch (1964) and Asplund (1972) without consideration of what the theory achieves once further steps are taken, with the analogies as a point of departure (Chadwick-Jones, 1970).

Homans' own counter-arguments to his critics have been notable; in his replies to Blau (in Borger and Cioffi, 1971) and to Blain (1971) he makes the point, in each case, that sociological theories have no general propositions other than those derived from psychology. Asplund (1972) who considers *Social Behaviour* "both barren and confused" yet gives Homans the pre-eminence of a place next to Durkheim: "we have here two conflicting views: that the individual is prior to society (Homans), and that the society is prior to the individual (Durkheim)" (p. 267). Homans' views are continually developing and he is likely to revise them again, yet he is entirely consistent on this point concerning the contribution of psychology to the explanation of social behaviour; we have seen it illustrated especially in his discussion of the distributive justice principle and its origins (see Homans, 1974).

We have not encountered in the recent developments of the theory much emphasis on economic concepts; instead, Homans' theory is revealed as developing together with Thibaut and Kelley's model, growing closer to this and to other perceptual-cognitive-symbolic theories in social psychology such as Festinger's (1954, 1957) theories of dissonance and the comparison other. Heider's balance theory is often cited as a joint reference with social exchange theory in research reports (see for instance Tallman, 1967, and others discussed in this chapter). Campbell and Alexander (1966) discuss basic notions concerning interpersonal influence which are shared by the theories of Festinger, Heider, Newcomb and Homans. Curry and Emerson (1970) take a fairly typical approach when they discuss social exchange theory as an alternative explanation to balance theory, and possibly a more parsimonious one. These tendencies, which were discussed at the beginning of Chapter 9, underline my view that it would be a mistake to classify the theory, following Nord (1969), as an "economic exchange theory" and more accurate to include it under "reward theory" (Sigall and Aronson, 1967) or "reinforcement-exchange-theory" (Shaw and Costanzo, 1970). While there is no doubt that economic concepts are reconcilable with the propositions of social exchange, this can be shown only at the most general level, as I pointed out in Chapter 8 (p. 183). Going down the deductive chain, the corollaries, hypotheses and concepts belong to social psychology. For that matter, it is not at all unusual for psychological theories to borrow from theoretical economics, which has contributed quite widely in situations "to do with the voluntary choices individuals make between objects of value" (Restle, 1971, p. 21). I emphasized in Chapter 8 that Homans drew attention to the limits in using economic concepts, a caution which Restle also makes when he points to the complexities of social evaluations and their multiple dimensions—so different to the one-dimensional, convertible prices of economics.

Borrowing from economics does not make the theory any less dependent on psychological interpretations and, as we have seen, these interpretations should not be labelled "behaviourist" even if behaviouristic analogies have been used in the theory. It is true that Homans restricts his theoretical discussion to the context of empirical studies where rewards and costs can be observed, inferred or measured. But, as was noted in Chapter 8, this is not a theoretical constraint, it is practical research procedure. Many critics have made the same oversimplification as have Miller, Buckler and McMartin (1969) when they term the theory "behavioural" as distinct from "perceptual". Kunkel (1967), however, recognizes that his "socio-behavioural" approach differs from that of Homans—after all, the latter is very much concerned with a person's expectations and draws no line between cognitive, symbolic and other forms of behaviour. We have also had examples of references to the theory as utilitarian *and* non-utilitarian, reflecting a tendency by different authors to isolate different parts of the theory.

Thus, one of the features of the critical appraisals of Homans' theory is an over-emphasis on its behaviourist antecedents. So much is this so that some critics completely miss out his discussion of equity and distributive justice and the applications which are a preponderant positive influence on current research. The notion of distributive justice which Homans derives from the body of earlier work summarized by Gouldner (1960) has become a major influence in social psychology; the experiments by Stephenson and Barker (1972) on redress of injustice seem to augur the continuation of this trend. It seems that the statements connecting with Proposition 5 may separate into a theory of distributive justice which is relatively independent of the other general propositions and their corollaries. One can, however, ask whether the "equity" propositions have necessarily to connect to the four reinforcement propositions. Clearly they do. The first four propositions deal with differential effects and conditions of rewards and costs; Proposition 5 presents the principle of justice in allocation of rewards and costs. The attainment of justice is also a reward in itself, as well as qualifying the way in which rewards and costs are perceived. It is therefore complementary and necessary to the basic propositions.

In this chapter we have seen the presentation of a good deal of evidence supporting the theory. The majority of it is experimental. This points to error in the statement made by Shaw and Costanzo (1970) that the theory "has not generated independent research and thus has not been subjected to test" (p. 80), with their further suggestion that the theory is "not very conducive" to experiment. In fact, interesting applications of the theory are to be found in the many factorial and other experimental designs described in this chapter and in research using the Prisoner's Dilemma game.

However, there are numerous studies where Homans' propositions have influenced the analysis and description of natural events in occupational, industrial and classroom studies. A recent example is the discussion of the reward-cost outcomes for Cuban refugees (Portes, 1969). Hamblin, Buckholdt, Ferritor, Kozloff and Blackwell (1971) cite the theory simply for its background support to their classroom and child-guidance reinforcement programmes where rewards (food, attention, praise), are administered repetitively and according to rule; nevertheless they attempt to systematize "streams of social interaction" (p. 242) a difficult assignment, more feasible with children than with adults because children's intentions are less covert. While the theory is manifestly useful in this kind of study carried out in situations approximating to natural classroom conditions, few appear in the academic journals, although they are more likely to appear in books or monographs. This presents a contrast to the burgeoning of laboratory experiments, which are more practicable in the short term and more easily published. While it must be noted that Homans' theory is a very widespread influence on experiments, we have no assurance that the proliferating of laboratory tests is a favourable development. It may merely be a by-product of current conventions for research in the discipline of psychology, with experiments as a safe option rather than a dangerous one in the sense used by Moscovici (1972, p. 62) who holds that much of social psychology has become a minor pursuit, where the experimenter pursues data instead of significant problems. One might wish to see the theory applied more to actual situations than to experiments, because it may be more worthwhile to use the theory in order to analyse and interpret existing problems, than to apply it to a convenient experimental paradigm.

12

Peter Blau's Prolegomenon to an Exchange Theory

Introduction

Blau (1964) states his intention to present an analysis of social process between individuals as a step *towards* a theory of more complex social structures. Blau does not intend to search for the psychological roots of interpersonal relations, but he does believe that the most complex aspects of social structure are to be explained by working from the basic social process between individuals. At the same time, Blau argues for the importance of relationships in social life mediated by friendship, status and the division of labour, which are properties additional to, and not described by, the characteristics and behaviour of individuals. Social exchange between persons is itself an instance of emergent properties. He concludes that the psychological process of reinforcement, which he accepts for each individual taken separately, is not sufficient to explain the exchange relation between them. This relation is a joint product of their interdependent actions. Blau lays an emphasis on *interdependency* as his subject matter, as other exchange theorists have done (see Chapter 3, p. 25).

In resting his theoretical argument on reinforcement ideas, even though he argues for the importance of the emergent phenomena of social relationships, Blau takes up a starting position which is identical with that of Homans and Thibaut and Kelley, and which he acknowledges (p. 2). It is his intention to advance from this position to a sociological theory of collectivities and institutions. Later in this chapter we will examine how far he implements this intention. However, the sheer fact that he starts from a base of psychological concepts has drawn sociological criticism as, for example, when Stanley (1968) criticizes Blau for treating macro-structures *merely* in terms of emergent properties "resting upon a presumably universal theory of primary relationships" (Stanley, 1968, p. 859).

Blau considers exchange to be a social process of central significance rooted in "primitive psychological processes" (p. 4) and from it many complex phenomena are derived. He maintains that considerations of exchange in a variety of forms are important for all socially mediated goals. Exchange behaviour covers a very wide substantive content, such that it may be "oriented to the pursuit of ultimate values rather than to the pursuit of immediate rewards" (p. 5). At this point Blau brings in a distinction between intrinsic and extrinsic rewards in interpersonal relations: the former term referring to value that inheres in a relationship itself: in mutual liking or companionship. In this case individuals may exchange favours for one another in order to express their commitment to the relationship and to encourage commitment on the part of the other (see pp. 286, 296 below). However, in an exchange of extrinsic rewards the relationship is only instrumental to achieving material or other rewards.

Blau recognizes the temptation to explain all social conduct by means of the notion of exchange. Therefore, to avoid the tautological use of the notion in such a way that all behaviour is "explained" as exchange, it is necessary to specify a criterion that restricts its use. What are the conditions under which exchange concepts do not apply? Here Blau touches on the most important question for any theory—does it provide empirically testable hypotheses? Blau states his intention of giving some examples of operational hypotheses.* Secondly, he raises the question of whether social exchange explanations are culture-bound and concludes that there is inevitably some bias, both in the choice of this theory and in the evidence which he adduces to support it, because it is suited to Western society.

Blau is particularly interested in the conditions which hold for different forms of power in social relations and he asks: how do status differences and power structures develop out of the interpersonal process of exchange? He intends to answer this question in the earlier part of the book and then, later on, he will devote his attention to the complex nature of collectivities and institutions. In discussing *status* he introduces economic concepts of marginal utility and rates of exchange,

* See below, pp. 301, 303, 326–329.

bilateral monopolies and supply or demand variations. He recognizes
that the "predictions" drawn from these analogies would in many cases
prove incorrect. However, he returns to his previous point that, at least,
statements incorporating these ideas provide operational hypotheses
which, if rejected, may lead to improved reformulations. In the course
of this chapter we will appraise the extent to which Blau realizes these
aims.

In the second half of his book Blau discusses the complex structures of
large collectivities and refers to the indirect (secondary) exchanges
which develop from the direct (primary) ones, when individuals receive
their rewards from a group rather than from another individual. Social
transactions are now considered which go well beyond direct exchange
between individuals. Integration, status differentiation and organization are some of the concepts considered at the level of social institutions, as are opposition, reorganization and conflict as structural
phenomena.

Social association: basic process

So, for Blau, the study of face-to-face interaction is only the first stage
towards a more ambitious sociological analysis and this explanatory
progression reflects a natural development wherein "the associations
between individuals tend to become organised into complex social
structures, and they often become institutionalised to perpetuate the
form of organization far beyond the life span of human beings" (p. 13).
Blau sets out to illustrate this main theme, beginning with a series of
examples of the basic process of social exchange. He gives some indicators of the richness and variety of social rewards between friends,
lovers, in families and in occupations, pointing out also that

> the rewards individuals obtain in social associations tend to entail a cost
> to other individuals . . . individuals associate with one another because
> they all profit from their association. But they do not necessarily all profit
> equally, nor do they share the cost of providing the benefits equally . . .
> (p. 15).

He elaborates on the differences between intrinsic and extrinsic rewards
and he introduces one of his favourite illustrations—the case of two
lovers which, strangely enough, is not discussed either by Homans or
Thibaut and Kelley. Thus, illustrating *intrinsic* rewards, Blau writes:
"It is not what lovers do together but their doing it *together* that is the

distinctive source of their special satisfaction—not seeing a play but sharing the experience of seeing it" (p. 15). _Extrinsic_ rewards come from the activities rather than the relationship itself between persons— examples are the giving of favours and the expressions of gratitude that are made in return for them. After some discussion of anecdotal instances Blau adds that "There are, to be sure, some individuals who selflessly work for others without any thought of reward and without even expecting gratitude, but they are virtually saints, and saints are rare . . . we require some incentive . . . if it is only the social acknowledgement that we are unselfish" (p. 17). Following his argument, altruism may be encountered infrequently but psychological hedonism would be an over-simple general explanation of behaviour. Blau emphasizes the part played by social approval as a prized reward from others, in diminishing tendencies to outright egotism and disregard of others' opinions. He notes that while social disapproval effectively deters persons from certain conduct, there are many subtleties in the expression of social approval. Many verbal expressions of apparent social approval are literally conventional and more meaningful signs of approval may be sought from others' behaviour over the long term. Blau comments that: "The social approval of those whose opinions we value is of great significance to us, but its significance depends on its being genuine" (p. 17).

Rationality

Blau raises an important question when he asks whether a rationalistic conception of human behaviour underlies the notion of social exchange. Like Homans he does not assume that the participants in social exchange have complete information of the rewards available to themselves and to others, nor that they are entirely consistent in their behaviour, such as would be assumed in the rationalistic model of game theory. The only assumption made is that persons choose between alternative courses of action or associates, according to a preference ranking. Like Homans, Blau accepts that the course of action a person takes may not be the one that yields greatest material profit or be the most efficient means to realize his goal. However, psychological interpretations of motive in social behaviour are not of interest to Blau, who is more concerned with "the social forces that emanate from them" (p. 19). Nevertheless, he gives a good deal of attention to what he calls "the simpler social processes . . . that rest directly on psychological dispositions" (p. 20). These "psychological dispositions" underlie the "feelings of attraction between individuals" and their "desires for various kinds of rewards". Social attraction—the attraction of associating with others, for whatever reason—is presented as a fundamental process leading to exchange relations. The exchange may be in the nature of reciprocal intrinsic rewards which inhere to the association, or it may take the (extrinsic) form of exchanging mutual favours; for instance, the provision of advice or help in exchange for expressions of gratitude.

Next he illustrates how exchange between persons can lead to differences in their power. Power is here defined as the capacity to obtain compliance from others. For Blau, power is based on the supply of rewards to others. It is illustrated as appearing in the relationship of lovers and the relationship of employer and worker. The latter may have equally good alternatives, may be able to do without the employer's benefits, may offer coercion as a counter; all these are limiting conditions on the employer's power. Blau continues:

> But given these limiting conditions, unilateral services that meet basic needs are the penultimate source of power. Its ultimate source, of course, is physical coercion. While the power that rests on coercion is more absolute, however, it is also more limited in scope than the power that derives from met needs* (p. 22).

It may be, says Blau, that a person rewards another with power over himself, undertaking to comply with the latter's wishes in return for a service. Blau emphasizes that this strategy is an important one, sufficiently frequent to create what he sometimes terms "status", sometimes "power", as a generic social reward, parallel to money. "The power to command compliance is equivalent to credit, which a man can draw on in the future to obtain various benefits at the disposal of those obligated to him" (p. 22). In this way exchange relations lead to the differentiation of power.

Blau now gives attention to the uses of different forms of power and of compliance. He considers the possibilities of *opposition* when power turns to exploitation. Here we have the first hint of Blau's later analysis of conflict and it is characteristic of his exposition that the examples range from lovers' power over each other to the formal organization of a factory. Legitimization of power, its collective recognition, occurs

---

* See Blau's discussion of coercive power below (p. 300).

through the consensus of a subordinate group and constitutes the basis of stable authority, he argues. On the other hand, collective disapproval of power leads to organized opposition movements or parties.

At this point Blau draws his first parallel between the social process among individuals and that among groups. But he also notes that there are fundamental differences between these processes. In complex social structures individuals and groups are without any direct contact and there is a network of indirect (secondary) exchanges. At this level the equivalent of the feelings of personal attraction in dyads or in small groups, is found in the *value consensus* which binds together the members of large collectivities. Blau holds that an analysis of social values and norms will complement the analysis of direct exchange and power transactions at the level of interpersonal contact.

A second "emergent property" is the complex, intricate pattern of relations between and within collectivities which constitutes a great contrast to the simpler analysis of exchange process. Blau indicates that the analysis of this pattern is his eventual aim in the final chapters. A third difference between inter-related groups (macrostructures) and interacting individuals (microstructures) is that formalized institutions of the macrostructures exist independent of any individual members and transmit social values and norms over long periods of time.*

Reciprocity

Blau has affirmed the tendency for social relations to become reciprocal exchanges of mutual advantage but he accepts that there is a tendency for one party to do better than another; for the exchange to be unequal. He now develops a very interesting discussion of what he calls "the strain towards imbalance", whereby individuals and groups strive to accumulate credit, to make their power or status superior to that of others. On this topic, Blau offers a more adequate discussion of social behaviour than that of Gouldner (1960) and others who have emphasized only the prevalence of reciprocity. As Ellis (1971) has mentioned, Blau does include the negative tendencies in social relations. Reciprocity is seen as resulting from an inclination to associate with others, to give

---

* Note that Thibaut and Kelley (1959, pp. 256–272) discuss the process by which group norms are formed and the various means by which groups exercise control over individuals. However, they do not advance the discussion beyond primary groups and are not concerned with the analysis of macrostructures.

and receive rewards, or to stay out of debt in social transactions, but a complete explanation of interpersonal relations is attained only when it is admitted that there is also a tendency to imbalance. Reciprocity explanations would give only a partial analysis. Blau goes into some detail to demonstrate that balance and imbalance exist together, as in his example of lovers whose reciprocal relationship "has been established by an imbalance in the exchange . . ." (p. 27) because, in this case, the boy has made special efforts so that the girl's association with him is rewarding to her. Blau continues:

> The reciprocal attraction in most intimate relations—marriages and lasting friendships as well as more temporary attachments—is the result of some imbalance of contributions that compensates for inequalities in spontaneous affection, notably in the form of one partner's greater willingness to defer to the other's wishes (p. 27).

Now he refers briefly to the psychological theories of Newcomb (1961), Heider (1958) and Festinger (1957) which postulate that individuals seek to avoid imbalance in their social relations. However, Blau discounts a psychological treatment of individual motives from his own discussion, preferring to give his attention to what he considers more important, the actual process and interplay of imbalance and balance in social relations: "that a given balance in social associations is produced by imbalances in the same associations in other respects" (p. 28). So, he points to the imbalance that unilateral benefits produce, when one person only has the power to provide services to another, this imbalance itself creates reciprocity of exchange since the person receiving benefits is obligated to reciprocate them. Thus, the individual who has power to provide unilateral benefits "accumulates a capital of willing compliance on which he can draw whenever it is to his interest to impose his will upon others" (p. 28). An imbalance in power may lead to a positive exchange, satisfactory to the person with less power but it may also lead to his opposition where the reciprocal obligation is on unsatisfactory terms. In the former case there is what Blau calls a positive imbalance of benefits which is acceptable to the person with less power, while in the latter, if the demands of the more powerful produce hardship, there is a negative imbalance of exploitation. Such effects and alternatives can be followed through, Blau assures us, from simple social process into complex macrostructures "where forces that sustain reciprocity and balance have disequilibrating and imbalancing repercussions . . ." (p. 31). As an example of positive imbalance Blau mentions industrial employees who "receive benefits, such as financial remuneration, in exchange for complying with the directives of superiors and making various contributions to the organization" (p. 29). His example of a negative imbalance stimulating opposition is the obvious one of trade unions in strike action.

Beyond the dyad

Blau ends this introductory outline of the topics he intends to discuss, with some comments on the inadequacy of the dyad as an illustrative case for the study of social relations. If the dyad is examined, then it should not be discussed in isolation, he argues, from the alternative social opportunities which each member may have outside this particular pair relationship. Blau refers to Simmel's distinction between a pair and any group of more than two, particularly in the conditions for the exercise of power, where strategies of forming coalitions, dividing the opposition or mediation by third parties cannot be manifest in a dyad. Blau therefore advises that an analysis of social association between individuals should be undertaken in networks of multiple relations in groups and not in isolated pairs, bearing in mind that "most associations are part of a broad matrix of social relations" (p. 32).

At first, this view of dyads seems to be in contrast to Homans' view of the dyad as the nucleus of all social relationships (see Chapter 8, p. 195). However, Homans also seeks his factual sources for generalizations in studies of larger primary groups and for him the dyad seems only to have served as a means to illustrating some of the conditions for reciprocity. Other conditions which pertain to larger groups are those involving conformity or collusive behaviour, collective approval (esteem) and leadership. Concepts of authority and justice require testing in groups of greater complexity than the dyad. So here are definite limits to an explanatory framework based only on the dyad although much of the argument employed in social exchange theory rests on the two-person illustration. Since Homans attempted to adduce research evidence from 60 studies in support of hypotheses derived from his basic propositions, it must be significant that only a small number of these concern dyads and most of them are based on observations of primary groups, as these are usually understood, comprising six to nine members. This confirms the necessity to look beyond two-person relationships; indeed it may only be possible in the laboratory to confine our subject matter in this way. Recalling our discussion in Chapter 3, Thibaut and Kelley have chosen to apply their model almost exclusively to individuals or to the dyad and in doing so they have created a problem that arises on every occasion when they argue for generalizing their empirical results; it is a difficulty which they frequently discuss (see Chapter 4, pp. 67–73). Some further clues to the restrictiveness which a dyadic model involves is found in the review of research in small groups by Delamater, McClintock and Becker (1965). They list the variables included in hypotheses from six sources, namely, the works of Bales, Cartwright and Zander, Homans, Moreno, Newcomb, Thibaut and Kelley. Subsequently they classify these variables as being available through observation (a) of individuals (b) of dyads and (c) of primary groups. Out of a total of 166 variables, 66 are available by observing individuals, 25 by observing dyads and 75 require observing three persons or more.

Blau points to the multiple relations occurring simultaneously in a group of persons and he is therefore not in favour of observing two-person relationships to the exclusion of the broader social context. He has thus stated his position on the unit for study and he thereby gives support to the conclusion that research in interpersonal relations has to be carried out in situations of greater social complexity than the experimental dyad.

Social integration

Blau gives a good deal of attention to integration within groups by means of the development of ties of attraction between members. He gives examples of groups with diffused boundaries such as friendship cliques in schools or neighbourhoods and groups which have an institutional origin such as work groups or families. In these varied groups the integral forces developing from social attraction are the same, notes Blau, and he asks: What are the processes of attraction? Blau suggests that these derive from the individual's "proclivity to associate with others" (p. 34) which earlier he has termed a "primitive psychological process" but now he states that attraction is closely involved with the capacity to reward—other persons are attractive if the individual anticipates that association with them will be rewarding. Thus, a reinforcement proposition is the implicit starting point of all Blau's explanations. He does not discuss reward hypotheses as such but he has fully acknowledged his debt to Homans and to Thibaut and Kelley in this respect. To be accepted as an associate, the individual must be attractive to others and he will therefore wish to show that he can offer them *rewards*. This is the "primitive process", Blau argues, from which the more complex forms develop when individuals enter into competition for social acceptance and when they become differentiated in status.

Impressing others

Blau is very interested in the ways in which a person sets out to make a good impression on others, to gain their acceptance as a potentially attractive member of the same group. Blau (1960) has discussed this effort at impression-making together with the somewhat contradictory tendency which a person may express to ingratiate himself with his future associates—as we shall see below.

It is important, Blau suggests, for a person to impress others that he is someone with whom it will be rewarding to associate. Beyond such a general statement, he distinguishes between relationships which are intrinsically rewarding and those where the association is only a *means* to obtaining rewards. In the former, where there is intrinsic attraction, the association itself has supreme value as an end in itself—for example, a person's devotion to loved ones transmits no obligation for specific returns. Even so, there is an expectation of rewards, or favours, as an expression or confirmation of the other's reciprocal commitment to the relationship.

In the case of extrinsic rewards a person may make comparisons between different associates, by independent standards of the "best", or rational choice. No such comparison is possible for associations which are intrinsically rewarding "except in the purely subjective terms of the gratifications they provide" (p. 36)—this is entirely a matter of individual judgement. Blau points out that many associations carry mixed intrinsic and extrinsic rewards and he suggests trade union membership as one example of these, not only as a means of improving the individual's employment conditions but it is a means of enjoying the fellowship of the union. By his attendance at meetings the individual does not merely derive material rewards* but enjoys the support,

---

* For a description of these mixed benefits in union activities see Chadwick-Jones, 1969, Chapter 3, pp. 28–37.

friendship and status rewards from other members of the group. The analytical distinction between intrinsic and extrinsic, breaks down in these cases of mixed benefits; not only do the intrinsic and extrinsic operate together but how does one decide if a reward is of one or other kind? Despite this difficulty, Blau says, it seems clear that the *initial attraction* of one person for another rests on extrinsic factors—at least, in the sense that they can be compared with rewards to be offered in alternative relationships. New acquaintances try to show that they would make attractive associates, displaying possibilities of sharing similar interests, or providing social support, or having admired qualities. In discussing this topic Blau refers to Goffman (1956, 1961) for a number of illustrations of ways of impressing others—for instance, the public performer in treating a difficult act with casual detachment. Blau cites Goffmann's description of "role distance", that is, the "attempt to show that the demands of a role are beneath one's capabilities" (p. 40), for instance, by clowning during the performance of a task and simulating noninvolvement—the chief surgeon's jokes—particularly where the task is an exacting one.

Next, the paradoxical situation is considered where an individual's impressive qualities are at once an advantage and a threat to other members of his group. The rewards for associating with him also make for dependency by others.* The person who shows only that he has qualities equivalent to those of other group members, that his claims are modest, will not constitute such a threat but ingratiating tactics alone are likely to achieve only minimal acceptance and so he may try a more aggressive assertion of skills that command respect. Again, respect brings anticipation of his expected contributions but anticipation too of future dependence, of future obligations. The result of this paradox is a reluctance to be impressed, as a defensive reaction which is an important strategy in the competition between individuals for the regard of others. Blau sees this kind of competition between several persons each trying to make an impression "as a series of interlocking mixed games, in which group members have some common and some conflicting interests" (p. 45). An individual may choose between expressing regard for another (and risking a subordinate position for himself) or withholding his regard (and endangering the possibility of an association). Blau holds that an individual (A) would prefer to enjoy B's high regard, but unless he is himself prepared to offer something

* Here Blau cross-references Thibaut and Kelley, 1959, pp. 21–24 and 66.

similar to B there may be no chance at all of them associating together. The choice of outcomes is represented in Fig. 17.

	A's choice	
	Expressing regard	Withholding regard
B's choice Expressing regard	Peer relation (2nd choice of both)	A superior to B (A's first choice)
Withholding regard	B superior to A (B's first choice)	No relation (Last choice of both)

Fig 17 (Blau, 1964, p. 45).

Blau states that this matrix schematization misses the most dynamic elements of group processes, particularly the continual modifying of behaviour that occurs in sequences of social interaction. He refers to the same point mentioned by Thibaut and Kelley (1959, pp. 18–19) when they call attention to the importance of successive choices, although they decide to ignore sequential effects in their matrix and he comments that this imposes a serious limitation.* Blau refers to interlocking games presumably to reflect the fact that there will be many such games concurrently between individuals in even a small group—in a group of ten there could be 45; the outcomes of some of them will affect others; "there is not merely a series of interlocking pair relations but a group structure with its own dynamics" (p. 46)—later in his book Blau will give full attention to such "emergent structural conditions".

A number of anecdotal or self-evident examples now follow illustrating how, after initial attempts to make a positive impression and to claim superior status, those who are not successful may become self-depreciating. By this means they can be accepted into the group as peers and settle at last for social support rather than for recognition. This strategy succeeds by overcoming the former defensive reactions of others, but it assumes that the others already feel some attraction for those who now adopt the more modest approach. Withdrawal from the competition for status permits an emphasis on shared interests and strengthens positive ties in the group otherwise under strain from competition. Those who no longer compete for superior status therefore

* Homans makes a similar point (see Chapter 9, p. 205).

gain acceptance in exchange for the contribution they can now make to group solidarity.

Following the preceding discussion of a number of illustrative cases, Blau discusses the research report of Jones, Gergen and Jones (1963). The findings tend to support the speculations on impression-making that have already been described. For instance, Jones and his colleagues (1963) tested the tendency to ingratiate as affected by status. Naval trainees on a university course were divided into pairs. In the pairs of the experimental group one member was told he was senior, the other that he was subordinate in status (and in fact they were, respectively, senior class students and freshmen). The experimenter announced that he was interested in finding out at the end whether each liked the other —this was the experimental variable—which constituted, in effect, "pressure to become integrated". In the control group, participants were told that this was *not* the experimenter's interest: "We are not especially concerned with whether you end up liking each other or not. . . . We are interested only in how well you can do in reaching a clear impression of the other person" (Blau, 1964, p. 52). Participants were asked to rate themselves on lists of personal characteristics, the results showing that those in the experimental group were more modest in their ratings—thus suggesting that, as Blau comments, "the pressure toward integration promotes self-depreciation" (p. 52). Both superiors and subordinates in the experimental group were more modest about themselves than those in the control group. There was also an interesting tendency for the experimental subordinates to agree more, on average, with opinions which the experimenter presented as having been made by their senior partners, than did those in the control group. In addition, subordinates tended to agree more with seniors, than the converse—confirming the hypothesis that such a strategy would be more congenial for subordinates. This was qualified by superiors' readiness to compromise on matters irrelevant to their authority. Blau doubts that this evidence shows conclusively that conformity is a strategy to gain approval; in this case it might merely have reflected acknowledgement of the superiors' greater competence. He mentions Kelley and Shapiro's (1954) experiment as demonstrating that low rank persons have a more general tendency to conformity than those of high rank.

In conclusion, Blau states that these findings provide support and some further refinement for a theory of social integration; in other words that much of the behaviour of members of groups results in establishing and maintaining integrative ties in the face of competitive strains which would otherwise dissolve them. Individuals have to impress on others that they possess superior competence in order to be granted high social rank but they may often indulge in some self-depreciation in order to minimize the resentment which their higher position and privileges may draw onto them.

In the first sixty pages of his book Blau has emphasized the paradoxes of imbalance and reciprocity; he cites four empirical studies and gives many anecdotal or self-evident illustrations. And he says that he will give further examples. To what end? Simply to the conclusion that the incompatible phenomena of social life are the source of its dynamics. Fundamentally, Blau presents us with a conflict theory. He gives a much greater emphasis on conflict than is to be found in the other contributions to exchange theory. This important difference can be traced back to his postulate that in social life there is almost always a strain to accumulate credit, a tendency not towards balance but towards imbalance.

Social support

After a brief discussion of the characteristics of cohesive groups which exercise strong control over their members but also offer them support, Blau considers two important elements of such support—expressions of social approval and intrinsic attraction. Both of these are social rewards but "they cannot be directly bartered in exchange without losing their intrinsic value" (p. 62), they have to be spontaneous reactions and not calculated to gain outcomes in exchange.

Let us first examine Blau's use of "social approval". As we saw in Chapter 9 Homans gives the same meaning to the terms "social approval" and "liking" but Blau uses social approval in a different sense: he equates it with the support that comes from agreement and consensus of opinions. Blau makes clear that men attach great significance to social approval because "the approving agreement of others helps to confirm their judgements, to justify their conduct, and to validate their beliefs" (p. 62). To have value, this kind of social approval must be genuine* and it must also be discriminating and therefore used sparingly. For Blau, furthermore, *respect* and *esteem* are a

---

* Homans makes a similar point when he discusses gift giving as a superiority ploy. For both Blau and Homans, contrived strategies are "counterfeit currency" and risk detection as such.

specific type of approval involving *unilateral* acknowledgement of abilities—they are more likely to refer to a general evaluation of a person, whereas approval usually refers to a particular decision or action. Other sorts of approval are multilateral (and therefore do not involve esteem or respect)* such as the mutual agreement which occurs when there is general conformity to norms in a group. When there is mutual approval between persons this does provide an initial basis for what becomes diffuse intrinsic attraction.

Blau now proceeds to illustrate the tendency for intrinsic attraction to develop between persons of similar opinions and he refers to Newcomb's (1961) study of the acquaintance process and to Thibaut and Kelley (1959, p. 42) who suggest that attraction involves "ability to reward" and "cost of providing the reward". Thus, if a person has similar opinions to another he merely has to express his own opinions in order to reward the other and there will be little cost to himself because it is easy to express what one really feels. There is much evidence that a person's agreement with another will increase the attraction that the other feels for him and we have already discussed this as part of Homans' exposition in Chapter 8 (p. 164 above).

Blau calls attention to the effect of first impressions on intrinsic attraction, how such impressions may become self-perpetuating because a person is encouraged to fulfil the expectations created by the first impression itself. There are further illustrations of, for example, how bluffing as a strategy is more likely to succeed in short-lived encounters. He next makes what he calls an "excursus on love" mentioning Thibaut and Kelley's (p. 66) commentary on lovers' quarrels—where one partner may test the other's dependence by temporary separation. Although Blau has said earlier that he will seek explanations of social behaviour in groups offering a complexity not to be found in only a pair of persons, nevertheless he now takes some time to illustrate the relationships—and intensely emotional ones—unique to a pair. Underlying these illustrations there are economic analogies, particularly in the notions of a depreciating currency where one partner grants favours too readily, and in the discussion of various courses of action available to either partner in the "courtship market". However, the point of all this is to underline Blau's conclusion that courtship "is a mixed game with some common and some conflicting interests, just as is the establishment of other social relations . . ." (p. 83), as shown earlier in Fig. 17 (above).

* But compare Homans' discussion of "mutual esteem" in Chapter 9.

He does, however, draw attention to the differences between dyads and larger social groups in that attraction between partners in the dyad although not independent of the surrounding social context, is still a matter of largely personal feelings whereas social approval in groups of three or more rests on multiple relationships, and forms part of a more extensive social structure. The significance of the approval bestowed by a person occupying a superior rank in a group structure is inherently greater, irrespective of the particular person bestowing it. Blau is here showing us that structural variables are of greater importance in group contexts than personal attributes. This view appears as a natural reflection of his emphasis on the emergent phenomena of social behaviour. In a group, moreover, there are more or less objective criteria for granting status as distinct from the idiosyncratic ones of personal attraction.

Although much of Blau's exposition is anecdotal, consisting of fairly convincing illustrations, it is nevertheless notable that in this discussion Blau refers from time to time to Thibaut and Kelley and to Homans in order to illustrate notions which are similar to theirs, or to support hypotheses which they too have put forward. It is surprising that while he discusses particular hypotheses he does not refer to the propositions, as such, of Homans' theory and far from constructing an alternative theory, Blau's explanation, at least at this stage, seems to be only a presentation of plausible hypotheses. However, this is consistent with his aims as stated at the beginning, to attempt an approach *towards* a theory.

Social exchange and its limitation

At the beginning of his chapter "Social Exchange" Blau mentions again that Homans' *Social Behaviour* has been his source of inspiration and he reiterates Homans' view that exchange occurs in most social associations: "not only in market relations but also in friendship and even in love, as we have seen, as well as in many social relations between these extremes in intimacy" (Blau, 1964, p. 88). He discusses the pervasiveness of exchange, tangible or intangible, in social relations but he warns that this interpretation cannot be applied to all social conduct: "People do things for fear of other men or for fear of God or for fear of their conscience, and nothing is gained by trying to force such action into a conceptual framework of exchange" (p. 89). Blau now makes his own distinctive contribution to the analysis of exchange. Discussing the studies of simpler societies by anthropologists such as Mauss (1954), he emphasizes two functions of social exchange: as contrasted with its *economic aspects* social exchange serves two general functions—establishing bonds of friendship and establishing superordination over others, contradictory as these two consequences seem.

As we have seen, the basic explanation of exchange is sought by Blau in the influences of rewards on behaviour. Rewarding services rendered by one individual to another create obligations which, in turn, must be discharged. Emphasizing mainly extrinsic rewards, Blau heavily underlines the importance of expectations of reciprocity. This appears in the influences on behaviour of obligations, and efforts to avoid social "debt". Blau also sees it as important for a person to provide incentives to others in order that they may increase their supply of rewards to him. With the latter, he is, in fact, approximating to Homans' Propositions 2 and 3 which state conditions where rewards are reciprocal. He also paraphrases Homans' Proposition 4: the more a person receives from another, the less valuable any further unit becomes or, in economic terms, the marginal utility diminishes. The exchange settles, as described by Homans, at the point where costs balance rewards and Blau expresses this with an economic analogy when he states that this point occurs where "the declining marginal utility of additional benefits is no longer worth the cost of obtaining them" (p. 90). Although he mentions that considerations other than these rational or economic ones will influence a decision (for example, a desire not to offend someone), this is Blau's basic model. Thus, he postulates that calculation of rewards influences social relations although the calculation need not be made with awareness of it, in an explicit sense. It need only be that something like a calculation occurs, but quite unconsciously. This is, of course, very similar to the views of Homans and Thibaut and Kelley. Blau comes now to a discussion of the limits on exchange explanations, which we have already noted briefly (see p. 278 above). The first limiting case involves conscience. When a man acts, following internalized ideas or standards, for reasons of conscience, without thought of reward, there is no social exchange. Furthermore, an exchange must be voluntary and, therefore, actions which are compelled by physical threat, or when a person is coerced, are not to be included.* This is the

* Because Thibaut and Kelley give so much emphasis to power conditions, they are often concerned with relationships where no exchange occurs. Their own reluctance to use the term "exchange theory" is justified, for this reason.

second limiting case—there is no exchange where physical coercion is used. This is not to say that compliance which is made voluntarily to the wishes of persons with other forms of power (and especially "reward power"), does not constitute social exchange. Power, in the sense of power to reward, is Blau's main concern rather than coercive power. So, an exchange may be entered into with persons who have superior power through the benefits they can supply. A voluntary exchange may also occur through a person's conformity to norms which are shared with others and mediated by them.

Differences from economic exchange

Another clarification supplied by Blau consists of his conjecture that social exchange does not start with the norm of reciprocity but with the "existential conditions of exchange" (p. 92), out of which the norm tends to develop. The most important difference of all between social and economic exchange, Blau continues, is that the former entails unspecified obligations; the exact nature of future returns is not specified in advance. Social exchange creates diffuse future obligations not precisely specified ones as in economic exchange; one has therefore to trust others to discharge their obligations—and, Blau argues that the nature of the return, certainly in many instances, cannot be bargained about.* Nor can the other party be forced to reciprocate. Trust is of the essence of a social exchange and as mutual trust flourishes so does the extent and commitment to the exchange. Typically a social exchange builds up slowly from minor transactions requiring little risk, until a relationship of mutual trust is established. A further aspect of unspecified social obligation is that benefits received do not have an exact price. Blau expresses this very clearly: "It is not just the social scientist who cannot exactly measure how much approval a given helpful action is worth; the actors themselves cannot precisely specify the worth of approval or of help in the absence of a money price" (p. 95).

Blau recognizes the weakness of any attempt to measure what is exchanged in an actual social relationship, Homans has recognized this by suggesting that measures must take a relatively modest form (Chapter 8, p. 176). From what Blau has said, it becomes all the more obvious

---

* Note that Blau speculates that there can be many situations where bargaining is not possible. For a discussion of bargaining and negotiation, see Chapter 6, pp. 109, 118 and Chapter 14, pp. 345–354.

that if the return in a social exchange cannot be precisely specified (or if it cannot be bargained about), these are conditions which are entirely different from an economic exchange. His argument at this point, although he is not consistent about it later, suggests that much of social exchange does not lend itself to a payoff treatment with quantified outcomes. This is the limitation of the game theory matrix used by Thibaut and Kelley who treat only with quantified outcomes within the control of laboratory designs, so that experimenters can allocate points or money to the alternative outcomes (see Chapter 3, p. 33). We find that Blau takes quite a different position to this but one which is very similar to that of Homans, when he points to the obstacles to obtaining measures of social rewards and costs. We can infer from this that relatively modest measuring techniques may often have been used and that it is more important to hold to terms of reference that are exploratory and broad in the matter of selecting research designs.

Continuing with his distinctions between social and economic exchange, Blau states yet another major difference: only the former engenders personal obligations and feelings of gratitude. These are *intrinsic* benefits of an exchange in which, rather than the acts themselves, it may be an underlying mutual support or friendliness that is being exchanged. For instance, seeking advice may be an occasion for conviviality and for confirming the friendly relations between two persons. Since there are no ways of establishing exact prices or of keeping separate the "utilities" of extrinsic from intrinsic rewards, Blau refers to Homans' statement that the economic notion of maximizing utilities cannot therefore be applied to social exchange, in any precise way. And while it is helpful to abstract extrinsic benefits* for the purpose of analysis, these may not in fact be detachable from the person who bestows them. Even, in economics, Blau remarks, multiple factors confound rational decision-making; in consumer behaviour, for a given choice, the significance of the alternatives available is rarely confined to a single factor: "People's job choices are affected by working conditions as well as salaries, and their choices of merchants by the atmosphere in a store as well as the quality of the merchandise" (p. 96). This is the problem of incomparability which Wiberg (1972) has recently discussed as, essentially, the problem of finding an indifference curve, and how to find such a curve "describing how people trade off one value against another". Wiberg adds his comment that "At least on the indi-

---

* Blau mentions advice, invitations, assistance or compliance as extrinsic benefits.

vidual level, the empirical problems connected with this issue appear to be still unsolved" (p. 310). Later in this chapter we shall discuss Blau's own attempt to apply indifference curves, by analogy, to social exchange (see p. 308).

We will examine Blau's treatment of indifference curves under *Consultation in groups: an economic analogy* later in this chapter, but for the moment we continue with his comments on measurement. Blau mentions that economists meet this difficulty by avoiding any direct attempt to measure utilities, for instance, they will do no more than *infer* marginal utilities from the distribution of consumer expenditures. He suggests that similar inferences concerning the value of social rewards can be made from conduct observed in social exchange.* In this way, Blau promises that testable hypotheses will be derived about the group structure emerging from the exchange of rewards, and he intends to state these later (see pp. 316–327, 329–331 below).

The conditions of exchange

Blau discusses the degree of commitment of either partner to an exchange. The one with fewer alternatives will have the greater commitment and this is a situation again resembling a mixed game, like the previous two examples he has discussed, social integration (gaining acceptance in a group) and love (achieving a reciprocal intensity of commitment). In a mixed game there are common and conflicting interests between the advantages of the common partnership and the conflicting consideration of who makes the greater commitment because the person who "shows his hand" will be the more dependent and, therefore, the more vulnerable of the two.

The discussion which follows gives further ammunition to the argument that social exchange and economic exchange have crucial differences. For instance, some social rewards cannot easily be part of a calculated exchange—as examples Blau refers to the attraction felt for another person, approval of his opinions, or respect for his abilities. These are spontaneous reactions not calculated to gain a return. Furthermore, such evaluations are rewarding only if they are clearly not being used as a means to exchange (see above, p. 173). On the other hand, the case of rewarding actions is different: these *can* be offered as induce-

* This is also Homans' argument, see Chapter 8, p. 163.

ments and examples of them are—accepting a newcomer in a group, or giving instrumental services, or offering to comply with someone's wishes. All these may anticipate benefits expected in the future. Within each of these two categories of evaluations and actions, attraction and acceptance are *intrinsic*, that is, pertaining to personal characteristics of the individual, while approval of opinions and instrumental services are *extrinsic*, they are not tied to a particular relationship. Blau adds a third category of rewards, which are *unilateral* evaluations such as the respect that bestows prestige on a person and unilateral actions such as compliance with a person's requests, giving him superior power. Blau presents this attempt to classify* social rewards in the form of the following scheme.

	Intrinsic	Extrinsic	Unilateral
Spontaneous Evaluations	Personal attraction	Social approval	Respect-prestige
Calculated Actions	Social acceptance	Instrumental services	Compliance-power

(From Blau, 1964, p. 100)

By means of economic analogies, Blau offers an analysis of the different kinds of cost incurred in providing social rewards. These are "investment cost", "direct cost", and "opportunity cost". The first entails the investment of skills necessary to supply many instrumental services and even to make a person's expression of approval carry worth for another. A direct cost is the subordination involved in a social exchange where a person expresses his respect for another, or manifests his compliance with another's wishes, and thus rewards him with superior power. A general cost in any social exchange is the time it requires and since the significance of this time depends on the alternatives which are forgone, it may be considered as an opportunity cost.† Both receiving and giving reward entails costs of surrendering alternative possibilities for reward or mutual benefit.

A special case exists in a situation where the person provides rewards for himself and simultaneously provides a social reward to another,

---

* Compare this classification with that suggested by Turner, Foa and Foa (1971). See Chapter 2, p. 22.

† Compare Homans' treatment of opportunity costs in Chapter 8 (pp. 177–183).

without further cost. These "costless" rewards are found in Blau's examples of mutual love. Underlying this discussion has been the distinction between the costs to a person A of obtaining a reward and the costs of B of supplying it. If B's costs in alternatives forgone are repaid by the gratification he receives in the very process of rewarding A, he supplies rewards at no net cost to himself. In another instance, Blau argues that exchange can be less costly and more profitable if rewards are supplied which simultaneously obligate several others and the leader who makes important contributions to an entire group illustrates this way of multiplying the benefits produced.

Blau makes some initial reference to the influences of context on exchange, although a more complete analysis is reserved for later (see pp. 322–327 below). For example, the entire exchange transactions in a group will set the prevailing rate of exchange; the demand for certain skills, potential coalitions among members, differences in power between them, all constitute such influences. It is quite likely that apparently unselfish behaviour in one exchange may profit an individual by earning him approval in other exchanges. The opposite case is where an individual extracts maximum benefits in one exchange despite the disapproval he accumulates therein, because he needs these benefits to court the approval of other parties outside the exchange. Multi-group affiliations resolve to some extent the conflicting individual desire of gaining approval and gaining advantage. Thus resources gained in one group while incurring disapproval may be used by an individual to his advantage and to gain approval in other groups, for example, gaining advantage by driving hard bargains in one group may allow a person to be generous in another. Behaviour in a given group, we can infer, is often to be understood only by taking into account memberships in other groups and by means of these examples Blau has once again forced our attention to the importance of a wider social context, the relationships between groups as well as between individuals within them.

Another example of the influence on exchange of social context and structure is encountered when Blau refers to the *segmental* nature of modern society,* contrasting its complexity of structure with the simple primitive societies described by Malinowski (1961). In the primitive

---

* Note that in the experiment by Kelley and Grzelak (1972) the authors fail in their explicit attempt to generalize from a small group to behaviour in the wider society, because they do not take into account the segmental nature of society.

society, wealth is dispensed with, is shared among others and the more generous individuals are the more renowned and the higher in status. In complex modern societies the approval of most persons in society is irrelevant to the possessor of wealth and he is only generous among his immediate associates, the narrow circle whose approval is significant to him. So, Blau illustrates convincingly that because our society is segmental, the approval of most of the persons with whom we come into contact is of little significance: clearly, this would apply to many other forms of behaviour where the individual refers himself to a relatively small group and where his accountability to others is also confined to a small number.

Blau demonstrates the importance of status structure as an influence on interpersonal behaviour; he cites Levi-Strauss (1957)* for an illustration of how the one-sided bestowal of favours may create crushing obligations and a diminution of rank and prestige in the recipient. Thus, a failure to reciprocate validates the superior status of the giver. In this way, Blau follows his theme of showing how structural characteristics of society both influence and develop out of the exchange process. For instance, a person's refusal to enter an exchange has different implications depending on his position in a larger social structure. Either he lacks the resources to reciprocate and in this case he merely reveals his inferior status or, if he declines to reciprocate when he is well able to do this, this has a completely different meaning. In this case, the giver is now rejected. Blau emphasizes that it is the existing social positions of the giver and recipient which determine the significance of the acceptance of gifts and whether or not they are returned.

Power and status

In his discussion of power, Blau distinguishes coercive power resting on deterrents, from the influence that is based on rewards; both are characteristic of exchange transactions. Power relations are inherently asymmetrical, the dependence is one-sided and if there is mutual influence or interdependence, this indicates, in fact, a lack of power.†
The kind of power which most concerns Blau involves the capacity to

---

* As does Homans in his discussion of reciprocal gift-giving (Homans, 1961, pp. 318–319).

† For a different viewpoint, as stated by Emerson (1962, 1972) see Chapter 13 below.

obtain compliance from others. Anyone who can supply services which are in high demand finds himself in a position of power with others dependent on him for those services and they may subsequently be obliged to comply with his wishes.

As we have seen, Blau's interest in power concerns the *power to reward*, a positive interpretation of the term referring especially to exchange relationships. He contrasts this meaning of the term with *coercive power* based on negative sanctions, not merely on force but on threats to incur detriment or loss of some kind. Although he recognizes the part played in some forms of power by threats or punishment he gives more emphasis to the power which comes from "supplying services in demand to others. . . . Providing needed benefits others cannot easily do without is undoubtedly the most prevalent way of attaining power . . ." (p. 118). He argues that power is closely related to obligations which are created by unilateral dependence. Thus Blau focuses almost entirely on "reward power" and goes on to state a general proposition that "the greater the difference between the benefits an individual supplies to others and those they can obtain elsewhere, the greater is his power over them likely to be" (p. 120). Here we have a proposition very similar to the hypotheses tested in experimental designs which incorporate varying degrees of dependency and which have been influenced largely by the *comparison level for alternatives* concept of Thibaut and Kelley (see above Chapters 3 and 5).

A little later, Blau draws attention to the process of power differentiation in primary groups and its parallel in complex structures. In primary groups this process develops when the superior attributes of some members allow them to command the compliance of others. As status begins to be differentiated, those who are more successful go on to compete among themselves for positions of power and leadership. Now a separation occurs between exchange and competitive relations. The high status members compete with each other for power, but between high and low status members there is only an exchange relationship, essentially a non-competitive one. In this exchange, the benefits afforded by high status members are exchanged for the compliance of low status members. Blau takes the further step of illustrating the effect as it has been found by anthropologists in simpler societies, for entire social classes rather than between individuals. Thus "families in the lower-middle class compete for staying in the middle class, while families in the upper-middle class compete for entry into the upper class, and since they are too far apart to compete, exchange relations develop between these two strata that serve the members of each in their distinct competitive struggles" and he adds "it is evident that the situation in Western societies though more complex, is strikingly similar" (p. 128). Still with these structural differences in mind, Blau notes that most exchange relations between high and low status individuals contribute to separate competitive systems within each class; and that, without the compliance of the "lows", the "highs" cannot attain pre-eminent positions of power. He does not, of course, omit the possibility of highs and lows clashing over the general distribution of rewards in society.

"Status, like capital, is expended in use" (p. 133). Blau gives some plausible examples of how such "capital" can be augmented by associating with prestigeful persons or decreased by submitting to another's wishes. Another example of direct expenditure is where a person commands others to do what he wants, thereby enabling them to discharge their obligations to him and depleting his power over them. If a person discharges his obligations to another, he thereby implements a transaction between them which means that their relationship will aproximate more to reciprocal exchange than to one of unequal power. It is therefore more favourable to a person's power that he should allow the obligations of others to accumulate, to have "a large asset of obligations" (p. 138). In this discussion of status and power Blau refers frequently to Homans' arguments and in general maintains close agreement with them.* We can see, as in Homans' exposition, that here is a source of hypotheses concerning status and reciprocal behaviour, multiple group membership, degrees of dependency on others, alternatives to submitting to others' power, exchange and competition between persons of different status. Potentially this is a source of propositions from which many working hypotheses may logically be derived.

Expectations

Blau next discusses the origins and nature of a person's expectations in social exchange. The influence of past experience is the first source of such expectations. He refers to a reference standard which an individual acquires, a notion very similar to the comparison level concept of Thi-

* See Chapter 8, pp. 180–181.

baut and Kelley. He applies this to groups, as well as to individuals, taking two examples from industrial field research in order to illustrate how the past experiences of organizational groups can influence employees' reactions to new leadership. This standard is partly the result of benefits a person has attained in the past and is partly the result of learning what others in comparable situations can obtain. Blau himself mentions the comparison level as a criterion of satisfaction with a given social relationship. He also notes the definition, given by Thibaut and Kelley, of dependence in a given relationship, as a matter of whether or not there are available alternatives; so Blau also incorporates the *comparison level for alternatives* and assumes an identical position with Thibaut and Kelley. But he does take the discussion into more detail, on the effects of social context, when he emphasizes the importance of the *prevailing rate* at which rewards are obtained for services in an individual's group or in groups which are similar.

We shall return to his exposition of the "going rate" of exchange in a moment (see pp. 304–307). Before we do so we will consider Blau's interesting discussion of aspirations. First he states two characteristics of levels of aspiration. One consistent finding is that those who successfully attain a given level of aspiration subsequently raise this level; those who fail to attain it subsequently lower their aspirations. The term "comparative expectation" is used for the comparison standard that individuals may use in making comparisons between possible future partners; to expand further on this comparative standard Blau takes up the idea of the ratio of rewards to costs and the idea of a fair return for investment. At the same time, in his discussion of comparisons between propective partners or group memberships, he is careful to avoid the comparisons of the utilities which a given relationship or group may have for different individuals.

Discussing the question of aspirations, Blau reverts to an economic idea when he states that attaining rewards that meet expectations is more important than gaining further rewards in excess of them—"a manifestation of the economic principle of the ultimately diminishing marginal utility" (p. 148). He also notes the similarity to the physiological principle of satiation but comments that there is no equivalent effect with prestige, or money, or power: "Social rewards do not have a point of complete satiation instead, as more of them are attained, their significance declines, either gradually or more abruptly" (p. 148). Here, he holds that the economic analogy is more appropriate than the physiological one, for social rewards, because ever if the drop in significance is abrupt, for example after attaining a specific goal, there may still be no satiation.

Blau asks his readers to note well the difference between this marginal principle stating the decline in significance of rewards following increasing attainments and the principle of rising aspirations which states that rewards grow in significance following increasing attainments. In the former, there has to be an assumption that general expectations remain constant (even though the level may be anything from low to extremely high, but it is a constant). If this assumption is removed, then we take into account that increasing attainments raise levels of expectation, an effect opposite to that of the principle of diminishing marginal utility and, as Blau concludes, it mitigates its influence.

The argument continues with a discussion of the going rate of exchange between two social benefits. This rate is determined, roughly, by supply and demand but is modified by other benefits that simultaneously enter the exchange, such as companionship. Here Blau draws an analogy to the equilibrium price in economic exchange: the equilibrium point occurs where supply and demand are equal but continual changes in economic forces prevent the actual price from matching the equilibrium price. Similarly, in social relationships the actual rate of exchange between two individuals may differ from the prevailing going rate in a group as various pressures induce some members to offer, for instance, more compliance for the advice of a highly skilled member or for the latter to offer more advice for the other's compliance with his wishes. The going rate merely sets an approximate standard of expectation that influences the actual rate of exchange.

Next, Blau raises a question which is a continual preoccupation in exchange theory. How can operational measures for these rates be devised? Blau argues that indices can be constructed for the benefits exchanged, for example for compliance and advice. A measure for the degree of compliance could be obtained through sociometric questions testing the relationships between different members of a group and their relative status. Or direct observations of day-to-day behaviour might be made.* For these purposes suitable indices of compliance and advice would need to be constructed to take into account both quality and quantity; as an example Blau cites Longabaugh's (1963) coding method (see also Chapter 13, p. 340 below).

* Compare the similarity of Homans' views on measurement (Chapter 8, p. 155).

Having stated these general and relatively modest aims for descriptive data-collection, Blau suddenly suggests a more comprehensive measurement of going rates and equilibrium rates in social exchange, dropping the use of analogy for something much more ambitious. This is what I had in mind earlier in this chapter (see p. 295) when I wrote that Blau is not consistent in his views on the differences between social exchange and economic exchange—particularly when he states that social exchange does not lend itself to the precise treatment of economic commodities. He argues:

> For this purpose, it would be necessary to determine how changes in the price of advice in (terms of) compliance affect variations in its supply and its demand. A market schedule would have to be made for each individual to show how much advice of a given quality he would be willing to supply at various prices in compliance and how much advice he would demand at various prices. Such a schedule could be based on answers to hypothetical questions, or, preferably, observations in situations in which the compliance received per unit of advice is experimentally varied and subjects are permitted to supply and request as much advice as they wish. By summing the schedules of all members of a group, a total demand-and-supply schedule would be obtained . . . The price at which demand and supply are equal is the "equilibrium price", which clears the market, and toward which the going rate is presumed to move (p. 154).

This statement of purpose is very similar to assumptions underlying the payoff model of Thibaut and Kelley. If anything, it assumes that even more can be done in precise measurement and Blau seems to suggest a more literal adaptation of the economic model. This is hardly consistent with Blau's more cautious views on measurement stated earlier in his book. As we shall see in a moment, the economic model requires empirical operations which are not feasible, at least, so far as we can foresee. This is a conclusion which will be confirmed in the next chapter, when we consider more recent research following on from Blau's book. There has been very little empirical follow-up in research projects since the publication of *Exchange and Power*.

The going rate and fair exchange

The going rate may not be identical with what is considered a fair rate of exchange. To demonstrate this, Blau extends the analysis from specific groups to larger communities and to a longer time span over the lives of individuals. Ideally, the call for a particular kind of expert advice in a community is expressed in adequate social rewards for it, and tends to equal the production of expertise by its members. This relationship corresponds to that between economic production and consumption and can be envisaged as governing the supply of, and demand for, advice in different groups and the degree of status superiority that can be earned with it. However, an important distinction which is now made between economic and social exchange (we have discussed others, see above, pp. 181–183 and p. 292), is that the intervening mechanisms in social exchange are the current norms of fairness. In a somewhat circular argument Blau states that normative standards of a fair return for a given service "have their ultimate source in society's need for this service and in the investment required to supply it" (p. 155).

In another economic parallel, he argues that the relationship between the fair rate and the going rate in social exchange is similar to that between the normal price and the average price in economic markets. The going rate in many groups may depart from the fair rate, and some individuals may not even be able to attain the going rate in their exchange transactions, possibly because of the power relations in particular groups.

A difference of emphasis now appears between Blau's derivation of the notion of fair exchange and Homans' derivation of distributive justice.* Blau attributes the notion of fairness to social norms, Homans starts at the individual level with justice as a natural sentiment and *only afterwards* does it become expressed through consensus in social norms.

Blau cites the industrial study by Patchen (1961) to illustrate how the expectation of fair exchange operates. The most relevant part of the findings shows that the oil-refinery workers, when asked to compare their earnings with those of other occupations with higher earnings, were on the average more satisfied if these others were professionals than if they were blue-collar workers; they did not object if the rewards of others exceeded their own provided that the educational investments of those others were correspondingly superior. These results support Homans' and Blau's conceptualization of fair exchange; Homans' Proposition 5 is mentioned in Blau's discussion for its focus on the consequences, to an individual, of inequitable treatment. Blau considers inequity as a source of group or community disapproval operating against anyone who deals unfairly with those under his power. His own study *The Dynamics of Bureaucracy* (1955) supplies some empirical support

* See Chapter 8, pp. 161–162.

for this. Lastly, Blau argues that because there can be independent measures of fair rates and going rates, these measures should prevent a tautological use of the exchange model.

Referring to the relative deprivation experienced when a person compares himself with others similar to him, who are more highly rewarded, Blau states that social rewards have an "invidious significance". This reflects the importance of comparisons and the use of reference groups as standards of comparison, a tendency which has been discussed already by Homans (see Chapter 8, p. 183). But Blau brings the economic analogy to bear once again, translating relative deprivation into a principle of diminishing *collective* marginal utility. By the principle of marginal utility, applying this to an individual: the more a person has of a benefit the less he values further amounts of it. Applying the principle to a group: in the case of relative deprivation, the member of a group who sees other members receiving a certain benefit in abundance, while he does not, values it more. However, the recipients value it less. Thus, in an organization where the number of promotions increases, those who have been promoted in company with numerous others, value promotion the less. The example given to illustrate this is the well-known one of the U.S. Air Corps as described by Stouffer *et al.* (1949). For Blau this study illustrates the close correspondence of social behaviour to an economic principle: "In brief, the marginal utility of increasing rewards eventually declines for entire collectivities as well as for individuals . . ." (p. 160). The major interest for us in this example is that Blau applies a proposition concerning individual effects to entire groups.

Although Blau seems close to the error of reifying the average decline in utilities as a collective property, nevertheless, his reference to the group average—the average reward received—as determining an individual's evaluation of a reward, provides a helpful explanation. Blau always emphasizes such collective factors, especially those that constitute an independent influence on exchange rates. Thus, he illustrates how the conditions of supply and demand in groups produce the going rate of exchange in a particular transaction. In a further example, he shows how economic competition between industries, and consequent innovations, disrupt the existing social commitments of individual members. Skills become obsolescent and an individual's investment no longer receives a fair return: "As a result, some men, due to no fault of their own, cannot obtain a fair return for the major investments of their lives" (p. 167). Blau has made the point that events in the wider social environment may often have to be admitted into explanation of exchange relationships at an interpersonal level.

Consultation in groups: an economic analogy

Continuing with his emphasis on collective or structural influences, Blau mentions the two critical reviews of Homans' *Social Behaviour* by Boulding and Davis (1962). Following Boulding's suggestion he now sets out to apply economic marginal analysis to social exchange; secondly, answering Davies' criticisms, he will attempt to demonstrate that specific predictions can be derived. He poses the question: Can economic principles of marginal analysis contribute to this aim? Blau has promised all along that he will show how operational hypotheses are derived from his basic assumptions of exchange. This section promises to be a significant part of Blau's exposition because he makes a detailed application of an economic model to social exchange, presenting two graphs to illustrate the application of marginal analysis, the basic underlying principle of which states diminishing marginal utility: in the long run, there is always a decrease in the marginal value, the value of yet another unit of a given benefit, for an individual. This trend is mitigated, as we have seen, by rising expectations but these expectations rarely cancel it out completely.

Blau intends to take as his exemplar, again, the exchange of advice for social status, the "pattern of consultation in work groups" (p. 168) as described in his *Dynamics of Bureaucracy* (1955), a study of relationships between white-collar employees. At its simplest, Blau considers these relationships between pairs of employees as a case of bilateral monopoly. Starting with one interpersonal exchange of advice for compliance Blau conjectures about "the ways in which exchanges in pairs proliferate into exchange processes throughout the group" (p. 169) as persons specialize in supplying services of different kinds. He argues that this leads to processes of social differentiation and to adjustments in group structure. By applying economic forms of analysis to social exchange, he hopes to clarify these processes.

He starts with the questions raised by a person's choice between two different commodities: where is the point at which he will prefer less of one and more of the other and what is the optimal combination of the two—where will the exchange settle? Blau uses indifference curves from Boulding's *Economic Analysis* (1955) representing, on the horizontal axis, the amount of status (defined as obtaining compliance from others to one's wishes) and, on the vertical axis, the amount of advice or help to be sought from a work colleague. Status and advice take the place of economic commodities and prices in Boulding's original graphs. Thus, in Fig. 18 Blau shows the indifference curves at their simplest in order to illustrate the amount of one commodity that, we infer, has equivalent utility to a given amount of another. This represents the basis for the decision that an individual makes between having different amounts of two commodities—he may have equal amounts of both or more of one and less of the other. In Fig. 18, argues Blau, the individual is indifferent about any combination X and Y that lies on I_1 although he may prefer combinations on the higher indifference curves I_2, I_3 or I_4. On each of these curves he is indifferent about any combination actually on that curve. AB is the opportunity line, (the "budget constraint" in economics), showing the resources available to the individual in obtaining the two commodities. Thus, a person may seek to obtain OB of Y and no X, OA of X and no Y, or any other combination on the opportunity

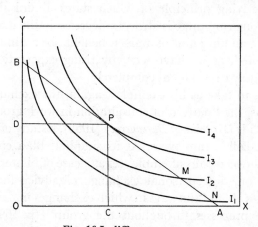

Fig. 18 Indifference curves.

line; the most profitable being where the opportunity line is a tangent to the highest indifference curve at P, where he obtains OD of Y and OC of X. Other attainable combinations, such as those at M and N, are on lower and less desirable indifference curves.

Arguing for the representation of social relations by such a graph, Blau proposes the case of an expert in a work group who may devote his surplus time (after doing his own work) either to relaxation *or* to advising others. The graph would show the division of spare time between relaxation and advising others, that yields most utility (P).

Blau's next step is to match the preferences of two persons on a box diagram with two facing pairs of co-ordinates representing the indifference curves of both persons in an exchange of compliance (giving status to the other person) for advice; such a graph as this would show the varying combinations that might be satisfactory and the points at which joint advantage could be maximized. In Fig. 19 below O_a is the

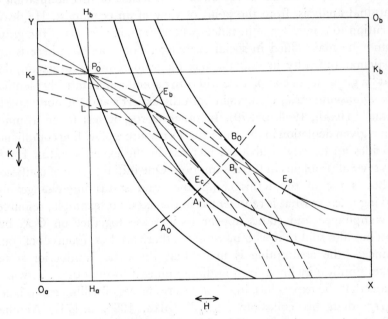

Fig. 19 Exchange in bilateral monopoly.

origin for the consultant, O_b for the colleague who consults him. K represents problem solving ability, conceived as the time devoted to problem solving weighted by the competence applied to the task. "$O_a Y$ (or $O_b X$) is the total problem solving ability available in the pair, with $O_a K_a$ representing the greater ability of the expert and $O_b K_b$ the lesser one of the colleague at the initial point P_o, before any consultation takes place. H indicates the compliance each is willing to express to raise the other's status . . . the expert's superior status makes him less inclined to subordinate himself . . ." (p. 174).

A fair rate of exchange based on current social norms is represented by the "opportunity line" $P_0 E_b E_a$. One such line might be at E_b where the consultant would furnish $P_0 L$ units of advice in exchange for LE_b units of compliance. The line connecting all points of mutual tangency $A_0 E_c B_0$ is the contract curve or "Paretian optimum", the condition that maximizes the joint advantage.

Some criticisms

Heath (1968) has made some incisive criticisms of this adaptation of marginal analysis, from the point of view of an economist. He draws attention to a number of instances where the conventions of the graph cannot be maintained in social exchange. For example, there is one particular difficulty in that the box diagram requires an assumption that "a given act of compliance will bring about quantitatively identical (though asymmetric) changes in both the expert's and the non-expert's status" (Heath, 1968, p. 279). In other words, it has to be assumed that a given depletion in the non-expert's resources of willing compliance provides an exactly equivalent increase in the expert's status. Heath sees several problems in this assumption. One initial source of confusion is Blau's use of the terms compliance and status interchangeably, making unclear what is represented in the axes. For example, resources of compliance and status appear to increase together on $O_a X$, but Blau has also said that with more status there are less resources of compliance: "the assumption is made that the expert's superior status makes him less inclined to subordinate himself to the other . . . which means that the expert has, in effect, less resources of willing compliance $(O_a H_a)$ than his colleague $(O_b H_b)$" (Blau, 1964, p. 174). Another difficulty inheres in the distinction drawn earlier by Blau between secure and insecure status. Acts of compliance are likely to have relatively greater effects on persons with insecure status. In the case of an exchange of advice for compliance between an expert and a non-expert, assuming insecure status in the latter leads us to expect a relatively greater fall in the non-expert's status and a relatively small rise in the expert's. Heath presents this as evidence that Blau would be unable to use the box diagram as he wishes. In brief, he denies the plausibility of Blau's translation of the model on the grounds that certain of its scalar conventions cannot be satisfied. As well as the difficulties in satisfying the conventions of the box diagram there is also a problem of empirical measures. As Heath points out, Blau implies that an act of compliance lowers the actor's status as much as it raises the recipient's, but there is little possibility of verifying this proposition with the degree of measurement currently practicable. Heath concludes: "we shall be able to test merely the weaker proposition that an act of compliance lowers the performer's status and raises the recipient's; we shall be unable to say whether the magnitude of the changes is the same" (p. 282). He sees as the main problem

that Blau is assuming isomorphism between the mathematical operations that can be performed on the numbers representing level of status or resources of compliance and the empirical processes that occur in practice. This is a problem which does not arise in economics to the same extent, . . . dealing with stocks of commodities or money, and processes *do* occur with these which are isomorphic with some mathematical operation. Thus we can be sure that if A gives B say £10. his stock of money is reduced by £10. and B's increased by £10., but we cannot be sure if A expresses compliance to B, B's status will increase by any given amount of A's or fall by a similar amount (p. 279).

Lastly, Heath has argued that the use of the indifference curves assumes aggregate conditions where trends are the result of a number of separate individual acts in response to market conditions. He questions the appropriateness of aggregate supply and demand curves because it has to be assumed that individuals act atomistically and normative controls are ignored. Not that Blau overlooks the norm of fair exchange, but Heath emphasizes the point that Blau fails to take up a position on its importance as a predictor. Heath asks this question: where there is a difference between a fair rate set up by the group and a rate predicted on the basis of summing individual demand curves, "which is the better predictor of what actually happens? That is to say, does the assumption that individuals act atomistically give a better prediction than the assumption that they act, in some respects, as a cohesive group?" (p. 286). He suggests Blau should have tried to clarify this issue, rather than leaving it open.

It is evident that, as a direct adaptation of marginal analysis, Blau's attempt does not succeed. At the present empirical stage of measurement the difficulties are very great, too great for the model's requirements. However, we cannot conclude that the attempt will not have some useful influence in the future merely becasue it has not yet been applied under the current limits on research sophistication. Blau's speculative discussion can be considered as successful to the degree that it emphasizes the importance of structural variables. As an outright application of an economic model, the attempt fails, of course. But, as an "in principle" demonstration of how structural variables can be incorporated into hypotheses about social behaviour, the argument succeeds. It will by now be quite obvious that we should accept Blau's use of the economic model only as an illustration of certain conditions and events that may help to explain what happens in social relations. Blau has been able to illustrate the effect of special conditions by showing their similarity with familiar economic situations. Fundamentally, the attempt raises again the problems of measurement which, as we have seen, are encountered in the other branches of exchange theory. Blau does not show how this type of economic model can be carried through to predictions at the level of working hypotheses; or how empirical data can be fed back to the graphs. It should not surprise us, therefore, if there have been no subsequent applications in any empirical study. Although he has argued that in social exchange certain effects similar to those in economics may occur, he has not overcome the differences, some of which he has already mentioned several times, between economic and social situations. In this respect Heath's cautious conclusion that it *might* in future be possible to apply the model to *some* forms of extrinsic social reward is a fair one: "What Blau is really doing is saying that some exchanges occur in social life that resemble those of economic behaviour, and hence that economic models can possibly be applied to them" (Heath, 1968, p. 286).

What are the operational hypotheses which Blau has promised to spell out? In the discussion following his presentation of the graphs, what kind of proposition does Blau have in mind? First, he sets out with statements about the exchange of advice for compliance. He suggests a number of possible combinations for the exchange of more or less of each activity. Taking the example of a work group where some members have more expert knowledge than the remainder, who may therefore seek their advice, he considers the effects of changes in group composition. If some experts leave the group, advice becomes more scarce and more compliance will have to be given in return for it. Again, more experts may arrive in the group and this may mean advice is available at less cost in compliance. Or, if there is an influx of unskilled recruits this may push up the cost of compliance. In order to predict whether or not these effects will occur Blau makes use of the economic concept of elasticity of demand or supply. If demand is inelastic, when experts leave the work group, more compliance will now have to be rendered and status differences will increase. If demand is elastic this will not take place, because advice will now be sought from other colleagues who will substitute for the experts. In another example, when there is a flow of new recruits to a group, only if the supply of advice is inelastic will more compliance have to be rendered and status differences increase.

Blau is interested in the effects of such conditions as group size, composition and status structure on the quantity of interpersonal activities —the amount of help, advice, compliance exchanged. His entire discussion focuses on the significance of these structural effects for relationships in a primary group; the discussion is carried out at a speculative level and conclusions are drawn that, in principle, certain events are probable. The hypotheses as Blau presents them are *structural* in that they demonstrate the influence of group and collective characteristics on behaviour between persons. Quite simply, the structural variables consist of (1) changes in the number of experts in a group, (2) changes in numbers of recruits, or derive from (3) the difficulty level of tasks entrusted to the group members. Although hypotheses can, in any case, be stated concerning these material effects, Blau seeks a translation of the problem into forms of marginal analysis borrowed from economics and while this appears to increase the degree of precision with which conditions or interacting variables (elastic or inelastic supply and demand) can be predicted, the enterprise cannot proceed beyond the terms of a general analogy. It appears, clearly, that a more direct application would fail at the point where empirical measures of social interaction have to be included—there is nothing here equivalent to the impersonal economic scale of prices. Let us not forget though that if the hypotheses are accepted simply as working propositions, in their own right, leaving aside that they have been suggested by economic "parallels", they still have the merit of including variables of context.

Concluding summary of the economic model

I have already pointed out that Blau's use of economic concepts may at first seem to give a greater precision in stating conditions which could be tested by empirical research. However, the transference of the economic model, as presented in Figs. 18 and 19 above, into the field of social behaviour also requires that we take into account certain assumptions in economics which cannot hold for social activities. Blau himself recognizes this, although also emphasizing that within classical economics such models introduce over-simplification, for instance, where assumptions of full employment or perfect mobility are concerned. The "unrealities" of simplifying are, for Blau, again much more evident in the case of social behaviour. Blau therefore thinks it worthwhile to examine the prerequisites of simplifying models as they are introduced as part of the borrowing of economic terms. These principally involve the rate of exchange as it settles between two persons and presumably, it is governed by such conditions as the costs of alternatives forgone and the reallocation of activities as these costs arise. In the economic model, as mentioned, *perfect competition* between alternatives is an unrealistic assumption and Blau now illustrates that it will also be unrealistic for social behaviour: many factors will prevent an exchange settling at the "market" level of the going rate. For instance, the individual may have to submit to a disadvantageous exchange through the use by others of superior power, or, when a person has to choose between several advisers, one cannot assume perfect competition between them because the value of their advice may be influenced by other factors in the relationship with an adviser. The "product" may not be homogeneous, as assuming perfect competition requires and, as Blau remarks, "transactions involving specific services are not completely insulated from other aspects of and other benefits derived from the exchange relation" (p. 191). He discusses several similar limitations but maintains that despite unrealistic assumptions, despite the abstraction of only a few variables and the neglect of others, the explanatory enterprise will still be useful if the variables abstracted are significant ones. It must be added that this comment seems appropriate for any theoretical model and could apply to any experimental paradigm; it remains to be seen if Blau's exposition is especially influential, more than others, in subsequent research.

In summary, Blau has presented the two graphs of indifference curves and bilateral monopoly in order to argue that marginal analysis may be applied, with benefit, to social exchange. We are shown the graphs in order to affirm the point that equivalent ones could describe combinations of social rewards and costs and therefore could explain social interaction as a process proceeding from laws similar to economic exchange. To achieve this, it would be necessary to obtain measures of social activities, namely, for the two hypothetical activities selected by Blau: giving advice and complying with another's wishes. It is therefore imperative to indicate how the empirical measures of these "amounts" and combinations of them are to be derived. Blau cites only one *empirical* example during all the argument in this section. This is the study by Blau and Scott (1962) of case workers in twelve work groups in a public welfare agency; here, increased work pressure and, therefore, demand for advice, led to increased consultation where the supply of advice was abundant and elastic, that is, in those groups where many reciprocal partnerships made mutual help easily available.

In the course of the discussion, Blau has continued to argue his view that status, defined in his own special sense of informal status among colleagues in a work group—and affording to the possessor the compliance of other group members with his wishes—is a predominant and generalized means of social exchange "similar to money in an economic exchange (except that it is far less liquid than money), since a person's command of the compliance of others enables him to obtain a variety of benefits, just as his possession of money does" (p. 170). Thus, status is given primacy as an exchange resource.

All through his book, Blau discusses exchange processes in terms of advice and social status as the most important elements in exchange, and whenever he illustrates these elements we notice that the exchange takes place in *work groups*. Indeed, there is a strong focus on work situations in the evidence which Blau and Homans introduce to support their theoretical discussion. For Homans his basic illustrations of the exchange process in dyads are taken from Blau's research study of office workers who exchange advice for status (see Chapter 8, p. 180). More than this, over half of all Homans' references to empirical studies are to work situations (see p. 199 above). Blau refers mainly to his own research observations of white-collar employees in public welfare agencies. This emphasis on work groups, in order to exemplify the exchange process, could be a weakness if it led to the relative neglect of play, family, love, friendship relationships, or groups formed, fleetingly, for whatever purpose but that of the formalized, stratified organization of office or factory. It could be a weakness because work groups are most likely to be entrenched in the trading ethos of a particular economic structure, so that this ethos will tend to pervade social relations to a stronger degree than in groups which are not committed, even indirectly, towards economic profit. This is a suggestion which can only be countered by extending the exchange model to other empirical situations. Such counter-evidence, in fact, does exist. Blau and Homans frequently cite and give examples from anthropological studies, and Homans often uses social-psychological experiments and surveys. Blau provides a wealth of different sources and gives much attention, as we have seen, to love as an exchange relationship and this has been followed up more recently in the current literature, and will be discussed in the next chapter. We can recall that the model of Thibaut and Kelley rests on a variety of citations extending from anthropology to experimental psychology, but the model itself is usually tested by one kind of experimental paradigm and this fact raises the restrictive problems discussed in Chapters 4 and 5.

Collective forms of power: legitimate authority

Blau next moves on with his declared intention of extending the analysis of exchange, by the same concepts, from small groups to larger social structures and collectivities. He discusses the co-ordination of activities in formal organizations. Here, power is the resource that makes it possible to direct and co-ordinate activities and power, when it is legitimate, becomes *authority*. Blau views authority as involving agreements or norms among subordinates to comply with a superior's directive. In contrast to other forms of power, the source of influence is here the collectivity rather than the individual leader. Collective approval of an individual possessing power is what legitimates his use of it and Blau refers to several field and experimental studies of the 1950s in order to illustrate that those leaders who attract approval are likely to be more effective. Note that he uses Festinger's (1957) concept of cognitive dissonance to explain how an individual may resolve his choice between carrying out the orders of a superior and noncompliance as a possible alternative, arguing that a process of rationalization occurs through which the individual adapts to his subordinate position by emphasizing the benefits of compliance.* He then points out that: "social processes, however, transform the individual rationalizations into common values" (p. 208). In this way, a social consensus develops among sub-

---

* Later in his book Blau calls on the cognitive dissonance explanation again, in a political context, in order to explain how members of a left-wing minority party reduce the dissonance in belonging to a party with little prospect of success, by an emphasis on their ideological commitment.

ordinates which validates their beliefs and expresses them as "a common value orientation." Thus, Blau has moved from an explanation of how compliance to a superior may be rationalized *by the individual* and, immediately, he takes the further step to a *group* process where individual rationalizations become embodied in social norms that transform power into authority. Instead of one exchange process between the individual and his superior, the former providing compliance in return for the latter's services, there are now two. A second exchange is added—between the individual and his group—in which the individual submits to authority because social norms require it and the "individual exchanges compliance with the directives of the superior for social approval from his peers" (p. 209). Furthermore, Blau sees a further indirect process of exchange between the collectivity of subordinates offering compliance, as the result of its social norms, in return for contributions to the common welfare supplied by those in authority. We shall consider additional examples of such exchanges in a moment (see pp. 319–322).

This discussion, maintained at the level of collective behaviour and the structure of organizations, also takes into account the process by which authority becomes transmitted through institutions over long periods of time, and Blau gives illustrations of cases where the obligations to comply with an authority's commands no longer develop out of social exchange, in return for contributions to common welfare, but are a *moral* obligation "inculcated by socializing agencies" (p. 212). Such an institutionalized authority is the political authority of a national government.* In a similar vein, discussing the organization of collective effort in associations, political, economic or military, Blau emphasizes that exchange is normatively regulated and that individuals conform to these standards rather than negotiating a direct exchange for their services.

A further effort to apply the concepts of individual psychology to group processes occurs when Blau applies the concept of relative deprivation, in the following way. In large organizations comprising many different groups of employees, comparisons referring to the better lot of others are especially likely to occur. Blau has shown how this concept can explain the importance of comparisons between individuals (see p. 306 above) and now argues for the same effect in comparisons between groups. So, in a work organization the management may

* For a discussion of this form of power see Goode (1972).

satisfy the demands of one group but this leads to relative deprivation and dissatisfaction in other groups. Blau points out that when one group receives an increase in earnings another may consequently experience "relative deprivation as a result of the decline in the comparative level of their income and social status . . ." (p. 219). He refers to the concepts of deprivation and relative deprivation in order to explain the differences between left-wing and right-wing revolts: the former as a reaction to deprivation by the least privileged social strata; the latter as a reaction of the lower-middle class to their relative deprivation, as their traditional superiority over working-class strata is reduced by economic improvement of the latter.

Referring to the inferences from animal experiments which suggest the ineffectiveness of punishment as a means of lasting influence on conduct, Blau also mentions Homans (1961, p. 26) and Thibaut and Kelley (1959, pp. 240–246) for their discussion of the implications for human behaviour. Blau asks "why do people so frequently hurt and punish others not only inadvertently but also intentionally?" (p. 225). He discusses a number of possible answers, for instance punishment may be used as a last resort when all else fails or punishment may be used as "an effective social deterrent even when it has little deterrent effect on the specific individuals that have been punished" (p. 226)—in this way, punishment may serve to emphasize the commitment of the majority to a given normative standard. Less directly, other forms of punishment appear as the cessation of existing regular rewards, even a failure to receive a regular increase in salary tends to be taken as a penalty. In another case, the high rewards that some people receive may produce feelings of relative deprivation in others, which is equivalent to punishment. However, Blau is mainly concerned with deliberate punishment, the most important factor in which is a desire to retaliate for harm done. He points out that people may "sometimes forget their own self-interest due to the strong desire for revenge" (p. 227). The argument is again conducted from individuals to the relationships between social groups and classes and Blau notes that if a social class or group holds an advantage stemming from conditions of society that create hardships for others, opposition will emerge "since power cannot escape the responsibility for the social conditions in which it is rooted" (p. 227).

Most of his subsequent discussion deals with exchange between political parties and groups in society. Blau discusses what the parties may offer, in ideologies or material success, to different social groups or classes. His case is therefore based on an underlying reward assumption, as expressed in forms of exchange between voters and the parties in a democratic society. A party's ability to offer rewards is considered as the means to success both in keeping its members and in obtaining votes.

Blau points out that the fundamental distinction between small groups and the complex structures of large collectivities is found in the way that structure is mediated. In the former it is developed by direct social interaction between individuals; in the latter, by value consensus and norms which are perpetuated in institutions over long periods of time. Blau quickly emphasizes that the legitimating values of complex structures are only one of their characteristics and that an adequate study of these structures must include power relations, exchange transactions between collectivities, changes produced by mobility or by opposition forces. Conflict is not to be ignored.

Here is evidence of a social exchange theorist taking a clear position on the study of conflict without by-passing the issue as some social psychologists have been accused of doing. Plon (1972) reiterates a criticism familiar in the sociological literature but directs it against a number of social psychologists and their assumption that conflict is necessarily negative, and therefore to be avoided, as reflecting a doctrine of established political and economic interests; he is critical of attempts by social scientists (for example, Deutsch, 1962) to evaluate the nature of conflicts as either constructive or destructive. We will return to this topic later.

Social norms and indirect exchange

Blau gives yet another example of the connection between individual and group process. For his present purpose the study of social norms is "justified because they provide the connection between the simpler process in micro-structures and the more complex ones in macro-structures" (p. 254). This is Blau's persistent aim—to indicate the connections between a theory of complex structures and of the social process he has discussed in great detail in the earlier part of his book. He reminds us of the indirect exchanges (see above, pp. 316–317) which social norms make possible, and now refers to the norms prohibiting force and fraud, protecting conditions of trust. Deriving from general cultural values such norms prohibit some forms of exploitation, for instance, sexual exploitation. Here Blau mentions Gouldner's (1960) discussion of exploitation of minors or of women by men of comparative higher status. Gouldner notes the paucity of empirical studies of exploitation. Sexual exploitation has been an exception since the analysis of courtship behaviour by Waller (1951) and we will discuss this topic again in the next chapter. Gouldner tries to minimize the value-laden, pejorative implications of the term "exploitation" by using it to refer to some forms of *unequal exchange* and he advocates the study of varied forms of "exploitation of students by teachers, of workers by management or union leaders, of patients by doctors . . ." (p. 167). These should be studied, he adds, as cases of a larger class of the same phenomenon and treated within the framework of systematic theory rather than by an *ad hoc* treatment in specific empirical contexts. Blau continues with a reference to the Prisoner's Dilemma; he summarizes this as a situation where both parties cannot realize their own interests because of the absence of a norm (of mutual trust) to preclude "the very choices that appear to be most rational" (p. 255). Only the operation of a social norm permitting trust can refrain the participants in this situation "from acting in a selfish manner that actually defeats their own self-interest" (p. 257). From this, Blau argues to the case of the individual who decides not to vote in a political election since his single vote can make hardly any difference and therefore, on strictly rational grounds of purely individual interest, it is not worth the trouble of voting. To prevent this becoming a general form of behaviour social norms are necessary, especially to "prohibit actions through which individuals can gain advantages at the expense of the common interests of the collectivity" (p. 257). Similar norms discourage rate-busters in work groups because competition between members may threaten the existence of the group as a whole, although in many groups competition can, in fact, be tolerated as, for example, between members of a sales force, or in professions (Blau, 1964, pp. 187–193; and see Chadwick-Jones, 1969, p. 158).

Blau continues with a discussion of how violation of group norms leads to an individual experiencing guilt feelings and drawing on to himself the disapproval of others. As group sanctions are brought to bear, these outweigh the rewards that he might otherwise have expected from deviating from the norm. In this way, Blau concludes that "sanctions convert conduct that otherwise would be irrational into a rational pursuit of self-interest" (p. 258). He refers to Thibaut and Kelley

(1959, pp. 127–135) for a fuller discussion of internalized norms and how these are functional in providing shared and depersonalized rules for social behaviour, which an individual will follow more readily than commands of another person.

Thus, Blau argues that social norms substitute indirect exchange for direct transactions between individuals, and that exchange between the collectivity and its individual members replaces direct transactions, as the result of conformity to norms. For instance, in groups of friends each one feels obliged to help others without thought of return, and while there is no direct exchange of favours the group norm assures that each will receive help when he needs it. This norm generates indirect chains of exchange such as might be found also in among groups of workers or professional colleagues. Blau illustrates this as follows: "Long chains of social transactions occur in complex organizations, in which the work of some members contributes to the performance of others, and which typically do not involve reciprocal exchanges. What these chains of transactions do involve is conformity to official obligations on the part of members of the organization in an exchange for rewards received from it" (p. 260).

Indirect exchange also occurs when rich donors of philanthropic contributions are rewarded by social approval of their peers. Arguing this further, Blau holds that the sum of such donations will provide an upper class, as a collectivity, with a claim to moral superiority, and thus entitle it to deference from the collectivity of recipients—so that the exchange has helped to sustain a class structure. Here again, Blau has applied an explanation, first at the individual level of charitable contributions from rich donors to individual recipients, and then at the level of collectivities in order to suggest that the exchange contributes to a particular social structure.

Professional services also provide examples of indirect exchange. In this instance, normative standards may forbid reciprocal social exchanges between a professional and his client "lest his decisions be influenced by the exchange instead of being based only on his best judgement in terms of professional standards" (p. 261). Parsons' (1951) analysis of psychotherapy constitutes a prototype in this respect: the professional detachment of the psychiatrist permits him to refrain from reciprocating either the friendly overtures of patients or their aggressive behaviour, as he is not concerned (or should not be) with the social relationship as a direct source of rewards and costs. Instead, he engages in an indirect exchange with his professional group; treating patients according to these professional standards brings him social approval and respect from his colleagues. In this way "an indirect chain of exchange replaces direct social transactions based on considerations of reciprocity" (p. 262) and the indirect exchange extends, even further, to the community, as Blau suggests: "the community bestows superior social status and controlling power upon the profession as a corporate group, which enable it to control and reward its members" (p. 263). He applies this interpretation to bureaucracy, where officials treat clients in a detached manner, thus avoiding exchange transactions which would make it impossible to follow bureaucratic procedures. An essential element of this detachment is an absence of direct exchange relations. However, there are two criticisms to be made about these illustrations of indirect exchange. First, it is doubtful whether professionals and bureaucrats are similar cases since the bureaucrat is rarely in face-to-face relationships with his clients, as the professional is continually. Secondly, it must be remembered that Blau presents an idealized sketch of what may actually happen. In professional-client relationships there must be some direct exchange even if only of trivial social gestures and there may always be some degree of deviance from the normative impersonal standard—and psychiatrists sometimes marry their clients.

Structural influences on interpersonal behaviour

In the next section Blau discusses the common values or norms that perpetuate social structure over time. He refers to the distinction between values which are *universalistic*, general throughout society, and *particularistic* values confined to a given group, in order to apply the distinction to social exchange. Thus universalistic values "expand the range of exchange transactions and status structures beyond the confines of direct social interaction" (p. 268), because what is valued in many different groups throughout society becomes a generalized means of exchange. Blau argues along these lines in great detail, indicating how social approval of informal leaders in small groups has its counterpart in the legitimation of authority in large collectivities and how social disapproval similarly has its expression eventually in opposition ideologies and political movements aimed at institutional change. Much of this later part of the book consists of a discussion of sociological theories of complex social structures and Blau's reference to exchange considerations now tend to become repetitive, re-emphasizing the general currency of social approval and status throughout the whole of a society and its component groups and associations. A person's services in some segments of the community earn him approval which is translated to social status in the community and now affords him rewards (respect, deference from others) that often do not come from the same segment.

Blau discusses mobility between groups, referring to the nature and quantity of rewards which influence the rate of mobility. The distinction between particularistic and universalistic standards is useful in the explanation of conditions which obstruct or facilitate mobility. Members of groups in which their internal status is a matter of particularistic contributions to the group will find that these contributions do not make them acceptable in other groups with different value standards. Then, there are instances of individuals choosing between alternative roles in a vertical status structure. If a person has a high status, should he associate with others of similar status and upwards, thus improving his class affiliation, or should he associate with those of lower status thereby increasing the immediate rewards, respect and deference, that he receives on a day-to-day basis, although he thereby has chosen a position in the status stratum which is less advantageous. A parallel choice faces an individual whose occupational activities meet with failure, instead of choosing between two kinds of social gratification he has a choice between two kinds of social deprivation: either to stay with his own social group where he is inevitably reminded of his failure, or move to a lower stratum, for the sake of more rewards in daily social contacts. The receiving collectivity has an interest in accepting the upwardly mobile, partly through their potential to accomplish valued activities and secondly because the new recruit has initially to assume a deferential role and this is a source of social reward for established members. The downwardly mobile also bring rewards to the established group which they join; because of their education and qualifications they may make superior contributions and provide opposition leadership for the less privileged group.

Blau continues in this plausible, anecdotal vein for a considerable part of the remainder of the book and, in doing so he illustrates fully the influence of structure, hierarchy and inter-group connections on the individual's rewards and costs in specific social relations. This is a result which especially should interest social psychologists and I will discuss it more fully in a moment. First, let us finish Blau's account of relationships between large groups and collectivities which take parallel forms to those he has described between persons.

Social conflicts

Concerning social conflicts, Blau describes opposition as a "regenerative force" when rewards for individuals have become too sparse in an existing social structure; opposition movements "constitute counter-vailing forces against these institutional rigidities . . ." (p. 302). Blau relates conflict between collectivities and between substructures and macrostructures in society eventually to the fact that a situation may arise where "actual rewards of most people frequently fall short of the high expectations of achievement and success created by cultural values . . . which produces frustrations and deprivations" (p. 303). The drawing together of dissatisfied elements is helped, according to this sociological perspective, by the latent opposition between centralized authority (macrostructure) and the substructures which are dependent on it but also striving for autonomy. Opposition need not take extreme forms, since there is

> the multitude of recurrently emerging and subsiding, less extreme, oppositions of diverse sorts that produce continual change and reorganisation in societies. Opposition activates conflict by giving overt social expressions to latent disagreements and hostilities, but it also helps to remove the sources of these conflicts. It is a disturbing and divisive force that ultimately contributes to social stability and cohesion (p. 304).

Social arrangements formed by a successful opposition create new dissatisfactions in due course, stimulating further opposition. Thus, Blau argues that social change is a dialectical process because any form of social organization will "engender problems and conflicts that call for some reorganisation" (p. 304).* He goes on to discuss the paradox of democracy:

> that the freedom of dissent and opposition constituting the very foundation of democracy must surely include the right to advocate the suppression of dissent and opposition. . . . hence, the persistence of democratic institutions depends, to a still greater degree than that of other institutions, upon being supported by moral values and norms that are deeply ingrained in the

* Blau acknowledges Simmel and other sociologists as his sources.

consciousness of the people . . . Another mainstay of stable democracy is
the existence of many cross-cutting conflicts and overlapping oppositions
in the society (p. 305).

In a given society, interlocking memberships in many organizations on
the part of large numbers of individuals will cut across diverse social
segments and classes making it unlikely that the most intense hostilities
will occur. On the other hand, these multigroup affiliations "simultaneously protect other institutions and the existing power structure
from being fundamentally transformed by a radical opposition . . ."
and this is "a social cost that is paid by the most oppressed social classes
who would benefit from radical changes in the status quo" (pp.
307–308). These formulations are, no doubt, familiar ones in political
sociology but their significance for us here is that Blau has arrived at
them by way of propositions about direct interpersonal exchange. He
has arrived at them by analogies to the individual condition of relative
deprivation, or retaliation in interpersonal relationships. At the same
time, there is no doubt that such analogies fail to convince sociological
critics like Mulkay (1971) and Heath (1972).

Blau and social psychology: the Comparison Level

More than this, he continues with the study of conditions in collectivities which would influence individual behaviour. These are conditions which are entirely neglected by individual conceptualizations
such as those offered by Thibaut and Kelley. To illustrate this point
we can refer to the *comparison level for alternatives* as this concept is used
to account for an individual's forsaking a relationship or group for one
that offers better outcomes: it is a matter of a comparison standard,
with individual gains in the present group set against what is available
in an alternative relationship; the $CL_{alt.}$ represents the least a person
will accept before attempting to find the alternative (Thibaut and
Kelley, 1959, pp. 100–101, and above, Chapter 7, p. 140). Now Blau
considers the mobility of individuals between organizations as the
"core of the relations between substructures in a macrostructure" (p.
310) because by this means society is continually being modified.
Powerful groups may impose restraints on entry to them and there are
further conditions to be taken into account, as follows. If status in a
group is decided by particularistic criteria, as might be the case in
religious groups, low-status members are most likely to move (they will

lose nothing by doing so, but high-status members might have to start afresh in a new group). If the criteria are universalistic as, say, professional or financial success, high-status members are most likely to move (taking their rank with them) and low-status ones to do so only involuntarily.

In his discussion of conflict Blau has offered an exposition of the origins in interpersonal behaviour of social hierarchies, opposition groups and conflict between classes. Obviously, this does not detract from the study of the latter at their own level. It has been Blau's aim to apply exchange concepts to the study of organizations and collective behaviour but how this is done will not be our concern as social psychologists since our interest rests in the hypotheses explaining interpersonal behaviour which Blau suggests in the course of his prolegomenon to a theory of macro-structures. Blau's discussion of interpersonal relations is only a means to attaining a set of explanatory statements at a sociological level but, for us, this is an end—the core of our subject matter. At the same time it is important to realize that Blau does provide what may be termed a contextual framework for this subject matter which can be illustrated by the following example.

As social psychologists, we should be justified in thinking that Blau has amplified and completed the concepts which we need to apply in order to explain the mobility of individuals between groups. We are now better equipped to understand why an individual stays in a particular group or leaves it and we see that Blau has given us concepts which are adequate to explain an individual's choice in a given social context. If we were to rest our analysis of individual choice on the $CL_{alt.}$ we would have only a partial explanation of what actually happens. Blau offers a *sociological* explanation, it is true, expressed in status structures and the nature of the status criteria, but the application of these group phenomena to individual choices gives a more comprehensive social psychological theory of the influences determining that choice. In this particular example, in order to explain a social event—whether a person leaves his group or not—we should need to know something of several variables: his perception of a comparison level ($CL_{alt.}$); what other comparison groups are important to him; his position in a status structure; the nature of the structure; whether status is based on criteria centred on the group *or* generally recognized in society at large. Blau has identified for us at least two social influences that must be included in an appraisal of what such choices involve. We can conclude that this conceptual approach presents an obstacle to a psychological reduction but it gives access to the group factors which should be included in social psychological theory.

Dynamics: reciprocity and imbalance

Blau asks the question: What attracts individuals to a relationship? and he gives the answer that they may either be attracted by intrinsic rewards of the relationship itself, as in love, or by extrinsic benefits which are not attached to any particular individual, such as advice in carrying out a task. Next, he raises what he terms a second fundamental question: Is the transaction between individuals symmetrical or not? He distinguishes reciprocal from unilateral transactions and he emphasizes that this distinction recognizes "a dynamic force that transforms simple into increasingly complex social processes" (p. 314). Blau accepts that there is a tendency towards reciprocity in social exchange, a view similar to Homans' statement of a strain towards balance, which we discussed in Chapter 9 (p. 208). However, he draws attention to the wider implications of an exchange, because "reciprocity on one level creates imbalances on others, giving rise to recurrent pressures for re-equilibrium and social change. In complex social structures . . . every movement toward equilibrium precipitates disturbances . . . The perennial adjustments . . . find expression in a dialectical pattern of social change" (p. 314). Although his prototype of social exchange is the *reciprocal* exchange of *extrinsic* benefits, he now suggests that there are other possibilities along the two dimensions of attraction and symmetry; they are presented, broadly, in the following cross-tabulation.

	Intrinsic	Extrinsic
Reciprocal	Mutual attraction	Exchange
Unilateral	One-sided attachment	Power

At this point Blau summarizes some of his previous arguments. Thus, when an association is intrinsically rewarding the exchange of extrinsic benefits simply sustains the major intrinsic rewards. In the case of unilateral extrinsic services, power is established because those who cannot reciprocate in kind are obligated to comply with the other person's wishes. Blau refers to the similarities between social and economic exchange. For instance, those who do favours for others expect some in return, if only a gesture of appreciation, and the principle of diminishing marginal utility is easily applied to social relations. However, he calls our attention again to fundamental differences he mentioned earlier (p. 294). There are no formal contracts, since social exchange involves unspecified obligations, nor can exact prices be established; without enforceable contracts, social exchange requires trust. Usually the gradual development of an exchange permits the test of trustworthiness during the initial stages of a relationship where there is little commitment. As mutual trust grows the content of exchange becomes more varied and as it begins to include advice, help, social support, or companionship, these transactions will produce some intrinsic significance for the relationship—at this point, the differences between economic and social exchange are at their greatest.

Blau continues with a discussion of the personal dilemmas which become apparent when we analyse relationships as exchange. So, an exchange between two partners is seen as a mixed game in which both have a common interest in maintaining a stable relationship, but their interests diverge concerning the ratio of rewards which each obtains. The person who is less committed to the partnership gains a special advantage because the other's commitment stabilizes the relationship and permits him to explore alternatives. The individual's dilemma lies between withholding his commitment until the other has made a greater commitment, thereby possibly endangering the continuation of the relationship, or committing himself first in order to ensure its continuation, thereby worsening his position in the relationship. Another dilemma appears when a person demands approval from others, but in addition he may need their help. Blau illustrates this with the case of work colleagues, one of whom seeks approval but also seeks help to improve his performance and this might involve critical appraisal, implying the other's disapproval. Furthermore, if approval is offered irrespective of performance it will depreciate in value. Thus, a strong demand for approval and a need to withhold it to preserve its value, creates cross-pressures. In a relationship between lovers there is a demand for expressive behaviour and also a need to withhold it, in case its free expression depreciates its value. Blau gives attention to this dilemma of commitment and it is a plausible example. In his discussion, it exemplifies conflicts common to interpersonal relationships *and* to large collectivities, as we shall see in several further examples which Blau gives.

In order to obtain a position of leadership, a person must command power over others and yet receive their approval and the dilemma occurs because attaining dominance tends to antagonize and evoke disapproval. Next, in a parallel example of collective behaviour, he discusses how members of an emergent radical opposition must modify their extremist ideology to make new converts and yet in doing so they run the risk of alienating those most devoted to its existing ideals. Yet another source of dilemma is inherent in the distribution of social rewards in a group: the more rewards there are, the more likely individuals are to become fully committed members. However, an abundance of social rewards depreciates their value, following the principle of diminishing collective marginal utility. The dilemma is therefore how much of a given reward to offer, how much of approval, emotional support, or help. Too much will produce depreciation, too little will not gain the members' commitment. Now Blau proceeds with the full "application" of exchange concepts to organizations.

Competition and exchange

Discussing social transactions that occur between organized collectivities Blau distinguishes between two kinds of transaction, between competitive and exchange processes—a distinction which, he notes, is equally valid for transactions between individuals. Applying this distinction, it is soon clear that where there is competition there cannot be exchange since the parties each aim to maximize what they obtain of scarce resources while exchange, in contrast, involves sharing and interdependence. Persons, or organizations in competition have the same objective and compete for the same services or resources, whereas exchange is most likely to occur among those having different objectives. In this case, the services exchanged are complementary to each other. Blau notes that competition promotes hierarchical differences between the more and less successful, while exchange makes for horizontal differentiation between the providers of specialized services. Here again, we have an instance of how Blau extends his speculative explanation from relationships between individuals to those between collectivities. Exchange which promotes differences in the specialization of activities leads eventually to the formation of specialized organizations. Now another consequence appears. As a result of competition and the differential success of individuals or organizations that were once *alike*, they now become sufficiently *unlike* to develop from their former competition to exchange relations. Alternatively, those formerly enjoying an exchange of services may, because of their similar degree of success, become competitors and Blau gives some examples, referring to major business concerns or strong unions which, as they are more successful, begin to compete for a position of dominance in the community. So competition and exchange are seen to be closely related processes; Blau shows how either may develop from the other and, in fact, he is the only one of our exchange theorists to do so.

Relative deprivation in organizations

Earlier Blau discussed the relative deprivation perceived by some individuals in a group where others received rewards they themselves did not. He argues that essentially the same process is found for entire collectivities whose members become aware of their relative deprivation, as a group. Thus, individuals or organizations become differentiated so that the relative deprivation of some gives rise to their retaliation and opposition, some becoming more, and some less, successful than others. Blau comments that this is the source of dynamics of organized social life.

The dynamics arising from competition and exchange are described by Blau as "a dialectic in social life . . . governed by many contradictory forces" (p. 336).* Blau notes that equilibrium and inequilibrium interact. For instance, reciprocity is an influence towards equilibrium because "every social action is balanced by some appropriate counteraction"; however, balance on one level induces imbalance in others. This, says Blau, is exemplified where a person with superior access to resources performs a service for another who reciprocates the favour by his compliance with the former's wishes; at the same time creating imbalance of power. Reactions to this imbalance superimpose a secondary exchange on the primary one—the exercise of power with

---

* See Schneider (1971) for a discussion of a number of meanings of dialectic in theory and method, including Hegel's "development through conflict" and Renan's dictum "Les institutions perissent par leur victoires".

moderation earns social approval (from those exposed to it), its unfair use incurs disapproval. Collective approval of a person in a position of power legitimates his authority but reinforces the imbalance. Collective disapproval, in the case of an exploited subordinate group, tends towards a reorganization.

Other contradictory influences are seen in the process of social integration, where individuals attempt to impress others by their useful qualities in order to gain acceptance in a group. Those who succeed, by their outstanding qualities, become differentiated in status; this eventually lessens the degree of integration. Again, the very increase of rewards in a group tends to depreciate the value of those rewards, as Blau has illustrated in the instance of increasing promotions in a group. As a result the same promotion no longer creates the same satisfaction as formerly. In society, Blau continues, relative deprivations among an underprivileged class may lead to opposition movements, the success of which fosters opposition by the lower-middle class who now undergo relative deprivation. Blau argues that whole segments of society are interdependent but they may often come into conflict if the success of one brings opposition from others. In this fashion, he ends strongly, if speculatively, on the sources of conflict in society.

Empirical influences on research

Blau has put forward a great number of hypotheses suitable for guiding research. This, I suggest, is the essence of his potential contribution to social psychology. Many of these hypotheses have been discussed in this chapter. It is my aim in the following chapter to examine which of these hypotheses have already been influential empirically, since the value of so many of Blau's speculations can only be assessed against further empirical work.

There is, no doubt, a similarity between Blau's explanatory effort in extending exchange theory and the analogy drawn by some economists between microstructures and macrostructures—the analogy between an interpersonal relationship and the market in general (see Plon (1972) for a critical discussion of this analogy). *Exchange and Power* culminates with a para-theory of social exchange for collective behaviour and this is not of itself of interest to us as social psychologists, although it has been followed through in Blau's more recent publications (for example, Blau and Schoenherr, 1971).

There is yet another contribution to social psychology, incidental to his own purposes as a sociologist, but it is a central issue for us and the most important development of all. He has made a theoretical advance by introducing concepts which capture the variables of social situation and context. There are only a few, mainly dealing with status and conflict, but he states them in a clear analytical and measurable form. These are variables which are simply not present in the Thibaut and Kelley model and to which even Homans has given less attention. Now, what should be our criteria for assessing Blau's part as a theorist? The criteria I use are empirical and we will seek our assessment in answers to the following questions: has Blau's version of social exchange ideas influenced research; how productive has it been of later work; what forms has this work taken? Has it led to the posing of new questions?

13

Recent Developments from Blau's Hypotheses

Introduction

In *Exchange and Power in Social Life* Blau's contribution is to elucidate exchange concepts and to suggest topics for further work. His own publications since then have not involved him in research at the level of interpersonal behaviour, nor was it his aim in the book to present explanations at this level. He has simply used propositions which offer an interpretation of social behaviour as exchange in order to proceed, by analogy, to an explanatory scheme for organizations, large collectivities and classes in society; for relationships between them and their internal structures. This extension is not our concern as social psychologists nor, in fairness, has it been the aim of Blau to contribute to social psychological theory. Nevertheless, he has attempted an elucidation of concepts used in social psychology and, as we have seen, his contribution is often cited as a reference in company with those of Homans and Thibaut and Kelley. There are few instances of Blau's contribution acting as a direct influence on research on interpersonal behaviour, although such as exist will be discussed in this chapter. I shall also explore the nature of its potential influences on research and offer a view of how his efforts in refining concepts of reciprocity, power and status may be useful for our study of interpersonal behaviour.

Blau has adopted the propositions of Homans (1961) such as those touching on distributive justice (see Chapter 12, p. 305) and he incorporates, in general outline, the Thibaut and Kelley model when he considers relationships such as courtship similar to a mixed-motive game (above p. 291). As I have said Blau's discussion of the social process between individuals is intended finally (and this part of his argument is developed in the last third of his book) as a step towards a theory of more complex social structures. On the way to achieving this approach to a theory of collectivities Blau has made a number of clarifying statements about interpersonal behaviour which ought to be recognized—for example, his conceptualization of reciprocal relationships and their limits, of power and imbalance in social relations and of factors contributing to status differences—these are all directly important for our analysis of social exchange. Essentially, what Blau has done is to elucidate these exchange concepts and this may be why his contribution has been mentioned, as we have seen, as an extremely rich source of reference. It is natural that others have followed him in his attempt to arrive at a conceptually more clear framework, particularly sociologists like Stanley (1968), Ellis (1971), Meeker (1971), Blain (1971a). There is no denying this aspect of Blau's work but the question still has to be asked, and this is our concern here, about Blau's influence on empirical research. We shall consider this, in a moment.

There is also the possibility, important to social psychologists, that Blau's work has implications for research methodology. In this respect Blau holds a position between that of Homans on the one hand and Thibaut and Kelley on the other. Homans is eclectic in his choice of research methods and has no preference for one design over another although he states that quantification must at least be, and usually will only be, in the form of ordinal scales. One exception is his rejection of the Prisoner's Dilemma design, but even in this case there are researchers who have used the paradigm to test Homans' exchange propositions such as those touching justice or equity (see Chapter 11, p. 253). Thus Homans drew his propositions from a complete range of research studies employing a variety of methods, as was demonstrated in Chapter 8 and current research which tests or refers to his propositions is varied in design and comprehensively so. On the other hand, Thibaut and Kelley (1959) present their single experimental paradigm: the payoff matrix, the game format. Although they do not *derive* their model from this one source, nevertheless in the large amount of subsequent research which they have influenced, and in which they have actively participated, there is principally only one kind of design—the experimental paradigm. In contrast to this, Blau advocates that field observation should be the preferred research method. This is the kind of investigation which he himself has carried out in *Dynamics of Bureaucracy* (1955). It supplies one reason why there has not been a subsequent proliferation of research publications revealing his influence, on anything like the scale of influence of the other two contributions. This is only one reason, another factor is that Blau expounds the existing propositions of exchange rather than providing new ones of his own. Furthermore, he has extended his theoretical approach beyond the empirical area to which the exchange propositions refer, taking his explanations to the level of organizations, collectivities and the relations between them. In doing so he also takes his subject matter and his theoretical effort away from the area of inter-personal behaviour which concerns the social psychologist. Those who are interested in Blau's latest work (for example, Blau and Schoenherr, 1971) will have to pursue this beyond the boundary of our unit of study in social psychology. I cannot deal here with exchange in the context of structural elements and for our purposes we must focus our attention on Blau's contribution to social psychology, on his exchange concepts as far as they help to explain direct social relations.

There are four topics for our consideration in this chapter which empirically demonstrate Blau's influence and the significance of his contribution within the psychological critique of exchange theory. First, does he help us in finding answers to the criticism of tautological "weakness" as this is intended by several recent critics (for example, Abrahamsson, 1970)? Secondly, does his position on reductionism, as an anti-reductionist, give support to the postulates of social exchange as comprising a "theory", a body of explanations, in social psychology, with a degree of autonomy? I discuss the problems of reduction in the following chapter, but the general tendency of Blau's conclusions will be briefly summarized here because they do give us a rationale for rejecting reduction. Thirdly, how far are Blau's uses of economic concepts and analogies any more successful than those of Homans and Thibaut and Kelley? Do his views on rationality and calculative behaviour qualify those of his predecessors? We need to know this before we make a general statement on whether the connections of exchange theory to economics are anything other than tenuous. Lastly, while Blau may assist us in throwing light on the criticisms that exchange theory is tautologous, that it is reductionist or that economic concepts are a non-valid source, his major role as a theorist touches on a more far-reaching criticism of exchange notions and one of the most difficult to answer. Basically, because social exchange theory incorporates reinforcement assumptions, as we have seen in Chapter 2, it inevitably draws attack for the triviality of so many of its propositions. Of course, most of everyday social behaviour is trivial and we are therefore to some extent contaminated by our subject matter. If we choose to discuss equity as what may happen when an elderly professor marries a glamorous young wife, then we have probably taken up a very trivial subject for testing the validity of exchange propositions. In contrast, there should be nothing to prevent any social psychologist from observing the behaviour of politicians or of representatives of different interest groups in society—except the opposition of the groups themselves. Again, he can observe the process of conflict—so long as he does not also assume that his position is value-free.

Blau's major and significant contribution to social exchange theory is that he brings into the field of study for social psychology the possibility of considering conflict, status differences and political behaviour as subject matter even though he does little more than point to the direction. He does not show how this projection can be carried through or what methods are to be used other than that the context for research should be actual situations of social actions. For the moment, we have to settle for his providing us with the concepts of status hierarchy, of the hierarchical aspects of group relations in society, of imbalance in power, as variables to be included in the hypothetical statements which may guide future research.

Before I go on to discuss recent empirical studies developing out of Blau's treatment of exchange and power I would like to summarize one or two general issues which Blau helps to clarify. We have already discussed some familiar theoretical weaknesses, not unique to exchange notions, but which are sometimes used to criticize these notions—namely, that they are utilitarian, in the classical economic terms of maximizing, or tautologous and reductionist. We have discussed the first two criticisms, and Homans' replies to them, in Chapter 9. The third critique, of reductionism, is treated extensively in the next chapter. We have already accepted that tautologies are necessary in the premises of a formal, logical theoretical structure, at the most general level. Tautologies are inevitable, at this level, as "logical truths"; here, no question of verification or falsification arises. But we are not immediately concerned with this kind of theoretical structure. We are concerned with *contingent* explanatory statements. Now, the hypotheses which can be empirically tested are not tautological but *substantial* assertions, to be confirmed against a test of evidence. We have already seen that the description "tautology" can be used in another sense to refer to the kind of statement where there are two terms in the form of x varies as a function of y and the antecedent term is not defined independently of the consequent one. For example, such a statement would be: "the more activities its members share, the more cohesive is a group". As we saw earlier, such statements are called "relational tautologies", the terms are not defined independently yet they can be measured independently (we discussed a number of examples above in Chapter 9, pp. 214–218). Blau strengthens the case for exchange propositions as contingent statements by the attention he gives to measuring operations, for example, Longabaugh's (1963) coding method; to empirical situations of symmetrical or asymmetrical exchange; to the clearer specification of the limiting conditions on reciprocity. In this way he has made several points against the tautological possibility that "any and all behaviour in interpersonal relations is conceptualized as an exchange, even conduct toward others that is not at all oriented in terms of expected returns from them" (Blau, 1964, p. 6).

When he draws on economic analogies in his explanatory scheme, Blau places heavy reservations on their suitability. He emphasizes the many differences between economic and social exchange (above, in Chapter 12, pp. 293, 328). True, Blau thinks that the economic principle of diminishing marginal utility provides a convenient analogy for the effects observed when a person gains social rewards in excess of his expectations, but even here he takes into account interpersonal comparisons and rising levels of expectation which limit the analogy. There is one apparent inconsistency therefore in Blau's attempt to apply indifference curves to interpersonal relations, an "application" which yet awaits appraisal against empirical data. On the whole, Blau's position on the use of borrowed terms from economics is very similar to that of Homans; it is a cautious one, using illustrative parallels but qualifying them very stringently. Blau, for example, makes much of the "intrinsic" values in reciprocal relationships, such as friendship and personal attachment (see Chapter 12, pp. 295–297 Furthermore, Blau comes nowhere near to assuming a form of economic rationality in social behaviour, nor to assuming optimal or efficient strategies or rational criteria of this class. Like Homans, his only assumption is that persons will choose between alternative courses of action according to a preference ranking.

Interpersonal behaviour and social structure

Exchange and Power has been called "a vast quarry of a book" (Macintyre, 1967), "a mine of source material" (Heath, 1971) and "the
richest of the exchange contributions" (Israel and Tajfel, 1972). However, it is difficult to divide the work into clear divisions and major
topics because it is an exposition containing many anecdotes and some
references to empirical studies, with the aim of giving plausible support
to a number of hypotheses. The latter, derived from reinforcement
theory or from economic analogies, are used to explain interpersonal
behaviour. This exposition takes up almost one-third of *Exchange and
Power* and is followed by a gradual, speculative extension of the hypotheses to organizations, collectivities and social classes as parties to an
exchange of rewards and costs. For social psychologists, the main
interest of Blau's work is found in his efforts to specify a variety of conditions of social exchange, building on the formulations of Homans and
Thibaut and Kelley. In particular, Blau speculates on the effects of
social structure on interpersonal exchange. This is a valuable addition,
though it is, as yet, a relatively untested one.

In many instances throughout the previous chapter we have seen
how Blau draws attention to the importance of structure. One example
concerns leadership and authority in groups. Blau illustrates how power
asymmetry leads to differentiation of rank or strata, that is, to a group
structure of status differences. His argument takes the following steps.
Providers of scarce resources (rewards) receive esteem from the recipients but in associations which continue over long periods, the esteem
of those who have lower rank does not have sufficient weight as a return
and, for this reason, compliance is the only alternative that they can
offer. So, from the specialization of resources, there develops a structure
of power which, although it is achieved through provision of resources
or rewards, in its longer term operation means that those who possess
power can impose their will, and if necessary, despite resistance (Blau,
1964, p. 117). Authority also develops out of the exchange between
those who have more power and those who have less: if the exchange is
considered fair then a norm emerges which prescribes compliance. The
asymmetry of power is thus recognized as legitimate. Another example
is provided by the case of an individual entering a group as a newcomer,
subject to a demand for valuable resources as his contribution to the
general purposes of the group. At the same time, the nature of his con-

tribution must not threaten the wellbeing of others or their status position, so that his behaviour, to some extent is under constraint. Blau describes the nature of group criteria for membership and this forces our attention to influences outside the dyad, alerting us to the possible effects of relative status, shared norms and collective aims. Blau discusses a number of factors which might be salient to individuals transferring between groups and considers how structural factors would influence the decision to transfer. He raises the following questions: would the newcomer obtain a similar relative status position in the new group; do equivalent criteria for status or rank pertain in both groups; is the new group itself in a similar stratum to that of the existing group? (Chapter 12, pp. 322, 326).

Some of these structural aspects are relevant to a social psychological explanation and I shall give some examples as they appear in the recent literature. As we have mentioned, Blau's own purpose is to carry on the discussion at a sociological level which in fact takes the discussion outside our particular area of interest. Blau's aim is to study complex structures: our aim is to study interpersonal behaviour. At the same time, Blau's approach helps us towards understanding the important influences of group structure and intergroup relations. How can these be included in social psychological hypotheses? We must look to some recent publications in order to find an answer.

We have discussed some general issues of Blau's approach. We shall now consider specific empirical influences of *Exchange and Power*.

Empirical studies

Graves's (1972) research report is typical of descriptive studies of the behaviour of managerial staff in organizations, which refer to Blau. Graves mentions Blau's (1955) earlier observations of communication between members of work groups, and Homans' (1961) discussion of differentials in communications (initiated or received) between status levels. In this case, testing the prediction that persons of higher status receive more communications, Graves presents his analysis of managers' diaries recording their activities during two-week periods. He concludes that the multiple criteria of status (personal skills, characteristics, seniority and so on) will qualify any prediction based only on rank in a formal hierarchy. A recent survey of managers by Wager (1972) also reveals Blau's influence: this was carried out by questionnaires referring to actions in staff meetings. For example, do managers seek or give information, co-ordinate or settle differences, or comment critically? They were asked to say how they might act on two separate occasions, either in a senior or junior capacity. The tendency for junior positions to have a greater frequency of both information seeking and giving can be interpreted by referring to Blau's speculations on impression-making. Wager suggests that in a junior or subordinate status managers strive to impress others in order to secure and enhance their positions.

Empirical studies which test Blau's hypotheses are relatively few. That is not to say that there are no investigators who have found Blau's concepts useful. For example, Rieger-Shlonsky (1969) uses the extrinsic-intrinsic classification of rewards in classifying his data on the resources sought from relatives or friends. Wager (1971) refers to Blau's definition of legitimate authority in his discussion of possible infringements by employers of an employee's right to privacy. Walton (1969) cites Blau and several of his sociological predecessors for a definition of power as involving an *intention* to use superior resources; power is the capacity to mobilize forces for the accomplishment of intended effects.

Katz, Gurevitch, Peled and Danet (1969) carried out a descriptive and exploratory study of doctor-patient relations and of the bargaining that takes place between patients who say they suffer from more ailments, or require more treatments, than the practitioner wishes to allow. These authors offer a useful addition to definitions of bargaining, noting especially that bargaining involves refusals. It is also very interesting that their research study follows in direct line from Blau's suggestion in *Exchange and Power* that Longabaugh's (1963) observation categories be used for coding exchange behaviour.

In a further study, Katz and Danet (1973) explore strategies used by new immigrants to Israel faced by the bureaucratic rules of various organizations (police, workers' committees, banks, sick funds). 116 men of different immigrant origin were each asked to role-play in four hypothetical situations. How would they influence bureaucratic decisions in their favour? Katz and Danet concentrate their analysis on the kinds of reasons or persuasive appeals they might employ. They seek evidence of (a) the influence of regional origins of immigrants and (b) the influence of the type of organization on the tactics chosen. They are able to illustrate that immigrants of Western origin tend to adopt a more sophisticated approach—for instance, by insisting on legal rights rather than trying promises or rewards. Katz and Danet comment that insistence on rights reflects some awareness of bureaucratic norms. They also think that appeals to the altruism of officials will occur most frequently where the organization has greatest power against the client and especially where the organization holds a monopoly of services. Thus, they expect most appeals to altruism in relations with the police and Sick Fund officials and less with workers' committees and banks because presumably the client can take his business or his employment elsewhere. Katz and Danet claim no more than a cautious exploration of some possibilities. From this study there is no clear pattern of results, yet studies along these lines may provide useful evidence to adduce to the hypotheses suggested by Thibaut, Gruder and Murdoch (see above Chapter 7) in their bargaining experiments manipulating high and low alternatives. Their discussion of the difficulties of meaning in content analysis is illuminating: they show how an appeal to altruism may have several levels of meaning. For example, the appeal to a police officer to grant a personal favour may also be perceived by him as flattery: "In other words, the most altruistic of appeals—reflecting the powerlessness of the client—also has a component of reciprocity: status or subservience is being offered in return for the official's hoped-for compliance" (p. 180). They note that Blau has suggested "that appeals to altruism, like inducements, acknowledge one's indebtedness to the other, thus offering him status or power" (p. 189).

Of the considerable work referring to Blau's hypotheses at the organizational level, I shall mention only one, the treatment of competition and exchange between organizations by Yuchtman and Seashore (1967). They discuss some of the definitions involved and do not deal with interpersonal behaviour at all but their distinction between competitive (similar) organizations and co-operative (dissimilar and complementary) organizations can equally illustrate some conditions of exchange between persons. They argue that such a dichotomy does violence to the actual mixture of competition and complementarity in any given relationship between organizations. They suggest, on the contrary, that "exchange and competition are the extremes of a continuum along which interorganizational transactions can be described" (p. 899). Although they do not discuss it explicitly, these authors raise the idea of a continuum for competition and exchange resembling closely the notion of a mixed-motive relationship especially familiar in experimental games (see above Chapters 4 and 6).

Schwartz (1974) offers an essay on waiting, and making others wait as part of a "strategy of delay". From this point of view waiting periods can be interpreted as supporting the distribution of power between persons and would be associated with the scarcity value of an individual (Blau, 1964, p. 118). Schwartz discusses waiting as an indicator of the value of the service waited for and this leads him to a further discussion of time as a "marketable commodity" and waiting as "an inherent feature of the psychology of social exchange" (p. 859). In formal organizations there are marked differentials in the accessibility of those lower and higher in status; and there are rituals of waiting. Schwartz deals especially with duration of waiting (by others) as an indicator of a person's status, or as a means to asserting status. In the next section we will discuss some aspects of delay and duration of time between a person's action and its reciprocation in the much broader context of trust in family relations. But these are topics which require more research attention.

In our discussion of trust and bargaining in the family we will present a number of examples of an exchange process in familial relations. This does not mean to say that everything that happens in the family is an exchange. I do not intend to consider behaviour in the family as exchange but to consider some aspects which are explained as exchange, a very much more modest claim.

Studies of trust and uncertainty

We have seen that Blau discusses the differences between economic and social exchange (see Chapter 12, pp. 292–296 and p. 328). The most important difference concerns the necessity for trust in social relations, because there are no binding formal contracts. In economic exchange, obligations are specified in advance but in social relations neither the nature of the return nor its timing can be specified; there are only diffuse obligations, nor may it be possible to bargain about them. If there is no trust, then neither is there social exchange. Furthermore, Blau calls attention to the fact that distrust is expected in economic relations but will have a negative significance for social behaviour in general (see Blau, 1964, p. 107). Blau has illustrated that trust tends to build up gradually through cumulative commitment to a relationship (as do Thibaut and Kelley, 1959, pp. 64–70). He refers also to the impossibility of developing trust in the Prisoner's Dilemma game. We have seen, in Chapter 6, how trust can only appear in this kind of experimental situation where there are conditions of free communication allowing agreements to be formed or when the experimenter intervenes to suggest contractual agreements as happened in the Thibaut and Gruder (1969) experiments. In these experiments an agreement avoided the implementing of mutual or unilateral threats.

From another point of view, the importance of norms or agreements is that they avoid uncertainty. Anderson (1971) in his study of kinship relations argues that interpersonal trust reduces one principle source of uncertainty in actual social situations. Although there may be many other factors in a given situation which may operate to make another's behaviour uncertain in the future such as his health, financial security or availability of resources, yet the uncertainty, that one may in the future be able to rely for support or services from another, will be immensely heightened if one has doubts about his willingness to reciprocate even if he has the means to do so. Anderson's monograph on kinship, undertaken within an exchange theoretical framework, is extremely valuable as a source of ideas and hypotheses about trust and uncertainty. He argues that uncertainty in social relationships influences persons to be calculative and to seek shorter-term returns. And he makes two further points: that where there is extreme uncertainty in social or kinship relations "this calculativeness in turn leads to increased variability in behaviour within a population. Secondly, the arrival of calculative orientations in a community will logically lead to the termination of generalized exchange; for this to be viable, absolute trust that others in the community will conform to expectations, is required" (p. 15). He suggests that only where communities are highly homogeneous and stable will there be general norms governing kinship behaviour. When Anderson contrasts rural with urban areas, the latter, as one might expect, show a more calculative orientation towards their family relationships. But it is not so completely straightforward as this— in the sectors of the migrant, impoverished workers' communities described by Anderson, he suggests that there was also inadequate socialization and hence weak superego development: "reactions to situations by many people were more likely to take place at the ego level than at the superego level. This, in turn, would have almost inevitably resulted in a much more calculative orientation . . ." (p. 109).

Anderson's study gives useful leads to the specifying of conditions under which calculative behaviour may or may not pertain. He also

discusses the time span between one person's action and its reciprocation by another, an aspect of exchange which requires more research
attention.

His analysis is of interest to us because it is set entirely within a
number of explicit formulations about social exchange and particularly
from the work of Blau, Homans and Thibaut and Kelley. Among the
other factors contributing to uncertainty about the social "returns"
that a person obtains from others, there may be doubts about the
other's ability to make the return, or about the utility of it when it is
made. Anderson especially comments on the timing of a reciprocal
action. "The longer the gap between service and reciprocation, however, the greater is the uncertainty both about alter's ability and about
one's own needs. And, the greater the risk in terms of uncertainty about
alter's ability and one's own future needs the greater . . . will be the
tendency either to demand a large surplus in the future, or to demand
instant reciprocation in the form of some other desired resource . . .
to calculate the outcomes" (p. 14).

Anderson's thesis states that *under certain conditions* calculative behaviour
is likely to emerge in family relationships in place of behaviour expressing social norms of obligation to parents, or moral principles stating,
for example, responsibility for maintaining elderly relatives. Throughout his discussion Anderson states one proposition very clearly: where
there is uncertainty there will be calculation and preference for short-
term returns; there will be abandonment of norms or moral precepts
which induce a person not to calculate at all or to wait for returns over
the long term. His study suggests that research be directed to observing
situations of varying certainty to explore the conditions into these
variations and to confirm, or otherwise, the hypothesis that a given set
of conditions leads to calculative behaviour. Anderson cites anthropological studies of communities with a general uncertainty of life and
extreme poverty, creating situations where any service rendered, even
to close kin, is "mentally recorded and reciprocation demanded, and
where no long-run obligations are entered into . . ." (p. 117).

For us, the limitation of the study is its exclusive emphasis on
economic conditions and the discussion of exchange among family
members as it is affected by such pecuniary influences as regular
income, amount of weekly earnings, state aid and household rents.
Anderson assumes that family relations have to satisfy some notion,
held by the individual, of an optimal bargain. This assumption provides

him with an analytic framework for his ordering of data on household composition and on patterns of occupations and earnings.

We can note that Anderson concludes, from his historical study, that the factory system introduced a new economic factor into parent-child relationships in workers' families. When minors gained a weekly wage this meant either that a bargain was struck favourable to all parties, or the child took a better alternative by leaving home. Unfortunately Anderson has to depend on the sparse evidence of residence patterns to support his hypothesis about short-term calculative orientations and altogether he has to depend on socio-economic data as support for his hypotheses about the nature of relationships within families. He has a weak basis for drawing inferences. However, he develops ideas on uncertainty and trust in social relations and he sets out his argument clearly and in forms which suggest hypotheses for research in other contexts; for example, factors which are important in social relations involve

> certainty about one's own future needs and about alter's future resources and other prior demands on them; such certainty is likely to be reduced in such situations as the following: situations of rapid social change; situations where major crises are frequent; situations where sizes of available resources fluctuate greatly; situations where actors are not in frequent interaction with each other and are therefore likely to be unsure of each other's resources and prior commitments (p. 173).

He advances the discussion of uncertainty and trust from the brief reference given to them by Thibaut and Kelley (1959, p. 66) and from the fuller treatment by Blau. Anderson's discussion is least helpful where he depends on economic data (these are his main factual sources) and it is to be hoped that future research will focus on other variables.

Bargaining and the family: parents and children

Anderson's analysis of family relationships as exchange is anticipated by Richer (1968) in a brief article discussing the contention that "rational social exchange occurs in families as in other groups" (p. 462). Twelve hypotheses are discussed stating the effects of, among other variables, the number of adults (as reward sources) in the family, the number of children, and the operation of notions of fair exchange following Homans' discussion of distributive justice. Richer puts forward the basic assumption that the primary goal of parents is to maximize compliance from their children. While he recognizes that this is somewhat simplistic, he presents it as a means to formulating particular hypotheses which may lead to empirical work. He attempts an analysis of parental capacity to gain compliance in terms of the parents' resources, their reward power. Richer offers hypotheses like the following: "The more integrated into a peer group the child is, the more available are non-parental social rewards, the less valuable are parental rewards, and hence the less likely are parental dictates to be followed." He discusses a number of possible situations in middle-class homes where the child may "raise the price of his compliance". Thus, one parental strategy might be to offer rewards which will enhance the child's status among his peers: "The hope is that dependence for peer approval on parental rewards will restore some of the lost compliance" (p. 464). Richer probably underemphasizes the changing roles of parents at different stages of the child's development—for instance, the parents' authority over the young child and their responsibility for that child is quite dissimilar to their responsibility for, and authority over a near-adult adolescent. It is of interest that Barker (1972) describes the changing parental role in workers' families once children start to earn their own living and she notes the *positive* effects in family finances and parent-child relations: "a source of friction is removed, a step towards adult status is taken, and parents feel they and their children get closer (as they do again when the children marry) because they share experiences" (p. 579). We shall return to this study in a moment.

Edwards (1969) makes a discursive review, similar to Richer's, of social exchange explanations in family relationships and mentions that these explanations have been used as an implicit analytical framework in many studies. This framework should now be stated explicitly, he argues, and its antecedents and assumptions should be made clear. He starts with the statement that behaviour is purposive, that persons exchange resources and "a resource is that which an exchanger has to give in a relationship. From the point of view of the receiver, this same resource may constitute a reward. Unlike economic exchange, most resources in social exchange are inseparable from the giver" (p. 519). He cites Blau for his emphasis on social norms of fair exchange, and Homans on justice. He notes the asymmetry and intensity of relationships, and the multiple resources which are aspects of family behaviour and which make it a problematic subject of study. Edwards draws our attention to the general conceptual problem in treating family behaviour as exchange when he asks: what is it that is actually exchanged? We can recall Blau's definition of intrinsic value in parent-child relations as an indicator of the complexity that any form of analysis will need to comprehend.

Edwards prefers the social exchange framework for two main reasons. First it postulates rational goals *but* this is not an *a priori* formulation and so his second reason is that exchange propositions have been derived from a body of diverse empirical work. One interesting part of his discussion focuses on the bases of familial power as these are affected by occupational status of husbands and wives and by non-economic characteristics of behaviour; he notes the hypothesis that the higher the husband's occupational or educational status the greater is his power in influencing marital decisions. Then he shows how this is qualified in some cultures by egalitarian expectations so that highly educated husbands may accord their wives greater control. Edwards ends with a warning that there is little evidence available about the resources exchanged in different family situations or of their rank in a hierarchy of value; little is known of alternative exchange possibilities except perhaps of divorce as an alternative (see Scanzoni, 1972). An advantage of social exchange theory which Edwards underlines is that it focuses on both sociological and psychological phenomena in the interplay between social context and individual outcomes.

In her interview sample of workers' families in Britain, Diana Barker (1972) examines the reasons why the majority of young people, before marriage, do not leave home (86 per cent of young men and 90 per cent of women were actually living at home, in her sample). Barker interprets this situation within an exchange framework, suggesting that the parents' domestic services and economic and emotional support of children is reciprocated by intangible rewards from the latter such as "appreciation, respect, affection, esteem and companionship". The emphasis on "spoiling" (parents going beyond their duty) is described: "The parent is seen as always giving over and above what a good parent should be expected to give. In part the child thinks that the return for this cannot be expected from him or her, but comes from the parent's own pleasure, self-satisfaction and status achieved in the community. The child . . . stays more firmly in the house . . . The return may also be considered to be deferred and to be due to the parents when the child is married and in the parents' old age" (p. 586). Barker raises a question, taken from Blau (1964), about whether there are disagreements if equivalence in exchange is not maintained. She also asks why the general expectation that parents should "spoil" their children has not resulted in a redefinition of their duty which is closer to what they actually do. She gives the answer that parents are able to convince their children they are "generous" beyond what is to be expected of them and she utilizes Blau's political analysis to explain this result more fully. Blau has argued that the significance of an imbalance of power depends on the reactions of the less powerful, and so differentiation of power does not necessarily produce a strain towards change because the advantages gained may outweigh the hardships. Barker concludes "if the underlings agree that the demands made on them are only fair and just in view of the ample rewards, there are fostered feelings of obligation and loyalty . . . in material terms, the balance is so heavily in the child's favour . . ." (p. 586). Next she rephrases the question and now asks: why do parents acquiesce in so unequal an exchange? Here again the answer is given by the concept of spoiling which involves elements of exchange defined as lying outside the sphere of parental obligation. Thus, spoiling is the basis for establishing obligations on the part of the child to "keep close". Barker comments that the parents' desire to keep young adults close to them has to be justified in the face of general social influences towards individual achievement and this is done by spoiling the child, giving the child benefit over and above what is required by norms governing the parental role.*

These sociologists tend to over-emphasize material and economic factors in family exchange, although, as we have seen, Anderson may be justified in trying to show the effects of poverty and mobility on familial obligations. Barker sketches the intangibles in parent–child exchange and so indicates an extremely important research topic. Furthermore, sociological studies draw our attention to the influences of class and social context on parent–child relations, to the influence of other adults in the family, of siblings and peer groups—they do more

---

* Barker adds that there was an absence of peer groups for children (and thus of a strong positive youth culture) because of the short period of schooling. Note that Sprott's (1958) brief introductory (a book which incidentally reveals the strong influence of Homans' earlier theoretical propositions) makes a relevant comment: "It would seem, however, that in our own (British) society, with all its discontinuities between family life and occupation there are sections of the community in which family unity is preserved to such an extent that a 'youth culture' scarcely develops" (p. 73).

even than this, because they focus on exchange process as it develops through the child's life and as the content of exchange itself varies between pre-adolescence and adulthood. This focus on the family as an unfolding of phases over the life-cycle of parent and child will avoid over-emphasis on the child's short-term learning, by rewards and punishments.

The parent's role as an exemplar is one aspect which the exchange-oriented discussion does not appear to cover in any detail and it remains one of the many possible subjects for research in the difficult and "complex geometry"* of family behaviour. The exchange theorist's view of parents as resource-providers should prove to be a complementary notion. These authors—Anderson, Barker, Edwards and Richer—by using exchange concepts, indicate varied facets of family behaviour and, in doing so, they reveal the narrowness of viewpoint concerning family relations which is sometimes to be found in social psychology. Not that these particular sociologists (with the exception of Barker) have made direct observations of families. In the main they point to topics for future research.

Bargaining, negotiation: husbands and wives

The fullest recent discussion of family relations within an explicit framework of exchange theory is provided by Scanzoni (1972) who analyses the relationship of husbands and wives as a process of reciprocity that at certain times may evolve into conflict, which in turn may or may not be resolved. Scanzoni, like Anderson and Edwards, refers to Blau's distinction between "intrinsic attraction" in a relationship that is an end in itself, and the *extrinsic* (or secondary) relationship which is merely, or chiefly, a means to obtaining some service or reward. Scanzoni recalls Blau's argument that exchange processes occur in love relations, as in others, even though the partners are not using each other as a means to extrinsic ends. Following Blau, he states that exchange is the basis of the formation and maintenance of any social relationship and, Scanzoni remarks, "to conceive of love and marriage as purely altruistic is to miss the point that rarely, if ever, can human love be sustained unless it be requited . . . to posit value consensus or common

---

* I quote this description from Brown's (1973, p. 401) conclusion that the child's learning by identification with parents "is a complex geometry of which we know little more than the rudiments".

interests as the prime basis for love and marriage exhibits only a tiny fraction of the iceberg, and totally misses the dynamics of marriage formation and subsequent interaction" (p. 51). Essentially, Scanzoni considers courtship and marriage as a process, a continual process, of bargaining.* He develops his thesis as follows: in anthropological studies the marriage contract is shown to involve exchanges of an economic nature between kin groups and these serve as a long-term binding force but in contemporary society there is no once-and-for-all exchange, instead there is "an ongoing quest or seeking for rewards . . . Therefore, persons today bargain during courtship, during the decision to marry, and furthermore they continue this bargaining on through the length of their marriage" (p. 53). Nonrational or "person-centred" considerations to some extent obscure the presence of a bargaining process, contends Scanzoni. On the other hand, trial marriages are at the opposite pole, introducing an attempt at explicit rationality into the love relationship so that outcomes of marital exchange can be weighed in a daily routine of life together, although Scanzoni fails to mention the mistrust that may accompany the attempt. Incidentally, he adds that there are no data to indicate the frequency of such trial arrangements, their prevalence or otherwise in different socio-economic groups.

Considering reciprocity and exchange in marriage, Scanzoni notes a discussion by Sprey (1969) which suggests that marital consensus is a state of "negotiated order" open to a process of continuous renegotiation. Scanzoni asks: how do we analyse the process of negotiation? He relies largely on Gouldner's (1960) concept of reciprocity as accounting both for stability and instability of social relations. As Scanzoni has mentioned, social exchanges established during courtship relationships become the basis for a bargain, the decision to marry. Scanzoni adopts the definition of bargaining used by Turner (1970) who says it

> may seem like a cruel word to apply to the deliberations of members in the intimate family relationship. But bargaining is simply a general term for any interaction in which the concessions that one member makes to

---

* Concerning the process of bargaining in marriage, see also Harris (1969): "After marriage, exchange continues. The spouses acquire rights in each other by marriage: a relationship is established. Given that relationship, however, the actual way in which the marital roles are further defined will depend on a process of bargaining which will continue through the marriage and whose outcome will depend on the relative power of the spouses, which is determined not by their position in a market but by the various material and social conditions under which they act" (p. 161).

another are expected to be reciprocated in some manner, so that over the long run the sacrifices of each will balance out (Turner, 1970, p. 106).

Scanzoni adds that bargaining need not be conscious or rationally calculated and that empirical work suggests it may be entirely implicit, both partners being unaware of it. Equity considerations are also revealed by empirical studies and equity itself may be a bargaining point (as Homans has stated, see Chapter 8, p. 162) and a partner who is generous on one occasion may expect the other to act similarly in the future. Scanzoni hypothesizes that the rewards exchanged in marriage are broadly of two kinds: instrumental rewards from income and status in the occupational and class structure of society and expressive rewards from companionship, understanding (empathy), physical love and affection.* He argues that the hypothesis accounts for correlations found between social status and marital stability. At the same time, Scanzoni wishes to distinguish between bargaining as part of everyday exchange and bargaining as part of conflict. "In most marriages" he comments "most of the time, reciprocity is probably more frequent than conflict" (p. 67). It is too tempting for Scanzoni not to take an analogy from union-management bargaining—most of the time the interaction is an exchange of agreed-on rewards and when conflict over the distribution of rewards does occur, efforts are soon made to move on again with a settled rate of exchange.

But how does exchange evolve into conflict? This is explained by Scanzoni in terms of power relationships and here he calls on Blau's *Exchange and Power* as the basis of his exposition. Husbands and wives each have power to influence, to impose their wills and what they bargain over is the relative power they possess. Scanzoni mentions the index of power devised by Blood and Wolfe (1960) which is composed of items such as the following: who usually makes the final decision about buying a car, taking out life insurance, what house to live in, what job the husband has, whether the wife works, where to go on holiday? Empirical studies carried out since 1960 (for example by Lupri, 1969) show that husbands of high socio-economic status control more decisions. Scanzoni (1970) himself has collected some evidence by questionnaire to support this and gives his interpretation of this trend

---

* Discussing marriage Thibaut and Kelley (1959, p. 226) state that: "The interdependence upon which such relationships are founded usually means that there is some sort of bartering wherein kinds of contributions A makes to B are *qualitatively* different from those B makes to A."

with the simple statement that power rests on resources and higher status husbands have more. The statement is qualified by Scanzoni later, using Blau's distinction between legitimate and non-legitimate power. Referring to further questionnaire evidence, he sketches the conclusion that the higher the husband's social status the more legitimate power (and willing compliance) he possesses, whereas the lower the status of the husband the more non-legitimate power he seizes. The occurrence of conflict is discussed by Scanzoni entirely in terms of Blau's framework and he draws on the latter's distinction between individual opposition and collective opposition to power. Thus, if an isolated individual perceives a power situation as unjust, his disapproval is not of general significance but if numbers of other individuals share his disapproval then there may be far-reaching implications for social structure. Scanzoni's next step is to speculate about this kind of result for marital structure. Blau's conceptual frame again supplies a pointer to reference groups influencing individuals in feeling relatively deprived. Scanzoni mentions Women's Liberation as an illustration: "Women in the movement obviously want other women to feel deprived vis-à-vis men, but they also want them to feel deprived compared to women who are fulfilling more 'modern' behaviours" (p. 85).

Scanzoni has based his arguments on the notion of a reward-cost ratio; he has also provided a useful discussion of academic husbands and wives and particularly where he deals with the activities of each that are specialized or are interchangeable. Their control over the timing and scheduling of shared and alternating activities in home and work is a salient feature. One point to mention in passing, is that the academic community seems to be joining workers' families as the social strata most accessible to investigation.

Courtship and bargaining

McCall (1966) in a discussion of different modes of courtship, uses Blau's definition of exchange behaviour and (this is of special interest to us) a definition of bargaining "as distinguished from simple exchange", implying "a certain purposive awareness of the exchange of rewards" (p. 191). Moreover, he continues:

> Individuals bargain about whether they will reward one another, in what ways, under what conditions, and to what degree. In this sense, then, exchange behaviour may occur even though bargaining does not. Bar-

gaining entails some knowledge of other sources of reward and an ability to draw on these alternative sources (or to threaten to do so), as well as a sense of how much one can reasonably expect to get in social exchange of a given variety (p. 191).

McCall discusses bargains struck in courtship over the conditions of association but raises the possibility that courtship may not only be a period of determining the best bargains but, he conjectures, even a period of "training in bargaining" because "the emphasis in modern life is on keeping up one's bargaining skills, for one never entirely leaves the market" (p. 197). In making this comment, McCall has in mind the effect of high divorce rates. Next McCall mentions various forms of sexual exploitation* which involve, for example, the breaking of promises after getting the other person committed to the relationship. He notes this kind of exploitation can only occur when, say, a man promises marriage in return for sexual favours and then fails "to keep the terms of exchange", he adds that "exploitation of this kind could occur only in a period during which sexual favours were problematic . . . and in a time when the granting of them represented deep commitment (and) . . . expectations of a permanent relationship" (p. 199). McCall goes on to speculate about the conditions under which forms of exploitation may occur, leaving some open questions about their degree of prevalence. As I mentioned in the previous chapter, there is much evidence yet to be collected on exploitation phenomena.†

Murstein's (1973) work on marital choice raises similar questions to those we have found in the studies described above. Murstein's work is worth noting here (although he does not refer to Blau) because it illustrates points I have mentioned elsewhere. As a psychologist using social exchange explanations, he refers to Homans and Thibaut and Kelley but not to Blau. This is quite characteristic of the psychological literature on exchange (see, for example, Secord and Backman, 1974, pp. 220–234) as it is just as characteristic for sociologists to refer to Homans and Blau only. Murstein's research nevertheless illustrates a convergence between psychological and sociological approaches which support the exchange viewpoint: it exemplifies the tendency for exchange ideas to develop into a unitary body of explanations extending across many social psychological topics.

* We have also discussed sexual exploitation above, Chapter 12, p. 320.
  † Exploitation phenomena have been explored in experimental designs, especially the Prisoner's Dilemma, and are discussed above in Chapters 4 and 11.

In his attempt to explain significant factors in influencing interracial marriages, Murstein attaches great importance to "the equality of exchange subjectively experienced by its participants" (Murstein, 1973, p. 24). He comments: "Although romantics may believe that love overrides all material considerations . . . love depends on equality of exchange" (p. 26). From this proposition Murstein goes on to examine U.S. census data from which he is able to show that, compared to all-black marriages, black-white marriages reveal a higher educational level in the black spouse. The advantages of a "higher" racial status of the white partner are traded off against the educational attainments of the other.

Murstein (1972) has also discussed, and carried out research on, different stages of courtship as a reciprocal exchange of intimate information (and see Worthy, Gary and Kahn, 1969, whose work on self-disclosure is discussed above, in Chapter 11). He describes some influences which might affect such disclosure, focusing especially on the greater dependence of women in courtship relations:

> the cost of abstaining from marriage is still currently greater for women, since the former tend to improve their standard of living and status more by marriage than do men. To compound the difficulty for women, the age difference between marriageable men and women, the women's shorter age range of marriageability, and their longer-life span put them in greater supply and less demand than men (p. 621).

The effect of men's more powerful position means also that they tend to take the most active role in courtship. Murstein then hypothesizes that because a woman is less powerful in the courtship situation she has more reason to attach importance to her partner's needs and his "ideal-self image". Consequently she will be more accurate in her judgement of them than her partner will be of hers. Questionnaires were given to 98 young couples. The analysis provides some qualified support for the general prediction which Murstein treats cautiously in a speculative discussion.

Power and imbalance

It is worth recalling that in *Exchange and Power* Blau makes much of the tendency towards imbalance of rewards in social relations and he has clearly emphasized that reciprocal behaviour may often be unequal with one party gaining more from the exchange than another. As Blau argues, early in his book, social exchange between persons leads to the intrinsic attachments of friendship or liking, but may lead also to the superordination of some persons over others if their gains are relatively greater, placing them in a position where they have greater influence. This influence comes about in the following way: because their gains are more they have a surplus of advantages or services which they can distribute in exchange with those who comply with their wishes. This is the essence of Blau's definition of power: that a person can influence or prevail on others to comply willingly with his wishes. In the dynamics of social relations, Blau gives attention to competitive forces as well as forces towards integration. He describes them at the level of interpersonal behaviour, indicating that similar forces and counterforces will be found at the level of relationships between organizations and entire social classes. Unlike Homans, Blau does not draw for evidence on many empirical studies, preferring to use only a few to illustrate his major points which, in most cases, are elaborations of the exchange propositions stated by Homans and Thibaut and Kelley. Yet in his greater emphasis on the incompatible phenomena of social life as the source of its dynamics Blau is offering his particular contribution to the existing body of exchange explanations and placing beyond doubt that they comprehend interpersonal conflicts and social conflicts on a larger scale. Unlike Homans, who emphasizes the strain towards balance and therefore the conservative influences in society, Blau has made the fundamental postulate that there is always a tendency in individuals to accumulate credit in their social relationships, a tendency therefore to imbalance, inequity and to greater power of one person over another.

In the previous chapter we saw how Blau has emphasized aspects of social conflict. He shows how exchange can lead to conflict and he is interested in showing the limitations to reciprocal relations. In other words, Blau makes sure that we do not consider exchange, or exchange explanations, only in the aspect of consensus but that we must give due weight to his attempt to admit conflict into exchange hypotheses.

Thus, in his discussion of interpersonal power Blau illustrates the asymmetry of many relationships where one person (A) is more dependent on another (B) than the latter is on him. Person A has less resources, or fewer alternatives than B, he has less influence on B and has to comply with B's wishes. The balance of reciprocity in the relationship is thus brought into question—there may be greater costs involved for the person who has to defer to others, yet if the resources of these others are so much greater, as Blau has illustrated (see Chapter 12, pp. 299, 316), then the asymmetry of such an exchange may be considered equitable by the less powerful. However, this asymmetry may become exploitation by the more powerful and this may lead subsequently to negative exchanges, with opposition and retaliation. The usefulness of Blau's argument is that it qualifies the universal operation of a norm of reciprocity, drawing our attention to limiting cases and different degrees of the reciprocal exchange. Exchange is seen as infinitely more complex than when it occurs in mutual returns between equals.

However, the question of defining power in exchange relations has not really been settled and Blau's treatment of the asymmetrical dependency has been raised again by Wrong (1967) in a critical, discursive treatment of this aspect of interpersonal power. He points out that Blau has separated power and exchange relations for the purpose of analysis and has suggested that mutual interdependence indicates lack of power. Wrong disagrees with this, arguing that situations often occur where there is mutual power and he advocates the use of the term "intercursive" or countervailing power which "exists where the power of each party in a relationship is countervailed by that of the other, with procedures for bargaining or joint decision-making governing their relations when matters affecting the goals and interests of both are involved" (p. 674). This is clearly very similar to the counter-power influences discussed by Thibaut and Kelley (see Chapter 3).

Wrong seems to be arguing for a greater attention to counter-power. Although this is not something which Blau excludes, nevertheless it is true that Thibaut and Kelley give it much more explicit attention. Wrong's argument rests basically on the statement that reciprocity is a *defining criterion* of the social relation itself and is never totally destroyed even in relationships of unequal power. He argues that the more powerful person may exercise greater control in some ways but submits to the control of the less powerful person in other ways. Thus, the transactional view of leadership offered by Hollander (1964) suggests such a view of reciprocity. However, I do not think he would deny the importance of Blau's contribution in drawing our attention to the inequalities and to the dynamics of exchange, and in giving us useful qualifications to the view that reciprocity consists merely in equality of exchange.*

* Reciprocity as equality of exchange is discussed by Weinstein, De Vaughan and Wiley (1969), see Chapter 11.

Wrong's views follow the earlier discussion by Emerson (1962) who examines the mutual influence of persons with different degrees of power, considering power relations as illustrative of one form of inter-dependence rather than a limiting case to it. Emerson's (1962) hypo-theses concerning power and counter-power are similar to those of Thibaut and Kelley and Homans. In his recent (1972) treatment of exchange Emerson mentions that Blau chooses to play down power-balancing processes, preferring to treat power in terms of asymmetrical advantage.

Ellis (1971) commends Blau's discussion of the negative side of social relations, especially his emphasis on avoiding social debts as a spur to reciprocity. Furthermore, Blau has argued that our understanding of such debts, as costs to be avoided, requires also that we study the status structure of a particular group or society. It is an argument which has had some empirical support from an experiment carried out by Green-berg and Shapiro (1971) who postulate that indebtedness may be a threat to status (Homans, 1961) or to power (Blau, 1964). Their experi-mental results which we discussed in Chapter 11 confirm Blau's (1955) observation that persons equal in competence tend to seek help from each other rather than from a superior—a hypothesis similar to Homans' supposition that exchange between equals avoids the cost of acknowledging inferiority. Thus, one needs to know what are the relative status positions of parties in an exchange. What is the giver's status relative to the receiver? Can one or the other afford to receive a favour, or not to return a favour, without consequences for his status position?

Cohen (1968) presents an attack on Blau's treatment of power which can be considered as an excellent, representative and brief statement of criticism. He takes up the issue of Blau's definition of power as *power to reward*. Cohen says that, first, power may well be attained through ways other than exchange and, second, that persons often do not choose whether or not to comply nor whether to have this alternative rather than another, because their choices are already predetermined by the powerful. Thus, he argues, that it is not just a question of the powerful person supplying needed services, indeed power may be established coercively more often than through the free market:

It is not simply that men wait to be given power by those who need them to perform a necessary role. These possibilities certainly exist: men with charisma are needed by others who enjoy their favour in its own right; and men of ability are needed to perform tasks of leadership, co-ordination, etc. but in many cases men are only too ready to create the conditions in which they or others like them, are "needed". And they establish a structure of power which constantly generates the conditions for its perpetuation; among these conditions is a set of so-called "needs" (p. 123).

Next, Cohen considers possible refutations of this criticism. One of them, which he thinks would be acceptable, holds that after a given structure of power is set up by coercion or other means, there are now the conditions in which the powerful can provide facilities which others need and call upon them to do so. But Cohen mentions that Blau underestimates the extent to which power constitutes a condition for determining the rate of exchange. In addition, Cohen suggests that those who have power can control not only the means of meeting a number of wants but also create them.

One great weakness in "exchange theory", according to Cohen, is the tautological use of its explanations so that any interaction can be treated as an exchange.* He illustrates this with a hypothetical example, a situation where religious leaders would be said to have great influence over men because the latter "are willing to submit in exchange for religious certainty". Cohen argues that, in fact, there is no such exchange; that, in societies where a particular religious organization is well established, we cannot explain membership as a matter of individual choices. He makes his point: ". . . when men are raised in a society in which the Church dominates they are offered little choice in the matter. Exchange theory seems most profitably applied when there are real options which men recognise" (p. 125). Finally, Cohen warns against attempting to use exchange explanations for the intrinsic benefits obtained from adhering to an ideology or religious faith—the results would be "unenlightening". He recalls for us that the notion of exchange means assuming that choices are made between various alternatives, one has to be compared to the other and evaluated.

The critique of Blau's exposition has come entirely from sociologists, as one might expect, because his is essentially a sociological orientation. His aim is to provide exchange explanations for relationships between organizations or collective elements within society. Although he has stated his own position as an anti-reductionist one, nevertheless he makes much of explanation at the level of interpersonal phenomena and we have already noted that the position he has taken up towards psycho-

* At the beginning of this chapter we discussed this criticism.

logical explanations is quite similar to that of the other exchange theorists (Homans, Thibaut and Kelley) who are reductionist in so far as they give primacy to psychological, or social psychological, propositions as their starting point. So Blau is guilty, after all, of what Goodwin (1971) has termed "that most horrible of sins in sociology—reductionism" (p. 834). Stanley (1968) has hinted that to postulate structural phenomena *merely* as "emergent phenomena" does not avoid reductionism. But it is surprising that Blau's sociological critics concur with his emphasis on interpersonal exchange to the extent that they direct much of their criticisms against this part of his theoretical discussion, which he himself has presented as no more than an introductory to a theory of collective behaviour. Critics such as Mulkay (1971) and Heath (1968, 1971) concentrate on aspects of Blau's speculations about interpersonal behaviour rather than on his discussion of structural and collective exchange. This seems to be a diversion of their attack, unless the criticism can be brought to bear on his structural explanations. Criticism of the explanations of interpersonal behaviour *per se* is inappropriate for the following reason. As should now be patently clear from the discussion throughout this book, at the interpersonal level social exchange theory is a social psychological theory and *Exchange and Power* rests largely on the work of Homans and Thibaut and Kelley. The explanations Blau offers are an extension of their basic propositions or model and any subsequent influence he has had, at this level, is only to be appreciated as part of the joint influence of these authors.

One last question. Has Blau raised or settled a major problem of exchange theory? Surely he has raised many possibilities for research and suggested a large number of working hypotheses. We can see now that the contribution of Homans has been to sketch and argue for a theory of social exchange. Thibaut and Kelley have concentrated on the refinement of experimental designs. Blau has contributed a diversity of ideas, a wider perspective, yet to be taken up within social psychology.

14

Exchange Theory and Reduction Arguments

Introduction

It is interesting that the major contributions to exchange theory differ in their approach to a *theoretical structure*. Really, Blau and Thibaut and Kelley are *pre-theoretical* in their approach and in their actual contribution to a theory of reciprocal relationships since they claim only to be working towards a possible theory. Blau (1970, pp. 329–339) has stated that his exposition of exchange principles does not constitute anything like a formal structure. However, he does believe that such a theory will eventually develop. He disagrees with Homans only on its likely derivation, the nature of major premises from which corollaries and empirical hypotheses are to be drawn.* The latter makes an attempt to sketch, in outline, the forms that a theory of reciprocal behaviour may take: it is the familiar natural science formulation starting with general propositions and corollaries from which working hypotheses are derived. This derivation is only *promised* by Homans in his theory sketch and he actually proceeds from basic psychological "premises" by means of analogy; the derivation itself is only a possibility. To be sure, Homans' five propositions have been shown to hold for a variety of social situations but there is no direct link which can, at present, be established between them and basic propositions in psychology which are yet more general. So, the degree of formalization in exchange theory can only suggest a future programme of exploratory work.

If we look around in the psychological literature for attempts at

* See Blau's discussion of explicanda, premises and propositions (Blau, 1970, p. 332 *et seq.*).

formalizing a theory, the example which has greater sophistication than others is Hull's (1940) theory of rote learning. Here, eighteen basic postulates were stated with the derivations of a number of corollaries and theorems; even so, Koch (1954) comments on the many failings of this attempt. What Hull achieved was only an approximation to a derivation, described by Koch as "perhaps the closest approximation . . . yet attained in a non-natural science theory" (p. 86).* The most positive results were Hull's efforts to explore the connections between his explanatory statements and empirical tests. Koch takes the view that in the early stages of developing a theory such explorations of possible deductions are necessary.

In one sense, Blau and Thibaut and Kelley assume a realistic position in avoiding any approach to formal "deductions". This is because many of the hypotheses describing social behaviour could well be independent of the psychological "premises" from which they may be thought, ultimately, to derive. In fact, the fertility of exchange propositions need not depend on any particular set of "core" assumptions. For one thing, it is impossible to establish any exclusive commitment of exchange theory to one set of basic assumptions. Homans, who tries to make this link most explicit, states several general propositions and one of these is quite close to a "law" for the conditions of learning derived from reinforcement theory. Apart from this one proposition, the remainder refer to reciprocal relationships and they are meant to be tested in social situations. These propositions are not the "axioms" of individual psychology. Therefore, it must be understood that exchange theory effectively begins with the statement of propositions and hypotheses about interpersonal relationships, even though each of its exponents is concerned about the connection with individual psychology and states a position about this connection, right at the outset. In order to answer the question of whether a reduction to individual psychology is possible, it is necessary to answer the further one: what is the nature of the theory? And perhaps the differences of viewpoint between the exchange

---

* Koch refers to Hull's work as "the product of a period of heroic optimism in recent theoretical psychology" (p. 3). He points out that Hull's theory of rote learning has "the greatest degree of rigour and explicitness of any formulation in psychology" and he adds that "the possibility of achieving this level of explicitness and detail appears to result from the restriction of theory to a limited empirical domain, and one in which the variables are highly controllable and manipulable" (p. 83). In his analysis of the theory Koch draws attention to indeterminacies and ambiguities surrounding the basic postulates.

theorists which we have noted, are especially important. Perhaps they should incline us towards the conclusion of Koch who urges that Hull's formulations of "core propositions" are most fruitfully considered not as firm postulates but as showing certain orientating attitudes and guiding ideas which *look towards* theory (Koch, 1954, p. 96).

Homans, Blau and Thibaut and Kelley share the same, or very similar, economic and reinforcement analogies as their starting point, yet they each acknowledge a different connection with individual psychology. We have seen a large amount of evidence, in the earlier chapters, to suggest that social exchange explanations should be treated as a unitary theory or model; but their relationship with the formal theories of individual psychology is not at all clear. This is not a problem unique to the theory since it persists in many areas of social psychology. Thibaut and Kelley take up a *de facto* position, giving little attention to the derivations of their model but Blau and Homans clash explicitly over the issue of how much significance is to be given to the premises of individual psychology. More explicitly still, they take opposite views on whether or not explanations of social behaviour are to be *reduced* to these premises. Homans is a reductionist, Blau is anti-reductionist. It is true that Blau's work extends mainly into sociology but a great deal of what he has to say is of importance to social psychology also, although this has never been fully recognized. However, much of the discussion in *Exchange and Power in Social Life* is taken up with arguing the case against a psychological reduction. Because of these differences, it is important that we consider pretty thoroughly what is involved in the reduction issue, so far as it is a special problem of exchange theory, and as a general problem in social psychology. I will examine, in this chapter, the arguments presented in the recent literature concerning the possibility of expressing one theory (the secondary) in the statements and concepts of another (the primary). In previous chapters we have seen exactly how each of the exchange theorists treats these questions, implicitly or explicitly, as part of his theoretical exposition. Lately there has been some discussion, precisely on the reduction question, between Homans and Blau (1970) and other writers refer to exchange theory in order to illustrate the reductionist position or its counter-arguments. I intend now to discuss these developments in more detail than was possible earlier in the book.

"Reduction" is a term which has been used with several different meanings, a state of affairs tending naturally to produce some confusion.

There is strict or complete reduction (Bergmann, 1957); logical reduction (Nagel, 1961; Stotland, 1965) and, lastly, empirical reduction (Boden, 1972). There are many disagreements over the reduction issue and further confusion arises when authors ascribe different meanings even to these qualified terms. It can be useful to refer to reduction attempts in the physical or natural sciences as a source of ideas for reduction in the social sciences, as Bergmann (1957), Swanson (1965) and Boden (1972) have done. But there is little which has any immediate bearing on the problem for social psychology. It is not possible to say if a reduction may or may not be possible in the future, nor to indicate how such a solution might be achieved. There is some virtue in considering the concrete example of reduction in social exchange theory for two major reasons. Firstly, it may help us to explore the topography of this theory and especially to examine how it is related to other theories. Secondly, we can discuss social exchange theory as an exemplar which may assist in answering the question: are there autonomous theories in social psychology? As I have said, there is no way at present, in the social sciences, of resolving the question of whether or not one theory is reducible to another but at least we can set out to make more clear the nature of *reduction* as a social psychological problem.

Before we consider some of the general issues involved, let us summarize briefly the question as it is approached by social exchange theory. Homans and Blau discuss reduction explicitly because they both approach theory-building as a procedure which follows well-established rules of deduction (see Blau, 1970, p. 333). The former sees theory-building as an immediate, the latter as an eventual, aim of their work. Thibaut and Kelley pursue the narrower objective of testing hypotheses within the tentative framework of game theory matrices; and they are not concerned with problems of theoretical structure. Nevertheless they have assumed an implicit position: although rejecting the use of concepts from sociology—what they call "sociological expansionism"—they transfer to their explanations some of the concepts of individual psychology, mainly from Hull's postulates. By doing so they introduce the possibility of a reduction although in their empirical, eclectic approach they have avoided questions of formal theory in preference to more modest theoretical aims.

Homans alone makes the attempt to sketch a formal or logical reduction when he applies propositions from experimental, comparative psychology to human social behaviour, taking the view that no new general propositions are required. As we have seen, Blau makes an outright attack on the "reductionist fallacy of ignoring emergent properties". The reduction which Homans indicates is far from a complete reduction. It is an ultimate (i.e. to be discovered in the future) logical connection with the statements of individual psychology as the source of necessary but not sufficient explanations. Blau, in opposing reduction, emphasizes the importance of intermediate or emergent phenomena generating concepts which cannot be explained by those available from individual psychology. It is important to emphasize that the disputed issue here centres on whether it is possible to link up to the primary theory, or whether additional assumptions are such that social phenomena must be explained by an independent theory.

This issue appears as an outright clash between Homans and Blau in their dialogue: "The Relevance of Psychology to the Explanation of Social Phenomena" (in Borger and Cioffi, 1970, pp. 313–343). In this dialogue most of the argument deals specifically with the reduction topic. Homans reiterates views which he has expressed earlier (1964, 1967, 1969) in favour of psychological explanations of social phenomena, where theoretical propositions are traced back to their most general explanatory, and psychological, premises. Referring to this viewpoint as that of "methodological individualism"* he claims that "all social phenomena can be analysed without residue into the actions of individuals, that such actions are what is really fundamental in the social sciences" (p. 325). Blau's reply to this centres on the counter-argument that psychological propositions in themselves do not *logically* imply propositions concerning social *organization*. Additional terms have to be brought in, defining the social phenomena and these are the crucial part of the explanation.

Psychology and physiology: a complete reduction?

Reduction arguments have occurred very frequently in the discussion of scientific theory. The question of whether one theory can be reduced to or explained by another is considered, for example, by Braithwaite (1953), Nagel (1961), and, with arguments especially relevant for psychology, by Bergmann (1957), who raises the questions: "Can psychology be reduced to physiology? Can the group sciences in turn

* For a discussion of methodological individualism see K. R. Popper, *The Open Society and Its Enemies*, London, Routledge and Kegan Paul, Vol. 2, 1962. Beloff (1973, pp. 211–213) has a commentary on Popper's arguments.

be reduced to psychology?'' (p. 163). Although these questions are not in fact answered or discussed by Bergmann he does state that "The four classical situations are the reduction of (1) thermodynamics to mechanics in nineteenth century physics, (2) physiology (biology) to physics-chemistry, (3) psychology to physiology, and (4) the group disciplines to psychology'' (p. 168). Bergmann rejects the feasibility of reduction, taking as his point of reference the strong definition of reduction as the *complete* substitution of one theory by another. By this definition, for a reduction to take place, one theory has to be completely replaceable by another; there must be correspondence between each term and proposition in the theory to be reduced, and those of the primary, before reduction can be achieved. Bergmann points out that this has only happened, to such a complete degree, in the reduction of thermodynamics to mechanics; here it was temporarily successful, but eventually the reducing theory (primary) had to be changed to fit the (secondary) theory which was reduced to it—as Bergmann emphasizes '. . . in what sense, if any, can one then still speak of 'reduction'?'' (p. 169).

Jessor (1958) and, more recently, Bannister (1968) and Boden (1972) have considered some of the arguments relevant to the question of whether psychology might be reduced to physiology. Bannister points out that the languages of psychology and physiology are non-overlapping where they deal with different kinds of data; that furthermore the language of physiology deals with individual process in a form unrelated to this process in other individuals. Jessor takes as his main point the logical barriers to the statement that physiological concepts are more basic for explanation than those of psychology. His arguments include drawing attention to the absence in physiology "of any systematic terms for describing the functional environment or context of behaviour" (p. 173), since the terms of physiology refer to intra-organismic process and there are no terms to specify the environment, whereas "psychological laws refer to interaction between organisms and functionally defined environments" (p. 174). Jessor takes as an example of "environment" a social interchange between persons, and thus (implicitly) uses an illustration from the subject matter of social psychology in order to deny the logical possibility of reducing psychology to physiology. He has used a somewhat paradoxical illustration; it is paradoxical for the following reason: the fact that his distinction between psychology and physiology is of a kind which could quite easily be made between general and social psychology. While it is clear that the language of physiology refers to events within the organism and does not include terms for the environment, it is also the case that much of the discipline of social psychology deals with an environment—with reciprocal relations—that is not incorporated in the terms of individual psychology. By using this kind of illustration, Jessor has taken social psychology and psychology as one, where we should be concerned with facts that show social psychology as an area of study distinct from the subject matter and general propositions of individual behaviour.

Sociology and psychology

In sociology the persistent question involves the possibility of a reduction to psychology. For example, Alexander and Simpson (1964) discuss the view that "the sociologist should be an ultimate, though not necessarily approximate, psychological reductionist" (p. 182), by which they mean that psychology may one day provide a theory from which explanations of social behaviour can be derived. This is a view quite likely to be contested by sociologists, as we shall see in a moment when we discuss the counter-arguments of Buckley (1967) and Emerson (1970). However, Runciman (1970) raises the rather controversial view that the discipline of sociology is "parasitic to the laws of others"; that there is no distinctive sociological theory. He first reviews the arguments for considering sociology as an autonomous discipline, and draws attention to the fact that this is so, *in practice*: "social systems have properties which, although they may be reducible in principle to aggregations of the properties of the individuals composing them, must in practice be treated as predicates of the collectivity" (p. 5). Even if "in principle" reduction is claimed, this does not do away with the special province of sociologists in practice. Thus, a degree of autonomy is to be allowed for special fields in the social sciences, as defined by the distinction between "in principle" and "in practice". The distinction is expressed lucidly by Runciman: "Perhaps it is true that in principle (whatever that is worth) the whole of chemistry, physiology, biology and social science could be described in terms of the application of laws governing the behaviour of the elementary particles; but that is not of the smallest interest to the practising social scientist . . ." (p. 13). While he acknowledges this Runciman also draws attention to the funda-mental importance of settling the issue of reduction.

His view in favour of an "in principle" reduction is based on the argument that unavoidably the subject matter of sociology is still, basically, the behaviour of individual human beings.* He holds that it is easier to argue for the reduction of sociology to psychology than for psychology to physiology: "To explain the origins and workings of social systems is to explain the thoughts and actions of men" (p. 8), and he concludes that psychological propositions form the apex of the theoretical system to explain social behaviour. Since the search for social "laws" cannot stop at an explanation which refers to organized social collectivities, without referring also to the antecedent conditions of these collectivities, it follows that "there are not and cannot be laws of social systems as such. Sociology (together with history and anthropology) is a consumer of laws, not a producer of them" (p. 10) meaning that the laws are acquired from other fields of study. Thus, he argues, it would be mistaken to locate theoretical "axioms" at the level of social systems, and Runciman concludes that sociology can only adequately be described as "psychology and ethology plus social history" (p. 11).

Logical reduction and empirical generalizations of exchange

Lastly, Runciman emphasizes the requirement for a successful theory: that it must contain explanations linked to specified premises which, once stated, allow the derivation of many empirical, explanatory statements about particular events. If the explanatory statement cannot be linked, in this way, then it will stand isolated as an empirical generalization. If a hypothesis about empirical events is to involve *testing a theory*, then it has to be given an explicit connection in a logical structure extending back to more general propositions. Here we have *logical reduction* and it is in this sense that Homans is a reductionist.

Runciman gives one of the clearest available expositions of the meaning of logical reduction and since this is also the meaning pre-

* Note that there are others who do not see this as a convincing argument. For instance, Fallding (1965) comments: " 'the individual' is an abstraction that belongs equally to biology, psychology and sociology. Whether he yields biological, psychological or sociological facts depends entirely on how he is regarded. 'The individual' is in social organization as bricks are in a wall, and in all he does he is clothed with culture as he is with garments. The province of psychology is not 'the individual' but his experience and personal organization. As . . . an exponent of culture 'the individual' is turned over to sociology" (p. 230).

ferred by Homans it should be considered in some detail. For Runciman a theory consists of "laws" which are statements asserting "that the connection between X and Y is causal and also that this connection can be fairly precisely formulated" (p. 12) where "causal" is used in "a sense broad enough to include interdependence or feedback and not merely links-in-a-chain". Thus, a law is a proposition in the form of: if X then Y,* and a theory is "a set of connected disconfirmable laws" (p. 16). His reference to "causal laws" does not imply, he states, that such laws will form a mechanistic or determined structure of propositions and derivations; they will be laws in the weak sense that prediction is attainable in terms of statistical probabilities. However, a causal law must still express in its derivation a *logical structure back to basic premises*. Now, the point of his calling attention to these criteria is really to illustrate how sociologists often go no further than explanatory statements covering empirical data, that is, the *empirical generalizations*. Incidentally, it is relevant to our discussion of exchange theory that Runciman takes, as his example to illustrate the nature of empirical generalizations, the proposition of Homans (as cited by Zetterberg, 1965)† that social interaction promotes friendliness. The point is made that an empirical generalization must include a specification of precise conditions under which it will hold, if it is to be linked causally to a theoretical grounding. Thus the development of friendly relations in a given situation may be explained by reference to the proposition that a high frequency of interaction results in a greater degree of liking; but, if the explanation went no further, it would be an empirical generalization only. Besides this, it has to be pointed out that there is evidence of situations (for example, of constraint, or overcrowding) where liking can decrease with interaction. The result is only "an ostensibly precise generalisation plus a long list of exceptions—clauses including the specification of a minimum of physical distance" (p. 32). Runciman now argues that for the causal link to be made, we need more than this, we need to "set out in psycho-physiological and ethological terms the necessary and sufficient conditions of mutual liking" before we can specify the social situations or institutional framework in which these conditions may be realized. The interaction proposition must be

* For a rich discussion of the if-then condition, see Zetterberg (1965, pp. 64–66). A number of alternative and more complex forms of this conditional are discussed.

† This "interaction proposition" is discussed as part of Homans' more recent theoretical work in Chapter 11 above.

derivable from more general statements about individual responses. On its own, the empirical generalization that interaction promotes liking is not sufficient. Without having a theoretical grounding it cannot be treated as a causal law; it must be derived from statements which explain the phenomena of mutual liking, from statements which explain social-affiliative attraction. In fact, Homas has subsequently attempted this derivation (see Chapter 8, pp. 184 *et seq.*) and in his *Social Behaviour* (to which Runciman does not refer) Homans has, in my view, given this particular hypothesis a theoretical grounding, as far as this is possible at present.

A reduction in the future

A great deal of attention is thus given to the formal derivations of hypotheses, but Runciman places the greatest weight on an empirical argument: for reducibility of statements about social behaviour to psychological premises, definitional equivalence of terms is not necessary, and he expresses this in an unusually obscure sentence: "it is enough to be able uncontroversially to say that any empirical connection asserted between the terms of a social-scientific law can be tested only against the behaviour (including, of course, the verbal behaviour) of *individuals* (my italics). It follows that these social-scientific terms must be capable of operational redescription in psychological terms . . ." (p. 39). At the same time, he acknowledges that the redescription of social facts would be lengthy and complicated. And it is by no means a direct derivation. Psychology is seen as "an evolutionary theory of individual behaviour as determined by the combination of genetic and environmental influences in a manner analogous to biological speciation" (p. 41). He is stating the case for an ultimate reduction at some time in the future, to the premises in psychology as they may eventually become.

Runciman's position in favour of reduction in principle, extends furthermore to the inter-connection of psychology and physiology "on whose theories it must be presumed to depend . . . (although it) is still little more than a hope" (p. 38). The laws of psychology which, Runciman argues, would provide the theoretical grounding for the social sciences have yet to be found, but when they are found they will provide explanation both of individual variables *and* of complex cultural ones. Psychological explanations will give the initial, general conditions from which follow the specific hypotheses about social behaviour. Runciman is really presenting a statement of faith in a reduction at some time in the future; he comments that "to talk of 'social theory' at all is to presuppose psychological discoveries which, for the most part, have still to be made" (p. 40).

It seems, for Runciman, that social psychology is (or will be) indistinguishable from psychology in supplying the underlying explanatory grounding for studies of social behaviour. This does nothing to resolve problems arising in social psychology through attempts to build explanations which have only weak connections with individual psychology. So there still remains the task of making more explicit the theoretical development between social psychology and individual psychology and exploring the condition of connections between them.

Reduction in social psychology

Much of psychology deals with the individual operating on the environment, and whether the environment is social or nonsocial is not a central problem in understanding perception or motivation, cognitive process, or learning—the emphasis is clearly on individual process and on ranges of individual differences. In social psychology there is a fairly well marked-off area of empirical study, in the sense that it is distinguishable from individual psychology and from broader societal theories. Explanation of behaviour in the primary group stands clear of other systems of explanation involving either individual or societal variables in order to focus on the *special conditions* of primary groups. There is a subject matter and concepts which are not found in other areas of psychology. Here we have a special area of research and one could expect to find some movement towards a body of theory. There has been a gradual accumulation of studies and, as Brown (1965) has written, there is "a set of topics that have exceeded the grasp of nonsocial psychology but which are effectively investigated by a psychology that draws upon the social sciences" (p. xx). The very accumulation of studies invites attempts to systematize and if there is some degree of autonomy, it must also be recognized that a view of social psychology as an autonomous discipline is not a recent one; earlier on, the argument was touched on by Wallis (1925) and Blumer (1940). However, as more efforts are made to order empirical evidence, questions of theoretical derivation can be expressed more sharply. Brown's reference to "a psychology that draws upon the social sciences" gives an interesting lead into the particular form of the reduction problem which now presents itself. The variety of given conditions unique to social behaviour seems to require a qualitative difference in the explanatory statements. In a moment, we shall see how social exchange theory illustrates this process.

Social behaviour and psychology: individual or group laws?

Very little is resolved simply by claiming autonomy for social psychology, since there are more subtle issues. Stotland (1965) quite rightly made a distinction between two major parties within the discipline, one emphasizing the individual and the other the group. The first of these parties favours measuring and analysing the individual response in social situations: "the individual's reaction is the dependent variable" (p. 315). The second centres attention on relationships between persons, where the variables measured are indicators of *the relationship*—for example, frequencies of reciprocal communication, measures of leadership styles and group activities.

It can readily be seen how the propositions which belong to the first category are no different from those of general psychology, nor are they different from motivational, cognitive or perceptual propositions referring to social as well as nonsocial events. For instance, in the study of attitudes there would be a considerable shared content, as Stotland indicates. Whatever differences exist between social and nonsocial situations will only be a matter of measured variation of the individual response. To take Stotland's example, the perceived ambiguity of a situation would have similar effects along a continuum of individual responses, irrespective of whether the conditions producing ambiguity were social or nonsocial. Those who assume this position need employ no concepts or methods, in the analysis of social events, other than those already in use in individual psychology. Shaw and Costanzo (1970) appear to refer to this type of approach when they discuss areas of social psychology where hypotheses are tested by methods customarily applied to problems of individual perception, motivation and learning "where most of the theories formulated to account for such individual processes have been developed in general psychology and are not social psychological in nature. The theorist merely incorporates the effects of social variables into a more comprehensive theory" (p. 5). I think this

EXCHANGE THEORY AND REDUCTION ARGUMENTS

is a fair comment, that these are not social psychological theories, but an extension of theories from individual psychology—to explain the individual act in so far as certain conditions can be shown to hold in a social as well as a nonsocial environment. Stotland still wishes to admit the possibility, within this approach, that the variation of conditions discovered empirically in social situations may produce modifications in the basic theory, allowing the latter to become more comprehensive and precise. In this sense he maintains that: "Attempts to place the individual-social laws and nonsocial laws in the same rubric can have heuristic value" (p. 317).

In contrast, the emphasis on *group behaviour*, comprising the second of the two approaches identified by Stotland, introduces conditions which cannot be explained simply by extending the use of propositions from individual psychology. In this category, we have much more than an extension of techniques, and the propositions, the hypotheses, which are now required differ qualitatively because they include new concepts such as: mutual attraction, cohesiveness, collusion, norms, status or esteem. Each of these reflect, in Stotland's words: "a separation on the level of empirical laws". However, for Stotland these empirical differences do not imply a logical separation and he proceeds to illustrate this argument. Although the propositions of group behaviour are qualitatively different from individual ones, he concedes that what he calls "group laws" are eventually available to explanation in terms of the individual laws. This does not explain away the group laws: they are *logically* derived from the propositions of individual psychology but the derivation does not mean they are substituted or replaced, it serves only to link up the group laws with the "total body of psychological knowledge" (p. 317).* Stotland therefore concedes a logical reduction, in principle.

His interpretation of a *logical reduction* of group laws to individual laws includes his statement that it must remain a matter of *in principle* reduction, for the following reasons. While there may be a logical, eventual derivation of hypotheses about social behaviour back to individual psychology, it is not currently possible to embark on the lengthy chain backwards, deriving each proposition in turn. Thus, he thinks the group laws will be necessary "if only as a useful shorthand". There are also other likely obstacles, for example, "the exact theoretical formulation

---

* The interaction-liking proposition could be taken as an example of this derivation.

of the empirical basis of the explanation" in the primary theory may not have been clearly established, or the primary theory itself will not have reached an appropriate stage in the development of firm premises. Stotland follows, in the conclusions if not in the details of his argument, a number of authors who accept that social behaviour cannot now be explained by the propositions of individual psychology, although statements about social behaviour are in close harmony with them. The argument is the familiar one in the history of the development of specialized fields of study and it is also the weakest form of counter-argument to a reduction because it allows for an eventual logical reduction, in principle.

As we have seen in the case of social exchange theory, the present explanations of social behaviour allow "derivations" from individual psychology in only a very general way, by analogy. There are still many problematical issues in the individual theories, as is demonstrated in theories involving the S-R reinforcement principle. In a fairly recent instance, Bitterman (1967, 1969) shows that there are important differences in results obtained as between animal species but this was a difficulty recognized, together with other similar ones, by Hull (1951, p. 117) in the final appraisal of this theory. The argument in favour of an eventual logical reduction does not rest on anything approximating a step-by-step derivation. In fact, it can only be shown that explanations of social behaviour show *some* form of connection with psychological premises. As in the case of exchange theory, the connection consists of borrowing some concepts to provide tentative analogies—presumably as a temporary but constructive strategy. Before we consider some of the examples in exchange theory, it would be worth summarizing the most explicit attempt at an outline of a logical reduction in social psychology, that of Guy Swanson.

Reduction in the natural sciences: empirical reduction

It is not surprising that authors who discuss reduction in psychology have sought their criteria and exemplary sources in the natural sciences. Swanson (1965) and Boden (1972) both seek to evaluate the possibility of a reduction in different areas of psychology by referring to Nagel's (1961) statement of the formal conditions required for reduction in the natural sciences. These are of particular interest to Swanson who emphasizes the logical structure between primary and secondary theories; Margaret Boden is interested in the question of reducing psychology to physiology by means of an *empirical reduction* which requires that the functional equivalents of psychological processes be found in physiology.* This means that the empirical, or in Nagel's terms, the non-formal conditions may make possible a logical derivation. Boden emphasizes that the empirical reduction is only, in principle, a possibility and a distant one. She points out that very little has been done to substantiate any bridging statements between theories of physiological process and a person's molar behaviour and this, despite the fact that there have been some promising indications:

> For instance, recent work on the activating functions of the mid-brain reticular system affords a basis for hypothesising bridging statements linking particular levels of consciousness—and personality traits such as extroversion and neuroticism—with physiological activity in certain fairly grossly specified areas of the brain (p. 97).

Furthermore, she emphasizes that "Efforts to establish the cerebral localization of behaviour have met with remarkably little success" (p. 153) and concludes that psychology may be empirically reducible to physiology in principle while it is unlikely the reduction will take anything more than

> a highly schematic form. In other words, psychology may sensibly be said to be "empirically reducible" to physiology in a weak sense that implies a total dependence of teleological phenomena on physical causal mechanisms ... (this) does not imply that bridging statements will actually be found to correlate every psychological statement with a specific neurophysiological statement (p. 155).

Let us refer to Nagel's own discussion of reduction in the natural sciences. We will find in it more than a hint of the lure which reductionism offers and the reasons for this will become clear. If one theory can be explained by the concepts and laws of another, whether it involves reducing sociology to psychology, psychology to physiology—or thermodynamics to mechanics—if one reduction is conceded there is presumably no bar to reduction in other cases. The procedure may be followed down to successively more basic levels, wherever the propositions

---

* Empirical and logical aspects of a theory cannot really be separated although logical reduction and empirical reduction are discussed: the former emphasizes the internal criteria of theoretical structure, the latter may refer especially to reduction by means of empirical advances in the primary theory. Nagel uses a similar convenient division of formal and non-formal conditions for reduction.

of one area of study can be reduced to explanatory statements which are more general and where the elements are smaller, better defined. At this more basic level, variables are measured more precisely and may be assumed to be prior in time or development to those of the larger, molar levels of behaviour. Nagel comments that "the phenomenon of a relatively autonomous theory becoming absorbed by, or reduced to, some other more inclusive theory, is an undeniable and recurrent feature of the history of modern science" (p. 337), and he considers at length the conditions that must accompany a successful reduction. The reduction of thermodynamics to mechanics is very extensively treated by Nagel as his illustration of some of the main criteria which have to be satisfied if reduction is to be possible. In reducing the laws of thermodynamics, the primary theory was extrapolated from "domains where it was already well confirmed into another domain postulated to be homogeneous in important respects" (p. 359). This extrapolation had the effect of unifying conditions and produced new avenues for research. Subsequently, he raises an interesting point about the results of a reduction. It is not enough that the findings of a secondary theory be translated to the statements of the primary one, there must be a greater result than this, "the primary theory must also be fertile in usable suggestions for developing the secondary science, and must yield theorems referring to the latter's subject matter which augment or correct its currently accepted body of laws" (p. 360). Nagel distinguishes between two kinds of reduction: in the first—complete reduction—the data explained by two theories are very similar, and no concepts need be employed for one (secondary) theory that are not present in another (primary) theory. In this kind of complete reduction, the vocabularies of the two theories are the same, and explanation in terms of the primary theory follows as a matter of course.

Most of Nagel's discussion concerns a second type of reduction, where the subject-matter of two theories are distinctive, dissimilar. Here, in Nagel's words "the subject matter of the primary science appears to be qualitatively discontinuous" (p. 342) and the descriptive terms of the secondary theory are not found in the primary theory. Nevertheless a reduction may be feasible but it can take place only if "co-ordinating definitions" are stated to demonstrate the equivalence of the terms used in the secondary propositions with those in the primary theory. Nagel uses Newtonian gravitational theory as his example of a source of general axioms, applicable to a wide area, after the co-ordinating definitions are supplied. The primary theory is then supplemented by adding the conditions for the axioms to apply to specific propositions at the level of empirical study, and the reduction can still take place. The primary theory thus continues to supply the most general explanatory premises, as a basis for the development of theories less general in their scope, for special areas. Nagel describes a classical instance of such a reduction: the incorporation of thermodynamics within statistical mechanics. Although the former was (and still is) treated as a special discipline, its laws have been shown to derive from those of mechanics.

Certain formal conditions are required for reducibility. First, explicitness and clarity of both theories constitute a condition which is, in fact, difficult to satisfy. Theoretical statements can be classified into distinct groups, a class T of statements comprising the fundamental postulates of the discipline (premises or leading principles) and a class R of co-ordinating definitions which link specific theorems to the more general postulates. Theorems and experimental laws about *prima facie* different phenomena may be classified as belonging to *separate* areas of enquiry, but these areas may be augmented or diminished and the boundaries changed subsequently—it all depends, at a given moment, on the progress of enquiry and the scope of current theories. A second formal condition concerns the linguistic structure of explanation, the condition that there should be a class D of descriptive statements, some of them of a highly specialized nature. A third condition follows, that these statements, as part of a theory, "possess meanings that are fixed by its *own* procedures of explication" (p. 352) irrespective of whether or not the theory is to be reduced to another.

Assuming that these preliminary conditions are satisfied, Nagel discusses the formal steps for a logical reduction. First of all, if the statements of a theory are shown to be a logical consequence of the theoretical assumptions (with co-ordinating definitions) of another, then reduction can be effected. However, if the statements of the secondary theory contain terms that do not occur in the primary theory additional assumptions must be introduced which will allow "connectability" between the primary and secondary terms. With the help of these assumptions the secondary theory must now be logically derivable from the premises of the primary discipline—this is called the "condition of derivability".*

---

* See Nagel (1961, pp. 354–358). The discussion by Kemeny and Oppenheim (1956) is useful for understanding these two conditions particularly where they argue

Next, Nagel discusses some of the non-formal and empirical conditions which may be influential. First, a reduction attempt may not be worthwhile because the primary theory does not have a sufficient degree of sophistication in its established postulates—we have already noted this difficulty. Secondly, the secondary theory may be at a stage where the most important tasks are to survey and classify its empirical content. This may well be the case in social psychology. As if to emphasize once again the complexities of the reduction issue, Nagel sees reduction as appropriate only at certain stages of theoretical development, because "although one science may be reducible to another, the secondary discipline would be progressively solving its own class of problems *with the help of a theory expressly devised for dealing with the subject matter of that discipline*" (p. 362). Nagel concludes that attainment of a comprehensive theory may be an ideal, but a reduction attempt to a more general theory may not be the best way "if the secondary science at that stage of its development is not prepared to operate effectively with this theory" (p. 363). All these points make the future reduction of social psychological theories seem extremely unlikely.

Social behaviour: an outline of a psychological reduction

A full range of arguments for and against reducing theories of social behaviour to basic explanations of individual behaviour, is found in Swanson's (1965) discussion of the question: "What is the proper relation between general theory in psychology and explanations of social interaction?" (p. 101). Swanson searches through alternative answers to the question of whether explanations of social interaction might be derived from the prior statements of individual psychology. He discounts an extreme "reductionist" position which would lead one "to question the ontological validity of social interaction" (p. 118).*

---

that connectability on its own is not sufficient for reduction, but derivability is both necessary and sufficient because it entails connectability. Connectability would be followed by derivability if for every term "A" in the secondary science but not in the primary one, there is a term "B" in the primary science such that A and B are linked by a biconditional: A if and only if B. When this linkage can be shown "A" is replaced by "B". However, the linkage might not be biconditional, it could be a one-way conditional: if B, then A and in this case "A" is not replaceable by "B" and the secondary science would not be deductible from the primary.

    * See also J. O. Wisdom, Situational Individualism and the Emergent Group-Properties in Robert Borger and Frank Cioffi (eds), "Explanation in the Behavioural

Instead he argues in favour of an ultimate, *logical reduction* and deals with its implications in detail; furthermore he considers the obstacles even to this weak sense of reduction.

To paraphrase Swanson's discussion, he conceives of social inter-action—the process, that is "in which individuals take account of their own or their fellows' motives, needs, desires, means and ends, know-ledge"—as evolving, in time, out of a behavioural (individual) inter-action with the environment (in general) as object. While rejecting the extreme reductionist position, Swanson nevertheless argues for what he refers to as *logical reduction*, in order to connect the theories of social interaction to basic theories of individual behaviour. He proposes a deductive process extending from individual to social phenomena, by which the propositions of the latter are derived logically from the former. In other words, what happens as a matter of constructing any particular theory, i.e. the derivation of one proposition from another, is now argued by Swanson as between one theory and another, indi-vidual and social. In accepting the feasibility of a *logical reduction* there still has to be added the qualification that social phenomena cannot be fully explained, cannot be explained away, by propositions of individual behaviour. It is not possible to do justice to all of the many points which Swanson argues but a few will be mentioned to illustrate his treatment of the question.

He first deals with what he assumes are erroneous attempts to answer this question. In the first place, "general systems theory", protagonists of which are Boulding (1965) and Miller (1955), consists of an attempt to apply the framework of an organization or system both to individual behaviour and social interaction; the content of both are subject to an analysis by such concepts as feedback or entropy, and ignoring, for this purpose, the substantive differences. Swanson concludes that this treat-ment obscures rather than clarifies: "Such an approach obliterates the very occasion for a social psychologist" (p. 110). A second approach, this time by translation of one set of concepts into another, also glosses

---

Sciences", Cambridge University Press, 1970, pp. 271–296. Wisdom defines reduc-tionism as follows: "For ease of reference I propose to reserve the expression 'reduc-tionist' or 'reductionist individualism' for the extreme form of individualism, accord-ing to which all institutional wholes are 'reducible' without remainder to terms con-cerning the purposes of individuals, i.e. all institutions are epiphenomena of individual purposes" (p. 274).

over differences; the translation results in nothing more than a multiple classification of a given event, nor does it resolve anything of the differences between events which are superficially similar.

Swanson criticizes a position which is often characteristic of sociologists, that of "simplification through closure". This implies starting with a premise that *social interaction exists* and accepting it *as given* without the need for further explanation. As a simplifying strategy this is legitimate but there is also a tendency to "confuse analyses which proceed from the latent assumption that social interaction exists with explanations of social interaction itself" (p. 113). Swanson does suggest how to avoid such an exclusive concern with immediate empirical data and specifying hypotheses; how it may be possible to relate social explanations to general theories of behaviour. The manner of establishing this relationship cannot be that of a complete reduction, defined by Swanson as the entire assimilation of a secondary theory to the statements of a primary one. There remains an alternative way, and by means of *logical reduction* it may be possible to place explanations of social behaviour within a systematic scheme such as Swanson's figure represents.

Figure 20 shows the connection between individual-physiological interaction with the environment in the left-hand columns and social interaction on the right. Swanson comments that "the contents of each column of Fig. [20], being more general in conception than those in the column immediately to its right, may be employed as a source of universal laws governing events in the column to the right" (p. 114). There is no implication that the columns on the right are nothing more than instances of phenomena in columns on the left. On the contrary in proceeding across the Figure from left to right, *additional assumptions are added*. So the presentation is meant to reveal what the columns have in common and what distinguishes them. Starting from the left, each column adds some characteristic until in column 4 elements of social interaction appear. Interactions from left to right across the Figure reflect increasingly complex relations. However, while added assumptions are required, there are no new postulates, argues Swanson. One great difficulty to making explicit such a derivation as this would occur as the chain of assumptions grows longer; now the correspondence between empirical hypotheses and the earlier premises becomes less certain. Thus, Swanson points only to the possible direction of logical connections:

Fig. 20 Major topics in social psychology

Characteristics	Some Varieties of Interaction					
	I. Social Stimulation	II. Circular Reaction	III. Conversation of Gestures	IV. Interpretive Interaction	V. Symbolic Interaction	VI. Communication
A. Each actor acts towards himself and others as loci of:						
1. Directed towards his own behaviour, this action is:	stimuli	cues	gestures	signs	selves	identity
a. It results in some degree of:				insight self control		
2. Directed towards others' behaviour, this action is:						
a. It results in some degree of:				empathy social influence		
B. Actors so engaged may yet have difficulties in coordinating their relations as:	objects	actors	co-participants in several types of act	co-participants in a division of labor (*i.e.,* a role system)	co-participants in several role systems	
1. The difficulties may be resolved if they pay attention to and routinize their use of the wider context provided by:	cues	gestures	signs	selves	identity	

Some Changes from One Variety of Interaction to Another

A. Elementary collective behaviour: A change from types of interaction in Columns V or VI to those in Columns I–IV and back again.
B. Socialization: An actor is trained to engage in symbolic interaction or communication.
C. Institutionalization: Actors jointly define some relationship as legitimate and as necessary for their continued interaction.
D. Social control: Actors encourage others to engage in, or prevent their engaging in, some relationship because it meets or violates an institutionalized standard.

if explanations constructed in this fashion prove adequate for social psychology they would be instances of logical reduction . . . reduction, as such, does not require us to eliminate the distinctions among phenomena classified in Fig. [20] or to make the columns on the Figure's left rather than those on its right the centre of our interest (pp. 118–119).

Swanson's conclusion is that assimilation of one theory to another is not possible, but he suggests a framework for relating one to another, and this might be the means of clarifying both the objectives and the fundamentals of social psychology. A *logical reduction* is at present only a speculative goal. But it will not be necessary for the concepts of social psychology to be substitutable by others; only that these concepts be treated as representing special instances of variables in general psychology. Having said this, Swanson introduces some formidable obstacles to a successful logical reduction. The first is the non-feasibility of linking secondary to primary statements by complex chains of additional assumptions and of expressing these in an explicit formula. One difficulty lies in the fact that the primary statements do not imply the assumptions to be added, they have to be supplemented as more empirical evidence is collected and there is a certain arbitrariness in arriving at these new assumptions. Furthermore, a concept at one level, for example occurring in a premise of individual psychology (and conforming to individual data) may represent a different meaning to the same concept included in a working hypothesis, conforming to social data. Because of these considerations Swanson accepts that the pursuit of a logical reduction is unlikely to bring any conclusive results, but it may yet hold promise.

Social psychology reduced to sociology?

For social psychology one might have a reduction attempt by taking the explanations of social behaviour down to individual propositions but there might also be a reduction taking the explanation upwards into societal analysis. Thus, when sociologists argue their case against psychological reduction, they tend to include the entire field of social phenomena into sociology—in effect, proposing a reduction of social psychology to sociology. *Sociological expansionism* is a similar process to reduction, requiring the use of concepts from larger aggregates to explain phenomena in the relationships between persons. For instance, Thibaut and Kelley (1959) deny that the allocation of interpersonal status in small groups should be explained by referring to stratification in large social structures: "it seems unwise to rely too heavily on social stratification as a model for small group status systems or to test hypotheses about these systems by reference to evidence from larger aggregates" (p. 223). This is a fundamental issue, whether social psychological theories are to be clearly distinguished *both* from individual psychology *and* from sociology. I will now give an example of a sociologist's counter-arguments to psychological reduction. In this case, as in Runciman's pro-reduction argument which has been discussed earlier in this chapter, there is an uncomfortable over-sight. They present their argument so broadly in the psychology versus sociology debate that social psychology is left out.

The example to be described now is a particularly effective argument against the reduction of sociology to psychology; I have selected it because of its effectiveness in this sense but, at the same time, it does illustrate the frequent tendency in this general debate to miss out the subtleties entailed by the "interstitial" field of social psychology. Emerson's (1970) discussion of "operant psychology" and exchange theory* clearly states that there are emergent phenomena in social relations which cannot be explained by reference to individual psychology. He argues that the terms of one theory have attributes additional to those of the other; for instance, he asks what is added by exchange theorists to the propositions of operant psychology, concluding that they add considerably. As an example he takes the social observation that "in status hierarchies certain communicative acts tend to be addressed upwards from lower- to higher-status" (p. 380) which is a hypothesis from Kelley's (1951) experimental study of communication in social hierarchies. Emerson believes that the explanation of why rewarding contingencies should be associated with higher status is a sociological question and a sociologist's task "not subsumable within psychology" (p. 381). This is so because psychological propositions

---

* The term "operant psychology" as used by Emerson refers to laboratory studies of behaviour control. Emerson states that exchange theories are based on operant psychology. This statement seems to be too limited. Thibaut and Kelley use different psychological concepts from those of Homans as the starting point for their theoretical efforts. The former take concepts from Hull's hypotheses, the latter takes basic propositions from Skinner's work. These differences at source are discussed in Chapters 3 and 8.

Emerson's reference list of major publications in exchange theory consists of those by Thibaut and Kelley, George Homans, Alfred Kuhn and Peter Blau.

occur at the beginning of a theoretical structure: they provide the most general, least specific statements which therefore *have to be supplemented* in the course of theory-building to the point where explanation can include the situational variables influencing social behaviour.

The meanings which accrue as a result of the situational variables are shown in the following examples of concepts used for explaining social behaviour. An attempt to translate the specific (secondary) concepts into primary (or, more general) ones results in *loss* of these additional meanings. The concepts of "group norm" can be translated into "discriminative stimulus"; "group sanction" into "reinforcer"; "group member" into "organism"—but only with loss. The secondary concepts have additional empirical attributes and while each can, with loss, be translated into the more general or basic concepts, the latter cannot be substituted for the concepts of the more specific social propositions. Explanation of social behaviour requires concepts with such additional attributes, and they take their places in hypotheses which, by Emerson's view, are sociological as opposed to psychological. Examining these examples more closely, he shows that both "norm" and "sanction" have the additional empirical attribute of "action in concert" by members of a group (acting in social coalition). Thus, despite the general truth of the propositions that certain discriminative stimuli are followed by behaviour which is reinforced, this proposition is not, so far as it goes, empirically valid for social situations. As an illustration, Emerson gives the instance that "a parent's sanctions can go for nought if the child finds rewards from third parties who are not in coalition with the parent in the norm-stating, sanction-administering process. Hence, the problem becomes inherently sociological. Conformity can be understood only in small part through the direct application of operant principles" (p. 383).

In brief, Emerson's viewpoint is that operant propositions carry us part of the way towards explanation of social structure as a dependent variable, but he suggests a more constructive use than merely attempting to apply them to the behaviour of individuals in society, treating society as a given (this would be reduction). His argument is, in fact, identical with the argument in favour of autonomous theoretical development in social psychology. He holds that sociological propositions have to be added and incorporated with the propositions taken from operant psychology, because of the *reciprocal relationship* between individuals which their being in society implies. Moreover, his position is by no means inconsistent with a weak form of logical reduction. The propositions of operant psychology are therefore "*a base* upon which new principles of social structure and structural change are built" (p. 403). Emerson prefers to refer to this procedure as theory-construction rather than reduction: thus, he says, exchange theory shows an explicit connection to psychological propositions, but these evolve into forms which are relatively remote from them. His argument is, up to a point, similar to that of Runciman in allowing psychological statements as a base, but he gives much more importance to the conceptual distinctions and additions as discovered by sociological (i.e. structural) research. Emerson's error is only to ignore altogether the field of social psychology but this is not surprising in a discussion which presents psychology and sociology as two opposing disciplines contesting the ownership of exchange theory.

Another instance of this argument is found in Buckley (1967) who, like Emerson, takes the position that the emergent phenomena of social behaviour are of decisive importance in the terms and propositions of a theory. Buckley treats the reduction controversy as a side-issue in a general discussion of social exchange theories, which he criticizes as "rejuvenated utilitarian", but which are also seen as part of a wider movement towards more dynamic theories of social process in place of the more static consensus theories of society. The claim, as stated by Homans, for the psychological reduction of sociological explanation is rejected by Buckley in favour of Blau's endeavour to use "intermediate concepts in their own right as a basis for an understanding of the complex processes and structure of associations" (p. 143). Buckley's view, similar as it is to Emerson's, is mentioned here largely because it is indicative of a line of thought held by many sociologists towards reduction—although Buckley presents it as an assertion of a theoretical position without the supporting argument and without the benefit of convincing illustration, such as Emerson provides.

A weak reduction?

It is tempting to take a position similar to Boden (1972) in her discussion of physiology and psychology, when she comments that one can be anti-reductionist in the sense of denying the possibility of a complete reduction, but reductionist in the weak sense of accepting some fairly loose logical connection between the *primary* and the *secondary* theories.

In the latter case, the explanations of a theory are not replaced or substituted, the two theories offer complementary explanations, as Boden seems to argue when she states her intention* to "convince 'anti-reductionists' of their essential compatibility, and 'reductionists' of their necessary complementarity" (p. 4). If we accept this complementarity between exchange theory and more basic psychological explanations, it is as a relationship which can barely be outlined, leaving the connection still extremely vague. We will accept this weak degree of reduction because we regard it as an orientation which will be fruitful and constructive. It could be a declaration of intent, to fill in the existing bare outline with more systematic knowledge. The somewhat sketchy connections with psychological premises are recognized, they may be reappraised in the future, but the immediate strategy is to present and test empirical hypotheses in primary groups. Actually, such a tentative position is near to the viewpoint of Blau who recognizes the psychological roots, and accepts much of Homans' work as valid, but turns his attention to the social context and away from the psychological foundations.

In social exchange theory we have seen the strategy of proceeding by analogy, from individual psychology and economics, in order to generate propositions and hypotheses for social behaviour. Explanatory statements cannot be applied from these sources unless they are in the form of general analogies suggesting that similar processes may be in operation that may be understood by analysis combining concepts from both sources. These borrowed concepts now contribute to a distinct body of theory. Nagel (1961) illustrates this procedure as it occurred prior to the reduction of thermodynamics to mechanics, mentioning that it was "the normal strategy of the science to exploit on a new front ideas and analogies found to be fruitful elsewhere" (p. 358). To proceed on the basis of analogies is therefore not *inconsistent* with a reduction but what appears most clearly in social exchange theory is that the analogies, somewhat eclectic in their derivation, provide only an indirect connection with source theories and the strongest tendency in exchange theory is the development of its own explanations.

Nagel makes another relevant point, that a discipline should develop theories for its own special field, even if reduction is an eventual aim: "the secondary discipline may be progressively solving its own special

* Referring to physiology and psychology, to "mechanism" and "purpose".

class of problems with the help of a theory expressly devised . . ."
(p. 362). While further attempts may be made towards a reduction to
individual psychology (no-one has argued for a reduction to elementary
economics), even in its most explicitly argued form it is still a reduction
of the remote future. At its utmost, Homans' argument that social
behaviour is ultimately explained by psychological propositions is a
declaration of faith, at a moment when, "in the social sciences a kind of
sketchy logic is as much as we can ask and more than we usually get"
(1970, p. 314). But the argument has its most useful purpose in emphasizing the connection between individual psychology and the study
of social behaviour; exchange theory has had considerable influence in
establishing psychological propositions as an initial theoretical position
even if sociologists, among whom Peter Blau is pre-eminent, discount
reducibility altogether.

Exchange theory and reduction

At the same time, exchange theory exemplifies an increasing convergence of research on *reciprocal* behaviour as a focus of explanations,
making the connection with individual psychology less important.
Empirical advances in the specialized field of reciprocal relations must
augment this development. Not that there is no dependence on individual psychology for explanatory statements, but that the social
explanations build considerably on to them. There are some hints of
this in the recent literature. For instance, Levinger, Senn and Jorgensen
(1970) describe the conditions of courtship relations, the essence of
which constitutes a common property between the partners that is not
specified by referring to them separately. In these relationships where
there is a common investment "the product will supersede indices that
focus only on the partners' individualities" (p. 441) and they suggest
that an effective measure will have to focus on the commonality of
investment by the pair.

As we have seen, the arguments of sociologists against reduction refer
to emergent phenomena in collectivities for which there are no psychological explanations. Coleman (1966) uses his interpretation of exchange
theory in order to illustrate this point of view. He argues that many
social phenomena cannot be explained by an *individual calculus* of
exchange and that the connection is tenuous between collective decisions
and individual rationality. In large collectivities, he says, only in rare

cases does action by the whole realize all individual goals and, further-more, the participation of all individuals is quite unlikely. He discusses exchange explanations* as applicable in a case where an individual chooses an action with the highest utility from a number of alternatives and he points out that this theory cannot be applied to collective action where there is no action that is preferred by all. Arguments by sociolo-gists were discussed earlier in this chapter, either in favour of, or against, reduction to psychology: the argument by Runciman (1970), Emerson (1970) and Buckley (1967) ignored social psychology altogether. A similar example is Emerson's (1972) apparent attempt to claim exchange theory exclusively for sociology. In fact, exchange theory when it is applied to primary groups *and* to institutions spans social anthropology, social psychology and sociology; the reduction question when it is argued as between psychology and sociology offers too gross an alter-native. Surely this has been clearly demonstrated by Stotland (1965) and Swanson (1965) utilizing the emergent phenomena argument—for primary groups—in order to emphasize the relative autonomy of social psychology. In view of the tendency to sociological expansionism, it is interesting to find Blain (1971), a sociologist, expressing his fear that sociology will be reduced to social psychology:

> Homans' reductionism encourages us to be, not sociologists but social psychologists. One need go no further than the students in an introductory class for evidence that Homans is encouraging us to do what requires no encouragement, but rather comes quite naturally; namely, social psy-chology. A sociological perspective is far more difficult to achieve. Students are relatively at home with the social psychological approach. This is in part because such an approach is somewhat more compatible with the individualism of American culture and in part because the natural way in which people experience and perceive life is in social psychological "face-to-face" terms (pp. 3–4).

Blain proceeds to suggest that there is a class of sociological propositions that are general, and non-deducible from psychological propositions. As an example, he discusses the Bavelas-Leavitt patterns of group communication, the "circle", the "wheel", the "chain" and the "Y", in order to show that groups can be classified as units. He emphasizes that if a group rather than a person is the unit which is classified then

* Note that Coleman takes an extremely narrow view of what exchange explana-tions imply, a view not supported in the previous chapters (see, for example, Chapter 7).

the variable is sociological and propositions which define their relationships are also sociological. Secondly, if persons rather than groups are
classified, the variable is psychological. As a third possibility, if a proposition relates to both sociological and psychological variables (groups
and persons) it is a social psychological proposition. Next, he discusses
the methodology for testing this last class of proposition:

> In general, the methodology involves classifying groups on the basis of
> some property and then classifying individuals within those groups on the
> basis of the same or some other property. The analysis is then analogous
> to the statistical technique of analysis of variance in which "between cell"
> effects are separated from "within cell" effects. Thus, Blau (1960) shows
> that the attitudes of caseworkers in a federal agency could be explained in
> part by the attitudes that prevailed in the caseworker's group and in part
> by other attitudes of the caseworker (p. 9).

As we saw in Chapter 12, much of the argument in Blau's *Exchange and
Power in Social Life* is aimed at demonstrating that a position in favour
of a psychological reduction is untenable. He effectively argues (Chapter 12, pp. 322, 326) for the significance of group phenomena as influences
on an individual's choice behaviour. The particular choice, which he
considers, is between whether to stay as a member of a group or to leave
it in order to join another. He shows that an interpretation limited to
the individual's perception of outcomes in his present group and the
comparisons which he makes with what is available elsewhere ($CL_{alt.}$)
gives only a partial explanation, unless it includes certain structural
variables. Especially important, he emphasizes, is the relative position
of the alternative *group* as a "substructure in a macrostructure". Furthermore, not only is it important to know the individual's own current
position in a status structure but whether his status is based on criteria
unique to his group (particularistic) or those generally recognized in
society at large (universalistic). Here we have several sources of
influence on an individual decision, to be included in any interpretation
of the meaning of a choice, some of them involving classifications of the
social environment which seem quite independent of psychological
propositions—and this is Blau's conclusion. However, this does not
invalidate the hypotheses of Thibaut and Kelley that an individual
decides, either to leave, or stay in a group as a result of his making
comparisons. They would probably argue that the social hierarchy of
groups, the criteria of status within them are necessary to our understanding of the individual's actions, but are accepted as given condi-

tions rather than as topics of study. For social psychologists, characteristics of the structure of institutions must be included as *givens*, since they are outside the empirical area of primary groups. It is a matter of the different pieces of empirical evidence which different disciplines seek to comprehend. Yet, structural characteristics should be taken into consideration, otherwise the interpretation of such decisions will fail.

Exchange between groups

When Blau's arguments, later in his book (see Chapter 8, pp. 55–58) make clear how exchanges develop between *groups* and organized collectivities he is extending the range of exchange concepts very convincingly. At the same time, it must be recognized that this extension now introduces subject matter which is sociological, beyond the province of social psychology as a discipline. Quite simply, the properties of collectivities enter social psychological analysis as given conditions, and very important ones, as we have seen. Here we have exactly the same distinction as has to be made for physiological process which underlies the behaviour of individuals but is taken as given in studying their social behaviour. Yet, if a fuller and less incomplete* explanation of an individual choice is required then there is no doubt it will be more adequate if it includes some data on the relations between collectivities, or the status rating of groups in society. It would be yet more adequate if we were to examine the personality correlates of individuals. If exchange theory were to aim for a fuller explanation in this sense, it would be the result of very ambitious interdisciplinary effort. But the reciprocal relationship among individual members of groups happens to be our principal point of interest as social psychologists. From this point of view, the structural sociologists (those who take institutions as the unit of analysis) abstract the study of organizations away from the social behaviour of individuals. And a parallel stratagem can be seen on the part of neurophysiologists who, offering explanation in micro-units, abstract the individual out of his social context.

Despite the efforts of Blau and more recently of Emerson, to establish that exchange propositions are sociological, the major parts of the theory itself, of its substantive propositions and research material, deal with interpersonal relationships in dyads or primary groups. The theory

* As Homans has remarked: "of course there is an enormous number of possible given conditions that cannot be explained . . ." (1970, p. 342).

outline, as it exists at present, is largely social psychological although it is shared with other disciplines. As a body of theory, independent of "derivatory" or analogous sources, the constituent propositions will, in the future, be refined through the study of social processes and this will lead to greater empirical and explanatory distinctiveness. However, the nature of these propositions also indicates that there will be developments in the connections with other disciplines and, above all, with other specializations in psychology.

15

Conclusion

Cognitive theories and exchange

Campbell and Alexander (1966) consider that Festinger, Heider, Homans and Newcomb all share basic propositions to account for interpersonal influence and consensus. I have occasionally commented in earlier parts of this book that exchange hypotheses run parallel with either balance or cognitive dissonance explanations. I mention this here particularly to call attention to the cognitive and symbolic elements in exchange theory and to help locate some of the current research on exchange in relation to other explanatory efforts within social psychology. Other explanatory schemes such as those influenced by symbolic interactionism (Lindesmith and Strauss, 1968, especially p. 6; Singelmann, 1972, 1973) also touch on social exchange explanations as we shall see in a moment. These points of contact lead to the conclusion that exchange theory is not so much biased by "behaviourism" in the pejorative sense that it avoids giving attention to thought process.

Alexander and Simpson (1964) discuss the common ground between Homans' notion of distributive justice and balance hypotheses. They continue a line of discussion begun by Heider (1958, p. 188) when he mentioned Homans' (1951) hypothesis that, under certain conditions, interaction between persons leads to them liking each other (the interaction-liking hypothesis is discussed above, Chapter 8, p. 185). Alexander and Simpson do not hesitate to note that several theories have begun to cohere and "a convergence of theories is unmistakable. Theories of balance, congruity, dissonance, equity, expectation, and justice are based on the same general postulates and are headed in the same direction though they follow different paths" (p. 183). Alexander and Simpson discuss the less obvious predictions from assuming that persons will seek consistency in their relations with other people: for instance, the prediction that undeserved rewards induce reactions of discomfort (see Homans, 1964, p. 76). They continue with a discussion of notions of distributive justice; that expectations and outcomes should coincide and that rewards should be proportional to costs. Reviewing work in dissonance theory, they refer to the experiment by Adams and Rosenbaum (1962) in which notions of equity, dissonance reduction and exchange are discussed together. They also refer to the social comparison process in which a person may use the costs and rewards of others as reference points as a standard for evaluating his own, giving particular attention to Homans' concept of a person's investments which are additional to the immediate costs in a particular situation. However, such *personal* (background) investments, they note, may restrict or prevent social comparisons (and certainly hinder measurement) because of the many differences of personal characteristics and experiences which can confound any clear comparison. We have already seen something of these difficulties as discussed by Homans in Chapter 8. Lastly, they regard imbalance as a "special kind of cost" and suggest it as a negative value in Homans' general framework of exchange.

Curry and Emerson (1970) use an exchange explanation as an alternative to their main balance hypothesis. They attempt to repeat Newcomb's (1961) study of interpersonal attraction, by administering questionnaires over an eight-week period to students living in a university residence. Here Curry and Emerson compare exchange and balance explanations and find greater empirical support for the former. Moreover, they conclude that exchange theory can predict mutual attraction in a more parsimonious way—in exchange propositions the reciprocation between persons is "an irreducible social fact" but in balance theory one has to predicate the psychological balancing tendency and derive from this any reciprocation that occurs.

There are other examples where balance and exchange explanations are not set against each other but are referred to as providing alternative *but similar ex post facto* interpretations. For example, Priest and Sawyer (1967) in a study which has been described above (Chapter 11, p. 269) cite Heider (1958) and Newcomb (1961) and collect data to test their balance predictions. In their analysis of sociometric questionnaires which they administered to 471 students they expected to find a high degree of reciprocation of choice between pairs of students as an indicator of balance tendencies. This was supported by the results. However, when it came to comparing the effects of proximity (location in the students' residence) and peership (membership of the same class) they found it more useful to refer to Homans and Blau. Especially useful was Homans' proposition that interaction leads to liking, with proximity or peership as given conditions. The effects of proximity and peership were interpreted in terms of rewards and costs. Evidence that peership was a better predictor of liking than proximity fitted with the interpretation that proximity reduces costs; peership, or similarity, increases rewards.

Also in Chapter 11 we described an experiment by Blumstein and Weinstein (1969) who discuss distributive injustice as a condition where an individual's rewards and investments are out of balance. Emphasizing the tendency to redress the balance they follow Homans' own conclusion that exchange and balance explanations are basically similar. Blumstein and Weinstein mention the possibility that seeking redress has its motivational source either in a tendency to reduce disparities and to strive for orderliness in social relations or as an attempt to reduce cognitive dissonance. This is yet another indicator of the convergence of these cognitive explanations. We have already seen that Adams (1963), in his version of equity theory, holds that it is a special case of Festinger's (1957) cognitive dissonance model. Thus, Curry and Emerson provide our only example of an approach to a direct test of an exchange hypothesis against an hypothesis from another theoretical source. In most cases exchange, balance or dissonance hypotheses are all discussed together as possible interpretations. Jones and Schneider (1968) refer to exchange and cognitive dissonance explanations in their post-experimental conjectures about the meaning of their results. Savell and Healey (1969) attempted to measure the effects of prior agreement from another person on subsequent conformity with his opinion and they suggest that conformity may reflect a person's efforts "to restore balance to what was, until that point, unequal social exchange" (p. 316). They discuss exchange propositions as alternatives to several other theoretical approaches in social psychology.

The views of Homans, Blau and Thibaut and Kelley are given prominence in Singelmann's (1972) discussion of exchange as symbolic interaction. In order to achieve a translation, Singelmann has to play down the behaviouristic influences on social exchange theory. For instance, he points out that exchange is much more than a matter of immediate objective rewards since it involves subjective meanings, past experience and future anticipations. Singelmann tries to demonstrate by means of citations from exchange theory sources that great importance is given to the subjective meaning of social situations, to the shared meanings between actors, to the varied meaning of the same objective reward to different persons in different situations. He is able to show similarities between these aspects of exchange theory and the notions of symbolic interaction postulated by Mead (1934, 1964). Both kinds of explanation overlap in the recognition of "multiple selves" depending on the social context with which the self is in interaction, the so-called "situational self". Lastly, he touches on a point raised by Homans (see Chapter 8, p. 173) when he mentions that one man's rational behaviour may seem quite irrational to others. From the point of view of symbolic interaction, Singelmann argues that it is all a matter of a person's definitions and interpretations. This is why a traditional pattern of exchange may persist in the face of changed objective conditions; or why an observer's appraisal of objective reinforcements will fail to account for such persisting tradtions. On the other hand, a person may change his definition because of his ideas of a just exchange; he may therefore reject a traditional pattern even though there have been no observable changes in the available rewards. Another important idea involving exchange as symbolic interaction means that the hedonistic principle must be qualified:

> In exchange, the hedonistic strivings of actors are limited and qualified by the nature of the subjective and socially shared definitions of the objective world which includes the self and others (Singelmann, 1972, p. 422).

Lastly, Singelmann faces the counter-argument that "the postulate of meaningfulness is ultimately tautological since it permits an *ex post facto* explanation of any behaviour, regardless of what has been predicted" (p. 423). In other words, it could be said that a given reward will produce an effect, or if it does not, it is because the actor does not see it as a reward. In defence, Singelmann states that he is discussing theoretical premises at their most general level and at this level such premises are always tautological.* It follows that a more significant

---

* We have discussed tautologies as "logical truths" in Chapter 2, p. 17.

question is whether the premises lead to concrete predictions which can be tested.

When Singelmann argues for the similarity between symbolic interactionism and exchange theory he mentions that the concept of *self* is central to both kinds of explanation. According to Singelmann much of exchange theory deals with a person's view of himself, the self as seen by others and the self of the other person. Thus friendship is seen as a mutual support for the self-concept. He mentions reference group theory "according to which self-other comparisons are important determinants of expectations" and claims that this mode of explanations has been incorporated by exchange theorists and by symbolic interactionists (Thibaut and Kelley, 1959, p. 88; Homans, 1961, pp. 73–74, 151–152, 48; and Blau, 1964, pp. 151–160). He attempts to show that a bridge between exchange and self theories has been made by Thibaut and Kelley (1959, pp. 245–246) when they discuss internalizing roles. Singelmann argues that the self and social reinforcement are interdependent but autonomous sources of motivation, so that exchange theory and symbolic interactionism are complementary, each explaining "what the other leaves open" (p. 418).

I mention Singelmann's discussion here because it underlines the attention given by "exchange theorists" to the symbolic, which we mentioned earlier (p. 391).

Recently, Abbot, Brown and Crosbie (1973) have assembled some criticisms of Singelmann's attempt to demonstrate the common ground between symbolic interaction and exchange, but Singelmann (1973) has replied that the value of his discussion rests in drawing attention to the importance of subjective meaning, subjective evaluations and to their more explicit definition in social relations. Singelmann underlines that the arguments of Blau, Thibaut and Kelley imply the constructiveness of human acts. He also thinks it important that the notion of interaction between individual and social environment as a continuous process of reconstruction which occurs in Mead's (1934) writings is also found in Blau's discussion of the strains towards change (see above Chapter 12) and which Homans (1964, p. 152) also recognizes.

In the course of his discussion Singelmann refers to Emerson as a "more experimentally and behaviouristically oriented" exchange theorist. In order to highlight the attention to evaluative and symbolic process in the exchange authors we have discussed in this book, we can now take up, briefly, this reference to "behavioural sociology". Emerson's (1962, 1972) approach is similar to that of Kunkel (1967) and Burgess and Bushell (1969), who have espoused "behavioural sociology". It is an approach to social behaviour by means of hypotheses adapted from experimental psychology, emphasizing the observation of activities, de-emphasizing subjective meaning, and advocating a minimum of inferences concerning internal states. This position is not particularly, or at all, characteristic of exchange explanations. Kunkel, for example, recognizes that Homans' approach is different because of the latter's concern with a person's expectations. But Kunkel prefers the advantages achieved "by greatly reducing the investigator's concern with men's internal states and by focussing . . . on the actual operation of the social structure rather than on the individual's *perception* of, or his *orientation* to, social systems" (p. 21). Although Kunkel's major postulate states that most behaviour is learned and maintained by differential reinforcement, there is little development of any explanatory framework beyond this. Kunkel considers he has thus made a useful economy in the work of explanation but it should be pointed out that this still begs the question of how vital is the part which he has removed. The heavy emphasis on the environment as cause is a weakness of his proposed schema and although he argues that he does not deny the existence of internal states yet he does propose to drop them entirely from his explanations.* Paradoxically, Kunkel sees his reliance on variant learning principles as a means of avoiding too much dependence on psychology in explaining social phenomena. Emerson takes hypotheses from Skinner's operant psychology, "applying" these, by exposition, to human social behaviour. Whether or not it is theoretically useful to reformulate operant principles, to make further translations of operant concepts into exchange propositions, is a question which can only be settled by empirical criteria in the future. A reformulation similar to Emerson's in terms of operant psychology, is suggested by Burgess and Akers (1966) and a general discussion of this approach is found in Burgess and Bushell (1969). Empirical studies in this vein have followed, for example, by Burgess and Nielsen (1974). These reformulations are weakened (and Emerson acknowledges the weakness) by their avoidance of the cognitive dimension of exchange. It remains an open question, therefore, of whether restating the analogies from operant

* See Homans' reasons for including "internal states", which are discussed in Chapter 8.

psychology provide an effective new alternative. As I have argued, in the earlier chapters of this book, such analogies are a beginning tactic in theory construction which allow basic premises to be stated, as a point of departure, for the development of a theory-sketch of social exchange; but the tactic itself is of little importance compared to the actual development which has occurred within this explanatory framework in the last few years.

The achievement in exchange theory

As I have described the main issues in this book, exchange explanations state the conditions under which different degrees of reciprocity occur, and the limitations to reciprocity in interpersonal behaviour. Evaluations of persons and acts; expectations of justice and fair exchange, receive much attention. The ideas of Thibaut, Kelley, Homans and Blau have found expression in a number of empirical studies which have been the subject of Chapters 4–7, 9–11 and 13. Few of these assume only one view of rationality or of optimizing behaviour. They are more likely to raise multiple possibilities of alternative hypotheses, and above all, the question of justice in interpersonal behaviour.

I have mentioned that analogies form the starting position of exchange explanations, as they do for many another theoretical enterprise, but that we should not confuse the illustrative analogy that sets the theoretical effort in motion with the empirical work that develops and, subsequently, modifies the theory or leads it perhaps in directions which the original statements did not predicate. Nor do exchange explanations derive only from economic, or even reinforcement analogies. It should not be forgotten that they have a broader inheritance in the anthropological studies of exchange, as found in Marcel Mauss' study of the gift. This wider context of exchange also forms the basis of discussions of justice in social interaction by Eckhoff (1974) and Rawls (1972). Homans' treatment of "distributive justice" has now been tested in a variety of experiments and field studies and has received as much, or more, attention than other topics in exchange. Maximizing postulates as expressed by Homans, Thibaut and Kelley have received most criticisms but they are not, in fact, the liveliest current issue in exchange hypotheses. The statements found in exchange theory are qualified and tentative, since each of these authors encounters problems with the transfer of such postulates to social behaviour. Earlier, in Chapter 7 the concepts of maximizing, optimizing or satisficing were discussed.

Exchange concepts and hypotheses appear in theoretical and research studies of family behaviour, of courtship and marriage. A cumulative body of work now appears in experimental studies of negotiation, the informational component of bargaining. It has become clear that the major problematic areas for exchange concern the conditions of reciprocation, of equity, fair exchange, negotiation and bargaining in a variety of social situations.

We can recall Popper's (1959) statement that if an intellectual discipline is scientific, it is not because of the source of its hypotheses, but because of what is done with the hypotheses once they have been postulated. I have shown how social exchange theory is based on analogies taken from reinforcement and economic theory but I have especially aimed to show how it has developed through empirical studies. I have also illustrated how concepts like "maximizing profit" change their meaning when they are transferred to social psychology. Such economic terms can only be applied by metaphor and propositions containing them only by analogy. It is quite a customary approach in scientific endeavour to introduce concepts or explanatory models by analogy. However, what happens once the concepts have been borrowed, makes the significant point. Their empirical referents are now completely different. For this reason we should accept that analogies do not explain, they give an illustration, as Plon (1972) rightly comments, of what *might* be a relationship between concepts and the empirical variables which they are thought to represent. The important steps occur after the analogy has been borrowed, and we may now have explanatory propositions that comprise an autonomous body of theory. I have sought to demonstrate how this is happening in "exchange theory".

Do exchange propositions suggest our acceptance of the existing allocation and distribution of rewards, in society? I see no reason why social exchange theory has, necessarily, to support a conservative ideology. We have discussed such criticisms, especially criticisms of the research topics and techniques used in experimental games (Chapters 4 and 6). In the view of some, the alternatives available to social psychologists, in problems or methods, are themselves already foreclosed by the influence of existing loci of power in society or in academic hierarchies. For instance, Michel Pecheux (1970) discussing ideological influences in social psychology refers to the "illusion of autonomy", an illusion which overlooks that a set of problems, a "problematic" is defined by a view of what is an appropriate scientific and (or) ideological approach, as well as by the methodologies and models currently available.

However, exchange ideas have been explored by a diversity of research methods and there are many hypotheses from which to choose. I have presented evidence to show that the scope of exchange ideas is not foreclosed by a narrow interpretation of social behaviour solely in terms of economic or calculative rationality. Nor are they limited to any one kind of research design. This seems to be one of the sources of strength in exchange ideas, that they can be tested in a variety of situations by researchers using different methods. Finally, perhaps the most interesting development in recent years is the interest shown in the principle of "distributive justice", and its application to research within the explanatory framework of exchange.

In pointing out, as I have done in earlier chapters, that the exchange hypotheses most frequently discussed in the literature touch on such social topics as altruism, distributive justice, equality or equity, I was commenting on a trend in empirical studies since the publication of the major works of Thibaut and Kelley (1959), Homans (1961) and Blau (1964). Homans (1974) has now chosen to re-emphasize the derivation of his explanatory propositions from "behavioural psychology" but this in itself is no indicator, and certainly no predictor, of how social exchange theory has developed, is currently developing, nor how it may develop in the future.

References

Abbott, C. W., Brown, C. R. and Crosbie, P. V. (1973). Exchange as symbolic inter-action: for what? *American Sociological Review*, **38**, 504–506.

Abelson, R. P. (1968). Simulation of social behaviour. *In* Lindzey, G. and Aronson, E. (eds) *The Handbook of Social Psychology*, vol. 2, Addison Wesley, Reading, Mass.

Abelson, R. P. and Miller, J. C. (1967). Negative persuasion via personal insult. *Journal of Experimental and Social Psychology*, **3**, 321–333.

Abrahamsson, B. (1970). Homans on exchange: Hedonism revived. *American Journal of Sociology*, **76**, 2, 273–285.

Adams, J. S. (1963). Toward an understanding of inequity. *Journal of Abnormal and Social Psychology*, **67**, 422–436.

Adams, J. S. (1965). Inequity in social exchange. *In* Berkowitz, L. (ed.) *Advances in experimental social psychology*, **2**, Academic Press, New York and London.

Adams, J. S. and Rosenbaum, W. B. (1962). The relationship of worker productivity to cognitive dissonance. *Journal of Applied Psychology*, **46**, 161–164.

Alexander, C. N. and Simpson, R. L. (1964). Balance theory and distributive justice. *Sociological Inquiry*, **34**, 182–192.

Allport, F. (1924). *Social Psychology*. Houghton-Mifflin, Boston.

Alvarez, R. (1968). Informal reactions to deviance in simulated work organizations: a laboratory experiment. *American Sociological Review*, **33**, 895–912.

Anderson, M. (1971). *Family structure in 19th century Lancashire*. Cambridge University Press, Cambridge.

Annett, J. (1969). *Feedback and Human Behaviour*. Penguin Books, Harmondsworth, Middlesex.

Apfelbaum, E. (1966). Études experimentales de conflict: les jeux expérimentaux. *Année Psychologique*, **66**, 599–621.

Apfelbaum, E. (1967). Représentations du partenair et interactions à propos d'un dilemme du prisonnier. *Psychologie Française*, **12**, 287–295.

Archibald, K. (ed.), (1966). *Strategic Interaction and Conflict*. Original papers and discussion. University of California, Institute of International Studies, Berkeley.

Argyle, M. (1969). *Social Interaction*. Methuen, London.

Asch, S. (1959). A perspective on social psychology. *In* S. Koch (ed.) *Psychology: a Study of a Science*, vol 3: Formulations of the person and the social context. McGraw Hill, New York.

Asplund, J. (1972). On the concept of value relevance. *In* Israel, J. and Tajfel, H. (eds) *The Context of Social Psychology: A critical assessment*. Academic Press, London and New York.

Atack, W. A. J. (1973). Calculated, conditioned, and normative behaviour in social exchange: an integration of assumptions. *Canadian Review of Sociology and Anthropology*, **10**, 214–230.

Atkinson, J. W. (1957). Motivational determinants of risk-taking behaviour. *Psychological Review*, **64**, 359–372.

Attneave, F. (1954). Some informational aspects of visual perception. *Psychological Review*, **61**, 183–193.

Back, K. (1951). Power, influence and pattern of communication. *In* Petrullo, L. and Bass, B. M. (eds) *Leadership and Interpersonal Behaviour*. Holt, Rinehart and Winston, New York.

Baldwin, D. A. (1971). Thinking about threats. *Journal of Conflict Resolution*, **15**, 71–78.

Bales, R. F. (1953). The equilibrium problem in small groups. *In* Parsons, T., Bales, R. F. and Shils, E. A. (eds) *Working papers in the Theory of Action*. Free Press, Glencoe, Illinois.

Balkwell, J. W. (1969). A structural theory of self-esteem maintenance. *Sociometry*, **32**, 458–473.

Bandura, A. (1969). *Principles of Behaviour Modification*. Holt, Rinehart and Winston, New York.

Bannister, D. (1968). The myth of physiological psychology. *Bulletin of the British Psychological Society*, **21**, 229–231.

Barker, D. (1972). Young people and their homes: spoiling and "keeping close" in a South Wales town. *Sociological Review*, **20**, 4, 569–590.

Baron, R. M. (1966). Social reinforcement effects as a function of social reinforcement history. *Psychological Review*, **73**, 527–539.

Bartos, O. J. (1967). *Simple Models of Group Behaviour*. Columbia University Press, New York.

Beloff, J. (1973). *Psychological Science: A Review of Modern Psychology*. Crosby Lockwood Staples, London.

Benton, A. A., Gelber, E. L., Kelley, H. H. and Liebling, B. A. (1969). Reactions to various degrees of deceit in a mixed-motive relationship. *Journal of Personality and Social Psychology* **12**, 170–180.

Berger, J. and Fisek, M. H. (1970). Consistent and inconsistent status characteristics and the determination of power and prestige orders. *Sociometry*, **33**, 287–304.

Bergmann, G. (1957). *Philosophy of Science*. University of Wisconsin Press, Madison.

Berkowitz, L. (1960). Repeated frustrations and expectations in hostility arousal. *Journal of Abnormal and Social Psychology*, **60**, 422–429.

Berkowitz, L. and Connor, W. H. (1966). Success, failure, and social responsibility. *Journal of Personality and Social Psychology*, **4**, 664–669.

Berkowitz, L. and Daniels, L. R. (1963). Responsibility and dependency. *Journal of Abnormal and Social Psychology*, **66**, 429–436.

Berkowitz, L. and Daniels, L. R. (1964). Affecting the salience of the social responsibility norm: effects of past help on the response to dependency relationships. *Journal of Abnormal and Social Psychology*, **68**, 275–281.

Berkowitz, L. and Friedman, P. (1967). Some social class differences in helping behaviour. *Journal of Personality and Social Psychology*, **8**, 217–225.

Berne, E. (1964). *Games People Play, the Psychology of Human Relationships*. Penguin Books, Harmondsworth, Middlesex.

Berlyne, D. E. (1957). Conflict and choice time. *British Journal of Psychology*, **48**, 106–118.

Bevan, W. (1963). The pooling mechanism and the phenomena of reinforcement. *In* Harvey, O. J. (ed.) *Motivation and Social Interaction*, Ronald Press, New York.

Bitterman, M. E. (1967). Learning in animals. *In* Helson, H. and Bevan, W. (eds) *Contemporary Approaches to Psychology*. Van Nostrand, Princeton, N. J.

Bitterman, M. E. (1969). Thorndike and the problem of animal intelligence. *American Psychologist*, **24**, 444–454.

Bixenstine, V. E. and Wilson, K. V. (1963). Effects of level of cooperative choice by the other player on choices in a Prisoner's Dilemma game. Part II. *Journal of Abnormal and Social Psychology*, **67**, 139–147.

Blain, R. R. (1971). On Homans' psychological reductionism. *Social Inquiry*, **41**, 3–25.

Blain, R. R. (1971a). An alternative to Parsons' four-function paradigm as a basis for developing general sociological theory. *American Sociological Review*, **36**, 4, 678–692.

Blau, P. M. (1955). *The Dynamics of Bureaucracy: A Study of Interpersonal Relations in Two Government Agencies*. University of Chicago Press, Chicago.

Blau, P. M. (1960). A theory of social integration. *American Journal of Sociology*, **65**, 550–553.

Blau, P. M. (1964). *Exchange and Power in Social Life*. Wiley and Sons, New York.

Blau, P. M. (1970). Comment. *In* Borger, R. and Cioffi, F. (eds) *Explanation in the Behavioural Sciences*. Cambridge University Press, Cambridge.

Blau, P. M. and Schoenherr, R. A. (1971). *The Structure of Organizations*. Basic Books, New York.

Blau, P. M. and Scott, W. R. (1962). *Formal Organizations*. Chandler, San Francisco.

Bloch, E. L. and Goodstein, L. D. (1971). Comment on "influence of an interviewer's disclosure on the self-disclosing behaviour of interviewees". *Journal of Counseling Psychology*, **18**, 595–597.

Blood, R. O. and Wolfe, D. M. (1960). *Husbands and Wives*. The Free Press, New York.

Blumer, H. (1940). The problem of the concept in social psychology. *American Journal of Sociology*, **45**, 707–719.

Blumstein, P. W. and Weinstein, E. A. (1969). The redress of distributive injustice. *American Journal of Sociology*, **74**, 408–418.

Boden, M. A. (1972). *Purposive Explanation in Psychology*. Harvard University Press, Cambridge, Mass.

Borah, L. A. (1961). An investigation of the effect of threat upon interpersonal bargaining. Unpublished doctoral thesis, University of Minnesota.

Borah, L. A. (1963). The effects of threat in bargaining: critical and experimental analysis. *Journal of Abnormal and Social Psychology*, **66**, 37–44.

Borger, R. and Cioffi, F. (eds), (1970). *Explanation in the Behavioural Sciences*. Cambridge University Press, Cambridge.

Boulding, K. E. (1955). *Economic Analysis* (3rd ed.). Harper, New York.

Boulding, K. E. (1965). *The Image, Knowledge in Life and Society*. University of Michigan Press, Ann Arbor.

Boulding, K. E. and Davis, J. A. (1962). Two critiques of Homans' social behaviour: its elementary forms. *American Journal of Sociology*, **67**, 454–461.

Bovard, E. W. (1951) The experimental production of interpersonal effect. *Journal of Abnormal and Social Psychology*, **46**, 521–528.

Box, S. and Ford, J. (1969). Some questionable assumptions in the theory of status inconsistency. *Sociological Review*, **17**, 187–201.

Boyle, R. and Bonacich, P. (1970). The development of trust and mistrust in mixed motive games. *Sociometry*, **33**, 123–139.

Braithwaite, R. B. (1953). *Scientific Explanation. A Study of the Theory, Probability and Law in Science*. Cambridge University Press, Cambridge.

Brown, R. (1965). *Social Psychology*. The Free Press, New York.

Brown, R. (1973). *Social Psychology*, The Free Press, New York.

Bruno, P., Pecheux, M. Plon, M. and Poitou, J-P. (1973). La psychologie sociale: une utopie en crise. *La Nouvelle Critique*, **62**, 72–78; **64**, 21–28.

Buckley, W. (1967). *Sociology and Modern Systems Theory*. Prentice Hall, Englewood Cliffs, N.J.

Burgess, R. L. and Akers, R. L. (1966). Are operant principles tautological? *The Psychological Record*, **16**, 305–312.

Burgess, R. L. and Bushell, D. (1969). *Behavioural Sociology: Experimental Analysis of Social Process*. Columbia University Press, New York.

Burgess, R. L. and Nielsen, J. M. (1974). An experimental analysis of some structural determinants of equitable and inequitable exchange relations. *American Sociological Review*, **39**, 427–443.

Campbell, D. T. and Stanley, J. C. (1963). *Experimental and Quasi-Experimental Designs for Research*. Rand McNally, Chicago.

Campbell, E. Q. and Alexander, C. N. (1966). Structural effects and interpersonal relationships. *American Journal of Sociology*, **71**, 284–289.

Chadwick-Jones, J. K. (1969). *Automation and Behaviour. A Social Psychological Study*. Wiley and Sons, London and New York.

Chadwick-Jones, J. K. (1970). Recent interdisciplinary exchanges and the use of analogy in social psychology. *Human Relations*, **23**, 253–261.

Cheney, J. Harford, T. and Solomon, L. (1972). The effects of communicating threats and promises upon the bargaining process. *Journal of Conflict Resolution*, **16**, 99–108.

Chomsky, N. (1959). Review of Verbal Behaviour by B. F. Skinner. *Language*, **35**, 26–58.

Cloyd, J. S. and Bates, A. P. (1964). George Homans in footnotes: the fate of ideas in scholarly communication. *Sociological Inquiry*, **34**.

Cohen, P. S. (1968). *Modern Social Theory*, Heinemann, London.

Coleman, J. S. (1958). Relational analysis: the study of social organizations with survey methods. *Human Organization*, **17**, 28–36.

Coleman, J. S. (1963). Comment on "On the concept of influence". *Public Opinion Quarterly*, **27**, 63–82.

Coleman, J. S. (1964). *Introduction to Mathematical Sociology*. Free Press of Glencoe, New York; Collier-MacMillan, London.

Coleman, J. S. (1964a). Mathematical models and computer simulations. *In* Faris, R. E. L. (ed.) *Handbook of Modern Sociology*. Rand McNally, Chicago.

Coleman, J. S. (1966). Foundations for a theory of collective decisions. *American Journal of Sociology*, **71**, 615–627.

Collins, B. E. and Raven, B. H. (1969). Group structure: attraction, coalitions, communication and power. *In* Lindzey, G. and Aronson, E. (eds) *Handbook of Social Psychology*. Addison-Wesley, Reading, Mass.

Copi, I. M. (1961). *Introduction to Logic*. (2nd ed.). MacMillan, New York.

Costner, R. L. and Leik, R. K. (1964). Deduction from "Axiomatic theory". *American Sociological Review*, **29**, 819–838.

Curry, T. J. and Emerson, R. M. (1970). Balance theory: a theory of interpersonal attraction? *Sociometry*, **33**, 216–238.

Daniel, W. J. (1942). Cooperative problem solving in rats. *Journal of Comparative and Physiological Psychology*, **34**, 361–368.

Daniels, V. (1967). Communication, incentive, and structural variables in interpersonal exchange and negotiation. *Journal of Experimental Social Psychology*, **3**, 47–74.

Darley, J. M. and Berscheid, E. (1967). Increased liking as a result of the anticipation of personal contact. *Human Relations*, **20**, 29–39.

Dashiell, J. F. (1935). Experimental studies of the influence of social situations on the behaviour of individual human adults. *In* Murchison, C. (ed.) *Handbook of Social Psychology*. Clark University Press, Worcester.

Davidson, D., Suppes, P. and Siegel, S. (1957). *Decision-making: An Experimental Approach.* Stanford University Press, Stanford, Calif.

Davies, J. C. (1962). Toward a theory of revolution. *American Sociological Review,* **27,** 5–13.

DeLamater, J., McClintock, C. G. and Becker, G. (1965). Conceptual orientations of contemporary small group theory. *Psychological Bulletin,* **64,** 6, 402–412.

Demerath, N. J. and Thiessen, V. (1966). On spitting against the wind: organizational precariousness and American irreligion. *American Journal of Sociology,* **71,** 674–687.

Deutsch, M. (1949). A theory of cooperation and competition. *Human Relations,* **2,** 129–152.

Deutsch, M. (1949a). An experimental study of the effects of cooperation and competition upon group process. *Human Relations,* **2,** 199–232.

Deutsch, M. (1958). Trust and suspicion. *Journal of Conflict Resolution,* **11,** 4, 265–279.

Deutsch, M. (1960). The effect of motivational orientation upon trust and suspicion. *Human Relations,* **13,** 23–140.

Deutsch, M. (1962). Psychological alternatives to war. *Journal of Social Issues,* **18,** 2, 97–119.

Deutsch, M. (1964). Homans in the Skinner box. *Sociological Inquiry,* **34,** 156–165.

Deutsch, M. (1967). Strategies of inducing cooperation: an experimental study. *Journal of Conflict Resolution,* **11,** 345–360.

Deutsch, M. and Krauss, R. M. (1960). The effect of threat upon interpersonal bargaining. *Journal of Abnormal and Social Psychology,* **61,** 181–189.

Deutsch, M. and Krauss, R. M. (1962). Studies of interpersonal bargaining. *Journal of Conflict Resolution,* **6,** 1, 52–76.

Deutsch, M. and Krauss, R. M. (1965). *Theories in Social Psychology.* Basic Books, New York.

Doreian, P. (1970). *Mathematics and the Study of Social Relations.* Weidenfeld and Nicolson, London.

Doreian, P. and Stockman, N. (1969). A critique of the multidimensional approach to stratification. *Sociological Review,* **17,** 47–65.

Dumont, R. G. and Wilson, W. J. (1967). Aspects of concept formation, explication and theory construction in sociology. *American Sociological Review,* **32,** 985–995.

Eckhoff, T. (1974). *Justice. Its Determinants in Social Interaction.* Rotterdam University Press, Rotterdam.

Edwards, J. N. (1969). Familial behaviour as social exchange. *Journal of Marriage and the Family,* **31,** 518–526.

Eiser, J. R. and Tajfel, H. (1972). Acquisition of information in dyadic interaction. *Journal of Personality and Social Psychology,* **23,** 340–345.

Ellis, D. P. (1971). The Hobbesian problem of order: a critical appraisal of the normative solution. *American Sociological Review,* **36,** 692–702.

Emerson, R. M. (1962). Power-dependence relations. *American Sociological Review,* **27,** 31–41.

Emerson, R. M. (1970). Operant psychology and exchange theory. *In* Burgess, R. L. and Bushell, D. (eds) *Behavioral Sociology. The Experimental Analysis of Social Process.* Columbia University Press, New York.

Emerson, R. M. (1972). Exchange theory, Part 1: a psychological basis for social exchange and exchange theory; Part 2: exchange relations and network structures. *In* Berger, J., Zelditch, M. and Anderson, B. *Sociological Theories in Progress,* vol. 2. Houghton-Mifflin and Co., Boston.

Evans, G. W. and Crumbaugh, C. M. (1966). Effects of Prisoner's Dilemma format on cooperative behaviour. *Journal of Personality and Social Psychology*, **3**, 486–488.

Fallding, H. (1965). A proposal for the empirical study of values. *American Sociological Review*, **30**, 223–233.

Faucheux, C. and Moscovici, S. (1968). Self-esteem and exploitative behaviour in a game against chance and nature. *Journal of Personality and Social Psychology*, **8**, 83–88.

Faucheux, C. and Thibaut, J. (1964). L'approche clinique et expérimentale de la genèse des norms contractuelles dans différentes conditions de conflit et de menace. *Bulletin du Centre d'Etudes et Recherches Psychotechniques*, **13**, 225–243.

Festinger, L. (1954). A theory of social comparison processes. *Human Relations*, **7**, 117–140.

Festinger, L. (1957). *A Theory of Cognitive Dissonance*. Stanford University Press, Stanford, Calif.

Festinger, L., Schachter, S. and Back, K. (1950). *Social Pressures in Informal Groups*. Harper, New York.

Fiedler, F. E. (1967). *The Theory of Leadership Effectiveness*. McGraw-Hill, New York.

Feigenbaum, E. A. and Feldman, J. (eds) (1963). *Computers and Thought*. McGraw-Hill, New York.

Foa, U. G. (1971). Interpersonal and economic resources. *Science*, **171**, 345–351.

Fouraker, L. E. and Siegel, S. (1963). *Bargaining Behaviour*. McGraw-Hill, New York.

Gallo, P. S. (1966). Effects of increased incentives upon the use of threat in bargaining. *Journal of Personality and Social Psychology*, **4**, 14–20.

Gergen, K. J. (1969). *The Psychology of Behaviour Exchange*. Addison-Wesley, Reading, Mass.

Gibb, C. A. (1969). Leadership. *In* Lindzey, G. and Aronson, E. *The Handbook of Social Psychology*, vol. 4, Addison-Wesley, Reading, Mass.

Goffman, I. (1959). *The Presentation of Self in Everyday Life*. Doubleday, New York.

Goffman, I. (1961). *Encounters*. Bobbs-Merrill, Indianapolis.

Goode, W. J. (1972). Presidential address: the place of force in human society. *American Sociological Review*, **37**, 5, 507–519.

Goodman, L. (1964). Mathematical methods for the study of systems of groups. *American Journal of Sociology*, **70**, 170–192.

Goodwin, G. A. (1971). On transcending the absurd: an enquiry into the sociology of meaning. *American Journal of Sociology*, **76**, 831–846.

Goranson, R. E. and Berkowitz, L. (1966). Reciprocity and responsibility reactions to prior help. *Journal of Personality and Social Psychology*, **3**, 227–232.

Gouldner, A. W. (1960). The norm of reciprocity: a preliminary statement. *American Sociological Review*, **25**, 161–178.

Graves, D. (1972). Reported communication ratios and informal status in managerial work groups. *Human Relations*, **25**, 159–170.

Gray, D. (1971). Some comments concerning Maris on "logical adequacy". *American Sociological Review*, **36**, 706–709.

Greenberg, M. S. and Shapiro, S. P. (1971). Indebtedness: an adverse aspect of asking for and receiving help. *Sociometry*, **34**, 290–301.

Gruder, C. L. (1968). Effects of perception of opponent's bargaining style and accountability to opponent and partner in interpersonal mixed-motive bargaining. Doctoral dissertation, University of North Carolina.

Gruder, C. L. (1970). Social power in interpersonal negotiation. *In* Swingle, P. (ed.) *The Structure of Conflict*, Academic Press, New York and London.

Gruder, C. L. (1971). Relationships with opponent and partner in mixed-motive bargaining. *Journal of Conflict Resolution*, **15**, 3, 403–416.

Gullahorn, J. T. and Gullahorn, J. E. (1963). A computer model of elementary social behaviour. *In* Feigenbaum E. and Feldman, J. (eds) *Computers and Thought*. McGraw-Hill, New York.

Gullahorn, J. T. and Gullahorn, J. E. (1965a). The computer as a tool for theory development. *In* Hymes, D. (ed.) *The Use of Computers in Anthropology*. Mouton, The Hague.

Gullahorn, J. T. and Gullahorn, J. E. (1965b). Computer simulation of human interaction in small groups. *Simulation*, **4**, 50–61. (also published in *American Federation of Information Processing Societies Conference Proceedings*, Spring Joint Computer Conference, Spartan Books, Baltimore.)

Gullahorn, J. T. and Gullahorn, J. E. (1965c). Some computer applications in social science. *American Sociological Review*, **39**, 353–365.

Gullahorn, J. T. and Gullahorn, J. E. (1969). Social and cultural system simulations: research report. Michigan State University, East Lansing.

Gullahorn, J. T. and Gullahorn, J. E. (1972). A non-random walk in the Odyssey of a computer model. *In* Inbar, M. and Stoll, C. S. (eds) *Simulation and Gaming in Social Science*. The Free Press, New York.

Gumpert, P., Deutsch, M. and Epstein, J. (1969). Effect of incentive magnitude on cooperation in the Prisoner's Dilemma game. *Journal of Personality and Social Psychology*, **11**, 66–69.

Hamblin, R. L. (1971). Mathematical experimentation and sociological theory: a a critical analysis. *Sociometry*, **34**, 423–452.

Hamblin, R. L., Buckholdt, D., Ferritor, D., Kozloff, M. and Blackwell, L. (1971). *The Humanization Processes: A Social, Behavioural Analysis of Children's Problems*, Wiley and Sons, New York.

Hamblin, R. L. and Smith, C. R. (1966). Values, status, and professors. *Sociometry*, **29**, 183–196.

Harris, C. C. (1969). *The Family: An Introduction*. Allen and Unwin, London.

Harsanyi, J. C. (1962). Bargaining in ignorance of the opponent's utility. *Journal of Conflict Resolution*, **6**, 29–38.

Heath, A. (1968). Economic theory and sociology: a critique of P. M. Blau's "Exchange and power in social life". *Sociology*, **2**, 273–292.

Heath, A. (1971). Review article: Exchange theory. *British Journal of Political Science*, **1**, 91–119.

Heider, F. (1958). *The Psychology of Interpersonal Relations*. Wiley and Sons, New York.

Helson, H. (1948). Adaptation-level as a basis for a quantitative theory of frames of reference. *Psychological Review*, **55**, 297–313.

Hempel, C. G. (1965). *Aspects of Scientific Explanation*. The Free Press, New York.

Himmelfarb, S. and Senn, D. J. (1969). Forming impressions of social class: two tests of an averaging model. *Journal of Personality and Social Psychology*, **12**, 38–51.

Hollander, E. P. (1958). Conformity, status and idiosyncracy credit. *Psychological Review*, **65**, 117–127.

Hollander, E. P. (1964). Leaders, groups and influence. Oxford University Press, New York.

Hollander, E. P. and Julian, J. W. (1969). Contemporary trends in the analysis of leadership processes. *Psychological Bulletin*, **71**, 387–397.

Homans, G. C. (1951). *The Human Group*. Routledge and Kegan Paul, London.

Homans, G. C. (1954). The cash posters. *American Sociological Review*, **19**, 729.

Homans, G. C. (1961). *Social Behaviour: Its Elementary Forms*. Routledge and Kegan Paul, London.

Homans, G. C. (1964). Contemporary theory in sociology. *In* Faris, R. E. L. (ed.) *Handbook of Modern Sociology*. Rand McNally, Chicago.

Homans, G. C. (1967). *The Nature of Social Science*. Harcourt Brace and World, New York.

Homans, G. C. (1967a). Fundamental social process. *In* Smelser, N. J. (ed.) *Sociology: an Introduction*, Wiley and Sons, New York.

Homans, G. C. (1969). The sociological relevance of behaviourism. *In* Burgess, R. L. and Bushell, D. (eds) *Behavioural Sociology: The Experimental Analysis of Social Process*. Columbia University Press, New York.

Homans, G. C. (1970). The relevance of psychology to the explanation of social phenomena. *In* Borger, R. and Cioffi, F. (eds) *Explanation in the Behavioural Sciences*. Cambridge University Press, Cambridge.

Homans, G. C. (1972). Review of B. F. Skinner, "Beyond Freedom and Dignity", 1971, Alfred A. Knopf, Inc., New York. *In American Journal of Sociology*, **78**, 3, 696–708.

Homans, G. C. (1974). *Social Behaviour: Its Elementary Forms* (revised edition). Harcourt, Brace, Jovanovich, New York.

Horai, J. and Tedeschi, J. T. (1969). Effects of credibility and magnitude of punishment on compliance to threats. *Journal of Personality and Social Psychology*, **12**, 164–169.

Horowitz, I. A. (1968). Social responsibility as a function of regression-sensitization and social exchange. *Journal of Social Psychology*, **75**, 135–146.

Hull, C. L. (1943). *Principles of Behaviour*. Appleton-Century, New York.

Hull, C. L. (1951). *Essentials of Behaviour*. Yale University Press, New Haven.

Hull, C. L., Hovland, C. I., Ross, R. T., Hall, M., Perkins, D. T. and Fitch, F. B. (1940). *Mathematico-deductive Theory of Rote Learning: a Study in Scientific Methodology*. Yale University Press, New Haven.

Israel, J. (1956). Self-evaluation and rejection in groups. *Stockholm Studies in Sociology*, vol. 1, Almqvist and Wiksell, Stockholm.

Israel, J. and Tajfel, H. (eds) (1972). *The Context of Social Psychology: A Critical Assessment*. Academic Press, London.

Jaques, E. (1961). *Equitable Payment*. Wiley and Sons, New York.

Jennings, H. H. (1950). *Leadership and Isolation*. Longmans, Green, New York.

Jessor, R. (1958). The problem of reductionism in psychology. *Psychological Review*, **65**, 170–178.

Jones, E. E. and Davis, K. E. (1965). From acts to dispositions. *In* Berkowitz, L. (ed.) *Advances in Experimental Social Psychology*, vol. 2, Academic Press, New York and London.

Jones, E. E. and Gerard, H. B. (1967). *Foundations of Social Psychology*. Wiley and Sons, New York.

Jones, E. E., Gergen, K. G. and Jones, R. G. (1963). Tactics in ingratiation among leaders and subordinates in a status hierarchy. *Psychological Monographs*, **77**, no. 566.

Jones, E. E. and Jones, R. G. (1964). Optimum conformity as an ingratiation tactic. *Journal of Personality and Social Psychology*, **32**, 436–458.

Jones, S. C. and Schneider, D. J. (1968). Certainty of self-appraisal and reactions to evaluations from others. *Sociometry*, **31**, 395–403.

Jourard, S. M. (1958). A study of self-disclosure. *Scientific American*, **198**, 77–82.

Julian, J. W., Regula, C. F. and Hollander, E. P. (1968). Effects of prior agreement by others on task confidence and conformity. *Journal of Personality and Social Psychology*, **9**, 171–178.

Kahan, J. P. (1968). Effects of level of aspiration in an experimental bargaining situation. *Journal of Personality and Social Psychology*, **8**, 2, 154–159.

Kandel, D. B. (1966). Status homophily, social context and participation in psychotherapy. *American Journal of Sociology*, **71**, 640–650.

Karpik, L. (1967). Three sociological concepts: the reference objective, social status and the balance of transaction. *Human Relations*, **20**, 131–154.

Kasl, S. V. and Cobb, S. (1967). The effects of parental status incongruence and discrepancy on physical and mental health of adult offspring. *Journal of Personality and Social Psychology*, **7**, 1–15.

Katz, E. and Danet, B. (1973). Petitions and persuasive appeals: a study of official-client relations. *In* Katz, E. and Danet, B. (eds) *Bureaucracy and the Public: A Reader in Official-Client Relations*. Basic Books, New York.

Katz, E., Gurevitch, M., Peled, T. and Danet, B. (1969). Doctor-patient exchanges: a diagnostic approach to organizations and professions. *Human Relations*, **22**, 4, 309–324.

Kelley, H. H. (1951). Communication in experimentally created hierarchies. *Human Relations*, **4**, 39–56.

Kelley, H. H. (1963). Review of Irving Goffman "Encounters". *Contemporary Psychology*, **8**, 71–72.

Kelley, H. H. (1964). Interaction process and the attainment of maximum joint profit. *In* Messick, S. and Brayfield, A. H. (eds) *Decision and Choice*. McGraw-Hill, New York.

Kelley, H. H. (1965). Interdisciplinary study of interdependence: a review of Fouraker, L. E. and Siegel, S., "Bargaining behaviour". *Contemporary Psychology*, **10**, 49–50.

Kelley, H. H. (1965a). Experimental studies of threats in interpersonal negotiations. *Journal of Conflict Resolution*, **9**, 79–105.

Kelley, H. H. (1966). A classroom study of the dilemmas in interpersonal negotations. *In* Archibald, K. (ed.) *Strategic Interaction and Conflict*. University of California, Institute of International Studies, Berkeley.

Kelley, H. H. (1967). Attributional theory in social psychology. *Nebraska Symposium on Motivation*, **15**, 192–240.

Kelley, H. H. (1968). Interpersonal accommodation. *American Psychologist*, **23**, 399–410.

Kelley, H. H. (1972). Distinguished scientific contributions award: citation and biography. *American Psychologist*, **27**, 60–63.

Kelley, H. H. (1973). The processes of causal attribution. *American Psychologist*, **28**, 107–128.

Kelley, H. H., Beckman, L. L. and Fischer, C. S. (1967). Negotiating the division of a reward, incomplete information. *Journal of Experimental Social Psychology*, **3**, 361–398.

Kelley, H. H., Shure, G. H., Deutsch, M., Faucheux, C., Lanzetta, J. T., Moscovici, S., Nuttin, J. M., Rabbie, J. M. and Thibaut, J. W. (1970). A comparative experimental study of negotiation behaviour. *Journal of Personality and Social Psychology*, **16**, 411–438.

Kelley, H. H. and Grzelak, J. (1972). Conflict between individual and common interest in an N-person relationship. *Journal of Personality and Social Psychology*, **21**, 2, 190–197.

Kelley, H. H. and Shapiro, M. M. (1960). An experiment on conformity to group norms where conformity is detrimental to group achievement. *American Sociological Review*, **19**, 667–677.

Kelley, H. H. and Stahelski, A. J. (1970a). Social interaction basis of cooperators' and competitors' beliefs about others. *Journal of Personality and Social Psychology*, **16**, 66–91.

Kelley, H. H. and Stahelski, A. J. (1970b). Errors in perception of intentions in a mixed-motive game. *Journal of Experimental Social Psychology*, **6**, 379–400.

Kelley, H. H. and Stahelski, A. J. (1970c). The inference of intentions from moves in the Prisoner's Dilemma game. *Journal of Experimental Social Psychology*, **6**, 401–419.

Kelley, H. H. and Thibaut, J. W. (1969). Group problem solving. *In* Lindzey, G. and Aronson, E. (eds) *Handbook of Social Psychology*, vol. 4. Addison Wesley, Reading, Mass.

Kelvin, P. (1970). *The Bases of Social Behaviour, An Approach in Terms of Order and Value*. Holt, Rinehart and Winston, London.

Kemeny, J. C. and Oppenheim, P. (1956). On reduction. *Philosophical Studies*, **7**, 10.

Kershenbaum, B. R. and Komorita, S. S. (1970). Temptation to defect in the Prisoner's Dilemma game. *Journal of Personality and Social Psychology*, **16**, 110–113.

Kimberly, J. C. (1967). Status inconsistency: a reformulation of a theoretical problem. *Human Relations*, **20**, 171–179.

Kimble, G. A. (1967). *Foundations of Conditioning and Learning*. Appleton-Century-Crofts, New York.

Koch, S. (1954). Clark L. Hull. *In* Estes, W. K. (ed.) *Modern Learning Theory*. Appleton-Century-Crofts, New York.

Koestler, A. (1967). *The Ghost in the Machine*. Hutchinson, London.

Komorita, S. S. and Brenner, A. R. (1968). Bargaining and concession making under bilateral monopoly. *Journal of Personality and Social Psychology*, **9**, 15–20.

Komorita, S. S., Sheposh, J. P. and Braver, S. L. (1968). Power, the use of power and cooperative choice in a two-person game. *Journal of Personality and Social Psychology*, **8**, 134–142.

Krebs, D. L. (1970). Altruism—an examination of the concept and a review of the literature. *Psychological Bulletin*, **73**, 258–302.

Kuhn, T. S. (1970). *The Structure of Scientific Revolutions* (2nd edition). University of Chicago Press, Chicago.

Kunkel, J. H. (1967). Some behavioural aspects of the ecological approach to social organization. *American Journal of Sociology*, **73**, 12–29.

Lammers, C. J. (1967). Stratification in a small group. *Human Relations*, **20**, 283–299.

Levinger, G., Senn, D. J. and Jorgensen, B. W. (1970). Progress toward permanence in courtship: a test of the Kerckhoff-Davis hypotheses. *Sociometry*, **33**, 4, 427–443.

Levi-Strauss, C. (1957). The principle of reciprocity. *In* Coser, L. A. and Rosenberg, B., *Sociological Theory*. Macmillan, New York.

Lindesmith, A. R. and Strauss, A. L. (1968). *Social Psychology*, Holt, Rinehart and Winston, New York.

Liska, A. E. (1969). Uses and mis-uses of tautologies in social psychology. *Sociometry* **32**, 444–457.

Logan, F. A. and Wagner, A. R. (1965). *Reward and Punishment*. Allyn and Bacon, Boston.

Longabaugh, R. (1963). A category system for coding interpersonal behaviour as social exchange. *Sociometry*, **26**, 319–345.

Loomis, J. L. (1959). Communication, the development of trust and cooperative behaviour. *Human Relations*, **12**, 305–312.

Louch, A. R. (1966). *Explanation and Human Action*. Basil Backwell, Oxford.

Luce, R. D. and Raiffa, H. (1957). *Games and Decisions*. Wiley and Sons, New York.

Luetgert, J. (1967). Generalized effects of social reinforcement on paired-associate learning by grade-school achievers and under-achievers. Ph.D. dissertation, Indiana University.

Lupri, E. (1969). Contemporary authority patterns in the West German family: a study in cross-national validation. *Journal of Marriage and Family*, **31**, 34–44.

Macintyre, A. (1967). A review of P. M. Blau, "Exchange and power in social life". *Sociology*, **1**, 199–201.

Malinowski, B. (1961). *Argonauts of the Western Pacific*, Dutton, New York.

Mann, L. (1969). *Social Psychology*. Wiley and Sons, Sydney.

Mann, L. (1969a). Queue culture: the waiting line as a social system. *American Journal of Sociology*, **75**, 340–354.

Maris, R. (1970). The logical adequacy of Homans' social theory. *American Sociological Review*, **35**, 1069–1081.

Maris, R. (1971). Second thoughts: uses of logic in theory construction. *American Sociological Review*, **36**, 713–715.

Marsh, J. F. and Stafford, F. P. (1967). The effects of values on pecuniary behaviour: the case of academicians. *American Sociological Review*, **32**, 740–754.

Marwell, G., Ratcliff, K. and Schmitt, D. R. (1969). Minimising differences in a maximising difference game. *Journal of Personality and Social Psychology*, **12**, 158–163.

Mauss, M. (1954). *The Gift: Forms and Functions of Exchange in Archaic Societies*. Cohen and West, London.

McCall, M. M. (1966). Courtship as social exchange: some historical comparisons. *In* Farber, B. (ed). *Kinship and Family Organization*, Wiley and Sons, New York.

McClintock, C. G. and McNeel, S. P. (1966). Reward and score feedback as determinants of cooperative game behaviour. *Journal of Personality and Social Psychology*, **4**, 606–613.

McClintock, C. G. and McNeel, S. P. (1967). Prior dyadic experience and monetary reward as determinants of cooperative and competitive game behaviour. *Journal of Personality and Social Psychology*, **5**, 282–294.

McDavid, J. W. and Harari, H. (1974). *Psychology and Social Behaviour*. Harper and Row, New York.

McDougall, W. (1908). *Introduction to Social Psychology*, Methuen, London.

McGrath, J. E. (1966). A social psychological approach to the study of organizations. *In* Bowers, R. V. (ed.) *Studies on Behaviour in Organizations*. Georgia, University of Georgia Press, Athens.

McGuire, W. J. (1969). The nature of attitudes and attitude change. *In* Lindzey, G. and Aronson, E. (eds) *Handbook of Social Psychology*, vol. 3. Addison-Wesley, Reading, Mass.

McNeel, S. P., McClintock, C. G. and Nuttin, J. M. (1972). Effects of sex role in a two-person mixed-motive game. *Journal of Personality and Social Psychology*, **24**, 372–380.

Mead, G. H. (1934). *Mine, Self and Society from the Standpoint of a Social Behaviourist*. University of Chicago Press, Chicago.

Mead, G. H. (1964). *On Social Psychology: Selected Papers*. Edited by Strauss, A. University of Chicago Press, Chicago.

Meehl, P. E. (1950). On the circularity of the law of effect. *Psychological Bulletin*, **47**, 52–75.

Meeker, B. F. (1971). Decisions and exchange. *American Sociological Review*, **36**, 485–495.

Mehrabian, A. and Ksionzky, S. (1970). Models for affiliative and conformity behaviour. *Psychological Bulletin*, **74**, 110–126.

Merton, R. K. (1940). Bureaucratic structure and personality. *Social Forces*, **18**, 560–568.

Messick, D. and Thorngate, W. B. (1967). Relative gain maximization in experimental games. *Journal of Experimental Social Psychology*, **3**, 85–101.

Miller, J. G. (1955). Toward a general theory for the behavioural sciences. *American Psychologist*, **10**, 513–531.

Miller, N. E. (1951). Learnable drives and rewards. *In* Stevens, S. S. (ed.) *Handbook of Experimental Psychology*, Wiley and Sons, New York.

Miller, N. E. and Dollard, J. (1961). Reward. *In* Birney, R. C. and Teevan, R. C. (eds) *Reinforcement. An Enduring Problem in Psychology*. Van Nostrand, New York.

Miller, N., Buckler, D. C. and McMartin, J. A. (1969). The ineffectiveness of punishment power in group interaction. *Sociometry*, **32**, 24–32.

Mills, T. M. (1953). Power relations in three-person groups. *American Sociological Review*, **18**, 351–357.

Mintz, A. (1951). Non-adaptive group behaviour. *Journal of Abnormal and Social Psychology*, **46**, 150–159.

Moore, J. C. (1969). Social status and social influence: process considerations. *Sociometry*, **32**, 145–158.

Moore, O. K. and Anderson, A. R. (1962). Some puzzling aspects of social interaction. *In* Criswell, J. H., Solomon, H. and Suppes, P. (eds) *Mathematical Methods in Small Processes*. Stanford University Press, Stanford, Calif.

Moreno, J. L. (1934). *Who Shall Survive?* Nervous and Mental Diseases Publishing Co., Washington.

Moscovici, S. (1971). Préface à D. Jodelet, J. Viet, P. Bernard. *La Psychologie Sociale. Une Discipline en Mouvement*. La Haye, Mouton, Paris.

Moscovici, S. (1972). Society and theory in social psychology. *In* Israel, J. and Tajfel, H. (eds) *The Context of Social Psychology: A Critical Assessment*. Academic Press, London and New York.

Mulkay, M. J. (1971). *Functionalism, Exchange and Theoretical Strategy*. Routledge and Kegan Paul, London.

Murdoch, P. (1967). Development of contractual norms in a dyad. *Journal of Personality and Social Psychology*, **6**, 2, 206–211.

Murdoch, P. and Rosen, D. (1970). Norm foundation in an interdependent dyad. *Sociometry*, **33**, 264–275.

Murstein, B. I. (1971). What makes people sexually appealing? *Sexual Behaviour*, **1**, 75.

Murstein, B. I. (1972). Person perception and courtship progress among pre-marital couples. *Journal of Marriage and the Family*, November, 621–626.

Murstein, B. I. (1973). A theory of marital choice applying to interracial marriage. *In* Stuart, I. and Abt, L. (eds) *Interracial Marriage*. Grossman, New York.

Nagel, E. (1961). *The Structure of Science, Problems in the Logic of Scientific Explanation*. Routledge and Kegan Paul, London.

Nemeth, C. (1970). Bargaining and reciprocity. *Psychological Bulletin*, **74**, 297–308.

Nemeth, C. (1972). A critical analysis of research utilizing the Prisoner's Dilemma paradigm for the study of bargaining. *In* Berkowitz, L. (ed.) *Advances in Experimental Social Psychology*, **6**, 203–234.

Newcomb, T. M. (1953). An approach to the study of communicative acts. *Psychological Review*, **30**, 393–404.

Newcomb, T. M. (1961). *The Acquaintance Process*. Holt, Rinehart and Winston, New York.

Newell, A. and Simon, H. A. (1959). The simulation of human thought. *RAND Report*, 1734.

Nord, W. R. (1969). Social exchange theory: an integrative approach to social conformity. *Psychological Bulletin*, **71**, 174–208.

Opsahl, R. L. and Dunnette, M. D. (1966). The role of financial compensation in industrial motivation. *Psychological Bulletin*, **66**, 94–118.

Organ, D. W. (1971). Some variables affecting boundary role behaviour. *Sociometry* **34**, 524–537.

Osgood, C. E. and Tannenbaum, P. M. (1955). The principle of congruity in the prediction of attitude change. *Psychological Review*, **62**, 42–55.

Ost, J. W., Allison, J., Vance, W. B. and Restle, F. (1969). *A Laboratory Introduction to Psychology*. Academic Press, New York and London.

Parsons, T. (1951). *The Social System*. The Free Press, Glencoe, Illinois.

Parsons, T. (1963). On the concept of influence. *Public Opinion Quarterly*, **17**, 37–62.

Parsons, T. (ed.) (1964). *Max Weber. A Theory of Social and Economic Organization*. The Free Press, New York.

Patchen, M. (1959). Study of Work and Life Satisfaction. Report No. 11: Absences and attitudes toward work experience. Institute for Social Research, Ann Arbor.

Patchen, M. (1961). A conceptual framework and some empirical data regarding comparisons of social rewards. *Sociometry*, **24**, 136–156.

Pecheux, M. (1970). Sur la conjoncture théorique de la psychologie sociale. *Bulletin de Psychologie*, **281**, 290–297.

Pilisuk, M., Kiritz, S. and Clampitt, S. (1971). Undoing deadlocks of distrust: hip Berkeley students and the R.O.T.C. *Journal of Conflict Resolution*, **15**, 81–95.

Pilisuk, M. and Skolnick, P. (1968). Inducing trust: a test of the Osgood proposal. *Journal of Personality and Social Psychology*, **8**, 121–133.

Plon, M. (1967). Problèmes théoriques et experimentaux posés par l'emploi des "jeux", dans l'étude des conflits interpersonnels. *Bulletin du C.E.R.P.*, **16**, 4, 393–433.

Plon, M. (1968). Observations théoriques et experimentales sur le role des représentations dans des situations de choix conflictuels. *Bulletin du C.E.R.P.*, **17**, 205–244.

Plon, M. (1970). À propos d'une controverse sur les effets d'une ménace en situation de négociation. *Bulletin de Psychologie*, **23**, 268–282.

Plon, M. (1972). Sur quelques aspects de la rencontre entre la psychologie sociale et la théorie des jeux. *La Pensée*, **161**, 53–80.

Plon, M. (1974). Sur le sens de la notion de conflit et de son approche en psychologie sociale. In press. *European Journal of Social Psychology*.

Plon, M. and Preteceille, E. (1972). La théorie des jeux et le jeu de l'idéologie. *La Pensée*, 166, 36–68.

Popper, K. R. (1959). *Logic of Scientific Discovery*. Hutchinson, London.

Popper, K. R. (1962). *The Open Society and Its Enemies*. Routledge and Kegan Paul, London.

Portes, A. (1969). Dilemmas of a golden exile: integration of Cuban refugee families in Milwaukee. *American Sociological Review*, **34**, 505–518.

Premack, D. (1965). Reinforcement theory. *Nebraska Symposium on Motivation*, University of Nebraska Press, Lincoln, Nebraska.

Price, R. (1971). On Maris and the logic of time. *American Sociological Review*, **36**, 711–713.

Priest, R. F. (1964). Pair similarities: IBM 709–7090 program for scoring and analysing similarities between pairs of individuals. *Behavioural Science*, **9**, 291.

Priest, R. F. and Sawyer, J. (1967). Proximity and peership: bases of balance in interpersonal attraction. *American Journal of Sociology*, **72**, 633–649.

Pruitt, D. G. (1967). Reward structure and cooperation: the decomposed Prisoner's Dilemma game. *Journal of Personality and Social Psychology*, **7**, 21–27.

Pruitt, D. G. (1968). Reciprocity and credit building in a laboratory dyad. *Journal of Personality and Social Psychology*, **8**, 143–147.

Pylyshyn, Z., Agnew, N. and Illingworth, J. (1966). Comparisons of individuals and pairs as participants in a mixed-motive game. *Journal of Conflict Resolution*, **10**, 211–220.

Rapoport, A. (1966). *Two-Person Game Theory: The Essential Ideas*. University of Michigan Press, Ann Arbor.

Rapoport, A. (1970). Conflict resolution in the light of game theory and beyond. *In* P. Swingle (ed.) *The Structure of Conflict.* Academic Press, New York and London.

Rapoport, A. and Chammah, A. M. (1965). *Prisoner's Dilemma: A Study of Conflict and Cooperation.* University of Michigan Press, Ann Arbor.

Rapoport, A. and Guyer, M. (1966). A taxonomy of 2 × 2 games. *General Systems*, **2**, 203–214.

Rawls, J. (1972). *A Theory of Justice.* Clarendon Press, Oxford.

Restle, F. (1971). *Mathematical Models in Psychology, an Introduction.* Penguin Books. Harmondsworth, Middlesex.

Richer, S. (1968). The economics of child rearing. *Journal of Marriage and the Family*, **30**, 462–466.

Rieger-Shlonsky, H. (1969). The conceptualization of the roles of a relative, a friend and a neighbour. *Human Relations*, **22**, 4, 355–369.

Rogers, D. L., Heffernan, W. D. and Warner, W. K. (1972). Benefits and role performance in voluntary organizations: an exploration of social exchange. *Sociological Quarterly*, **13**, 183–196.

Rosenhan, D. and White, G. M. (1967). Observation and rehearsal as determinants of prosocial behaviour. *Journal of Personality and Social Psychology*, **5**, 424–431.

Ross, E. A. (1908). *Social Psychology*, Macmillan, New York.

Ross, M., Thibaut, J. and Evenbeck, S. (1971). Some determinants of the intensity of social protest. *Journal of Experimental Social Psychology*, **7**, 401–418.

Rothbart, M. (1968). Effects of motivation, equity and compliance on the use of reward and punishment. *Journal of Personality and Social Psychology*, **9**, 353–362.

Rotter, J. B. (1966). *Generalized Expectancies for Internal versus External Control of Reinforcement.* American Psychological Association, Washington.

Rubin, J. Z. and DiMatteo, M. R. (1972). Factors affecting the magnitude of subective utility parameters in a tacit bargaining game. *Journal of Experimental Social Psychology*, **8**, 412–426.

Runciman, W. G. (1967). Justice, congruence and Professor Homans. *Archives of European Sociology*, **8**, 115–128.

Runciman, W. G. (1970). *Sociology in its Place, and Other Essays.* Cambridge University Press, Cambridge.

Runciman, W. G. and Bagley, C. R. (1969). Status consistency, relative deprivation, and attitudes to immigrants. *Sociology*, **3**, 359–375.

Sampson, E. E. (1963). Status congruence and cognitive consistency. *Sociometry*, **26**, 146–162.

Samuelson, P. A. (1955). *Economics: an Introductory Analysis.* McGraw-Hill, New York.

Savell, J. M. and Healey, G. W. (1969). Private and public conformity after being agreed and disagreed with. *Sociometry*, **32**, 315–329.

Sawyer, J. (1966). The altruism scale: a measure of cooperative, individualistic and competitive interpersonal orientation. *American Journal of Sociology*, **71**, 407–416.

Scanzoni, J. (1970). *Opportunity and the Family.* The Free Press, New York.

Scanzoni, J. (1972). *Sexual Bargaining: Power Politics in the American Marriage.* Prentice Hall, Englewood Cliffs, N.J.

Schelling, T. C. (1963). *The Strategy of Conflict.* Oxford University Press, London.

Schneider, L. (1971). Dialectic in sociology. *American Sociological Review*, **36**, 667–678.

Schopler, J. and Bateson, N. (1965). The power of dependence. *Journal of Personality and Social Psychology*, **2**, 247–254.

Schwartz, B. (1967). The social psychology of the gift. *American Journal of Sociology*, **73**, 1–11.

Schwartz, B. (1968). The social psychology of privacy. *American Journal of Sociology*, **73**, 741–752.

Schwartz, B. (1974). Waiting, exchange and power: the distribution of time in social systems. *American Journal of Sociology*, **79**, 841–870.

Scodel, A., Minas, J. S., Ratoosh, P. and Lipetz, M. (1959). Some descriptive aspects of two-person, non-zero-sum games. *Journal of Conflict Resolution*, **3**, 114–119.

Sears, R. R. (1951). A theoretical framework for personality and social behaviour. *American Psychologist*, **6**, 476–483.

Secord, P. F. and Backman, C. W. (1974). *Social Psychology* (2nd edition). McGraw-Hill, New York.

Sermat, V. (1962). Behaviour in a mixed motive game as related to the possibility of influencing the other's behaviour. Paper read to the American Psychological Association, St. Louis.

Sermat, V. (1964). Cooperative behaviour in mixed motive games. *Journal of Social Psychology*, **62**, 217–239.

Sermat, V. and Gregovich, R. P. (1966). The effect of experimental manipulation on cooperative behaviour in a chicken game. *Psychonomic Science*, **4**, 435–436.

Seward, J. P. (1965). Choice-points in behavior research. *In* Wolman, B. J. *Scientific Psychology*. Basic Books, New York.

Shaw, M. E. and Costanzo, P. R. (1970). *Theories of Social Psychology*. McGraw-Hill, New York.

Sherif, M. and Sherif, C. W. (1953). *Groups in Harmony and Tension*. Harper and Row, New York.

Shomer, R. W., Davis, A. H. and Kelley, H. H. (1966). Threats and the development of coordination: further studies in the Deutsch and Krauss trucking game. *Journal of Personality and Social Psychology*, **4**, 119–126.

Sidowski, J. B., Wyckoff, L. B. and Tabory, L. (1956). The influence of reinforcement and punishment in a minimal social situation. *Journal of Abnormal and Social Psychology*, **52**, 115–119.

Siegel, S. (1957). Level of aspiration and decision making. *Psychological Review*, **64**, 253–262.

Siegel, S. and Fouraker, L. E. (1960). *Bargaining and Group Decision-Making*. McGraw-Hill, New York.

Sigall, H. and Aronson, E. (1967). Opinion change and the gain-loss model of interpersonal attraction. *Journal of Experimental Social Psychology*, **3**, 178–188.

Simon, H. A. (1953). A formal theory of interaction in social groups. *American Sociological Review*, **17**, 202–211.

Simon, H. A. (1956). Rational choice and the structure of the environment. *Psychological Review*, **63**, 129–138.

Simon, H. A. (1957). *Models of Man*. Wiley and Sons, New York.

Singelmann, P. (1972). Exchange as symbolic interaction: convergences between two theoretical perspectives. *American Sociological Review*, **37**, 414–424.

Singelmann, P. (1973). On the reification of paradigms: reply to Abbott, Brown and Crosbie. *American Sociological Review*, **38**, 506–509.

Singer, E. (1971). Adult orientation of first and later childen. *Sociometry*, **34**, 328–345.

Skinner, B. F. (1938). *The Behaviour of Organisms*. Appleton-Century-Crofts, New York.

Skinner, B. F. (1953). *Science and Human Behaviour*. The Free Press, New York.

Smelser, N. J. (ed.) (1967). *Sociology: An Introduction*. Wiley and Sons, New York.

Smith, W. P. (1968). Precision of control and the use of power in the triad. *Human Relations*, **21**, 3, 295–310.

Smith, W. P. and Emmons, T. D. (1969). Outcome information and competitiveness in interpersonal bargaining. *Journal of Conflict Resolution*, **13**, 262–270.

Smith, W. P. and Leginski, W. A. (1970). Magnitude and precision of punitive power in bargaining strategy. *Journal of Experimental Social Psychology*, **6**, 57–76.

Solomon, L. (1960). The influence of some types of power relationships and game strategies on the development of interpersonal trust. *Journal of Abnormal and Social Psychology*, **61**, 223–230.

Sorokin, P. A. (1966). *Sociological Theories of Today*. Harper and Row, New York.

Sprey, J. (1969). The family as a system in conflict. *Journal of Marriage and the Family*, **31**, 699–706.

Sprott, W. J. H. (1958). *Human Groups*. Penguin Books, Harmondsworth.

Stanley, M. (1968). Nature, culture and scarcity: foreword to a theoretical synthesis. *American Sociological Review*, **33**, 855–870.

Stephenson, G. M. and Barker, J. (1972). Personality and the pursuit of distributive justice: an experimental study of children's moral behaviour. *British Journal of Social and Clinical Psychology*, **11**, 207–219.

Stephenson, G. M. and Fielding, G. T. (1971). An experimental study of the contagion of leading behaviour in small gatherings. *Journal of Social Psychology*, **84**, 81–91.

Stevens, C. M. (1963). *Strategy and Collective Bargaining Orientation*. McGraw-Hill, New York.

Stotland, E. (1965). Experimental social psychology and its neighbours. *Journal of Social Psychology*, **67**, 315–323.

Stouffer, S. A., Suchman, E. A., DeVinney, L. C., Star, S. A. and Williams, R. N. (1949). *The American Soldier*. Princeton University Press, Princeton, N. J.

Swanson, G. E. (1965). On explanations of social interaction. *Sociometry*, **18**, 101–123.

Swingle, P. G. and Gillis, J. S. (1968). Effects of the emotional relationship between protagonists in the Prisoner's Dilemma. *Journal of Personality and Social Psychology*, **8**, 160–165.

Tajfel, H. (1972). Experiments in a vacuum. *In* Israel, J. and Tajfel, H. (eds) *The Context of Social Psychology: A Critical Assessment*. Academic Press, London and New York.

Tallman, I. (1967). The balance principle and normative discrepancy. *Human Relations*, **20**, 341–355.

Tannenbaum, P. M. (1966). Mediated generalization of attitude change via the principle of congruity. *Journal of Personality and Social Psychology*, **3**, 493–499.

Tedeschi, J. T., Bonoma, T. V. and Brown, R. C. (1971). A paradigm for the study of coercive power. *Journal of Conflict Resolution*, **15**, 197–223.

Tedeschi, J. T., Burrill, D. and Gahagan, J. (1969). Social desirability, manifest anxiety and social power. *Journal of Social Psychology*, **77**, 231–239.

Tedeschi, J. T., Schlenker, B. R. and Bonoma, T. V. (1971). Cognitive dissonance: private ratiocination or public spectacle? *American Psychologist*, **27**, 685–695.

Teger, A. I. (1970). The effect of early cooperation on the escalation of conflict. *Journal of Experimental Social Psychology*, **6**, 187–204.

Terhune, K. W. (1968). Motives, situation, and interpersonal conflict within Prisoner's Dilemma. *Journal of Personality and Social Psychology*, Monograph Supplement, **8**.

Thibaut, J. (1968). The development of contractual norms in bargaining: replication and variation. *Journal of Conflict Resolution*, **12**, 102–112.

Thibaut, J. and Faucheux, C. (1965). The development of contractual norms in a bargaining situation under two types of stress. *Journal of Experimental Social Psychology*, **1**, 89–102.

Thibaut, J. and Gruder, C. L. (1969). Formation of contractual agreements between parties of unequal power. *Journal of Personality and Social Psychology*, **11**, 1, 59–65.

Thibaut, J. and Kelley, H. H. (1959). *The Social Psychology of Groups*. Wiley and Sons, New York.

Thibaut, J. and Ross, M. (1969). Commitment and experience as determinants of assimilation and contract. *Journal of Personality and Social Psychology*, **13**, 322–329.

Treiman, D. J. (1966). Status discrepancy and prejudice. *American Journal of Sociology*, **71**, 651–664.

Turner, J. L., Foa, E. B. and Foa, U. G. (1971). Interpersonal reinforcers: classification, and some differential properties. *Journal of Personality and Social Psychology*, **19**, 2, 168–180.

Turner, R. H. (1970). *Family Interaction*. Wiley and Sons, New York.

Turner, S. (1971). The logical adequacy of "the logical adequacy of Homans' social theory". *American Sociological Review*, **36**, 709–711.

Tversky, A. (1972). Elimination by aspects: a theory of choice. *Psychological Review*, **79**, 281–299.

Voss, J. F. (1971). Are reinforcement concepts able to provide reinforcement for theorizing in human learning? *In* Glaser, R. (ed.) *The Nature of Reinforcement*. Academic Press, New York and London.

Vroom, V. H. (1964). *Work and Motivation*. Wiley and Sons, New York.

Wager, L. W. (1971). The expansion of organizational authority and conditions affecting its denial. *Sociometry*, **34**, 91–113.

Wager, L. W. (1972). Organization "linking pins": hierarchical status and communicative roles in interlevel conferences. *Human Relations*, **25**, 307–326.

Wahrman, R. (1970). High status, deviance and sanctions. *Sociometry*, **33**, 485–504.

Waller, W. (1951). *The family: A Dynamic Interpretation*. (Revised by R. Hill.) Dryden Press, New York.

Wallis, W. D. (1925). The independence of social psychology. *Journal of Abnormal and Social Psychology*, **20**, 147–150.

Walster, E., Aronson, E. and Brown, Z. (1966). Choosing to suffer as a consequence of expecting to suffer: an unexpected finding. *Journal of Experimental Social Psychology*, **2**, 400–406.

Walster, E., Berscheid, E. and Walster, G. W. (1973). New directions in equity research. *Journal of Personality and Social Psychology*, **25**, 2, 151–176.

Walton, J. (1969). Development decision making: a comparative study in Latin America. *American Journal of Sociology*, **75**, 828–851.

Weber, M. (1947). *A Theory of Social and Economic Organization*. (Edited with an introduction by T. Parsons) The Free Press, New York, 1964.

Weinstein, E. A., De Vaughan, W. L. and Wiley, M. G. (1969). Obligation and the flow of deference in exchange. *Sociometry*, **32**, 1–12.

White, H. C. (1972). Simon out of Homans by Coleman. *American Journal of Sociology*, **75**, 852–862.

Whyte, W. F. (1943). *Street Corner Society: the Social Structure of an Italian Slum*. University of Chicago Press, Chicago.

Wiberg, H. (1972). Rational and non-rational models of man. *In* Israel, J. and Tajfel, H. (eds) *The Context of Social Psychology: A Critical Assessment*. Academic Press, London and New York.

Wilke, H. and Lanzetta, J. T. (1970). The obligation to help: the effects of amounts of prior help on subsequent helping behaviour. *Journal of Experimental and Social Psychology*, **6**, 488–493.

Wilson, K. V. and Bixenstine, V. E. (1962). Forms of social control in two-person, two-choice games. *Behavioural Science*, **7**, 92–102.

Wilson, T. P. (1970). Conceptions of interaction and forms of sociological explanation. *American Sociological Review*, **35**, 697–708.

Wisdom, J. O. (1970). Situational individualism and the emergent group-properties. *In* Borger, R. and Cioffi, F. (eds) *Explanation in the Behavioural Sciences*. Cambridge University Press, Cambridge.

Woodworth, R. S. and Sheehan, M. R. (1964). *Contemporary Schools of Psychology*. (3rd ed.) Ronald Press, New York.

Worthy, M., Gary, A. L. and Kahn, G. M. (1969). Self disclosure as an exchange process. *Journal of Personality and Social Psychology*, **13**, 1, 59–63.

Wrong, D. H. (1967). Some problems in defining social power. *Journal of Sociology*, **73**, 673–681.

Wyer, R. S. (1968). Effects of task reinforcement, social reinforcement, and task difficulty on perseverance in achievement-related activity. *Journal of Personality and Social Psychology*, **8**, 3, 269–276.

Wyer, R. S. (1969). Prediction of behaviour in two-person games. *Journal of Personality and Social Psychology*, **13**, 222–238.

Wyer, R. S. and Bednar, R. (1967). Some determinants of perseverance in achievement-related activity. *Journal of Experimental Social Psychology*, **3**, 255–265.

Wyer, R. S. and Schwartz, S. (1969). Some contingencies in the effects of the source of a communication on the evaluation of that communication. *Journal of Personality and Social Psychology*, **11**, 1–9.

Yuchtman, E. (1972). Reward distribution and work-role attractiveness in the Kibbutz-reflections on equity theory. *American Sociological Review*, **37**, 581–595.

Yuchtman, E. and Seashore, S. E. (1967). A system resource approach to organizational effectiveness. *American Sociological Review*, **32**, 891–903.

Zaleznik, A., Christensen, C. and Roethlisberger, F. J. (1958). The motivation, productivity, and satisfaction of workers: a prediction study. Harvard University Division of Research, Graduate School of Business Administration, Boston, Mass.

Zetterberg, H. L. (1965). *On Theory and Verification in Sociology*. The Bedminster Press, New Jersey.

Author Index

Subject Index